Studies in Cognitive Growth

An earlier collaboration of the Center for Cognitive Studies:

Jerome S. Bruner, Jacqueline J. Goodnow, and George A. Austin.
   A study of thinking, Wiley, 1956.

Studies in Cognitive Growth

A Collaboration at the
Center for Cognitive Studies

JEROME S. BRUNER

ROSE R. OLVER   PATRICIA M. GREENFIELD

and

JOAN RIGNEY HORNSBY

HELEN J. KENNEY

MICHAEL MACCOBY

NANCY MODIANO

FREDERIC A. MOSHER

DAVID R. OLSON

MARY C. POTTER

LEE C. REICH

ANNE McKINNON SONSTROEM

John Wiley & Sons, Inc.,   New York · London · Sydney

For Jean Piaget

Friend and mentor, whose brilliant insights have given new and powerful form to the study of cognitive growth.

In honor of his seventieth birthday.

Preface

As the title page indicates, this book is a collaboration, and it is so in several specific senses. It is not a book "written by a committee," but rather one that has grown over a period of six or seven years out of the communal efforts of a professor, his students, and a number of postdoctoral fellows who had come to Harvard to work with him. As far as I know, there has never been a time when all the collaborators were simultaneously in Cambridge, and there has never been a proper "committee meeting" to hammer out elements of agreement. However, there have been many seminars, many laboratory lunches, numberless exchanges of letters, research memoranda, and repeated drafts of manuscripts. There have been disappointments and quarrels and surprises. All in all, the work reported in these pages is the outcome of an intensive period in a research "shop" that was applying its attention to the problem of how intellect develops.

This preface is written by one of the group, the professor. Although in the dictionary sense I am the teacher, I am perhaps also the principal learner. This is a distinction none of my collaborators can share, for I am the only one who has worked closely with all of them and have learned, I hope, from each. Indeed, some of the members of the collaborative, given the transiency of life in a university, have never met some of the others. Six years between one man's thesis and another's probably constitute an academic generation. Mine has been the role of transmitting the culture of the group through six years. The seminars and lunches and parties and quarrels have been central to the enterprise.

The mode in which the chapters have been composed has also

been part of the picture. Many of the studies reported subsequently were originally carried out as baccalaureate honors theses or doctoral dissertations at Harvard and Radcliffe Colleges. Most of us would grant that the writing of any thesis or dissertation is an extraordinary exercise and in the main a memorable one for both professor and student. I am not one who takes the theses and dissertations of his students coolly—I may indeed get overly involved. The effect of this perhaps unfortunate trait is to make me very susceptible to the points of view of the students working with me, but I am also strong-willed and will debate long and hard with anyone who has taken an issue seriously enough to conduct research on it.

The arguments continued in each case past the thesis stage and, as theses were converted into articles and articles into chapters, the debates have continued. They have gone on right through galley proofs, and indeed a word of gratitude is owed our publishers, John Wiley and Sons. When the galley proofs were distributed among the collaborators, many interesting suggestions cropped up that resulted in extensive changes. Most of the authors commented on most of the chapters, and all were gone over in great detail by myself, by Dr. Rose Richardson Olver, and by Dr. Patricia Marks Greenfield. In a fashion hard to describe I have been editor-in-chief, with the aid of Dr. Olver and Dr. Greenfield.

After the first drafts of all the chapters were completed in the spring of 1965, I escaped the distractions of the home base by going into hiding in London, where I had the wonderful experience of "reworking" the manuscript for ten hours a day, six days a week, for a month. My principal task then was to tie together the various threads of the different research enterprises carried out over six or seven years. Since that time the main task has been to resolve the fresh debates set off by my "reworking."

❊   ❊   ❊

As a matter of fact, this book began well before its first page was envisaged. In 1956 after completing *A Study of Thinking*, I spend a term as Guggenheim Fellow at Cambridge University. My intellectual companion and research assistant at that time was Michael Wallach, then a graduate student at Harvard University and now a professor at Duke University. During those months in England we read widely in the literature on cognition and on cognitive development, we visited research centers in Britain and on the Continent, and made a first visit to Professor Jean Piaget in Geneva. After all our reading and discussion, it seemed to us that the best approach to understanding the growth of cognitive processes would be in a study of the nature of efficiency and inefficiency in the strategies employed by human beings in thinking and in solving problems. That winter I gave a series of lectures at University College, London, on this subject. On returning to this Cambridge I soon became involved in a research project on the factors affecting the efficiency of learning.

This project was organized around the idea that we should study learning in children at its normal efficiency and, for comparative purposes, at its lowest. The assumption was that we would compare a group of children who had been referred by schools to a child-guidance clinic as cases of "learning block" with a group of children of like age who were operating within the normal range of efficiency in a regular school setting. For reasons described elsewhere (Bruner, 1966), that study did not produce a neat comparison, because "learning block" turned out to be not so straightforward a manifestation of cognitive inefficiency as we had anticipated.

It was work with the "control group" of some sixty normal ten-year-olds in a suburban school near Boston that in fact proved to be the beginning of this book. It provided us with a group of children with whom we became very well acquainted over a period of two years and on whom we were able to try out a wide variety of investigatory procedures. Indeed, several of the research techniques employed in the following chapters were first developed for the purpose of studying aspects of learning efficiency in normal school children.[1]

The objective in those studies was to find reliable patterns of individual difference. Could we characterize in children generic modes of functioning that manifest themselves in a variety of activities? These studies were never completed—not that they "failed," for they generated a good deal of fruitful thinking and a modest number of publications. The main harvest of this early work, however, was reaped by two members of our original research team nearly a decade later. I refer to two books that emerged from the collaboration of Dr. Nathan Kogan and Dr. Michael Wallach, *Risk-Taking: A Study*

---

[1] Among the investigators who worked with us at Harvard during this formative period from 1957 to 1959 were Dr. Michael Maccoby, now at the National University of Mexico, Dr. Frederic Mosher of the Carnegie Corporation, Professor Michael Wallach of Duke University, Dr. Albert Caron of the National Institute of Mental Health, Professor Salvadore Maddi of the University of Chicago, Professor Philip Daniel of Brigham Young University, Dr. Nathan Kogan of Educational Testing Services, Dr. Henri Tajfel of Oxford University, Professor Betty Fraser of the University of Aberdeen, Dr. Rhea Mendoza Diamond of Harvard University, and Mrs. Jean Yeomans.

in Cognition and Personality (1964) and _Modes of Thinking in Young Children_ (1965). These two investigators brought to maturity the ideas that first appeared in those early studies of cognitive organization in normal school children.

It is the lot of each investigator that he must live with his own demons. Because of either inclination or training, I have never been drawn to studies of individual difference and consistency. Indeed, I doubt whether I would have been capable of the kind of ingenious analysis that went into Wallach and Kogan's _Modes of Thinking in Young Children_. Dr. Tajfel and I have published some work on cognitive risk-taking (1961) which he later developed far beyond those original studies; for my part, I have gone on to other, though related, kinds of work.

These latter studies sprang from my desire to find out _how_ children come to develop different strategies of problem solving—those strategies that were so apparent in our early studies of individual differences and that have since been so beautifully explicated by Wallach and Kogan. I went directly from observational studies of school children performing school-like tasks in the laboratory to studies in which we were able to alter the pattern of activity in the classroom. There followed an intensive two-year period of experimentation whose object was to try to teach children the strategies of problem solving, principally in the field of mathematics, in which the nature of the material being taught permits a closer analysis of what is being learned. In a word, I went from studies of individual differences in cognitive operations to a study of intervention and change in cognitive functioning. There have since appeared two works reflecting this research, _The Process of Education_ (1960) and _Toward a Theory of Instruction_ (1966). In neither book was the conventional concept of growth a central concept. In fact, both books urge rather that there is a way of communicating ideas to children that is appropriate to a particular age and that it is futile educationally simply to wait passively for the child to grow into readiness.

A new series of experiments was begun in 1960, with the objective of exploring the course of human intellectual development. These were not directly concerned with individual differences or with the effects of school instruction proper but rather with the maturing of various cognitive operations. Indeed, it would be misleading to describe the opening of this phase of research as a "series" of experiments. The approach was too inductive and exploratory from the outset to merit so purposeful a description. The first work was carried out by an informal seminar consisting of a few graduate students and a few faculty members at the newly established Center for Cognitive Studies. Work on the development of equivalence formation, information seeking, and perceptual recognition was undertaken with techniques very similar to those developed for use with the school children studied several years before.[2]

The results of this early work highlighted a number of issues that became perennial concerns over the next five or six years. One was the speed and seeming discontinuity of the change that occurs in the intellectual life of a Western child somewhere between the ages of five and seven. When this change begins it seems to go on very swiftly and definitely in the direction of what in Geneva is now called "operativity." What this means in barest terms is that the child moves from a technique of dealing with things one aspect at a time in terms of their perceptual appearance to dealing with sets of invariant features several at a time and in some structured relationship. There is much discussion, theoretical and empirical alike, on this matter in the following chapters.

A second issue raised by these first studies (fuller versions of which constitute Chapters 3, 4, and 5 of this book) was the question of complexity and its relation to growth. One of the first reports to grow out of this work (Bruner and Olver, 1963) went so far as to propose the hypothesis that in one respect cognitive growth might be conceived as achieving a capacity for simplicity in dealing with information.

Finally, the early work made us keenly aware of the role of heuristics in the growth of perception and problem solving—ways of proceeding that the children picked up from the culture around them. We were very early convinced that these were crutches that aided growth and that growth came as much from the outside in as from the inside out.

In the following year, 1961–1962, the "development project" was fairly launched. Several compelling forces sped us along. The most important was the presence at the Center of Professor Bärbel Inhelder of the University of Geneva. She was not only a willing and able participant in the research seminar on development but was also a superb tutor in Genevan research methods and theory. It was in the course of our debating the issues of conservation and invariance that research of the kind reported in Chapters 8 through 11 was first

---

[2] This group consisted of Mrs. Rose Olver, Mr. Frederic Mosher, Mr. Philip Daniel, Dr. Mary C. Potter, Dr. Helen Kenney, Mr. Samuel Anderson, Mr. Daniel Slobin, Mr. Gerald Davison, Miss Joan Rigney, and myself—our titles written as of 1960–1961 are now, of course, more exalted.

conceived. During the next two years there was a steady exchange of visits and data with Geneva, thanks to a special grant from the Ford Foundation. It was chiefly during and after this period that we incurred the intellectual debt owed Professor Jean Piaget, to whom this book is dedicated.

Several other things served to push us irreversibly into developmental studies. Professor Roger Brown's return to Harvard was one. He set up at the Center a small research group concerned with writing grammars of the developing speech of two children, and the cognitive problems posed by learning grammar soon penetrated our own thinking. There were psycholinguistic problems of the first order encountered in Dr. Olver's developmental study of equivalence, in Dr. Mosher's work on question asking, and in my own work on problems of classification and conservation. First Dr. Dan Slobin (before his departure to teach at Berkeley) and then Dr. David McNeill (before he went to Ann Arbor) provided a bridge between the grammarians and our developmentalists. And in the background there was the stimulating research of Professor George Miller and his collaborators on the relation of grammatical transformations and the operations of thought to remind us that the general problem of language and thought required attention over and above its developmental side.

This last reminder, though it needed no reinforcements did receive several from unexpected quarters. One came from visits exchanged with colleagues from the Soviet Union. We were fortunate in our guests. Professor Luria and Professor Zaporozhets of Moscow were both deeply involved in developmental studies and both were particularly concerned with the role of language in mental growth—the impact of the famous Second Signal System. In the midst of the research reported in these pages I also had an opportunity to visit the Soviet Union for several weeks to discuss and observe. That visit was enormously helpful, thanks to the tireless hospitality and tutorial zeal of Professor Luria, who brought me together with Professors Elkonin, Zaporozhets, Tikhomirov, and many other young investigators, who could start talking shop at eight in the morning and keep at it until far into the night, the conversation interspersed with visits to the laboratory, to the ballet, and to that beehive of discussion, the cafeteria of the old University of Moscow.

Finally, there has been a strong impact of anthropological ideas on the work here reported. It is not a fortuitous influence. It has grown out of an initial conviction about the shaping influences of a culture on thought: that culture provides amplifiers in the form of technologies to empower human cognitive capacities. I was early determined that our work should not be limited to Western suburban children. Through circumstances unrelated to our research, I had an opportunity to explore school-learning problems in West and East Africa and to observe some striking differences in the behavior of children in class (see the *Report of Working Group on the Application of Technology to Educational and Cultural Affairs*, 1961). At the University of Dakar I found a lively group of investigators concerned with the differences in development among Wolof and European school children: Professor Henri Collomb, Dr. Serge Sauvageot, Mme. Madeleine Collomb, Mme. Simone Valantin, and others. Mme. Valantin came to the United States for several months in 1962 to study our research techniques at the Center, and later that year a small group from Harvard went to Senegal and worked out some preliminary procedures that promised interesting results. Finally, through a special grant from the Ford Foundation to the University of Dakar and a fellowship from the same foundation to Dr. Patricia Marks Greenfield, we were able to carry out parallel studies in Senegal—matters reported in Chapters 11 and 13.[3]

At approximately the same time Dr. Maccoby was undertaking studies of child development in rural Mexico. He is a veteran in our long campaign in the study of development. The results of his imaginative collaboration appear in Chapter 12. So, too, do some results of a parallel study of the conceptual behavior of Eskimo children undertaken by Mrs. Lee Reich in Anchorage, Alaska.

We have not entirely escaped ethnocentrism in this volume, but I hope we have raised a sufficient number of questions so that the reader will not leap easily from what is observed in the suburbs of Boston or London or Geneva to what exists in a subsistence culture or even in the subcultures of our inner cities. It is plain, to be sure, that there are deeply ingrained universals in human growth. The impact of culture is one of those universals. Even though human cultures have great differences on the surface, they also have certain notable communalities. It would be a mistake to take these universal cultural traits for granted and to forget their huge role in aiding and empowering the growth of individual human beings. But culture produces great differences as well, and these we shall attempt to explicate while keeping in mind the universals.

In a venture as long-drawn-out and as extensive as this one there

---

[3] A special word of thanks is needed here, to Philip Kaiser, former United States Ambassador to Senegal, and Mrs. Kaiser, who helped us with all our arrangements, provided us with hospitality and good counsel, and opened many doors. They even guided our apparatus through a skeptical customs office!

are many people to thank and many donors whose generosity in providing research funds must be signaled. Grants, research contracts, and enabling fellowships are listed on the page following this preface. We are grateful to school authorities in many places who provided access to children for our various tests and experiments—in Boston and its suburbs and surrounding cities, particularly Newton, Brookline, Arlington, and Worcester; in Dakar and Taiba N'Diaye in Senegal; in Anchorage, Alaska; in Mexico City and in a small Mexican town that must remain unnamed.

Numerous people have contributed to the making of this book. Those who have directly assisted in the research as faculty aides and research assistants are noted in the several chapters in connection with particular experiments. Their help has been invaluable. Three of them have been particularly gifted in working with children and thus in helping us to a sense of how to design experiments for them: Jennifer Campbell-Pitt, Betty Burgoon, and Jan Bettman. Their tact and their wisdom with children has been a source of delight to those of us for whom they served as assistants.

We are especially grateful to several people for maintaining peace and order in the "shop" over the six years of our work—in preparing reports and manuscripts, in checking bibliographies, and in scheduling experiments and meetings. Maryse Anderson, Marjorie Mayer, Barbara Graf, Ellen Plakans, and Ann Chait have been intelligent and patient in these pursuits. Betty Gardner has aided us by drawing the several dozen figures designed to summarize our data. John Crowley has skillfully and swiftly designed and built apparatus. In the preparation of any book there are many chores to be done. The chief editorial task of rendering the manuscript more readable fell to Mrs. Katharine Strelsky.

The major task of running the "shop"—that is, seeing that the human and material assistance was ready without fuss—was accomplished with grace by Mrs. Paul Bartlett, the Assistant to the Director, and her small but able staff.

There are many colleagues to whom we would acknowledge our gratitude for ideas and suggestions. Most of these must remain unsung, though their influence is pervasive throughout the book. Several, however, have been especially contributory. Professor George Miller and Professor Roger Brown have been continually available for talk and have been generous with their critical aid. Several Visiting Senior Fellows at the Center have also been particularly helpful at different stages. I have already mentioned our great debt to Professor Bärbel Inhelder of Geneva. Professor Nelson Goodman of Brandeis University, Professor Jan Smedslund of Oslo, Professor Mary Henle of the New School for Social Research, Professor Sheldon White, then of the University of Chicago and Dr. Peter Wason of University College, London, are others. We are grateful to Dr. David McNeill, Dr. Dan Slobin, and Dr. Janellen Huttenlocher for much good discussion and advice. They barely escaped the burden of being coauthors.

Several colleagues have provided useful guidance on different matters. One of these, Professor Roman Jakobson, would very likely insist that, in spite of his most convincing efforts, I still treat language as if it bore too arbitrary a signifying relation to the world of experience, that there are ikonic aspects of language that are neglected in this book. I would agree. And another colleague, Professor I. A. Richards, would argue that I separate images from action too sharply, that images are "full of muscles." Again I agree. I hope that later work will show a proper acknowledgment of these criticisms.

One person was particularly generous and supporting during the long process of preparing this book. He was Mr. Gordon Ierardi of John Wiley and Sons, our publisher. When the idea of a book of this sort was proposed to him in 1963 during a dinner conversation at the Harvard Club in New York, he responded by mailing us a contract the next morning. When I was discouraged with a late draft of the book, he heartened us by telephoning from New York immediately on receipt of my letter. He died on February 17, 1966. We mourn a good friend, a fine editor, and a champion of psychological writing.

Many points of disagreement are nevertheless minor by comparison with the points of fundamental agreement we share with Professor Jean Piaget. This volume would have been impossible without his monumental work. His genius has founded modern developmental psychology. It gives us all deep pleasure to dedicate this book to him on his seventieth birthday and to present it to him on that occasion at the XVIIIth International Congress of Psychology in Moscow on August 9, 1966.

Cambridge, Massachusetts
May, 1966

Jerome S. Bruner

The following grants and contracts were made available to the Center for Cognitive Studies, Harvard University for support of research that resulted in Chapters 1, 2, 5, 6, 7, 8, 9, 11, 13, and 14, for the period 1960–1965: Carnegie Corporation of New York, #B-3004; The Ford Foundation; National Institutes of Health, #M-1324-C3 and -C4, #MH-05120-02, -03, and -04, #2G-1011, #5T1GM-1011-02 and -03; U. S. Office of Education, #OE-4-10-136. The project reported in Chapter 6 was also supported in part by research grants from the Canada Council and from Dalhousie University to Dr. David Olson. The investigation in Chapter 12 has been supported by a grant from the Foundations Fund for Research in Psychiatry to Dr. Erich Fromm, who is directing the study of the Mexican village, and by a Public Health Service Fellowship (M7888) to Michael Maccoby from the Institute of Mental Health of the U. S. Public Health Service.

Contents

CHAPTER 1

On Cognitive Growth

Jerome S. Bruner

We shall be concerned in the pages that follow with the nature of cognitive growth—how human beings increase their mastery in achieving and using knowledge. The body of the book consists of chapters dealing with particular manifestations of this growth, such as the growth of classification, of information seeking, and of perceptual recognition. A final chapter then sets forth some general conclusions.

The function of these two opening chapters, then, is to set the stage, to describe in a general way the rationale of the research and the theoretical point of view that gives that research coherence. There are several central themes that recur, themes that are almost axiomatic to our conception of growth and the conditions that shape it.

The first theme relates to the means by which growing human beings represent their experience of the world; and how they organize for future use what they have encountered. There are striking changes in emphasis that occur with the development of representation. At first the child's world is known to him principally by the habitual actions he uses for coping with it. In time there is added a technique of representation through imagery that is relatively free of action. Gradually there is added a new and powerful method of translating action and image into language, providing still a third system of representation. Each of the three modes of representation—enactive, ikonic, and symbolic—has its unique way of representing events. Each places a powerful impress on the mental life of human beings at different ages, and their interplay persists as one of the major features of adult intellectual life.

A second major theme centers around the impact of culture in the nurturing and shaping of growth. We take the view that cognitive growth in all its manifestations occurs as much from the outside in

1

as from the inside out. Much of it consists in a human being's becoming linked with culturally transmitted "amplifiers" of motoric, sensory, and reflective capacities. It goes without saying that different
cultures provide different "amplifiers," at different times in a child's
life. One need not expect the course of cognitive growth to run parallel in different cultures, for there are bound to be different emphases,
different deformations. But many of the universals of growth are also
attributable to uniformities in human culture. Cultural differences
are not all that is produced by human culture. Cognitive growth,
whether divergent or uniform across cultures, is inconceivable without
participation in a culture and its linguistic community.

A third theme relates man's growth to his evolutionary history,
particularly to his immediate past as a product of primate evolution.
The increased emphasis in primate evolution upon distance receptors
that accompanied arborealization, and on the gradual despecialization
represented by the evolution of the cortex, has a notable significance
for understanding human growth. Man seems to have evolved with
a unique capacity for helplessness that can be relieved by outside
shaping and external devices. It is enough to note here that, although
man has only about a quarter of his adult brain volume at birth
and does not achieve it all until the end of his second decade, most
monkeys have more than two-thirds at birth and reach full brain
weight within a year. It is as if, to paraphrase Le Gros Clark (1963),
man's neural equipment favored his mode of adapting to the environment by social and technical means rather than by morphological
adaptation.

These are the major themes. There are also some "points of view"
to be made explicit at the outset. They concern the nature of explanation where cognitive growth is concerned. The first is that psychological events require explanation in terms of psychological processes
and are not fully explicated by translation into sociological, physiologi-
cal, evolutionary, linguistic, or logical terms. Cognitive growth is a
series of psychological events. A child does not perform a certain
act in a certain way at a certain age *because* the culture he lives
in exhibits a certain pattern, *because* it is inherent in the evolution
of primates that vision is a dominant sense, *because* his language
has or does not have an easy or an obligatory way of making a
significant distinction, or *because* the child's act exhibits a certain
underlying logical structure. Nor, obviously, does it suffice to explain
any aspect of human growth to say merely that "this is typical of
the five-year-old."

Such final causes, formal causes, material causes, and historical causes are all interesting and challenging to the psychologist who seeks to understand the growth of mind. But for him they must remain insufficient. For what is needed for a psychological explanation is a psychological theory. *How* does a culture in which a child lives affect his way of looking at the world? Does the dominance of visual and auditory cues in early life (primate in origin though they may be) operate by a channeling of attention, by selectivity of memory, or how? Why do *some* linguistically available distinctions *not* affect thought: for example, the obligatory masculine-feminine distinction in the nouns of some but not all Indo-European languages? If a syntactical distinction is reflected in thought, how does it achieve this status? Finally, are we any nearer an *explanation* of a child's solution to a problem to say that the solution presupposes some kind of grasp of the principle of logical implication? Is this not only a more refined and conceivably more useful way of describing the formal properties of the behavior observed—much as it would be useful to say that a return by a player in a tennis match indicated that he was able to intersect the ball's trajectory in a fashion that could be described by a particular set of equations? Such equations would indeed be a useful formal description of an act, for they might permit one to compute decision-time estimates, the amount of lead time required, and so forth, and therefore permit a better estimate of the kind of sensorimotor mechanism required in tennis (or any sport of its kind).

So, too, with a linguistic description; if language *can* affect thought, it is obviously crucial to specify as powerfully as possible the *formal* nature of the language under examination. Later, for example, we shall examine the psychological basis for the widespread early appearance of the $R(x)$ syntactical structure in the baby talk of languages as diverse as English, Russian, and Turkish—none of which exhibits the form in adult syntax. The linguistics must be moderately clear before the relevant psychological question can occur to us. A formal linguistic description is *not* a psychological explanation of the origin or nature of the speaker's behavior. And so, also, to consider an evolutionary example, it is useful to know that among higher primates there have evolved certain nongenerative gestural languages for the expression or communication of emotions. Do these patterns appear in children before the appearance of language proper? Can appropriate responses to such gestures be learned more easily than responses to arbitrary gestures? One does not *explain* such phenomena simply by reference to evolution. What determines the behavior in a human being here and now? Moreover, if one finds that children

in a particular culture have a certain trait, he does not understand
the matter psychologically until it is known what, exactly, the culture
"did" to encourage such behavior (or to discourage certain other
behavior).

Another matter relating to explanation has to do with the "push"
propelling growth. It is a vexing question, and there is some basis
for doubting its fruitfulness in shaping the problem of growth. For
one thing, it translates too easily into the language of teleology, into
notions like "actualization" or "unfolding" or, indeed, unadorned
"maturation." We shall, in keeping with our emphasis upon the shaping effect of both evolution and culture, take the view that growth
requires explanation both from the outside and the inside; the
"pushes" and "unfoldings" need further specification. The early helplessness of man, for example, seems to be accompanied by a propelling
curiosity about the environment and by much self-reinforcing activity
seemingly designed to achieve competence in that environment.

Whether one calls this complex a "will to learn" (Bruner, 1966)
a "competence motive" (R. W. White, 1959), intrinsic motivation
(Hunt, 1965), or *Funktionslust* (K. Bühler, 1930), its internal "push"
seems to be dependent upon an external supply of stimulation in
the form of what Tolman (1932) called *discriminanda* and *manipu-
landa,* things to look at and handle. Indeed, the degree to which
a supply of stimulation creates a demand for it may be crucial for
a species in which morphological adaptation has become so supplemented by technological adaptation—a species that, in Weston La
Barre's striking phrase (1954), survives by grace of prosthetic devices.
Piaget (1951) suggests still another general "push" to growth that
also has both an inner and outer aspect. Intellectual growth, for him,
is propelled by disequilibrium, by a failure of accommodative and
assimilative processes to keep pace with one another—by the failure
of the child's models of the environment to suffice in coping with
the newly learned complexities of that environment. We have in the
past criticized the concept of disequilibrium as used in this way
(Bruner, 1959), both for its lack of specificity and for its circularity
of prediction about growth; yet there is clearly an important truth
in such a "trouble theory of mental development," as an irreverent
undergraduate once called it. Overcoming "trouble" because of the
bad fit to nature of one's models or representations is one aspect
of seeking competence. The rub is that there are many cognitive
conflicts of this kind that do *not* lead a child to grow. We shall
have to return later to this issue.

One last procedural problem must concern us before we turn to a detailed consideration of the main themes of these chapters: whether it is more fruitful to postulate "stages" of growth or to think in terms of gradual processes of growth. We believe the issue is a fruitless one, and for several reasons. For one thing, the smoothness of the growth curve is very much a function of the kind of behavior one is looking at—and, in some instances, how carefully one looks. Language provides a nice case in point. There are ample actuarial studies to show that in some general sense the child gradually acquires "more" language. But current studies of language development (e.g., Brown and Fraser, [1964] or Miller and Ervin [1964]) usually proceed by writing "grammars" for a child's speech at different ages. A child moves from a grammar of single-word holophrases to one in which syntax proper begins with two form classes, a pivot class and an open class, the $P(x)$ construction of Braine (1963b) in which a pivot word like *allgone* precedes virtually all other words in the child's vocabulary except those that are also used as pivots; for example, "allgone Mommy" or "allgone bye-bye." Each grammar one writes, particularly if there are marked differences in rules, represents a "state" or a "stage" in language development. It is perfectly legitimate and necessary to recognize such discontinuities, even though they may disappear if one seeks to average a population of children rather than studying one at a time. So, too, in many aspects of intellectual growth, one can find countless pages in *Child Development* devoted to showing a gradual increase in mastery.

For *a* particular child, however, considered in the light of his capacity to solve *a* particular type of problem, there appear to be important discontinuities. One sees, for example, that a particular child at a particular age cannot use indirect questions in the game of "Twenty Questions." He interprets questions as direct probes for the answer. Some weeks later, the notion of organizing information hierarchically and of using bracketing questions appear with all the abruptness of a rash. The child is suddenly asking indirect, information-seeking questions rather than guessing the answer. If one were studying the childs' study habits, however, the change might appear quite gradual, given what the Geneva school calls "horizontal *décalage*" (Flavell, 1963) or the tendency of newfound structures and strategies to be generalized gradually over an array of related tasks. Kessen's admonition (1962) must surely be taken seriously: one does not describe growth by describing the different states through which it passes. Nonetheless, one does well to note discontinuities however ill equipped we may be to explain them.

To reiterate, then, we shall be concerned with intellectual growth as it is affected by the way human beings gradually learn to represent the world in which they operate—through action, image, and symbol. We shall attempt to show that these representations or constructions of reality cannot be understood without reference to the enabling powers of a culture and the heritage of man's evolution as a primate. At the same time, and almost as a methodological credo, we believe that intellectual growth can be understood only in terms of the psychological mechanisms that mediate it and that the explanation of growth cannot be effected by involving the nature of culture, the nature of language, the inherent logic of child thought, or the nature of man's evolutionary history. One finds no internal push to growth without a corresponding external pull, for, given the nature of man as a species, growth is as dependent upon a link with external amplifiers of man's powers as it is upon those powers themselves.

ON REPRESENTATION

There are two senses in which representation can be understood: in terms of the *medium* employed and in terms of its *objective*. With respect to the first, we can talk of three ways in which somebody "knows" something: through doing it, through a picture or image of it, and through some such symbolic means as language. A first approach to understanding the distinction between the three can be achieved by viewing each as if it were external—though our eventual object is to view representations as internal. With respect to a particular knot, we learn the act of tying it and, when we "know" the knot, we know it by the habitual pattern of action we have mastered. The habit by which the knot is represented is serially organized, governed by some sort of schema that holds its successive segments together, and is in some sense related to other acts that either facilitate it or interfere with it. There is a fair amount of sensorimotor feedback involved in carrying out the act in question, yet what is crucial is that such a representation is executed in the medium of action.

Representation in imagery is just that: the picture of the knot in question, its final phase or some intermediate phase, or, indeed, even a motion picture of the knot being formed. It is obvious, yet worth saying, that to have a picture before one (or in one's head) is not necessarily to be able to execute the act it represents, as those who have invested in books called "Skiing Illustrated" know all too well. A picture or image has certain properties as a medium. A picture is a selective analogue of what it stands for, and only in a trivial sense is it a "copy" of its referent, as Nelson Goodman (1965) and

E. H. Gombrich (1960) remind us. Yet it is not arbitrary. One cannot fathom the word for something by looking at the something. One can learn to recognize an image of something just by looking at the something. Finally, it is most usually "like" something else one has experienced as well, and again by selective resemblance. A particular knot is *like* overlapping circles or a pretzel or a three-leaf clover—at least to the particular people who tie it. The representation of a knot in symbolic terms is not so readily stated, for it involves at the outset a choice of the code in which the knot is to be described. For symbolic representation, whether in natural or mathematical "language," requires the translation of what is to be represented into discrete terms that may then be formed into "utterances" or "strings" or "sentences," or whatever the medium uses to combine the discrete elements by rule. Note, too, that whatever symbolic code one uses it is also necessary to specify whether one is describing a process of tying a knot or the knot itself (at some stage of being tied). There is, moreover, a choice in the linguistic description of a knot whether to be highly concrete or to describe *this* knot as one of a general class of knots. However one settles these choices, what remains is that a symbolic representation has built-in features that are specialized and distinctive. We need not pause here to examine the properties of such a system, for we shall do so in some detail later.

How do we know what kind of representation someone has "in his head?" Obviously, "representation" must be inferred from behavior we can observe. We draw inferences from the manner in which a person segments events, groups them, or organizes, condenses, and transforms them. To infer a person's representation of the world, if we are canny experimenters, we design tasks that permit us to infer how he does these things. We ask him to tell us the fifty states of the Union. If he "reads out" in this order, "Maine, New Hampshire, Vermont . . . ," we can guess that the supporting representation for his recital is spatial. If the order is "Alabama, Alaska, Arizona, Arkansas, California . . . ," the support is inferred to be more list-like, ordered by an alphabetic rule.

We shall consider in a later section the specific nature of internal representation by action, image, and symbol and the difficulties of inferring their presence-in-operation; but before we do so it is necessary to talk first of the *objective* of a representation—not simply the medium by which things are represented, but what they are represented *for*. We have already touched on the question in trying to elucidate symbolic representation, whether it is designed in a particular instance to represent process or state and at what level of abstraction. An utterance can be, in effect, a recipe or prescription or step-by-step account to guide some action. It can represent in language a sequence of acts. Its discrete elements segment the action and its rules of formation then reconstruct the elements into something like the original. This is a representation in symbols *for* action. When the child says, "A hole is to dig," he is defining in words the process of hole making. Luria (1961) makes a great deal of this "pragmatic function" of speech to account for the early process by which the child brings overt behavior under the control of language with the advent of the "Second Signal System." In this form, language can provide a basis for "self-instruction."

Language, of course, is classically useful for the description of states and images. Children use language to describe things and their rela- tion. Here the process involves the abstraction of features in terms of which an object is to be depicted, and a synthesis of these features in an utterance. There is, on the face of it, a sharp distinction between the prescriptive language of recipes and the descriptive language of things.

There are certainly other properties of symbolic representation that relate neither to recipe nor to description. One in particular is relevant here: the use of language (or symbol systems generally) to describe abstract relations among states and processes. We shall deal with this very interesting matter in Chapter 8 and see to what extent the child has difficulty in grasping the symbolic representation of abstract relations that depict neither images nor actions. The last thing to enter the child's vocabulary are the functors—*to, on, at, above,* etc.— the small coin of such relational representations.

Pictures can also be used for representing states, actions, or, in a "symbolized" way, relations. J. Z. Young (1964, p. 3) notes the difference between three pictures (see Figure 1).

Picture *a* is a reasonable "sketch" or "blueprint" of a battery, a switch, and a lamp. It provides a selective picture of a state and, indeed, by taking one part at a time, one could "follow" it in order to reproduce the state depicted. Picture *b*, if it is indeed a picture, is highly symbolized and is, of course, called a circuit or wiring dia- gram. It "includes" Picture *a* as a case but could also include many other kinds of batteries or generators, switches, and resistances. It is puzzling whether to call *c* a picture at all, for in fact it is only a spatial representation of a highly formal set of ideas, and the "blocks" of the block diagram are empty of content. It could stand as easily for an organic system in which sugar was being metabolized (power supply) under the regulation of a temperature-regulating

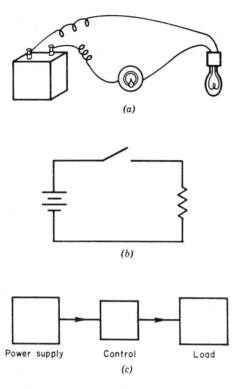

(a)

(b)

Power supply   Control   Load

(c)

Figure 1. Three degrees of pictorial literalness: (*a*) the "blueprint" type of diagram; (*b*) the "circuit diagram" type; (*c*) the "block diagram" type.

mechanism (control), to produce muscle action (load). And indeed, the point of a block diagram is precisely to locate isomorphs, to render such cases as Picture *a* into exemplars of a more generic case.

Often one can translate a symbolically encoded relationship into a spatial image to deal better and more directly with the problem at hand. De Soto (1965) has shown, for example, that three-term problems such as, "Alice is taller than Mary; Elsie is shorter than Mary: Is Elsie taller than Alice?" are translated into an "up-down" image and the answer "read off" the image.

It is not so plain, as we have already commented, how a picture can serve easily as a guide for action or a support for action. The kind of sensorimotor schema that guides skilled activity is usually marked by temporal segments to guide the course of action. These seem to get lost in the simultaneity of a picture or diagram. Yet there is a technology of constructing flow charts that appears to be of considerable use for representing action spatially. Likely as not, diagrams do this by the use of certain language-like features: "the beginning" at the left; "the end" at the right; and so on.

A moment's thought dispels the apparent obviousness that surrounds the question of how a picture guides or supports "looking." Nelson Goodman (1965) has long since warned us off the simple notion that pictures merely reflect "reality." They are obviously and universally selective in what it is they depict and also highly conventionalized. For all that, it is evident that a picture bears a relation to visual experience that words do not, just as there are some ideas that cannot be expressed freely and properly in anything but words. As the philosopher Etienne Gilson (1959) wryly concludes, "It is as impossible to paint by means of words as it is to speak by means of paintings."

Finally, with respect to the uses to which representation by action can be put, the matter is difficult. Indeed, Piaget (1964) doubts whether what we have been calling enactive representation ought to be called representation at all, for it is questionable whether action "stands for" or represents anything beyond itself. Note that earlier we suggested that what was representative about action was its "habitual" pattern, that past events had, so to speak, been inscribed in the form of a persisting and, to some degree, transferable habit pattern. We shall urge later that it is possible for such habit patterns to become programmatic and amenable to being regulated by symbolic activities such as language. Such a programmatic pattern is best illustrated by skilled tool-using. What is at first a habitual pattern for using sensorimotor activity to achieve some end later becomes a program in the sense that various "substitutes" can be inserted without disrupting the over-all act. Even a chimpanzee who is unable to get a hand into an opening to extract a desired object can substitute a stick in place of reaching. Or in skilled tool-using by humans the carpenter who forgets his plane can substitute a chisel in the smoothing routine, a pocket knife, or the edge of a screwdriver, if need be.

We generally speak of such motor skills as "know-how," but they might better be called generative habits in the analogy of generativeness in language, referring to the capacity to recombine and substitute elements to produce a rich area of language from a relatively small stock of language elements. Let us propose that representation by such an action system is designed to guide and support symbolic activity. We believe that motoric representation for symbolic use makes possible the marvelously subtle articulatory side of language and lies at the base of the skills involved in technology.

Can one properly speak of enactive representation in support of looking? Again, one need only cite the literature on preparatory set (e.g., Gibson, 1941) or "orienting reflex" (Sokolov, 1963) to recall that searching for a particular object or pattern is mediated by a response that is specifically geared to a visual or auditory pattern. Granted that such sets are usually rather loosely tuned, as a runner poised to start a race is sprung by virtually any sharp sound, they nonetheless have the property of channeling an organism to be sensitive to some class of external events.

To close this preliminary discussion, there is, the principal use to which enactive representation can be put—the guidance of action itself. Because the issue is discussed in considerable detail later, particularly in connection with Lashley's celebrated Hixon Symposium (1951) paper on serial behavior, we need comment here only on one feature of enactive representation through "habit" as a guide to overt action. It is precisely the manner in which "habit" provides a pattern which is *not* serially determined for the guidance of behavior that *is*. That is to say, it is in the nature of habit to free serial behavior from being ordered in an inflexible chaining, such that *c* must follow *b*, which must follow *a*, etc. Indeed, the idea of enactive *representation* (rather than simply action) is premised on the conviction that, insofar as action is flexibly goal-directed and capable of surpassing detours, it must be based on *some* form or representation that transcends the mere serial linking of stimuli and responses.

To sum up, we have seen that representation can be effected in the media of symbols, images, and actions and that each form of representation can be specialized to aid symbolic manipulation, image organization, or the execution of motor acts. Each of the media accomplishes each objective in its own terms. Plainly, the three representational systems are parallel and each is unique, but all are also capable of partial translation, one into the other. And here lies one very important "impulsion" to cognitive growth. For, as we shall see, there is serious disequilibrium when two systems of representation do not correspond—what one sees with how one says it, or how one must act overtly and how the world appears. Indeed, we shall see that it is usually when systems of representation come into conflict or contradiction that the child makes sharp revisions in his way of solving problems—as, for example, there may be a conflict between "appearance" and "reality," the one being ikonic and the other symbolic. However, these are matters better reserved for the specific content of experiments.

ENACTIVE REPRESENTATION

In setting forth his view of emotion William James proposed that we cry not because we are sad but are sad because we cry. Toward the closing months of the first year of life there is a cognitive phenomenon comparable to the James-Lange view of emotion. By then the identification of objects seems to depend not so much on the nature of the objects encountered as on the actions evoked by them. Two observations by Piaget (1954, p. 22) illustrate the point:

> So also Laurent at 0:7 loses a cigarette box which he has just grasped and swung to and fro. Unintentionally he drops it outside the visual field. He then immediately brings his hand before his eyes and looks at it for a long time with an expression of surprise, disappointment, something like an expression of its disappearance. But far from considering the loss as irremediable, he begins again to swing his hand, although it is empty. After this he looks at it once more! For anyone who has seen this act and the child's expression, it is impossible not to interpret such behavior as an attempt to make the object come back. Such an observation . . . places in full light the true *nature of the object peculiar to this stage: a mere extension of the action.*

Or consider Lucienne, a month younger:

> At 0:6 Lucienne is alone in her bassinet and, watching what she is doing, grasps the material covering the sides. She pulls the folds toward herself but lets them go at each attempt. She then brings before her eyes her hand which is tightly closed, and opens it cautiously. She looks attentively at her fingers and recommences. This goes on more than ten times.
> It is therefore sufficient for her to have touched an object, believing she grasps it, for her to conceive of it as being in her hand although she no longer feels it. Such a behavior pattern . . . shows the degree of tactile permanence the child attributes to objects he has grasped.

For the infant, then, the actions evoked by stimulus events may serve in major part to "define" them. At this age he is unable to differentiate clearly between percept and response. The sight of the box leads Laurent to swing it, but when the box disappears the action is used to evoke the sight of the box. Lucienne expects to see the fold of cloth in her hand, having clenched her hand "as if" the cloth were still in it. In later childhood this first technique of representation does not fully disappear, and it is very likely the origin of the phenomenon that Freud remarked in children, "the omnipotence of thought"—a confusion between thinking something and doing it.

We find behavior in toxic regression and in severe cortical damage that also has enactive features, though different from the child's behavior. Here is a description by Hanfmann, Rickers-Ovsiankina, and Goldstein (1944, p. 5) of a carefully studied case, that of Lanuti, who has suffered massive lesions in the occipital cortex. He is given various objects and asked what they are.

> [Hard-boiled egg in its shell]: Lanuti takes the egg, turns it, knocks it lightly on the table, shakes it in front of his ear, then makes a motion to throw it saying, "Ball . . . want play?" The examiner cracks the egg and returns it to Lanuti, who now immediately starts shelling the egg very carefully and says, as if making a discovery, "Egg!"
> [Match and matchbox]: When a box of matches is opened for the patient, he takes out a match and repeatedly strikes it on the box, but when the match finally lights, he stares at it at first in complete amazement and only then as if he were making a discovery. "Match this!" and asks for permission to keep the box. In repeating the experiment after a few minutes, Lanuti happens to strike the match on the wrong surface. He says with a puzzled and bewildered expression: "No more, no good this . . . no start this . . . no match . . . this strike and no match . . . ."
> [Ball]: Lanuti takes it, squeezes it, bites into it, and shakes his head in disapproval. Throws the ball on the floor and when it rebounds, exclaims joyfully, "Ball!"

An interesting question is how this tight link between action and perception becomes established by the latter half of the first year of life. Although the data on perceptual development from birth till the sixth month are unfortunately scarce, there are still sufficient indications in the contemporary work to suggest an interesting hypothesis.

Let us begin with the reasonable assumption that in the life of an organism there is a point at which that organism "begins to see." Now, this point is in fact many points, for "seeing" is an achievement in which primitive forms are integrated into more powerful ones. There is plenty of evidence from human and subhuman primate neonates to indicate that from birth organisms are capable of discriminating a great many features of the environment. Four lines of work support this "nativistic" view.

The first is anatomical and comes from the work of Hubel and Wiesel (for a general account, see Hubel, 1963) on the nature of anatomical arrangements in the visual system. Their findings indicate that groups of cells in the geniculate and in the cortex of the monkey respond to edges in the visual field oriented dark in one direction and light in another; others respond to the obverse; still others respond to light centers surrounded by white, showing that there are systematic built-in response patterns to changes in orientation in a line, etc. It is quite plain that from birth the primate nervous system has a sufficiently large array of independently operative analyzers to register on many features of the visual world. It may also have an equal richness in other modalities, although no work comparable to the above has yet been accomplished. Yet, as Hubel (1963) remarks,

> One cannot expect to "explain" vision, however, from a knowledge of the behavior of a single set of cells, geniculate or cortical, any more than one could understand a wood pulp mill from an examination of the machine that cuts the logs into chips. . . . "Higher" structures build on the information they receive from these cortical cells, rearranging it to produce an even greater complexity of response (p. 62).

We shall consider that process shortly, but the other sources of evidence must be examined first.

The work of Kessen (1965) provides another clue. He has examined the manner in which day-old human babies scan with eye movements a solid-colored triangle on a contrasting field. Indeed, it is quite apparent from the tracings obtained that neonates are able to locate corners and lines, along with a sharp contour separating dark and light; and what is just as important, there is not only discrimination at the start but also appropriate motor activity, a matter that will concern us shortly.

A related set of experiments carried out by Bower (1965) on human infants from four to nine weeks of age suggested how wide a range of features of the visual field are discriminated at a surprisingly early age. He used two different techniques: an operant conditioning technique in which slight head movements by the child activated a switch, which in turn signaled the child's mother to appear from hiding and coo at the child, and a technique for recording heart rate to determine whether the appearance of a stimulus in the visual field produced a change in the heart rate. By the use of both techniques it was possible to determine that very young children discriminate many features of the visual figures presented to them—even an oblique plane from one that is orthogonal to the eye, or orientations of lines, as well as various simple features like size and brightness. Bower also reported that if a moving stimulus is passed behind a screen and emerges unchanged within approximately a second little change in heart rate occurs, but if the moving stimulus disappears and then reappears in altered form the reappearance produces a marked reaction—provided the emergence is within the critical time limit. Beyond that limit altered appearance has no effect. This suggests that there may be a very early mechanism for registering not only the many features of objects but also the continued identity of objects, at least over short periods of time.

The work of Fantz (1965) suggests much the same story, though his data are based on infants' *preference* for looking at one of two patterns presented to him. His results are, so to speak, *a fortiori* evidence, for in order to prefer one pattern to another the baby would obviously have to be able to discriminate them. Presumably, there would be some pairs of patterns discriminated that would not yield a "looking preference." Fantz finds for primates during the first ten days (including babies) that patterns are usually preferred to plain figures, irregular edges to regular, centered patterns to diffuse ones, three-dimensionally shaded ones to flat ones, moving ones to still ones—all of which, interestingly enough, are properties of "objects."

Fantz (like Kessen) takes the view that objects as such are constructed, a view also held by Piaget (1954), who even entitles one of his monographs *La Construction du Réel chez l'Enfant*. Fantz holds the view that a child's preference for certain features, leading as it does to his biased exposure to them, builds up a correlation among these features in the form of cell assemblies. The correlation inheres in the fact that the preferred features happen to be highly correlated in natural visual input—being properties of objects. Now, when the child reaches the stage of reaching and manipulating, Fantz argues, there is "added to" this correlated visual input the "reinforcement" of kinaesthetic feedback. This, in effect, leads the child to segment the world into further segregated correlated features, the objects we handle as well as look at. And so Fantz concludes that "perception is innate in the neonate, but largely learned in the adult" (1965, p. 400).

Now, it is quite plain that such a constructionist view leaves out of account many aspects of perceptual development that could be learned neither by a process of correlating features encountered nor by "tying" them together by the intermediation of kinaesthetic feedback. Anybody who has read the subtle accounts in von Senden's valuable book on the restored sight of the congenitally blind (1960) will recognize the uniqueness of a spatial framework. It seems to be given in the very nature of the visual modality and makes possible a perceptual locus. To such a spatially defined locus correlated features can be assigned to yield a simultaneous rendering of the visual and kinaesthetic features that are successively encountered. Indeed, logic alone compels recognition of the fact that "objects seen in a certain place" require a spatial framework to which they can be assigned, and von Senden's compendium (1960) of evidence makes reasonably plain that such a spatial framework cannot be achieved without sight. Therefore, though objects are "constructed," the construction takes place within a prepared and innate visual framework.

The work of Held and his colleagues provides a hint of what is involved in the process of "constructing objects." The medium of this work has been the experiment involving an organism's adaptation to prisms that displace the visual field in some order-preserving transformation—lateral, vertical, or oblique displacements. Held and his co-workers have found that adaptation to such displacements requires not only "visual experience" with the displacements but also motor activity, so that there can be reafference to provide the data necessary for recorrelating the visual and kinaesthetic fields. Reafference refers to the neural excitation that is systematically dependent on movements initiated by the sensing organism. In a recent review article Held (1965) concludes:

> In sum, the experiments I have described have led us to conclude that the correlations entailed in the sensory feedback accompanying movement—reafference—plays a vital role in perceptual adaptation. It helps the newborn develop motor coordination; it figures in the adjustment to the changed relation between afferent and efferent signals resulting from [physical] growth; it operates in the maintenance of normal coordination, and it is of major importance in coping with altered visual and auditory inputs (p. 94).

We suggest that the origin of enactive representation is found precisely in the reafference that serves to relate the requirements of action to the properties of the visual field. We know from the work of Kessen already cited (1965) that the effort at correlation begins on the first day of life. The initial form of action is "looking at," as in eye movements or orientation of the head. It is obviously innate. Later, the actions of grasping, mouthing, holding, and the like further "objectify" and "correlate" the environment. Action, in this view, is the necessary condition for the infant's achievement of the ecologically valid "correlations" that constitute the segmented and segregated objects of experience. Action and some input from the distance receptors provide the necessary and sufficient conditions for such progress— assuming now an intact nervous system.

These are the preliminaries that, in our view, set the stage for the sensorimotor phase of development of which Piaget (1954) has written so brilliantly, a stage in which action and external experience are fused. He refers to the first part of sensorimotor intelligence as one in which things are "lived rather than thought." He likens this type of intelligence to an irreversible and fixed succession of static images, each connected with an action. In time, Piaget notes, the child seems able to "hold an object in mind" by a less and less direct manual prehension of it. At first the child will respond with searching, or at least frustration, to the disappearance of an object *only* when it is actively removed from his grasp. Late in the first year it suffices to remove the object when the child has *begun to reach for it.* In another few months the child will search for an object removed from view *without the intervention of reaching,* and well before the second birthday he will not only search for hidden objects placed under a cover but also under various covers to see where the object has been transposed in the course of being hidden. The "existence" or "permanence" of the object becomes increasingly independent of direct action toward it. The terminus of this first period of development is the emergence of a world in which objects are independent of the actions taken toward them.

Piaget interprets this growth of an action-free world of objects in an interesting way. At the outset, sensorimotor intelligence is guided by highly specific action schemata that are totally irreversible; that is to say, each action has its own plan, and the action goes off from its beginning to its end, and only in that order. Action at this stage, moreover, is highly egocentric in the sense that it is carried out with no appreciation of an action taken from some other perspective than the child's—for example, when the child's pushing of an object is opposed by the counteracting push of another person. Moreover, the schema of a particular action is uncoordinated with other action schemata. Each action is momentarily sufficient unto itself and is not part of a longer-range, more hierarchical plan of action. Beyond sensorimotor intelligence the major vehicle of development is the coordination of action schemata into a more generalized schema, in which each action is now "fused" with others into something that is more genuinely a representation of the world. The fusion or coordination of action schemata thus produces a kind of simultaneous rendering of the alternative paths of action of which the child is master. He can finally deal with a set of alternatives rather than one line of action at a time.

Just as we know very little about the way in which action fuses with percept in the opening months of life, we know little about how the separation of the two spheres comes about. Piaget's observations are interesting but not explanatory. His theoretical account is so far removed from the specifics of the behavior he describes that one is again left without a sense of detailed explanation. There are a few detailed observations in the literature that are suggestive. One is an observation by Mandler (1962). In his experiment subjects were asked to master a rather complex maze of toggle switches without vision of the maze. A large number of trials was needed to achieve mastery. Fortunately, Mandler asked his subjects to go on "running through" the maze pattern for many trials, after achieving mastery. After a while several subjects reported that they were now going about the task differently. Now, they claimed, they had an image of the true path rather than a connected series of overt movements. Their image permitted a perspective of the maze outside action proper, one that served to render simultaneous what before was a sequence of acts. How this "print out" of stabilized action into imagery comes about we cannot say, but we cite this experiment on adults to indicate that the process of conversion from overlearned or serial response to summarizing imagery may be one key to the problem. It is a hint that leads us immediately to a line of inquiry about the relation of serial and simultaneous organization in perception and behavior.

When motor activity becomes "regularized" or "steady," is it converted from a "serial" to a "simultaneous" form? Here we may turn again to Lashley's famous Hixon Symposium paper, "The Problem of Serial Order in Behavior" (1951). In brief, he argues that it is inconceivable that serial motor activity can take place in an orderly fashion, as it does, without there being a matrix of background representational processes, built up through past encounters with the environment and not very amenable to change on the basis of immediate peripheral stimulation. That representation must be in the form of a simultaneous or "atemporal" representation. Let us suggest as an hypothesis that such a representation begins as a trace of a prior response. This primitive representation or trace guides a new response and makes some kind of anticipation possible. It thus "frees" behavior from complete peripheral control. In order for behavior to become more skillful, it must become increasingly freer of immediate or serial regulation by environmental stimuli operative while the behavior is going on. I believe that this "freedom" is achieved by a shift from response learning to place learning—in effect, the placing of the behavior in a spatial context or "layout" that makes possible its organization in more flexible ways, notably by making possible detours and substitutions to meet changed conditions. It is this spatialization that provides the "atemporal" rule for regulating serial behavior to which

Lashley refers, and it is this common feature of "place" that makes possible the translatability or transfer of schemata from one pattern of behavior to another. For example, over time all hammering behavior becomes translatable into a common schema, even though the different hammering acts may each involve different muscle groups. Just as in Mandler's experiment (1962), in the beginning there is response learning, and in time as the supporting schema becomes abstracted from particular serial acts there is place learning. It seems fairly evident on *a priori* grounds that such a shift could not take place without the intermediation of a spatial framework, even one that is completely egocentric with all dimensional origins starting at a figurative Cyclopean eye in the middle of the child's forehead! For it is the essence of such spatial representation that it be atemporal or simultaneous, and it is only through visual space that such simultaneity can be achieved. (One recalls the precocious blind child mentioned by von Senden [1960] who developed a tactile tape measure to no avail, as far as simultaneous spatial awareness was concerned.)

Once a schema becomes abstracted from a particular act and becomes related to serial acts in a one-many relation it can become the basis for action-free imagery. Then the child's way of representing the world can also become free of action. It is a slow procedure, this dissociation of a spatially organized schema from supporting actions. The degree to which the child, even after action-free imagery is well developed, continues to depend on some forms of enactive representation, is striking. An early experiment by Emerson (1931), extended by Werner (1948), and repeated in our laboratory with interesting variations by Drake (1964) illustrates the point. Emerson's study of delayed reaction in young children between the ages 2:3 and 4:11 deals with the child's ability to remember the position of a ring placed on a near-upright rack containing some forty-two regularly distributed pegs arranged in six columns and seven rows. A ring is placed on a peg on the experimenter's rack. The child is then asked to copy this position on his own rack. But the child's rack can be moved with respect to the experimenter's. It can be placed facing the experimenter's rack, at a right angle to it, or back-to-back with it. When a very young child moves to his own rack, he has great difficulty in placing the ring on the correct peg if his rack has been displaced. For all children, the greater the angular displacement required to go from the experimenter's rack to his own in order to copy what was on the experimenter's rack, the greater the difficulty of the task. The older children are less affected by bodily reorientation and seem to carry out the task more by perceptual orientation and less by the aid of body representation. Werner has repeated the study on older children and gives the following summary in his *Comparative Study of Mental Development* (1948, p. 166b):

> We repeated these experiments with children six to ten years of age and found that the peg position was accurately determined by many subjects through numerical-verbal means. Thus, with increasing age, delayed response patterns seemed to become reorganized in terms of functions of a genetically higher order. We are probably justified in distinguishing at least three genetic levels: At the primary level, the delayed response appears mainly based on bodily (sensory-motor) cues; at a higher level concrete perceptual relationships gain increasingly in importance; finally verbal conceptual activity may become a significant factor in the delayed response pattern.

Drake added several interesting variations to Emerson's basic experiment. For one thing, she included a condition in which the children, having been shown where the ring was to be placed, were then asked to hop to the corner of the room and back before placing it on the proper peg. The effect of this intervening motor activity was completely disruptive for the three-year-olds; but they were not disturbed by waiting quietly for a comparable period of time. Moreover, the older children seemed hardly troubled at all. The effect, of course, may be due to interference by interpolated activity. The matter is worth more careful inquiry.

Withal, the transition from dependence on motor representation to autonomous sensory control remains obscure. It is of some comfort to quote the shrewd and witty comment of Leeper (1963, pp. 404–405) on the relation of motor activity to underlying representational process.

> Much of what is attributed to motor habits is actually a matter of . . . representational habits and sensory-organization habits rather than what we will describe as "motor-discharge habits." For example, when a person learns to swim the crawl stroke, part of what he learns is skill in perceiving when his mouth is sufficiently out of water to permit safe breathing. The perceptual skill can be transferred to any other stroke . . . . In fact, many types of learned activity that involve motor activity have little or no development of new motor-coordination habits as part of what is learned. For instance, it is doubtful that maze learning or learning in a lever-pulling experiment is a matter of motor skills to any significant degree. More probably, these are merely cases where new representational habits are developed and govern the use of already acquired motor skills. A person who learns to walk over the necessary routes in a new town is not learning new movement patterns of walking. He is merely learning representational habits which, having been learned with reference to walking, could easily be transferred to bicycle riding or roller-skat-

ing. All such considerations help to explain why cognitive psychologists have been so dissatisfied with the proposition that habits are linkages between stimuli and effector responses. Maybe the whole point can be summed up by saying that movements often are like symbols or actually are symbols. Their significance is determined by the relations of those movements to a larger context of the situation. A person blows on his hands to warm them, he blows on his soup to cool it.

There is doubtless a whole range of factors affecting the gradual loosening of the world of perception and imagery from the world of action. The work of Werner and Wapner (1956) and other "sensoritonic" theorists suggests that the separation is never complete. We have been at some pains in this section to explore what might be involved in this course of development through which the child must first get the spatial world of vision in correspondence with the serial world of action and then, later, free the perceptual world and imagery from the control of action. In the course of the discussion we have tried to make a little clearer what is meant by enactive representation. Many issues must remain obscure, but the importance of the phenomena one observes during the period of growth that encompasses the opening year or two of life should not be overlooked simply because our theories are still so primitive.

IKONIC REPRESENTATION

A second stage in representation emerges when a child is finally able to represent the world to himself by an image or spatial schema that is relatively independent of action. By the end of the first year the child is well on his way toward this accomplishment. At the outset there remains a strong component of manipulation as a necessary aid to imagery.

Because it is so difficult to infer directly the nature of the images in terms of which the child organizes his cognitive activity (though we shall investigate the matter in following chapters), we would do well to begin with the organization of perception in the young child. It seems not unlikely that the properties one finds in visual perception at this age might appear in exaggerated form in the child's imagery or his spatial schematization. Perception in young children can be characterized by the following features, according to Gibson and Olum (1960): (1) it is "stuck" or nontransformable; (2) it is "autistic" or subject to the influence of affect; (3) it is "diffuse" in organization; (4) it is "dynamic," in the sense of being closely related to action; (5) it is concrete rather than schematic or abstracted; (6)

it is "egocentric," in the sense of having a central reference to the child as observer; and (7) it is marked by an unsteady attention. To this interesting list we would add one more entry: (8) the young child's perception is organized around a minimal number of cues, and these cues are usually the ones to which the child can most readily point.

With respect to the "stuckness" of early perception, a voluntary shift in set seems much more difficult for the young child. Characteristically, then, the young child is an easy victim of camouflage. The studies of Witkin and his colleagues (1962, p. 374) point strongly in this direction.

> The same developmental trend is revealed by the results of both the cross-sectional and longitudinal studies: children tend to be relatively field dependent early in their perceptual development and to become more field independent as they grow older. The ability to determine the position of the body apart from the tilted room, to perceive the position of a rod independent of the tilted frame, to pick out a simple figure obscured by a complex design, tends to improve on the whole, until about the age of 17.

To exemplify with a specific finding: the time required for children to find a simple figure "camouflaged" by a masking design of greater complexity is something of the order of one hundred fifty seconds per picture at age ten and about fifty seconds five years later. In fact, the task is too difficult for children much below ten, for they seem unable visually to decompose complex geometrical figures into their components. Goodenough and Eagle, in a study reported by Witkin et al. (1962), have designed a procedure for younger children, and it is interesting that they have had to make two compromises in doing so. For one thing, they have had to make the hidden figures "meaningful," that is, familiar objects. Then, to quote the authors (Witkin, Dyk, Fatterson, Goodenough, Karp [1962, p. 62]):

> In contrast to the Embedded Figures Test, the Children's Form is more of an action than a spectator situation. Each of the complex figures is mounted on a 21-inch-square board in the form of a multi-colored jigsaw puzzle. Knobs are attached to several of the pieces, but only the correct simple form can be removed from the board by pulling at the appropriate knob.

In short, imagery must be made *concrete*, and the task of isolating a simple figure within the complex figure must be rendered *manipulative*.

By the same token, as we shall see in Chapter 5, the young child (for example, the three-year-old) seems ill equipped to *reconstruct* a picture from its parts or *complete* it from partial cues. Mooney's (1957) study is characteristic. Children from seven to thirteen as well as adults were shown incomplete black and white figures of heads and faces, along with nonsensical items that were similarly cut up or "incomplete." The subjects had to sort the pictures into categories—boy, old woman, and so forth. There is a clear increase with age in the ability to recognize the incomplete pictures. Less redundancy is needed as we grow older. Piaget and von Albertini (1954) have also shown that below six years of age children have great difficulty in recognizing dotted outlines and figures familiar to them as wholes, such as squares, circles, triangles, and rectangles. These investigators examined not only their recognition of dotted forms but also their recognition of forms intersected by other forms—a simpler version of the Embedded Figures Test used by Witkin. From the fourth year on there is a steady increase in the child's ability to "maintain" the integrity of an outline form that is intersected by another. In the early stages of development the child is thrown off the track by the intersections and finds it hard to analyze one of the two different forms out of the mixture. Ghent (1956), also working with children under six, found that their difficulty in recognizing was not limited to intersecting figures but also extended to figures sharing a common contour. Four-year-olds, for example, had great difficulty in isolating figures that shared one contour.

To us these findings suggest two things. In the first place, it would seem that there is relatively little "economy" or generativeness in the representations supporting early childhood perception. We infer this from the child's inability to reconstruct a whole from the shreds of a picture. Second, there seems to be a considerable amount of "one-trackness" or need for serial integrity in the way figures are viewed—the child is easily thrown off by intersecting lines, by camouflage, or by shared boundaries. Perhaps it is for this reason that children so often help themselves out in trying to recognize a complex picture by "tracking" it with a finger, as if the finger guided them through and even provided a point to return to if the eye were distracted.

One might infer from these findings that the complexity of organization in the perceptual field of the young child would be strikingly less than in adults. In a later chapter on the development of perceptual recognition we shall be examining evidence on this point in some detail. In passing, it is worth noting that the literature, for all its imperfections, confirms the inference. Hemmendinger (1953), for example, using the Rorschach technique, has found that three-year-olds respond "globally" to the ink blots, giving whole responses and reporting virtually no details. Somewhere between the sixth and eighth year there is an increase in the number of details reported, but it is only around the ninth year that the details are integrated into a whole pattern. A study by Segers (1926) and a more recent one by Vurpillot and Zoberman (1965), in which children had to match one set of pictures to another, similarly indicate that young children have greater difficulty in noticing detailed differences between pictures, as if they were attending to the more general features of objects around them. Yet, at the same time, we know from the work of Elkind, Koegler, and Go (1964) and from other work by Vurpillot and Zoberman that on occasion children also respond to very small details in attempting to recognize and match design—but only to one detail at a time. If the task is more demanding, they fall back on a global impression. It is one side of this commonly noticed characteristic of children that has led experienced students of child development like Werner (1948) to remark upon diffuseness and "globality" as a major characteristic of childhood perception, whereas others speak of the child as being overly sensitive to small, single cues.

As already noted in other contexts, the perceptual life of the child is saturated with a motoric component—reflecting a transition from strong reliance on enactive representation. Gellerman (1933), for example, found finger tracing to be essential both in two-year-old children and in chimpanzees learning "triangularity *per se*"—as if the children and apes were translating the visual image into "three turns." An experiment by Jeffrey (1958), well summarized by Gibson and Olum (1960, p. 367), also points to the importance of accompanying action in discrimination:

> His criterion task was learning to press a button on the left in response to a low tone (128 cycles per second) and one on the right to a high tone (1152 cycles per second), and, after mastering this problem, to do the same for a closer pair (256 and 384 cycles per second). Three groups of kindergarten children took part. Group I did only the criterion task. Group II had pretraining consisting of trying to sing the two tones and were then passed to the criterion task. Group III had pretraining by striking the appropriate keys on a piano (the two keys were marked with red tape) and were then passed to the criterion task. Only one of the seven Ss in Group I was able to learn the criterion task in 72 trials. In Group II five of the seven learned it, and in Group III all did.

Many writers have commented upon the egocentrism of the young child's perceptual world. The child characteristically is not able to view the world perceptually from other perspectives than his own. If, as in the experiments of Piaget and Inhelder (1956), a six-year-old child is asked to match the position of objects on a toy landscape on another identical one rotated 90 degrees away from the axis of the first, he has great difficulty. He himself is at the origin of all the coordinate systems that order his perceptual field, and he cannot appreciate other origins. "Taking a view" external to himself is as difficult for him socially as it is perceptually and intellectually. If he is asked to recount the number of people in his family, he will give the correct number—save that he often leaves himself out of the reckoning—for his frame of reference in counting is not "outside" the family but "inside counting out."

In the same egocentric fashion the child represents his affective states by distortion in the perceptual field and in the systematic changes in imagery by which those fields are remembered. The experiments of Bruner and Goodman (1947), Tajfel (1957), and the "New Look" generally point in this direction.

Finally, the child's perceptual attention is highly *unstable*. He is notoriously distractible. Perhaps this trait accounts for the short supply of research on early perception! For young children can be astonishing in their distractibility. They are victims of the shifting sensory vividness and of the novelty of their environments. Titchener (1908) long ago distinguished between primary, secondary, and derived primary attention. Primary attention, he held, is governed by inherent sensory considerations: an almost involuntary attention to *changes* in the visual field, to movement, to brightness, and the like. Secondary attention is conceived of as the effort to focus upon some segment of experience that would not, under the laws of primary attention, be particularly compelling. With derived primary attention, the newly acquired cues become automatic through practice, as in the well-known experiments of Lawrence (1949, 1950) on the acquired distinctiveness of cues. The child seems to pass through some such progress as Titchener describes. What accounts for the growing stability we shall consider later. If we assume that the "inner image" is like the external percept, perhaps more so, the inference would be somewhat along these lines.

We have examined early childhood perception with a view to inferring the character of a child's "image of the world." Its inflexibility, its dependence upon small details imbedded in diffuseness, its self-centeredness and susceptibility to the distortions of need and affect, its action-dependence, its distractibility—all suggest a system that, unlike the serial ordering of action and enactive representation, is labile and highly lacking in the economy of which Attneave (1954) writes. It is as if the young child, having achieved a perceptual world that is no longer directly linked to action, now deals with the surface of things that catch attention rather than with deeper structures based on invariant features. Or, to put it another way, it is as if the child had as his next principal task to find precisely a way of getting to the base structure of the world of appearance. In one experiment after another in the following chapters we shall see the younger child failing to solve problems by virtue of using surface cues while the older child succeeds by learning to respond to such "invisible" or "silent" features as relations, hierarchies, etc.

Clementina Kuhlman (1960) has addressed her research most directly to this point.[1] Her initial hypothesis is that the major vehicle of "thinking" in children is imagery and its manipulation. Their subsequent intellectual development takes one of two related courses: "Either the habit of using imagery is suppressed as language is learned or it is retained during language acquisition and is adapted to the requirements of complex problem solving" (pp. 109–110). The cognitive operations of imagistic thinking, though serving to preserve past experience, are dominated by rules of organization that rest upon spatio-temporal-qualitative properties of experience. Thus the grouping of objects is carried out by principles of contiguity or on the basis of dominant perceptual similarity. One would expect, then, that certain intellectual tasks, even though associated with language acquisition, would be aided by imagery and certain others hindered. One might expect, for example, that the task of learning a vocabulary of concrete nouns would be aided by good imagery, for the nature of the task is to associate a relatively arbitrary label with a particular thing. On the contrary, learning a concept in which one had to discover the common property that tied together a set of perceptually quite diverse objects would be hindered by imagery.

To test this initial hypothesis, Kuhlman selected two groups of children from the first, second, third, and fourth grades of an American public primary school, one group scoring high in a test of imagery, the other low. For proper control she matched pairs of good and poor imagers in terms of their school grades, sex, and IQ's. Imagery was measured by a combined index of four standard imagery tests: Thurstone's Space Test in the battery for assessing Primary Mental Abilities, the Kuhlmann-Finch Space Test, the Minnesota Paper Form Board, and the Flags Test. These tests measured not only visualization

---

[1] Because Dr. Kuhlman's study is highly relevant to our concerns and is not published, we refer to it *in extenso* here.

but also the ability to recognize image isomorphs in different orientations.

Her first and, for our purposes, most interesting finding is that children with high imagery are indeed better at performing a task in which they must learn to associate arbitrary verbal labels with pictures. On the other hand, it is the child with low imagery who excels in a task that requires him to form a concept by recognizing the shared attribute of a set of pictures. She remarks about "meaning-categories" or concepts, "A functional attribute or a complexly patterned perceptual attribute is frequently criterial for the meaning-categories, and hence for the correct use of language." For the child who still searches for the vivid perceptual cue the task of attaining conceptual meanings is necessarily made more difficult. Yet for the child who uses the newly acquired conceptual categories and the language that goes with them there is also a cost. Language becomes the preferred mode of grouping, and as time goes on imagery is used less and less and "decays with disuse" (p. 133). The "low-imagery child," though intellectually more supple, seems progressively to lose his ability to preserve the distinctive quality of perceptual experience as such. He becomes slower in learning names for objects and less accurate in reproducing visual stimuli. "The price paid for the superior conceptualizing ability of the low-imagery child would seem to be a conventionalization of memory. Because he depends upon concepts for recall . . . his memory for visual stimuli [is] distorted toward stereotypes determined by those concepts" (p. 115).

It is of more than passing interest, then, that in the first two grades of primary school there is a *positive* correlation between the use of imagery and school achievement as measured by conventional school achievement tests. As likely as not, the emphasis upon identifying things and attaching names to them, as well as the relatively small reliance on reasoning in most early school curricula, would account for this. By the third or fourth grade, the correlation becomes negligible.

Kuhlman tried to ascertain in her research whether the poorer conceptual performance of children with high imagery was a result of their *failure to generalize* or of their *choice of attributes* for grouping. If early differences in conceptualizing were due to differences in generalizing, then achieving a next level of development would depend on mastering the new form of generalization. If, on the other hand, a lesser capacity for concept attainment derived from the choice of grouping attributes, the matter would be quite different. In the latter case the question would involve where the attention of the children was directed—whether to the vivid sensory aspects of objects or to the more subtle perceptual patterns and functional uses of the objects they were to form into conceptual groupings. The results point clearly to the latter conclusion: *the inferior conceptual performance of children with imagery preference is a result of their use of surface features in grouping*. Dr. Kuhlman concludes, "It seems likely that the basis of the inferior concept attainment in high imagery children is not a failure to generalize labels, but a failure in their awareness of the bases upon which generalizations are made" (p. 120).

These observations and others from the work of Reichard et al. (1944), of Werner (1948), and of N. E. Miller (1934) indicate that children up to age eight or nine prefer perceptual bases for sorting objects. They all point to the fact that nonschematized imagery is highly characteristic of early intellectual operations. It is a precursor of more properly "logical" operations which, under certain circumstances, it may even disrupt. The concentration upon surface properties of the environment and the conservation of these properties through imagery seem to constitute a stage of growth that bridges the gap between the rigid serial representation of earlier enactive representation and the language-saturated phase of later childhood that will concern us in the next section.

And, indeed, even progress in symbolic representation seems to rest upon a prior base established by imagery. Thus the child's vocabulary usually grows from small picturable categories to wider and more subtle "unpicturable" ones. Brown (1958, p. 277), for example, reaches the following conclusions about the growth of vocabulary:

> The vocabulary of preschool children in the United States is less abstract than the vocabulary of adults. In studies comparing the most commonly used words in these two vocabularies it was found that the adult list contained many more superordinates. It included words like *article* and *action*, which are not used by children. There were many more picturable words on the children's list, i.e., words naming categories having a characteristic visual contour. Without having made any controlled comparisons most adults are aware of this difference. The young child is likely to say *car* or *truck* but not *vehicle;* he will know *dog* and *man* and *bird* but not *mammal* or *quadruped.* Where he does use a very abstract term like *animal* or *flower* he does not usually possess the full category but only applies the term to some restricted subclass of the whole.

Let us see how we can sum up the matter of ikonic representation. Napoleon is reported to have said that men who think in images are not fit to command. Perhaps Napoleon had in mind this surface property of images. It would be hard for an image-bound general to have recognized Clausewitz's famous dictum that war is a continuation of peacetime policies. The two do not look enough alike. It may be true that a picture is worth a thousand words, but if the object is to locate its functional equivalent in another context then perhaps one word is worth a thousand pictures if it contains the conceptual key. Napoleon's image-struck general would, moreover, be a flighty fellow if he were at all like the perceptually dominated child. Watching a three-year-old child walk across an "attractive" room is an interesting experience. Each act is governed by some new novelty and terminated by a still newer sensory temptation that happens along the path.

In enactive representation there is a confusion of reference that arises from the lack of an autonomous, external frame of reference. By the time ikonic representation is established there is a sharp separation between the child and the world around him. There will often be some confusion even in the three-year-old between what is internal to his own experience and what is "external" in the sense of its being shared by others (as with respect to his dreams), but the separation by now is a relatively clear one. When he "matches" something in his mind to something he is encountering, he does so by pointing to some particular sensory correspondence between the two. Ostensive definition, as we shall see again and again in later chapters, is critical to the child's thinking in ikonic representation. It is only when he can go beyond this "match by direct correspondence" that he comes to deal with such "nonsensory" ideas as the relations between quantities, invariance across transformations, and substitutability within a conceptual category.

Consider now the origins and nature of symbolic representation. We turn to this problem in the following chapter.

CHAPTER **2**

On Cognitive Growth II

Jerome S. Bruner

In this discussion we take the view that symbolic representation stems from a form of primitive and innate symbolic activity that, through acculturation, gradually became specialized into different systems. The most specialized "natural" system of symbolic activity is, of course, language. But images, as we have already noted, can be infused with the properties of symbolic functioning, as can tool-using involving action. It can also be said that skilled motor activity can be shaped to the requirements of such a system, as in the articulatory aspects of speech, in the eye movements of readers, and the like.

It is a legend that during the fourth quarter of the nineteenth century the *Cercle linguistique de Paris* forbade the presentation of papers about the origins of language. Today it is a topic that is coming back into vogue, stimulated by inquiries into language universals (e.g., Greenberg, 1963). In trying to understand the origin of language not as a phylogenetic matter but as an ontogenetic one, one might follow a similar line and examine the universal properties of earliest infant language, regardless of what language community the child belongs to. Presumably there will be certain features of this early language that are general enough to suggest something about the basic or stock phenomenon of symbolic activity before it becomes specialized into language. One could also examine in the same way the ontogenesis of such symbolically relevant activity as tool-using with the same objective in mind, but unfortunately we can find no scientific literature that throws light on the subject.

If in the following paragraphs it may at times appear as if our search is for the nature of *language* growth, let the reader be assured that we are searching instead for the nature of the protosymbolic activity that supports language and all other forms of symbolization. We shall set down the properties of early language as "instances" and then try to attain the concept. We begin with reference.

Symbol Reference. The idea that there is a name that goes with things and that the name is arbitrary is generally taken as the essence of symbolism, and indeed White (1949) makes such "symboling" the unique basis of all human behavior. One cannot tell what a symbol stands for by sensing it: the color appropriate to mourning may be yellow, black, white, or irrelevant, depending upon what has been decided. It is apparent that a fully developed use of symbolic reference in this sense is not immediately available to the child who begins to talk. For one thing, the child first learns words as signs rather than as symbols, standing for a thing present before him (see Brown and Berko, 1960) and conceives of the word rather as an aspect of the thing. As Vygotsky puts it (1962, p. 129):

> The word, to the child, is an integral part of the object it denotes. Such a conception seems to be characteristic of primitive linguistic consciousness. We all know the old story about the rustic who said he wasn't surprised that savants with all their instruments could figure out the size of the stars and their course—what baffled him was how they found out their names. Simple experiments show that pre-school children "explain" the names of objects by their attributes. According to them, an animal is called a "cow" because it has horns, "calf" because its horns are still small, "dog" because it is small and has no horns; an object is called "car" because it is not an animal. When asked whether one could interchange the names of objects, for instance, call a cow "ink" and ink "cow," children will answer no, "because ink is used for writing and the cow gives milk." An exchange of names would mean an exchange of characteristic features, so inseparable is the connection between them in the child's mind . . . . We can see how difficult it is for children to separate the name of an object from its attributes, which cling to the name when it is transferred, like possessions following their owner.

Yet, for all that, the young child, like the young Helen Keller, comes early to the notion that things have names that they go by and that the name cannot be found by inspecting its referent.

We should like to propose, in line with a suggestion by McNeill (1966), that the learning of reference, that is, the "semantic function" of language, is a slow process (unlike the learning of syntax, discussed below) largely because it involves a basic type of cumulative process that has been very interestingly described by Katz and Fodor (1963).

It involves learning the semantic markers of a word—the senses that it has or the contexts into which it fits, much as the word *build* fits into contexts having to do with construction, with the shape of a body, with piling blocks on top of one another, and so on. In learning how to speak or to recognize whether what he hears is semantically sensible or anomalous, the child is learning to match the semantic markers of some words he has learned to the selection requirements of others that he is using in a sentence. It is not surprising that young children have more difficulty in distinguishing between a semantically anomalous sentence like "The flower ate the cheese" and one that is not anomalous like "The mouse ate the cheese." This conception of semantic learning is a far cry from the "learning by pointing" that is a stock in the trade of the older textbooks. The "original word game" may be characteristic of earliest semantic learning, but it is less and less frequent over the first years of language learning. It takes no elaborate investigation to know that we do not have to take five-year-olds into the presence of each "thing" for which they learn a word. Rather, their "What's that?" is increasingly directed to unfamiliar words that are being used and to the unfamiliar senses in which familiar words are being used. It is probably this feature of semantic learning that puts the children with strong imagery in Kuhlman's experiment (1960) at a disadvantage, for to learn the senses or semantic markers of words is to learn the constraints on their conceptual range—an intellectual task, not a perceptual one. Leopold (1949) in his classic observations of his own children also comments on this gradual progression "from coarse to fine" semantic distinction, and we shall return later to the point in discussing the relation of semantic and syntactic learning in the early acquisition of speech.

Categoriality. It is universally the case that, as Roger Brown (1956) has most persuasively put it, the child's *use* of language is categorial. Words cover classes of things, and these classes are, on close examination, found to be rule-governed so that new members can be added. Indeed, even morphological and syntactical rules, of which more is said in a moment, have a categorial use very nearly from the outset. In short, the type-token distinction is universal in all language, including early language.

Grammaticalness. All human language, once it passes the first stage of the comprehensive "one-word" utterance, the holophrase, is characterized by grammar. This is not the place to set forth a capsule characterization of what is meant by grammar, and indeed linguists are not in complete agreement as to how to characterize it. All languages, we can say, have a base grammar or structure that provides for at least three fundamental properties to sentences: *verb-object, subject-predicate,* and *modification.* There are no human languages whose sentences do not contain rules for these three basic sentential structures, and there are no nonhuman languages that have them. Languages use many devices, such as *order,* various kinds of *markers,* such as suffixes and function words, and different forms of prosody, as in intonation; but all reflect or respond to the basic grammar. One further universal of grammar, of the same fundamental status as the three basic relations of subject-predicate, verb-object, and modification, is *transformation.* All languages have rules for "rewriting" sentences: for example, rules for rewriting passive, interrogative, or negative sentences into basic-structures-plus transformation; that is, *The dog bit the boy* can be written with any one, two, or three of the optional transformations noted directly above—with all three of them yielding, *Was the boy not bitten by the dog?*

One can examine the nature of language more closely still by considering the classes of morphemes it contains, the minimum units that carry meaning, and the privileges of occurrence in sentences that they have. One can examine more carefully the small stock of phonemes in a language, combinations of which permit the production of a large stock of morphemes. Just as a morpheme is the minimum unit that carries meaning, a phoneme is the minimum sound element, a change in which alters meaning in a morpheme (or word) that contains it. These are matters which, though of great interest, need not concern us here.[1]

In general, when we speak of the grammar of a language we mean the set of rules that will generate any or all permissible utterances in that language and none that is impermissible. When a person speaks a language, he "knows" these rules in some fashion, though he cannot (like a linguist) recite them to you. In studying a child's grammar, we attempt to infer the rules that govern his utterances: we write a grammar for him much as we would write a grammar for some remote tribe. The difference is that, in the case of the child's language, we are interested in how he "moves toward" the model grammar of the adult linguistic community; therefore we study not only the differences between his grammar and adult grammar but also the transitions between his grammar at one age and at another.

The rules of grammar are, in effect, combinatory and "productive."

---

[1] The reader will quite properly sense that the present account is strongly influenced by the views of Noam Chomsky (1957, 1965) and George Miller (1965).

In the very nature of natural language these rules cannot be in the form of a device for "generating utterances from left to right," for all grammars ever studied have rules that permit imbeddings and forms of dependency that cannot be generated in this serial way. Chomsky (1957) illustrates this universal property with a set of declarative sentences, S_1, S_2, S_3 in some natural language, say English. It is possible in English or any language to generate these sentences:

(a) If S_1, then S_2.
(b) Either S_3, or S_4.
(c) The man who said that S_5 is arriving today.

In all three instances a simple serial rule of order is plainly inadequate. There must be a basic grammar that can govern the over-all sentence rather than only what word can follow a preceding word. This matter, perhaps a little abstruse on first encounter, becomes important shortly.

 ˙ Let it be clear at the outset that the kind of grammar we are discussing differs strikingly from other forms of communication that come before it in the child's life. Mere gesture or vocalization, for example, is agrammatical. Dorothea McCarthy (1954, p. 521) in her exhaustive review of the literature on speech development has this to say:

> It is quite generally agreed that the child understands gestures before he understands words and, in fact, that he uses gestures himself long before he uses language proper. He looks for objects he has dropped, he reaches for objects, etc., long before he can ask for them. These and other overt bodily movements which are used as means of early expression and communication are often accompanied by early vocalizations. It has been claimed that words constitute substitutes for actual gross motor activity.

Such substitution of vocalization for gesture is often interpreted as the route from prelinguistic to properly linguistic or symbolical reference. This is the view of the Sterns in their *Kindersprache* (1907): first there is gesture, then gesture and vocalization, and then gesture drops out and vocalization carries the main burden. Such a statement fails to notice the enormous discontinuity between mere "gestural vocalizations" and the complex and the highly constrained grammar of language.

As Meumann originally suggested a half century ago (1908), the first functions of vocalization are affective and volitional, expressive of inner states, on the one hand, and of demands on the environment, on the other. How does the child make the step toward a properly combinatory grammar capable of productivity? There is consensus in the literature that first sentential utterances usually contain one common restricted morpheme and a second open or free-varying one. Such sentences as *that truck, that baby,* and *where dolly, where truck* illustrate this. The unique thing about this first step toward sentence formation is a forming rule that permits the generation of new sentences, like *where baby* and *that mommy,* when *where* had previously been used only with *dolly* and *truck* and *that* with *truck* and *baby.* The bound or pivotal forms are combined with other words in a manner that is strikingly rule-bound. Braine (1963b, p. 13) gives the most succinct account of the process.

> The simplest account of the phenomena of the first phase of development seems to be as follows: out of the moderately large vocabulary at his disposal the child learns, one at a time, that each of a small number of words belongs in a particular position in an utterance. He therefore places them there, and, since he has not learned anything else about what goes where in an utterance, the complementary position is taken by any single-word utterance in his vocabulary, the choice determined only by the physical and social stimuli that elicit the utterance. As a consequence of this learning, the word combinations that are uttered have a characteristic structure containing two parts of speech. One part of speech, here called pivot, comprises the small number of words whose position has been learned. The other, here called X-class, is a part of speech mainly in a residual sense, and consists of the entire vocabulary, except for some of the pivots. During this first phase the language grows structurally by the formation of new pivot words, i.e., by the child learning the position of new words. The language grows in vocabulary by adding to the X-class.

To illustrate the rule-bound nature of the combinations, Braine considers the problem of rare word combinations not likely to be found in parental speech (p. 10).

> An objection which has been raised against the assumption that any pivot can occur with any x-word is that it puts into the children's mouths some implausible expressions which seem highly foreign to English. For example, the formulae would allow Gregory to generate *more hot, big dirty, allgone hot;* Andrew to say *see read, other fix, I short,* and Steven to say *that do, there up, high do.* This objection is sometimes based on the idea that the children's utterances are a recall or delayed imitation of things they heard adults say. As against this, there are a number of expressions in the corpora which are sufficiently strange to render it most unlikely that the children had heard them, e.g., *see cold, byebye dirty, allgone lettuce, no down, more high, want do pon* ("put on"), *there high . . . .* Moreover, several "strange" combinations, similar or identical to utterances generated by the

formulae, appear in the fifth and sixth months; [after the beginning
of the two-word sentences] examples are *more wet, allgone sticky*
(Gregory after washing his hands) . . . etc. Manifestly, the strange-
ness of an utterance is no criterion of its grammaticality at this age.

How rapidly the child avails himself of this new system of making
combinations in his utterances can be grasped from sampling the
record of one child studied by Braine during the first six months
after the appearance of the first two-word utterance: for each successive month the count was 14, 24, 54, 89, 350, 1400, 2500 plus.

Brown and Fraser (1964, p. 79) conclude their report on the acquisition of grammar with the following suggestion:

> For the present, then, we are working with the hypothesis that
> child speech is a systematic reduction of adult speech largely accom-
> plished by omitting function words that carry little information. From
> this corpus of reduced sentences we suggest that the child induces
> general rules which govern the construction of new utterances. As
> a child becomes capable (through maturation and the learning of
> frequent sequences) of mastering more and more of the detail of
> adult speech, his original rules will have to be revised and supple-
> mented. As the generative grammar grows more complicated and more
> like the adult grammar, the child's speech will become capable of
> expressing a greater variety of meanings.

None of the above accounts for the *first* appearance of grammar,
why for example, the child shifts to the $P(x)$ form. We shall return
to the point later. For the while it suffices to say that grammar does
come forth and is typical of the child's utterances from about the
second year on. It is an obvious point, but a powerfully important
one. What is less obvious is that from the very first appearance of
grammar the child seems to be master of the use of categories (as
in his use of pivot and open classes) and of hierarchies. The latter
are found in the form of "nested constructions" in which a single
class is replaced by a sequence of instances that are, in effect, an
unfolding of the original class. Ervin-Tripp and Slobin (1966) comment in their review of the literature on language acquisition that
a "layering of constituents in adult phrase structure is found from
the very beginning of grammar." We shall have occasion very shortly
to return to these two features of grammaticality.

Effective Productivity. As we have already seen, the rule-bound
nature of grammar assures that the child (once he has acquired it)
will be able to produce an endless number of utterances of a syntactically legitimate nature and will, moreover, produce none that is not.
In short, he learns rules. We know from the engaging study by Ruth

Weir (1962) that children practice pushing these rules to the limit. But the critical point for the student of symbolic representation is that these powerful productive rules of grammar are linked to the semantic function as well—to the "real world"; that is to say, having translated or encoded a set of events into a rule-bound symbolic system, a human being is then able to transform that representation into an altered version that may but does not necessarily correspond to some possible set of events. It is this form of effective productivity that makes symbolic representation such a powerful tool for thinking or problem solving: the range it permits for experimental alteration of the environment without having, so to speak, to raise a finger by way of trial and error or to picture anything in the mind's eye by imagery. "What if there were never any apples?" a four-year-old asked upon finishing one with gusto!

But it is apparent that much language is used without seeming awareness of the semantic implications of what has been said or of what our transformations imply for the world to which our words refer (e.g., Inhelder and Piaget, 1964); that is, although words can potentially be used to turn reality on its head for hypothetical purposes they are not often used in that way. This fact has been treated in various ways—this failure of the Whorfian hypothesis to predict as much as it should about a speaker's world view on the basis of the language he speaks. The popular approach is to follow the lead of Vygotsky (1962) and to assume that language becomes part of our apparatus of thinking when it becomes "interiorized" or "internalized," the assumption being that language starts as dialogue and then becomes monologue and finally "inner speech." It is a view whose chief flaw is that one can say too little about the nature of inner speech. In any case, it may be that one can avoid this problem of nonspecificity with respect to inner speech by examining how language becomes related to reality.

Now, to begin with, the very use of language presupposes certain underlying cognitive processes required for its use. We have just discussed some of these processes in considering the universal grammaticality of language. It seems as if these concepts are first used and perfected in the sphere of language and are only gradually transferred to thinking in general, and often not well transferred. How a child comes to transfer such formidable concepts as hierarchy and transformation from the linguistic to the nonlinguistic sphere is obscure, but a conjecture is in order. Brown and Bellugi (1964) speak of a contingent cycle between the child and the tutor in original language learning. Recall that the child makes an utterance in his own particular grammatical form: the adult "tutor" idealizes and expands the child's utterance into a more model grammatical form and the child matches his next utterance selectively to the adult model (if he is "ready"). Brown's observations are confined principally to the second and third years of age. Some such process as this goes on throughout childhood—with parents, with teachers, with older children. This exchange is as much a matter of learning to organize one's thoughts in a certain way as it is of learning the rules of *grammar*. Brown (1966) provides an example from the speech of Eve, one of his young subjects in her fourth year of life:

> Eve: *I sit table.*
> Eve: *I get big.*
> Mother: *That's right, when you get big you can sit at the table.*
> Now we look back and find that there has always been a latent structure in the order of the simple sentences the mother produced, seemingly with a more logical texture in the two more educated families (conditional, causal, disjunctive, and a more concatenative structure in the one less educated family).

It is at this point that McNeill's (1966) discussion is particularly useful. Recall that he comments upon the slow accretion of semantic markers in the child's grasp of the "meanings" of a language—the allowable contexts into which words are to fit. It is worth pursuing his argument in more detail, from the point at which the child first uses holophrases and then shifts to words.

> It is clear that children have some kind of semantic system at a very early point in their linguistic development. We have already mentioned that children first seem to use words holophrastically, a phenomenon that suggests that the *earliest semantic system consists of a dictionary in which single words are paired with several complete sentence-interpretations.* A holophrastic dictionary is burdensome for a child's memory and susceptible to ambiguity, two conditions that might lead to the creation of a sentence dictionary. Again, because of memory load, *a sentence dictionary is itself abandoned,* this time for the ultimate solution, a word dictionary. Each of these transitions effects a re-working of a child's semantic system. Of the two, however, the second transition is by far the most significant, and it is from this point that we can date the rudiments of a system that is basically similar to adult competence. In the case of the first change, from a holophrastic to a sentence dictionary, a child continues storing undifferentiated semantic information, in that the definition of one sentence is not related to the definition of any other. The transition from a sentence dictionary to a word dictionary, on the other hand, introduces a fundamental change in the format of the dictionary entries themselves, for in compiling a word dictionary, a child must begin to build up a system of semantic markers. The evidence is that the

accretion of semantic markers is, in contrast with the acquisition of syntactic competence, a slow process that is not completed until well into school age.

We can confidently place the first effort to compile a word dictionary as occurring not earlier than the use of base-structure rules in a child's grammar. *It is very difficult to conceive of a word dictionary that does not receive input from some sort of syntactic component.* Without such input, a word dictionary would constitute a retreat to a point even more primitive than the original holophrastic dictionary. A word dictionary without syntax would result in a loss of power to encode information that previously had been encoded, viz., sentence meaning, and the cause of the transition to a word dictionary, we assume, is the need to retain an ability to encode sentence meanings while reducing the load on memory.

It may well be that language provides a kind of temptation to form concepts of objects and events that have a structure comparable to those contained in words, form classes, and sentences—as Brown (1956) and Werner and Kaplan (1950) have suggested. What it takes to bring the two into correspondence is a topic we must postpone until a later section. These concepts refer to the properties of communication that are characteristic of human language, though they may also be characteristic of nonhuman communication (see Hockett, 1960).

Design Features. Some aspects of early language are so specifically specialized for the transmission side of communication that they need not concern us in our search for "protosymbolic" activity. There are others that, although "transmission specific," may nonetheless suggest some general properties of human symbolic functioning. Consider these briefly.

Hockett's (1960) list of design features of communication provides a guide for us. That all human spoken language *uses the vocal-auditory channel* probably tells very little. As Sapir (1921, p. 42) said more than forty years ago, "The mere phonetic framework of speech does not constitute the inner fact of language." Yet there may be some special significance in the fact that to produce language we must develop articulatory motor responses that are governed by rules as subtle and productive as those governing distinctive features, phonemes, and allophones. At very least, vocal production may provide a prototype of all "programmatic" motor skills, and one cannot help wondering whether at some future time in human history the skill of the human hand may be directed by some form of combinatorial program such as that involved in speech production. The performing musician may be a precursor. Closely related to vocal-auditory channeling are the *interchangeability* of heard and spoken signals in human speech and the *feedback* of the human voice to the speaker's ears. So too is the *specialization* of human speech in the sound channel—so that the sounds of speech are produced for communication alone and not as a by-product of some other activity. The *broadcast transmission* of speech and its *directional reception* are part of the same complex. Their significance concerning the general nature of protosymbolic activity is obscure, save in the sense that, like our first example, they connote a specialized development of skills.

We should probably take a moment to scrutinize the feature of *rapid fading* in human speech, for though it may not reflect anything "primitive" about a symbolic system it does suggest that symbolism is an extraordinarily swift system, particularly in contrast to the two rather sluggish modes of representation discussed earlier: action with its habitual sequences and imagery with its lag and its slow transformability. It may well be that some of the startlingly abrupt spurts in growth reported in later chapters are a function of the shift from slow to fast functioning. The processing time required to solve problems by ikonic or enactive means is prohibitively long for a child whose attention span is short.

Hockett's list then goes on to several features of greater importance for inferring the basic properties of symbolism in man. Several have already been mentioned in preceding pages: *semanticity*, the *arbitrariness* of human symbols and their lack of any resemblance to what they specify; the *productivity* of utterance made possible by grammatical rules; and the *traditional transmission* of the language rather than its environment-free transmission through the genes. This leaves three critical features still to be examined for their possible significance: *discreteness, displacement,* and *duality of patterning.*

Discreteness in language refers to the fact that at the sound level, as at the level of meaning, the material of human language is discontinuous: there is no intermediate step between *bin* and *pin* that produces a word: /b/ and /p/ are discontinuous phonemes, and, should one voice a word that uses a sound midway between, the hearer will interpret it as one phoneme or the other. So too with words or morphemes; they are neither organized by continuum with a range from *hat* to *helmet*, nor are they form classes, such that one goes imperceptibly from nominals (or "nouns") to, say, functors such as *to, by,* or *at.* What this imposes on the speaker of human language is the requirement that he analyze the domain of sound and of sense into discontinuous components that can then be constituted into a message. The rule of discreteness in symbolic representation contrasts sharply with the rule of representation by perceptual similarity: the

analogue rule of ikonic representation. Analysis and synthesis are ·
literally *forced* on anyone who would speak human language. Language, then, breaks up the natural unity of the perceptual world—or
at least imposes another structure on it.

Displacement as a design feature of language refers to the fact
that one can represent something in language, though it may be remote from the place of speaking (or writing) in place and time.
Save for the odd and fascinating cul de sac of bee-dancing, one
finds this feature in no other part of the animal kingdom save man.
What is interesting about displacement is that it is only gradually
acquired by young speakers who, as we have seen, begin their speaking careers by referring only to those things that are present. More
interesting still is the fact that, in problem-solving behavior dominated
by ikonic representation, the principal feature seems to be "ostensiveness" rather than "displacement"; that is to say, the behavior is dominated by the requirement that all features of the task to be dealt
with be present, present even to be pointed at. As we shall see repeatedly in experiments reported in later chapters, there is a critical
point at which the child is able to go beyond the immediate situation
of the problem-solving task to deal with features that are "remote
in space and time"; for example, in playing a game of "Twenty Questions." It may well be, then, that there is some primitive respect
in which a capacity for symbolic activity permits a human being
to get this "distance" from a task. Indeed, it may be that without
such distance it would be impossible to develop the analytic approach
necessary for decomposing tasks into the discrete features in order
to encode them better in the categories to which a language system
can be applied.

With respect to *duality of patterning*, again we are dealing with
a feature that is unique to human communication. Hockett (1960,
pp. 4–6) describes the feature succinctly:

> The meaningful elements in any language—"words" in everyday
> parlance, "morphemes" to the linguist—constitute an enormous stock.
> Yet they are represented by small arrangements of a relatively very
> small stock of distinguishable sounds [phonemes] which are in themselves wholly meaningless. This "duality of patterning" is illustrated
> by the English words "cat," "tack," and "act." They are totally distinct
> as to meaning, and yet are composed of just three basic meaningless
> sounds in different permutations.

Little indeed is known about the significance in the broader cognitive sense of a system of this sort for human symbolic activity.
What it suggests is again an enormous rule-governed capacity for

analysis-and-synthesis. Duality of pattern, or the capacity that makes possible our mastery of it, probably also makes possible our capacity to use other "artificial" systems for analysis that have many of the same properties as language—notably mathematics and logic.

After this survey, what shall we make of the basic nature of symbolic activity in humans? We have looked at what we choose to call its "specialized" manifestation in spoken language, in the conviction that, since there is a gap between the child's competence with language *per se* and his competence with "reality," the former cannot tell us the whole story about his symbolic representation of the latter. Yet we do well to try to sum up the inherent properties presupposed by the use of language.

We may begin with Roman Jakobson's account of the fundamentals of language. He says (1956, p. 58): "Speech implies a selection of certain linguistic entities and their combination into linguistic units of a higher degree of complexity." With respect to these two fundamentals, selection and combination, Jakobson then goes on to remark (p. 60):

> Any linguistic sign involves two modes of arrangement. (1) *Combination*. Any sign is made up of constituent signs and/or occurs only in combination with other signs. This means that any linguistic unit at one and the same time serves as a context for simpler units and/or finds its own context in a more complex linguistic unit. Hence any actual grouping of linguistic units binds them into a superior unit: combination and contexture are two faces of the same operation. (2) *Selection*. A selection between alternatives implies the possibility of substituting one for the other equivalent to the former in one respect, and different from it in another. Actually, selection and substitution are two faces of the same operation. The fundamental role which these two operations play in language was clearly recognized by Ferdinand de Saussure [1916].

To the psychologist, the two properties in question can be readily translated into *category* and *hierarchy*, the latter providing a system for nesting the former (See Bruner, Goodnow, and Austin, [1956]). Let us assume for the time being that these are two basic features of symbolic representation as well as of language.

To stop at category and hierarchy in describing the underlying structure of language is to leave out of account the nature of sentences and grammar taken in the fine. We have already commented on three universal properties of base-structure grammar, properties as characteristic of the child's grammar as of the adult's: subject-predicate relations, verb-object relations, and modification. Each of these presupposes an underlying logical form that can be simply stated. The subject-predicate relation is a linguistic expression of the argument of a function, "x is a function of y," where x is the subject and y the predicate. For "S-P" of the grammatical jargon, we can write $x = f(y)$ in logical jargon. Where the verb-object relation is concerned, it is a linguistic rendering of cause and effect. Modification in its turn is an instance of the intersect of classes—*green hat* is the intersect of *green* things and *hats*. The sentence, *The man wore the green hat*, contains the underlying relations, then, of a man wearing something (or x being a function of y), a hat being acted upon (being worn, which is causing it to be worn), and a certain kind of hat at that (modification by green). And so we might add to our list of language "fundamentals," to go on with Jakobson's term, the three symbolic operations of *function, causation,* and *intersection* (or logical addition of classes, as it is often called).

Now reconsider effective productivity. If linguistic categories organized in hierarchies are to have relevance to the "real world," then experience itself must be organized into hierarchically organized categories. We know that the child's language is organized in this way, and we know equally well from experiments that his experience is not. I am prepared to believe that in the linguistic domain the capacities for categorization and hierarchical organization are innate and so, too, are predication, causation, and modification; I will attempt to justify this belief later, but it is also plain that the child's experience is not organized by these principles. Here I find myself in fundamental agreement with Piaget's discussion (1961) in his difficult but rewarding book, *Les Mécanismes Perceptifs*. In discussing the difference between perception and intelligent thought he comments, "La perception primaire ignore l'abstraction." It is precisely the initial unanalyzability of perception that strikes Piaget: "Lorsque, par example, devant les figures classique de Müller-Lyer, le sujet est prié de comparer les deux médianes horizontales, il n'y a pas de problème déductif, puisque la question est seulement de comparer pour 'voir' " (p. 358).[2] This immediacy and nonabstract quality of perception is precisely what makes difficult the analysis-and-synthesis that is necessary for adult thought to be brought to the task—adult thought that has been organized to correspond to the properties of symbolic activity.

I would argue that language itself is not what is "imposed" on

---

[2] "When, for example, a subject is presented with a pair of classical Müller-Lyer figures and asked to compare their horizontal lines, it is not like a deductive problem, since the question is only one of comparing the two visually."

experience—as already suggested in my rejection of Vygotsky's idea that language is internalized and becomes inner speech, which is tantamount to thought. Rather, language comes from the same basic root out of which symbolically organized experience grows. I tend to think of symbolic activity of some basic or primitive type that finds its first and fullest expression in language, then in tool-using, and finally in the organizing of experience. It is by the interaction of language and the barely symbolically organized experience of the child of two or three that language gradually finds its way into the realm of experience.

Let us assume that at the outset, and concurrently with the earliest form of vocal or bodily gestural sign, the child has developed some working conception of identity: that an object now encountered is the same object previously encountered. Indeed, Bower's (1965) finding, using the method of moving objects behind a screen and then making them reappear in an altered form, even suggests that a primitive grasp of identity may be present in the first month of life, if not at birth. Primitive identity is surely, then, a sufficient beginning for semanticity—although it lacks the arbitrary quality of symbolic reference in full. It can be argued that it is not until the child has, in Piaget's (1954) full sense, achieved the *concept* of an object that there is naming, even by the beginning of the holophrase; for the use of an arbitrary name or holophrase requires some freeing of the object from its immediate context of action.

As McNeill (1966) properly points out, the shift from holophrase to words is inconceivable without a syntactic component that would give words a productive benefit over either holophrases or nondecomposable "sentences" in the child's repertory. That first syntax is simple, to be sure, but it is clearly a step beyond what went before—as for example in the pivotal grammar $P(x)$, already discussed. What nourishes the emergence, at just about eighteen to twenty-four months, of a syntactical system in language that contains our basic properties is anything but apparent. Is it the new achievement of a certain amount of freedom from enactive representation that permits this quick unfolding of syntactical learning? The suggestion comes indirectly from Lashley's paper on serial order (1951) already considered in Chapter 1. Lashley comments that serially ordered behavior, like grammatical language, requires that there be some atemporal principle of organization: "Syntax is not inherent in the words employed or in the idea to be expressed. It is a generalized pattern imposed upon the specific acts as they occur." Or, more specifically, "The facility with which different word orders may be utilized to express the same thought thus is further evidence that the temporal integration is not inherent in the preliminary organization of the idea."

We suggest that the strong motoric element in enactive representation that prevails during the child's first year of life—described so skillfully by Piaget (1954) and underlined by the work of Held and his associates (1963, 1965)—probably interferes with the development of this atemporal schema. Indeed, the speculation fits in well with the observations of Kagan (1966) that hypermotoricity interferes with "reflectiveness" in young children, seeming to delay language development and the development of linguistic ability. When the child cannot inhibit the motoric acting out of responses, he cannot organize a central pattern sufficient for language—or at least for any language more complicated than the immediate holophrase. It is important to bear in mind that there is a long period of delay between the appearance of the first holophrase and the first syntactically ordered sentence—in the case of Leopold's (1949) daughter, for example, from the ninth month to the twentieth. It may be a period for steadying and overlearning.

The maturing of the syntactical system, as we know, takes place by a process of reciprocal interaction between child and tutor—the expansion-idealization cycle to which Brown and Bellugi (1964) refers. Whatever the mechanism is that operates in this learning—it is certainly *not* a form of simple imitation, as we know from the work of Brown, Fraser, and Bellugi (1964)—is not clear. Brown uses the expression "Original Word Game" for semantic learning, and it is plain that this is a different activity from the "Original Sentence Game," in which the child is learning some sort of base-structure grammar. It is rather intriguing to consider that while the child is learning the ostensive referent of words and their semantic markers the very same words are already embedded in some form of syntactic hierarchy. In short (and we shall encounter the fact repeatedly in the studies reported in later chapters), the child is learning to use his words and their semantic markers for the picturable or ikonic aspects of his world, but the words themselves are enmeshed in a highly abstract and hierarchical system of categories used formally to signal causation, predication, and modification through sentences that the child can "rewrite" according to transformational rules that he early masters (see Brown, 1966 and Slobin, 1963). However, as we have said, these powerful, only potentially semantic features of language are rarely used by the child for giving structure to his experience. He can neither use the superordinate rule of categorization consistently (see Chapter 3) nor can he organize what he knows in a hierarchical organization (see Chapter 4). He has not, to use Herbert Simon's (1962) phrase, mastered the "architecture of complexity" for things, but only for words; and, as with Simon's mythical watchmakers, Hora and Tempus, he is never finished with his problem-solving tasks, though he is quite capable of finishing his sentences.[3] Nor can he deal adequately with causation (Piaget, 1930), functions (Inhelder and Piaget, 1959), nor modification (Piaget and Inhelder [1962]; Inhelder and Piaget, [1964]).

Then, if the child lives in an advanced society such as our own, he becomes "operational" (to use the Genevan term for thinking symbolically), and by age five, six, or seven, given cultural supports he is able to apply the fundamental rules of category, hierarchy, function, and so forth, to the world as well as to his words. Let it be explicit, however, that if he is growing up in a native village of Senegal (Chapters 11 and 13), among native Eskimos (Chapter 13), or in a rural *mestizo* village in Mexico (Chapter 12) he may not achieve this "capacity." Instead, he may remain at a level of manipulation of the environment that is concretely ikonic and strikingly lacking in symbolic structures—though his language may be stunningly exquisite in these regards. (The reader is reminded, in Sapir's words [1921] that "we know of no people that is not possessed of a fully developed language. The lowliest South African Bushman speaks in the forms of a rich symbolic system that is in essence perfectly comparable

---

[3] Simon's fable (1962, p. 470) is worth repeating: "There once were two watchmakers named Hora and Tempus who manufactured very fine watches. Both of them were highly regarded and the phones in their workshops rang frequently—new customers were constantly calling them. However, Hora prospered while Tempus became poorer and poorer and finally lost his shop. What was the reason?

"The watches the men made consisted of about 1000 parts each. Tempus had so constructed his that if he had one partly assembled and had to put it down—to answer the phone, say—it immediately fell to pieces and had to be reassembled from the elements. The better the customers liked his watches, the more they phoned him . . . .

"The watches that Hora made were no less complex than those of Tempus. But he had designed them so that he could put together subassemblies of about ten elements each. Ten of these subassemblies again, could be put together in a large subassembly; and a system of ten of the latter subassemblies constituted the whole watch. Hence, when Hora had to put down a partly assembled watch in order to answer the phone, he lost only a small part of his work, and he assembled his watches in only a fraction of the man-hours it took Tempus."

The five-year-old, very strikingly, goes about his manipulation of the real world in a fashion akin to that of Tempus, distraction being his undoing. But his language behavior prospers, like Hora.

to the speech of the cultivated Frenchman.") But Miller and Chomsky (1963, p. 488), after a searching analysis of the formal properties of languages, conclude:

> An organism that is intricate and highly structured enough to perform the operations that we have seen to be involved in linguistic communication does not suddenly lose its intricacy and structure when it turns to non-linguistic activities. In particular, such an organism can form verbal plans to guide many of its non-verbal acts. The verbal machinery turns out sentences—and for civilized men, sentences have a compelling power to control both thought and action.

We shall consider next how sentences might come to have this power.

To sum up our discussion of symbolic representation, symbolic activity stems from some primitive or protosymbolic system that is species-specific to man. This system becomes specialized in expression in various domains of the life of a human being: in language, in tool-using, in various atemporally organized and skilled forms of serial behavior, and in the organization of experience itself. We have suggested some minimum properties of such a symbolic system: categoriality, hierarchy, predication, causation, and modification. We have suggested that *any* symbolic activity, and especially language, is logically and empirically unthinkable without these properties.

What is striking about language as one of the specialized expressions of symbolic activity is that in one of its aspects, the syntactic sphere, it reaches maturity very swiftly. The syntactical maturity of a five-year-old seems unconnected with his ability in other spheres. He can muster words and sentences with a swift and sure grasp of highly abstract rules, but he cannot, in a corresponding fashion, organize the things words and sentences "stand for." This asymmetry is reflected in the child's semantic activities, where his knowledge of the senses of words and the empirical implications of his sentence remain childish for many years, even after syntax has become fully developed.

One is thus led to believe that, in order for the child to use language as an instrument of thought, he must first bring the world of experience under the control of principles of organization that are in some degree isomorphic with the structural principles of syntax. Without special training in the symbolic *representation of experience*, the child grows to adulthood still depending in large measure on the enactive and ikonic modes of representing and organizing the world, no matter what language he speaks.

In view of the autonomy of the syntactic sphere from other modes of operating and of its partial disjunction from the semantic sphere, one is strongly tempted to give credence to the insistence of various modern writers on linguistics that language is an innate pattern, based on innate "ideas" that are gradually differentiated into the rules of grammar (McNeill [1966], Chomsky [1965], Katz [1965]).

Considering now the interaction of the three systems of representation, we quickly find ourselves dealing with the question of how experience is organized to correspond in some measure to the structure of language.

THE INTERACTION OF SYSTEMS

Early in Chapter 1 the distinction was drawn between "representation by" and "representation for," the former referring to the medium in which a representation is couched, the latter to the uses to which it is put; doing, sensing, or symbolizing. We have already explored briefly the various ways in which systems of representation are translatable (or partially translatable) into each other. What we must do now is examine more carefully the nature of this interaction and its history. For it must be apparent from the preceding discussion that there is much more to this matter than first meets the eye.

The first and most general issue is raised by Lashley (1951), commenting on a dilemma of memory. Much of memory, he remarks, is spatially organized. Yet for even simple reproduction to occur, it is necessary to translate the images of memory into a serial order of their reproduction (or recall). We are constantly translating atemporal images into serially organized actions—as in the diagram of the battery, lamp, and switch, should we have to use the diagram as a guide to the reconstruction of the simple circuit it portrays. Even at a more primitive level the maintenance of postural equilibrium consists in monitoring the relation between an enactive, postural system governed by the semicircular canals, and a visual system with spatial coordinates. The coordination of the two systems, visual and kinaesthetic, most surely was the condition for survival of our arboreal, primate ancestors. The system must be well organized by the time the human child is able to crawl, for by that age he already displays avoidance of the visual cliff (Walk, 1965). One is tempted to look exclusively to the phenomenon of reafference as the source of the integration of the sphere of action and of sensory perception, as we did in Chapter 1. Plainly there is reason to think that the feedback between the two systems provides the basis for much of sensorimotor integration. But what of the integration of those systems with a symbolic system?

Before launching into that issue, we would do well to consider briefly the relations that can exist between two systems of representation, using the relation of the visual system and action as a model. In abstract terms, there are three basic ways in which two systems can relate to each other: by *matching*, by *mismatching*, or by *independence* of each other. In visual and labyrinthine definitions of space, for example, there is a kind of point-to-point correspondence between the systems so that independence is not possible. Where the two systems match, the organism goes on with its ordinary operations without any special problem solving. When the two systems mismatch, as in the experiments of Witkin and his collaborators (1962), one or the other is suppressed or some sort of correction is made in the schema that coordinates the two. In short, mismatch creates the kind of "trouble" that requires handling. In the Witkin experiments it is plain that before children are in adolescence they have come to deal with "mismatch troubles" either by developing a general preference for the visual representation of space or for the kinaesthetic-labyrinthine. What is remarkable about the long series of experiments carried out by the Witkin group (using the rod-and-frame procedure, tilting rooms, etc.) is not only that there is considerable consistency in these preferences for one or the other modality but also that many other features of behavior become correlated with the preference. This type of clustering suggests that there is a more general schema of adaptation than relates specifically to the preference for one or another medium of representation.

The existence of such a general schema suggests that when, in the history of the organism, mismatches occur between two systems there is a rather widely ramifying problem solving that is set up. There develops a range of "devices" and "preparations" that have to do with dealing with mismatch on the next encounter: trust in one's body image or strong reliance on a visual framework and the world of objects, etc.

Consider now the question of independence, match, and mismatch between two systems in which one system is symbolic. We have already commented on the fact that the syntax of language is mastered by the young child before he seems able to use it to organize his experience or his actions. It is as if independence prevailed in a major degree, but as soon as there develops an organization of experience that is in some sense capable of "matching" the properties inherent in language the state of independence between the two systems recedes. Consider this issue in connection with two quite different matters: the first, Sapir's (1921) analysis of imagery and language, and the second, the series of experiments stimulated by the early experiment of Carmichael, Hogan, and Walter (1932).

Sapir says (p. 12):

> The world of our experiences must be enormously simplified and generalized before it is possible to make a symbolic inventory of all our experiences of things and relations and this inventory is imperative before we can convey ideas. The elements of language, the symbols that ticket off experience, must therefore be associated with whole groups, delimited classes of experience, rather than with the simple experiences themselves. Only so is communication possible, for the single experience lodges in an individual consciousness and is, strictly speaking, incommunicable.

Pursuing the thought further, he says (p. 14):

> We have seen that the typical linguistic element labels a concept. It does not follow from this that the use to which language is put is always or even mainly conceptual. We are not in ordinary life so much concerned with concepts as with concrete particularities and specific relations. When I say, for instance, "I had a good breakfast this morning," it is clear that I am not in the throes of laborious thought, that what I have to transmit is hardly more than a pleasureable memory symbolically rendered in the grooves of habitual expression. Each element in the sentence defines a separate concept or conceptual relation or both combined, *but the sentence as a whole has no conceptual significance whatever.* It is somewhat as though a dynamo capable of generating enough power to run an elevator were operated almost exclusively to feed an electric doorbell. The parallel is more suggestive than at first sight appears. Language may be looked upon as an instrument capable of running a gamut of psychic uses. Its flow not only parallels that of the inner content of consciousness, but parallels it on different levels, ranging from the state of mind that is dominated by particular images to that in which abstract concepts and their relations are alone at the focus of attention and which is ordinarily termed reasoning. *Thus the outward form only of language is constant; its inner meaning, its psychic value or intensity varies* freely with attention or the selective interest of the mind, also, needless to say, *with the mind's general development.* [Italics ours.]

The reader will perhaps bear with this lengthy quotation from Sapir, for in fact we could not put it better. He notes very properly that, although at the outset language may be used for labeling, it is not until there is a certain level in the development of mind that it can be fitted to thought, particularly language's sentential or syntactical structure. Again, Sapir says it better than we can (pp. 14–15):

> From the point of view of language, thought may be defined as the highest latent, or potential, content of speech, the content that is obtained by interpreting each of the elements in the flow of language as possessed of its very fullest conceptual value. From this it follows

at once that language and thought are not strictly conterminous . . . .
To put our viewpoint somewhat differently, language is primarily a
prerational function. It humbly works up to the thought that is latent
in it, that may eventually be read into its classifications and forms.

How human beings work their way up to the point where they
derive the "fullest conceptual value" from their language is left rather
loosely formulated by Sapir, and his looseness of statement is probably
responsible for the misinterpretation of his position, which often goes
by the name of the Whorf-Sapir hypothesis. He says (p. 15):

> It is, indeed, in the highest degree likely that language is an instru-
> ment originally put to uses lower than the conceptual plane and that
> thought arises as a refined interpretation of its content. The product
> grows, in other words, with the instrument, and thought may be
> no more conceivable, in its genesis and daily practice, without speech
> than is mathematical reasoning practicable without the lever of an
> appropriate mathematical symbolism.

There is a curious contradiction in this last point: that thought
and the structure of experience depend for their growth on a reflective
consideration by the speaker of the language he uses. How, then,
would he have been able to *apply* language to experience and thought
had these not achieved a form that matched them to the properties
of the linguistic elements and sentences to which Sapir earlier refers?
He clearly senses this problem, for a few paragraphs later he remarks
(pp. 16–17):

> One word more as to the relation of language and thought. The
> point of view we have developed does not by any means preclude
> the possibility of the growth of speech being in a high degree depen-
> dent on the development of thought . . . We see this complex process
> of the interaction of language and thought actually taking place under
> our eyes. The instrument makes possible the product, the product
> refines the instrument.

In sum, then, there is some need for the preparation of experience
and mental operations before language can be used. Once language
is applied, then it is possible, by using language as an instrument,
to scale to higher levels. In essence, once we have coded experience
in language, we can (but not necessarily *do*) read surplus meaning
into the experience by pursuing the built-in implications of the rules
of language.

Until the time that this "surplus meaning" is read off from our
linguistic coding of experience, language and experience maintain
an important independence from each other. A child can say of two
quantities that one is greater than another, a moment later that it
is less than the other, and then that they are the same—using his

words as labels for segments of experience (Chapter 8). It is not until he inspects his *language* that he goes back to his experience to check on a mismatch between what he sees with his eyes and what he has just said. He must, in short, treat the utterance as a *sentence* and recognize contradiction at that level. He can *then* go back and reorder experience, literally *see* the world differently by virtue of symbolic processes reordering the nature of experience.

We do not wish to quibble over the point, but it is *not* language *per se* that provides the reordering of experience. Rather, it is a genuine restructuring of how we perceive. The child says, for example, "that one *looks* bigger, but they are *really* alike," and later there is a firm distinction drawn between "the looks of appearance" and "the looks of reality." There remain, to be sure, those anomalous instances, the *visual illusions* that persist in defying perceptual reorganization, though we "know better," but even they can be divided into those that decline with age and experience (like the size-weight illusion) and those that are intractable (like the Müller-Lyer illusion).

Sapir's striking image of language as the "dynamo . . . operated almost exclusively to feed an electric doorbell" brings us to the second matter at hand, illustrated by the experiment of Carmichael, Hogan, and Walter (1932). Note first that labeling a figure (even one that is "meaningless") is almost irresistible. The dynamo seems hitched up to the doorbell very early. In Chapter 5, where the visual recognition of children of different ages is examined, it is quite obvious that even the three-year-olds name ambiguous figures. The labeling, once it occurs, has a strong influence on the form in which the figure is recovered from memory, with the well-known assimilation of the form to the label that has been applied to it—an effect even greater than originally found when appropriate controls are introduced as in the study of Herman, Lawless, and Marshall (1957). Indeed, if the figure is labeled *in advance* of its being presented tachistoscopically, it can be shown (Bruner, Minturn, and Busiek, 1955) that its immediate reproduction will also be affected. Certain features will be made to conform with the defining properties of the class denoted by the label. Note that *if* the experiment is kept entirely within the ikonic mode—pictures are shown, labeled or unlabeled, and the subject's task is to *recognize* the pictures from among a set presented to him visually as in Prentice's (1954) experiment—then the effect of labeling is canceled out. If one has only to *match* a memory image to a present percept, the intervening aid of a label is not needed, but once the task becomes complex enough and involves a serial task such as reproduction, language is necessary as an aid to reconstruction. It is much as in a remark of Sapir's (1921, p. 15): "No one believes that even the most difficult mathematical proposition is inherently dependent on an arbitrary set of symbols, but it is impossible to suppose that the human mind is capable of arriving at or holding such a proposition without the symbolism." When the limits of direct imagery are reached (and they are soon reached), it is necessary to use another means—symbolic representation or even enactive, postural orientation, as in the experiment by Drake (1964) cited earlier. In Chapter 7 we examine the need for "outside" aid when a visual memory image fails to be adequate.

It is interesting that Vygotsky (1962) in his evocative book, *Thought and Language,* takes a view very similar to the one expressed here with respect to how thought comes to conform to language—this in spite of his rather loosely formulated view that "thought is inner speech." He clearly recognizes the separateness of "the stream of language" and "the stream of thought" and is sensitive to the need for organizing thought in a fashion that corresponds to language. He remarks that " we must uncover the means by which man learns to organize and direct his behavior" (p. 56). His famous sorting test, in which the subject has to form groupings of a set of blocks that themselves vary in width, color, shape, and height, is designed to explore this organization process. The very young child forms his groupings as "heaps," a seemingly unorganized congeries. In this phase "word meaning denotes nothing more than a vague conglomeration of individual objects that somehow or other coalesce into an image in his mind." At first, the child forming heaps picks up pieces at random to find out whether they will fit; a kind of grouping by doing. Later he chooses objects on the basis of "some other more complex relationship [produced] by the child's immediate perception" (p. 60). The somewhat older child organizes his groups by a process Vygotsky calls "thinking in complexes." A complex is a "family-relationship," and it may take several specific forms—the sharing of a common attribute with a nucleus object or the grouping of them by a theme rather than a universal property—"this is the mother block, this the baby." As Vygotsky puts it (p. 65),

> A diffuse concept in the child's mind is a kind of family that has limitless powers to expand by adding more and more individuals to the original group. The child's generalizations in the nonpractical and nonperceptual areas of his thinking, which cannot be easily verified by perception or practical action, are the real-life parallel of the diffuse complexes observed in the experiments.[4]

---

[4] For the role of such complexes in "intellectual pathology" in childhood, notably learning blocks, the reader may consult J. S. Bruner, *Toward a Theory of Instruction* (1966), particularly the chapter "On Coping and Defending."

Finally, the conventional superordinate category emerges governed by the logical rules of inclusion, exclusion, and overlap: "all tall, red figures here; all short, blue ones there," etc.

Interestingly enough, Vygotsky does not discuss the emergence of these grouping rules as an instance of external language becoming inner speech but rather as the effect of instruction—instruction, indeed, in "scientific thinking" and even in Marxist thinking. I take him to mean, although he is not clear on the point, that the contents of experience must be prepared and organized better to fit the requirements of being handled by language and that once this occurs there can also be a "reading off" of the surplus properties of the language in much the fashion that Sapir suggested. Indeed, it is only a little extreme to suggest that there are symbolic rules contained in the principles of grouping. Heaps are characterizable as isomorphic to the verb-object relation: "These are in the group because I was looking at them or had them in my hand"; or, in the case of complexes, the grouping conforms to a grammar of prediction (as we shall see more clearly in Chapter 3) in which, "This block is the baby of that bigger one." Finally, the principle of superordination is the introduction of categorial hierarchy and of modification, where "red circles" are opposed to "green squares."

There remains a puzzling problem about the interaction of symbolic representation and action. Why is it impossible simply to *tell* somebody how to ride a bicycle? Consider some Soviet experiments on the regulation of action by speech. The work of Luria and his students (1961) is a good instance to begin with, in particular an experiment by Anokhin. It had been discovered that if a child of two were asked to press a bulb when a light came on the *instruction* itself led the child to press whether the light had come on or not. To quote Luria (1961, pp. 59–60):

> Some assumptions by Sechenov, later reproduced by Anokhin, helped us in tackling this problem. These scientists maintained that the inhibition of a given action usually results from conflict between two excitations, the one inhibiting the other. Is it then possible to make use of the impeding, initiating action which adult speech already has for the child [as demonstrated by the experiments of Yakovleva] and on this basis to produce a conflict between two excitations which would result in the inhibition of the reaction already begun?
>
> With this aim in mind, we performed a very simple experiment, the results of which fully came up to our expectations. . . . We asked [the child] to perform two simple actions in succession: to squeeze the ball at the flash of an electric light signal, and then move his hand away at once (e.g., put it on his knee). When he had obeyed this double act of starting on instructions (which did not present

any difficulty to him), we gradually reduced the distance he had to move his hand after pressing the bulb. First he was told to put it not on his knee, but on the table by the [bulb]; then we reduced the distance still further, and at last after some time, we were able to cut out the second intermediary part of the experiment altogether. Having learned through performing the second action thus to inhibit the first, the child was now able to cope quite easily with a task which he had previously found impossible . . . . Verbal instructions, previously ineffective, could now produce the required effect, thanks to the preliminary influences prepared by the preliminary conflict between the two successive excitations.

In short, if the action itself could be organized first in a fashion that conformed to the instructions that were to come, the instruction could be effective. It is the same point made earlier about the structure of experience. Athletic coaches also recognize that *telling* an athlete something that is useful to him depends first upon his having the requisite motor behavior segmented or organized in a fashion that corresponds to words. Where no such preliminary correspondence exists, there is an independence between the two systems, and we have the ubiquitous case of "he who talks a better game than he plays."

In sum, then, if one is using symbolic representation to guide looking or to guide action, the success of the effort will depend upon the extent to which the sphere of experience or action has been prepared to bring it into some conformance with the requirements of language. If Lashley (1951) is correct about the atemporal, grammar-like control of most serially ordered behavior in human beings looking and acting alike—there should be a very considerable scope for the achievement of control by symbolic means in the growth of the child. So we would have to agree strongly with the view expressed earlier by Miller and Chomsky (1963) that "sentences have a compelling power to control both thought and action."

GROWTH, CULTURE, AND EVOLUTION

On the occasion of the one hundredth anniversary of the publication of Darwin's *The Origin of Species,* Washburn and Howell (1960) presented at the Chicago centennial celebration a paper containing the following passage (pp. 49f.):

It would now appear . . . that the large size of the brain of certain hominids was a relatively late development and that the brain evolved due to new selection pressures *after* bipedalism and consequent upon the use of tools. The tool-using, ground-living, hunting way of life created the large human brain rather than a large-brained man dis-covering certain new ways of life. [We] believe this conclusion is the most important result of the recent fossil hominid discoveries and is one which carries far-reaching implications for the interpretation of human behavior and its· origins . . . The important point is that size of brain, insofar as it can be measured by cranial capacity, has increased some threefold subsequent to the use and manufacture of implements . . . . The uniqueness of modern man is seen as the result of a technical-social life which tripled the size of the brain, reduced the face, and modified many other structures of the body.

This statement implies that the principal change in man over a long period of years (perhaps five hundred thousand) has been allo-plastic rather than autoplastic. That is to say, he has changed by linking himself with new, external implementation systems rather than by any conspicuous change in morphology—"evolution-by-prosthesis," as Weston La Barre puts it. The implement systems seem to have been of three general kinds: (1) *amplifiers of human motor capacities* ranging from the cutting tool through the lever and wheel to the wide variety of modern devices; (2) *amplifiers of sensory capacities* that include primitive devices such as smoke signaling, and modern ones such as magnification and radar sensing, but are also likely to include such "software" as those conventionalized perceptual shortcuts that can be applied to the redundant sensory environment; and finally (3) *amplifiers of human ratiocinative capacities* of infinite variety, ranging from language to myth and theory and explanation. All these forms of amplification are in major or minor degree conventionalized and transmitted by the culture, the last of them probably the most so, since ratiocinative amplifiers involve symbol systems governed by rules that, for effective use, must be shared.

Any implement system to be effective must produce an appropriate internal counterpart, an appropriate skill necessary for organizing sen-sorimotor acts, for organizing percepts, and for organizing our thoughts in a way that matches them to the requirements of imple-ment systems. These internal skills, represented genetically as capaci-ties, are slowly selected in evolution. In the deepest sense, then, man can be described as a species that has become specialized by the use of technological implements. His selection and survival have de-pended on a morphology and set of capacities that could be linked with the alloplastic devices that have made his later evolution possi-ble. We move, perceive, and think in a fashion that depends on tech-niques rather than on wired-in arrangements in our nervous system.

Where representation of the environment is concerned, it too de-pends upon learned techniques; and these are precisely the techniques

that serve to amplify our motor acts, our perceptions, and our ratiocinative activities. We know and respond to recurrent regularities
in our environment by skilled and patterned acts, by conventionalized
spatioqualitative imagery and selective perceptual organization, and
through linguistic encoding which, as so many writers have remarked,
places a selective lattice between us and the physical environment.
In short, the capacities that have been shaped by our evolution as
tool-users are those we rely on in the primary task of representation.

The consequence of the development of such a representational
system, as psychologists and anthropologists alike have pointed out,
is to make possible a kind of integration over space and time that
approaches the conditions necessary for dealing with past and future
in the present and for dealing with the distant as if it were near.
As Hallowell (1955) put it in his presidential address to the American
Anthropological Association,

> The psychobiological structure that the hominid evolved is one in
> which intervening variables which mediate between immediate stimuli
> and overt behavior come to play a more primary role. Such intervening
> variables include unconscious processes such as dreams, as well as
> conscious operations like thinking and reasoning, "Whereby the remote
> as well as the immediate consequences of an impending overt action
> are brought into the psychological present, in full force, so to say,
> and balanced and compared" [Mowrer and Ullman, 1945].

In time, there develops within human culture the traditionally transmitted means for making these activities more easily learned and
more powerful.

As Peter Medawar (1963) notes, the point in primate evolution
at which adaptation occurs almost entirely by the development of
techniques rather than by change in morphology is the point at which
evolution becomes reversible and, in a figurative sense, Lamarckian.
We depend for survival on the inheritance of acquired characteristics
from the culture pool rather than from a gene pool. Culture then
becomes the chief instrument for guaranteeing survival, with its techniques of transmission being of the highest order of importance.

Man's dependence on a cultural heritage is supported by the strikingly appropriate accidents of man's morphological evolution that
has produced a long period of early helplessness. Bipedalism, with
its need for a stronger pelvis, reduces the birth canal at a time in
evolution when brain size is increasing. The morphological compro-
mise is a neonate brain of marked immaturity and with few prepared
response patterns. This circumstance and the marked dimorphism

of the human sexes give ample time and woman-power for child-rearing and ample opportunity for enculturation.

What a culture "teaches" and how it goes about the task of doing so will concern us in much detail in later pages. What seems plain enough is that the most characteristic thing about the lessons that are imparted—whether with respect to matters of value, of existence, or of self—is their productive generality. Whatever is learned seems to be converted into general rules that are applicable to many contingencies never before encountered. In learning a culture, we learn rules, it would seem, and in this sense there is a great kinship to learning language. Obviously, "behaving culturally" is no more "caused" by the culture's "rules" than speaking a language is "caused" by the grammarian's rules. Kroeber and Kluckhohn (1952, p. 170) cite a letter by the present author directed to the section of their monograph dealing with implicit and explicit culture:

> The process by which the implicit culture is "acquired" by the individual (i.e., the way the person learns to respond in a manner congruent with expectation) is such that awareness and verbal formulation are intrinsically difficult. Even in laboratory situations where we set the subject the task of forming complex concepts, subjects typically begin to *respond* consistently in terms of a principle before they can verbalize (a) that they are operating on a principle, or (b) that the principle is thus-and-so. Culture learning, because so much of it takes place before very much verbal differentiation has occurred in the carrier and because it is learned along with the pattern of a language and as part of the language, is bound to result in difficulties of awareness. Thought ways inherent in a language are difficult to analyze by a person who speaks that language and no other, since there is no basis for discriminating an implicit thought way save by comparing it with a different thought way in another language.

Perhaps one should emphasize too that the "nonverbalizable" phase of concept learning, rule learning, and skill learning constitutes the *preparation* of motor, sensory, and intellectual life for assistance by language; the issue was discussed in the section just preceding. Once this learning occurs, the trait then emerges that is most characteristic of human behavior: its symbolic quality, through which we substitute words and sentences in place of events in order to have a vicarious trial run on reality.

We have also commented that the extent and shape of this intellectual development, since in its very nature it depends on assistance from a culture, will vary as a function of culture. Cultures, so goes the classic line of relativism, are all different. Yet to take this position in analyzing the impact of culture on growth dooms one to a study of what is different about growing up in different places, and that is surely a trivial pursuit in comparison with the study of the few powerful shaping forces in culture that produce enormous uniformities in growth and a few crucial differences. Consider now some of these differences.

We have recently had the opportunity to observe carefully on film the play of baboon juveniles and of Kung Bushman children in a similar African habitat.[5] The comparison extended, of course, to our own culture. It is typical of baboon juvenile play that it is virtually all interpersonal. The young males chase and mock-fight one another, developing the skills needed in filling the role of the adult dominant male. The females do a certain amount of chasing around, but soon center on the infants in the troop, whom they groom and try to carry or care for. The adults do no "instructing" and interfere only to place general limits on the juveniles. The limits are on such things as noise that gives away position, for one often sees an older male "policing" a great juvenile chase-about. Adults also herd the young animals into a proper position in the troop or in a tree when a predator is around. There is also intergeneration exchange of grooming. But in the juvenile group, generally, learning is mostly in the peer play that develops skills which, when orchestrated, make an adult repertory. The important thing about this play of the young baboons is that it exercises and develops skills that in rearranged pattern have a place in adult life.

Among the Bushmen there is also very little explicit teaching, but what is strikingly different is the amount of joint activity between the children and the adults. What the child knows, he learns from direct interaction with the adult community, whether it is learning to tell the age of the spoor left by a poisoned kudu buck, to straighten the shaft of an arrow, to build a fire, or to dig a spring hare out of its burrow. Yet in thousands of feet of film, one sees no *explicit* teaching in the sense of a "session" out of the context of action to teach the child a particular thing. It is all implicit. One does see children imitate in competition with one another what they have been participating in with the adults, as in one beautiful scene in which Bushmen children are shooting miniature arrows at beetles. The only exception is the well known teaching of rituals in some indigenous societies at the time of the *rites de passage*. But that ceremony, wherever it has been observed, is for teaching rituals,

---

[5] We are indebted to Professor Irven De Vore and to Educational Services, Inc., for the opportunity to use the baboon film footage, and to Mr. and Mrs. Laurance Marshall for the use of the Bushman footage. Their kindness and patience in discussing these matters are gratefully acknowledged.

chants, myths, and ceremonies—never skills (see Spindler, 1959). In
Bushman society, indeed, there is rather little of this kind of instruction. Usually one finds that the dances, games, and rituals are first
encountered when the young baby is still being carried in his mother's
karosse and miraculously held there while the mother goes through
the complicated steps of, say, the centipede dance.

By far the most detailed field study of the learning process of
children in an indigenous society is to be found in the monograph
by Professor Meyer Fortes (1938) of the University of Cambridge,
Social and Psychological Aspects of Education in Taleland. This
monograph, published as a supplement to the journal *Africa,* is not
readily available, so it is worth examining its contents here in some
detail. For one is struck by the extent to which certain of Fortes'
observations correspond to those of others who have looked at the
educational process in indigenous societies.[6] The first point that
Fortes makes about the matter is crucial (pp. 8–9):

> The process of education among the Tallensi, as among a great
> many other African peoples of analogous culture, is intelligible when
> it is recognized that the social sphere of adult and child is unitary
> and undivided. In our own society, the child's feeling and thinking
> and acting takes place largely in relation to a reality—to aims, responsi-
> bilities, compulsions, material objects and persons, and so forth—which
> differs completely from that of the adult, though sometimes overlap-
> ping it. This dichotomy is not only expressed in our customs, it comes
> out also in the psychological reactions which mark the individual's
> transition from the child's world to the adult's—the so-called negative
> phase of adolescent instability which has been alleged to be universal
> in our society. It is unknown in Tale society. As between adults and
> children, in Tale society, the social sphere is differentiated only in
> terms of relative capacity. All participate in the same culture, the
> same round of life, but in varying degrees, corresponding to the stage
> of physical and mental development, nothing in the universe of adult
> behavior is hidden from children or barred to them. They are actively
> and responsibly part of the . . . system. Psychological effects of
> fundamental importance for Tale education follow from this. For it
> means that the child is from the beginning oriented toward the same

---

[6] One does not find many careful studies of education in primitive society,
with education viewed literally as leading the child into the views, beliefs, and
skills of a society. For more than a quarter century, most American writing has
been dominated by the "culture-and-personality" point of view that concerned
itself with the handling of emotional crisis points in a child's life (bowel training,
weaning, the arrival of new siblings, etc.). It is difficult in such studies to find
much on the development of skills or the process for passing on attitudes and
values. Spindler's (1957) book has rich references and one can find occasional,
well-informed articles in the pages of *Africa.*

reality as its parents and has the same physical and social material upon which to direct its cognitive and instinctual endowment. The interests, motives, and purposes of children are identical with those of adults, but at a simpler level of organization.

The same point about continuity has been made about many indigenous societies and, indeed, an illustrative episode presented by Fortes (p. 11) finds an almost identical parallel among the Netsilik of Pelley Bay, so meticulously studied by the Danish anthropologist Rasmussen (1931). The Tale episode involves the nine-year-old girl Maanyeya, who had eaten none of the meat of the previous night's sacrifice. Asked why not, she replied:

> When they sacrifice to Zukek, women don't eat of the meat. If they do, they will never bear any children, they become sterile. [What's that to you?] Am I not a woman? Who wants to be sterile?

So too with a Netsilik girl of about the same age, loaded down with amulets, who, when asked why she wore them, listed a catalogue of adult woes from which she was guarding herself.

Everybody instructs among the Tallensi: adult to child, older child to younger, peers among one another; but the instruction is always in the context of the action or endeavor in progress. There is virtually nothing by way of standardized and deliberate methods of training children. The system is premised on the "expectation of normal behavior . . . . In any given social situation everybody takes it for granted that any person participating either already knows, or wants to know, how to behave in a manner appropriate to the situation and in accordance with his level of maturity" (pp. 25–26). The child is given tasks commensurate with his capacity and it is taken for granted that he will participate in and contribute to the economic, social, and ritual tasks of adult life, in however small a way. Even play, of which there is a fair share, is marked by the same centering on themes that are as much part of adult as of children's lives.

But because so much of the "meaning" of what is being learned is intrinsic in the context in which the learning occurs, there is very little need for verbal formulation. Fortes remarks (p. 30),

> The natives say that small children frequently ask questions about people and things they see around them. However, listening to children's talk for "why" questions, I was surprised to note how rarely they occurred; and the few instances I recorded referred to objects or persons foreign to the normal routine of Tale life. It would seem that Tale children rarely have to ask "why" in regard to the people" and things of their normal environment because so much of their learning occurs in real situations. . . .

Consider again the question raised earlier about why, under certain conditions, intellectual development moves toward an elaborated form of symbolic representation with all the powerful accompanying symbolic activity that becomes accessible for use. Five possible sources of this development were mentioned in the earlier discussion, and we are now ready to consider them in more detail. They were, in brief: (a) the use of words as invitations to form concepts; (b) contingent dialogue between adult and child; (c) the importance of "school" as an innovation; (d) the development in ·a culture of "scientific" concepts; (e) the possibility of conflict between modes of representation.

Note first that when a society grows more complex in its technology and division of labor, there are two deep changes that must necessarily occur. First, the knowledge and skill within the culture comes increasingly to exceed the amount that any one individual can know. Almost inevitably, then, there develops a sharp disjunction between the worlds of the child and of the adult. The unity of the Tale world becomes impossible in more complex societies. Increasingly, then, there develops a new and moderately effective technique of instructing the young based heavily on *telling* out of context rather than on *showing* in context. The school, of course, becomes the prime instrument of this new technique but by no means the exclusive one. For, in fact, there is also a great increase in telling by parents, again out of the context of action, for there come to be fewer spheres in which such learning *in situ* can be practiced. It is probably by virtue of this development that the "why" question becomes so important a feature of the child's response to his environment. It serves to provide a verbal context in the absence of the context of action characteristic of technologically simpler indigenous societies. Indeed, it has even been remarked that the world of learning of the child in school becomes detached from life as lived in the greater society, and one hears the voice of the reformer asking that school be drawn closer to life.

Yet, as commented upon in detail elsewhere (Bruner, 1965), it may indeed be that the important thing about the school as now constituted is that it *is* removed from immediate context of socially relevant action. This very disengagement makes learning an act in itself and makes it possible to embed it in a context of language and symbolic activity. For now indeed it is the case that words are the major invitations to form concepts rather than the action contexts so aptly described by Fortes (1938) and others. *Verbal* understanding, the ability to *say* it and to enumerate instances becomes the criterion of learning in such a context, in contrast to the Tale concept of "yam," which according to Fortes connotes wisdom and resourcefulness about how to *behave*—both practically and morally.[7]

In more evolved technical societies, then, the very nature of the learning situation *requires* a contingent dialogue between parent or tutor and the child, for once one is out of the task context in which learning occurs directly one can no longer point or "let the situation carry the meaning." We would predict, and the prediction is almost trivial because it is so obvious, that comparable tasks to be performed by a member of a more technical society and a member of a less technical society will always be more accessible to verbal description by the former. It is precisely in this application of symbolic recoding of "what one knows" that the process of translating action and experience into its symbolic, vicarious forms occurs. Little enough is known about the process, but at least a few studies (Crutchfield's study of increased inferential power in children [1964] and Saugstad's [1955] experiment on a solution of Maier-type problems) suggest the manner in which prior verbal analysis of a task can produce an increase in reasoning solutions. We need mention these matters only in passing, for they will concern us again in the discussion of the striking difference one finds among Wolof-speaking school children and their unschooled peers in Senegal (Chapters 11 and 13).

Finally, with respect to the problem of *conflict* between systems of representation as a source of impulsion to grow (the disequilibrium theory), there is striking evidence elsewhere in this volume for the efficacy of the conflict between verbal and visual formulations (Chapter 9) and for visual and enactive modes (Chapter 11). However, there is a deeper problem that is worth a moment's exploration. It can be introduced by a comment in *A Study of Thinking* (Bruner, Goodnow, and Austin [1956], p. 50) to this effect:

> It is curiously difficult to recapture preconceptual innocence. Having learned a new language, it is almost impossible to recapture the un-

---

[7] It goes without saying that the separation of thought and action has not been an unblemished blessing in technically mature societies. Hamlet, "sicklied o'er with the pallid cast of thought" or Goethe's contrast, "Gray is all theory/Green grows the golden tree of life" bespeak the problem eloquently. Yet it is all too evident that the unity of "the noble savage" fares poorly when the powers of analytic thinking work their separatist way. As McGranahan (1963, p. 16) remarks, ". . . in viewing the human implications of technological change we [must] not become so fascinated by the bad as to forget the good, and so protective of the present cultures of under-developed areas as to wish to preserve these cultures against the very idea of progress which we embrace for ourselves."

differentiated flow of voiced sounds that one heard before one learned
to sort the flow into words and phrases. Having mastered the distinction between odd and even numbers, it is a feat to remember what
it was like in a mental world where there was no such distinction.
In short, the attainment of a concept has about it something of a
quantal character. It is as if the mastery of a conceptual distinction
masked the preconceptual memory of the things now distinguished.

There is a dilemma here. In one sense it is a loss for the growing
human being to "lose" his older, more innocent conceptions and skills,
but at the same time it appears to be a necessary condition for acculturation (and, indeed, for cultural control of the individual) that
there be this "childhood amnesia," as Schachtel (1947) has called
it. It is perhaps Neisser (1962, pp. 63ff.) who deals most directly
with this problem from the point of view of the role that culture
plays in shaping the growth of the child:

> Essentially, the experiences of childhood are incompatible with
> the schemata of the adult. It is no wonder, then, that the adult cannot
> recall them. The events, activities, and emotions of childhood were
> assimilated in a way that is no longer open. Years of sophisticating
> accommodation have made it as impossible to remember our own
> childhood as to fully understand anyone else's. The early years are
> like a forgotten dream. The simile of the dream is appropriate: our
> inability to remember dreams is based on the same factors. The co-
> herent schemata of waking life have no room for their childlike illogic.
> It is worth noting the great individual differences in memory for
> dreams, as in memory for childhood experiences: not all persons are
> equally accommodating to society's demand.
>   This means that the universal amnesia for childhood is not primarily
> the result of anxiety or guilt, and is not based on an active process
> of suppression. It is, instead, a necessary consequence of the discon-
> tinuities in cognitive functioning which accompany growth into adult-
> hood. From preverbal to verbal, from naive to sophisticated, from
> carefree to responsible, from weak to powerful—the cognitive accom-
> modations which accompany these transitions seem to make the past
> inaccessible. Schachtel finds the changes repugnant, preferring the
> spontaneity of the child to the stereotype of the adult. For him, both
> the amnesia and its cause are a matter for deep regret. Over and
> over again he stresses the value of what is lost in the process of
> acculturation and accommodation, as if adulthood was an essentially
> impoverished condition. To me, his view appears one-sided. Childhood
> is not so simple, nor maturity so barren. Indeed, it is in the prematurely
> rigid schemata of early and middle childhood that the roots of adult
> neurosis are found. Psychotherapy does not aim at regressing the
> patient to the conceptual innocence of childhood, but at permitting
> him to grow beyond childhood. The healthy person is not the one
> who refuses to assimilate, but the one whose schemata are adequate
> to reality.

As the mental apparatus of a growing child develops, and the information-handling processes become more intricate, thinking goes through a succession of stages. These are semi-stable states of accommodation, phases through which the cognitive mechanisms must evolve on the route to intellectual maturity. A child assimilates and "distorts" the world of his experience in ways characteristic of his age. As he grows up, constant necessity for accommodation results in cognitive change. This change can come about in three fundamentally different ways, which we must clarify.

The first mode of accommodation is *absorption*. Later forms of cognitive schema may absorb earlier ones completely. This is what usually happens with repeated exposure to a piece of music. The inharmonious jumble that was experienced the first time simply ceases to exist. It cannot be perceived again and cannot be remembered. The new schema has swallowed up all the elements and interrelations of the old. Absorption is a common experience in hidden-picture puzzles. When we finally find the outline of the squirrel that the artist has cleverly concealed in the bark of the tree, we cannot lose it again; it is impossible to imagine how we could have failed to see it before. The same thing tends to happen in successful rote learning. One who knows a poem by heart usually does not recall the individual trials on which he practiced it. In a sense, he has an amnesia for them. Are they "forgotten"? Yes and no: they have a continuing effect (because they established the schema which now exists) but they cannot be individually recalled.

A second mode of accommodation might be called *displacement*. Part of the cognitive apparatus does not evolve, but continues to exist side-by-side with a new schema which assimilates the same environmental events in a different way. A trivial example of such dual mental functioning is the "double-take." The double-take occurs when you suddenly realize that something heard or seen a few moments ago actually had quite a different significance from that which you had, perhaps inattentively, ascribed to it. One assimilation process interpreted the event as unimportant. A second process, occurring simultaneously but unconsciously, interpreted it very differently; the double-take occurs when the second assimilation becomes conscious. More sustained instances of displacement are common among social scientists, who are able to react to a social situation either "personally" or "professionally." The behavioral results of these two ways of assimilating racial discrimination (for instance) can be poles apart.

Adequate consideration of the consequences of "displacement," in this sense, would go far beyond the intent of this paper. It is possible to interpret the classical evidence for unconscious cognitive processes in these terms. Suppose that an adult has preserved the assimilative mechanisms of a four-year-old with respect to certain events, for example, situations involving sexuality. These schemata will be "unconscious" from the point of view of his organized adult awareness, but will continue to process information and control behavior. The results will be perceptual defense, forgetting of intentions, and perhaps other symptomatic phenomena. This interpretation is not far from that implied by the concept of "dissociation," but here the displacement is viewed as one possible outcome of a developmental process that will take *some* form in any case.

The third mode of accommodation is the *integrative* one. In many cases it is possible for a new schema to make use of an old one without destroying its integrity. Integration requires a step to another level of abstraction or understanding, in which outputs of the older modes of processing are only part of a more comprehensive whole. This hierarchical organization can be taken for granted in some aspects of perceptual development. We do not lose our ability to see figure and ground when we understand the three-dimensional permanence of figured objects. Moreover, their perceptual solidity is not impaired when we endow them with cultural or personal meaning. To be sure, wide individual differences exist here. Some persons see much more than others of the natural shapes and colors about them. The artist's world is filled with shapes and colors that go unnoticed by the less perceptive. He has somehow maintained—and developed!—the integrity of assimilative systems that are absorbed or displaced in the rest of us.

The foregoing analysis of the accommodative process can be applied to the problem of childhood amnesia. Both absorption and displacement of earlier schemata must lead to "forgetting." Both types of change must almost inevitably occur as a baby becomes a child, and a child grows to adulthood. Indeed, even integration leads to a certain loss; a childish mode of functioning somehow preserved in an adult structure cannot be identical with its unintegrated form. However understanding a parent (or teacher or a therapist) may be, he remains an adult. But this change of perspective is insignificant compared with the total amnesia for infancy which we all share, and which I attribute to absorption and displacement. What circumstances lead to one mode of accommodation rather than another? An adequate answer can hardly be given. It is very likely, however, that the manner in which different developmental stages are handled by environment and culture are particularly important. Displacement will tend to occur where cultural factors emphasize the discontinuity and incompatibility between different phases of development, while integration must be easier where several stages of assimilation are welcomed and used together in a consistent way. Thus we must expect a close relationship between the continuity or discontinuity of developmental patterns on the one hand, and the continuity of memory on the other.

Neisser's comments are worth quoting in such detail not simply for the light they shed on the adult's inability to reconstruct his own development but because, in a deep sense, they provide a justification for doing research on intellectual development in children! Growth has a way of minimizing the conflicted ways of knowing, making retrospective efforts at creating a developmental psychology worse than hazardous. With that much said, we can turn directly to processes we have explored by examination of how they manifest themselves in the behavior of young children.

PLAN OF THE BOOK

The chapters that follow explore the points considered in these opening pages. These monographic studies are all carried out with the use of more or less controlled experimental conditions, all are concerned with how cognitive function changes with age, experience, and exposure to the instruments of a culture. Most have been carried out in the United States, virtually all around Boston. Some have been done in rural Mexico, in the Senegalese bush in West Africa, or among the Eskimo of Alaska. They do not constitute anything like an adequate base for drawing conclusions about the "role of culture," but at least they serve to guard us against the illusion that the child of Westchester County, or Geneva, or Hampstead, or Newton is the "standard child" from which all others deviate. There is no "standard child," and "natural childhood" is hard to imagine outside a cultural context.

Although the studies we report have grown out of a common point of view, they are in no direct sense "derived" from the theory. The theory is not of that kind, nor is it meant to be. Rather, the experiments are raids into new territory or revisits to old, guided by the theory. They have been designed to plumb the issues introduced discursively in these opening pages, issues that the authors have discussed, argued about, and helped jointly to convert into experimental form.

We now present these studies, each linked as closely as possible with the rest. The epilogue deals with the major points that have been raised.

CHAPTER **3**

On Equivalence

Rose R. Olver and Joan Rigney Hornsby

$\mathbf{T}$hat children and adults group discriminately different things and treat them as "the same" or "alike" is hardly debatable.[1] And indeed, were they not naturally prone to do so, the diversity of the environment would soon overwhelm them. Such equivalence-making is in large measure a learned achievement; it may be expected to change with growth and development in a manner consistent with more general changes in cognitive development. Elsewhere in this book a good deal is made of how the very young child represents and "knows" by doing, how there is added to this primitive mode a capacity for knowing by depicting in images, and finally how the growing child achieves the ability to give an account of his world in the powerful medium of language. This course of growth by which finally all three techniques of knowing come into force—enactive, ikonic, and symbolic representation—is reflected in the changing ways that children have for imposing equivalence on the things of their world.

Enactive, ikonic, and symbolic representation might each, for example, be expected to emphasize different features of the environment as bases for establishing equivalence. Under enactive representation, things should be seen as alike on the basis of a common role in some action. Equivalence with ikonic representation might more likely be accomplished by grouping items according to perceptual kinship or

---

[1] This chapter has grown out of two theses carried out at the Center for Cognitive Studies. The first is a doctoral dissertation, *A Developmental Study of Cognitive Equivalence*, and was completed by Rose R. Olver in 1961. The second, by Joan Rigney (Hornsby), entitled *A Developmental Study of Cognitive Equivalence Transformations and Their Use in the Acquisition and Processing of Information*, was submitted as an honors thesis one year later. Both were submitted to the Department of Social Relations at Harvard.

likeness. With the achievement of symbolic representation, equivalence might well be expected to be governed by such grammatical principles as synonymy, superordination, or syntactic substitutability. It is with such a course of growth that this chapter deals. The transitions with which we shall be concerned are interesting in their own right as a documentary on development. More interesting still is the picture of the underlying form of organization in thought that is revealed.

For example, it is not only the "semantics" of equivalence that changes with growth—the features of the environment used as the basis of equivalence—but the "syntax" of equivalence formation as well. Might equivalence groupings under enactive representation demonstrate the sequential properties of action sequences? Might groupings governed by ikonic representation, reflecting the domination of the perceptually vivid be based on a kind of conjunctive joining of attributes? Does the development of symbolic equivalence groupings take on the form of conventional categorization and hierarchical organization?[2]

The studies reported here trace the development of equivalence from age six to age nineteen, from the first year of regular school work to the first year in college. The materials we have used permit

---

[2] Vygotsky (1962), in tracing the development of concepts from "heaps" to complexes to "true concepts," also remarks upon changes in the syntax of equivalence. Initially, according to his account, "Word meaning denotes nothing more to the child than a vague syncretic conglomeration of individual objects that have somehow or other coalesced into an image in his mind" (pp. 59–60). The second major step toward "true" concept formation is "thinking in complexes." Here the child groups diverse elements into a complex on the basis of perceptually concrete and factual relationships. Complexes are thus distinguished from "heaps" in that the objects included are united not only by subjective impressions but also by "bonds actually existing between these objects" (p. 61) and from true concepts, in that "an object included because of one of its attributes enters the complex not just as the carrier of that one trait but as an individual, with *all* its attributes. The single trait is not abstracted by the child from the rest and is not given a special role, as in a concept. In complexes, the hierarchical organization is absent: all attributes are functionally equal (p. 64)." The final stage, that of "true concepts," occurs when the child guides his mental operations "by the use of words as a means of actively centering attention, of abstracting certain traits, synthesizing them, and symbolizing them by a sign" (p. 81). According to Vygotsky, this stage of genuine concepts is achieved during adolescence. The reader will see that Vygotsky has provided us with a framework with which to begin, but that we have diverged from him in several critical ways: in the separation of semantic and syntactic features of equivalence, and in a variety of other ways that become clearer in the description of experiments and results.

the child to demonstrate both the basis on which he renders things equivalent and the syntax or structure of the groups he forms.

Experiment 1: Equivalence Formation with Verbal Materials. We gave children from age six to nineteen the task of telling us how different items are alike. We presented the words *banana* and *peach*, each typed on a small white card and spoken aloud as well, and asked the child, "How are banana and peach alike?" We then added *potato* to the list, first asking, "How is potato different from banana and peach?" and then, "How are banana, peach, and potato all alike?" Next we added *meat*, asking, "How is meat different from banana, peach, and potato?" and then, "How are banana, peach, potato, and meat all alike?" This procedure was continued until the array consisted of: *banana, peach, potato, meat, milk, water, air, germs*. At the end of the array we included an item about which we asked only how it differed from the preceding items; for example, *stones* was presented as the final item in the banana-peach list. We presented a second array of items in the same manner: *bell, horn, telephone, radio, newspaper, book, painting, education,* and as the contrast item, *confusion*.

Note that the arrays are made up of successively more distant items, but, though the items become increasingly more diverse, they share a common characteristic. The items in the banana-peach array, for example, are all ingestible; those in the bell-horn array all carry messages, and so forth. As words are added, the task gets more difficult, and so it was intended, for we were interested in pushing our subjects to their limits. The two lists were constructed impressionistically. Could we have found a more systematic method—we tried several—it would have been better. The present lists do at least evoke responses that serve our purpose.

Sixty children formed the subjects in this investigation. The children in the youngest grades—from age six to fourteen—were enrolled in suburban public schools near Boston; the sixteen-year-olds came from a nearby suburban high school; and the oldest group (the college freshmen) were students of Harvard and Radcliffe Colleges. There were five boys and five girls in each age group, and their mean ages and IQ scores are shown in Table 1.

Children of different ages go about such a task in rather different ways. One six-year-old said that banana, peach, potato, and meat were alike because "a banana is yellow, and a peach is red and yellow, or sometimes red and sometimes just yellow, and a potato is light flesh, and meat is brown." Another responded, "Meat and potato are most of the time together, peach and banana can be for dessert, and

TABLE 1
Subjects in Experiment 1—Ages, IQ's, Number of Children

Grade	Mean Age	Mean IQ	Number
1	6 years 3 months	*	10
4	9 years 6 months	122	10
6	11 years 7 months	115	10
8	13 years 5 months	122	10
10	15 years 11 months	122	10
Freshmen	18 years 7 months	*	10

* IQ data not available.

the banana is close to the kind of vegetable." Older children, for example, the sixteen-year-olds, grouped the same items as "They're all something to eat," or "They're all food." The six-year-old, consistent with his reliance on ikonic representation, seemed caught by the way things look—their color or where they are found together. The sixteen-year-old spoke of the function of the items—what they are used for. Not only did the bases for grouping differ, but the syntax as well. While the older child used a common characteristic to form a class, some property shared by all members, the six-year-old linked each item only to the next one, or stated a characteristic separately for each item in the group.

Consider more closely now on what bases the items are judged to be "the same." Since they all vary from one another in a number of different dimensions, a variety of different characteristics could be used as the basis of equivalence. Five main modes can be distinguished: *perceptible, functional, affective, nominal,* and *fiat equivalence.* For each mode we can set forth a typical language frame for characterizing the basis of equivalence.

1. *Perceptible:* The child may render the items equivalent on the basis of immediate phenomenal qualities such as color, size, shape, or on the basis of position in time or space.

Perceptible Intrinsic They are ———. (X:adjective: ". . . both yellow.")
They have ———. (X:noun: ". . . writing on them.")

Perceptible Extrinsic They are (preposition) ———. (X:position in time or space: ". . . all in a house.")

2. *Functional:* The child may base equivalence on the use or function of the items, considering either what they do or what can be done to them.

Functional Intrinsic They _____. (X:verb: ". . . make noise.")
Functional Extrinsic You _____ them. (X:verb: ". . . can turn them on.")

3. *Affective:* The child may render the items equivalent on the basis of the emotion they arouse or of his evaluation of them.

Affective You _____ them. (X:value or internal state: ". . . like them both.")
             They are _____. (X:adjective indicating value: ". . . very important.")

4. *Nominal:* The child may group the items by giving a name that exists ready-made in the language.

Nominal They are (or are not) _____. (X:noun: ". . . both fruit.")

5. *Fiat Equivalence:* The child may merely state that the items are alike or are the same without giving any further information as to the basis of his grouping, even when he is prodded.

Fiat Equivalence "A" is (or is not) _____ "B." (X:like, similar to, the same as, and so forth: "They are the same thing, really.")

Six-year-olds do, indeed, group more often according to perceptible properties than do older children. Their protocols are laced with the colors, sizes, shapes, and places of things. More than a quarter of their groupings are of the perceptible intrinsic type; no older group forms even half that many on this basis. From age six on there is a steady increase in functionally based equivalence—from 49 percent of all responses at age six to 73 percent at age nineteen (Figure 1). Initially the turn to functional attributes as the basis of equivalence is extrinsic as we have defined it, and often it is seemingly arbitrary—the child speaks of what *he* can do *to* the objects: turn them on, roll them up into a ball, and so forth. At age nine half of the children's groupings are formed in this way. It is as if the child were taking himself as reference point in order to create a common basis for grouping an apparently diverse array.

What emerges at this point is a bit surprising. One is at first taken aback by the central role of "functionalism" as an arm or at least an

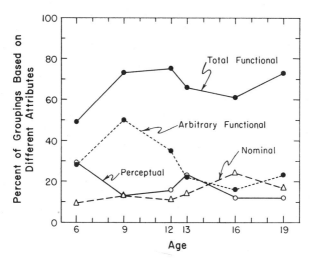

Figure 1. Percent of groupings based on different attributes.

accompaniment to intellectual growth. It has about it some of the properties of enactive representation—definition by an action taken. But a closer examination suggests that this new functionalism provides a means for the child to get free of responding to the more immediate, surfacy aspects of the things around him. Indeed, functionalism in its egocentric form is what permits the child to distinguish between objects and actions taken toward them. Yet a closer look at the syntactic aspect of grouping as it expresses itself at this time in the child's life—and we shall have a closer look presently—also makes it plain that functionalism is highly associated with more mature forms of grouping. It may well be that as the child breaks away from the perceptual domination of vivid things he must fall back on a more practical way of dealing with the environment—through action, or at least vicarious action. The common uses of things are pitted against their divergent appearances, and the conflict promotes growth. Whether functionalism is made possible by the child's ability to use new grouping principles, or the other way round, must remain a moot point.

Consider further this increase in grouping according to use, even arbitrary use. The nine-year-old, for all his functionalism, forms groupings that are neither particularly appropriate nor realistic for adaptive action. Without intending a philosophical point, we may say that their functional groups are often arbitrary and that they ignore the conventional or sensible uses to which objects are put. The child at this age ignores the possible reciprocal relations between himself and the objects he is sorting and, instead, imposes functions upon them. There is, for example, a sharp increase at age nine in the use of the pronouns "you" and "I" in answering the questions we pose. And the use of "you" and "I" in framing responses declines beyond age nine as the child turns from extrinsic to intrinsic functional properties as the basis of grouping. The shift is from responses such as, "I can crinkle up a newspaper and then it will make a noise like the bell and horn" to. "They all tell ideas in their own way." Figure 2 depicts the relevant data.

Consider now the structure or "syntax" of the groupings formed by children of different ages. We can distinguish three general grouping structures: *superordinate, complexive,* and *thematic* (Figure 3).

1. *Superordinate groupings* are constructed on the basis of a common feature or features characterizing the items included in a group or class. This is the classic category of Venn diagrams and the like. Any array of items has a number of common characteristics, any one or combination of which can serve as the criterion for their inclusion in a group. Thus, for example, banana, peach, and potato can be placed in a superordinate grouping because, "They all have skins," or "They are all food," or because "They all can be bought at a store," and so forth.

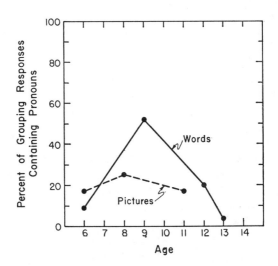

Figure 2. Percent of grouping responses containing pronouns "You" and "I"— verbal and picture array.

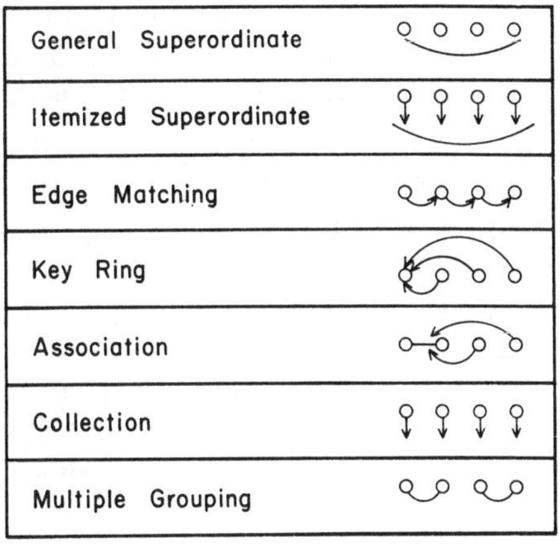

Figure 3. Grouping syntax diagrams.

General superordinate. The general superordinate construction consists of stating a common characteristic of the items in the group. For example, bell and horn are "both things that make noise."

Itemized superordinate. Itemization may be added to superordinate grouping such that, while the items have a generalized property that joins them, the basis on which each item qualifies is explicitly stated. For example, "Bell makes noise, horn makes noise too, bell says ding-dong, horn says doo-doo."

2. *Complexive structures* are formed by using attributes of an array so as to form local rather than universal rules for grouping and, in this sense, these are closer to Wittgenstein's[3] "family resemblances" than to the classic category. This general pattern is illustrated by five maneuvers for forming complexes: *collections, edge matchings, key rings, associations,* and *multiple groupings.*

Collections. The collection complex consists in finding complementary or somehow contrasting or otherwise related properties

---

[3] See L. Wittgenstein (1953, 1958). Wittgenstein is quite right in pointing out that such complexes as we describe have a useful status in scientific as in everyday thinking. We may at times in our discussion appear to denigrate complexive thinking, but that is not our intention. Rather, our concern is with the child's capacity to go beyond such grouping—not simply with whether he abandons or foreswears complexive grouping.

that all the things have, but not in tying them together in terms of attributes that are shared. For example, "Bell is black, horn is brown, telephone is blue, radio is red." Or, "Newspaper you can read, book you can read, telephone you get messages over, radio you get messages over, and a horn you can blow."

Edge matchings. The edge-matching complex consists in forming associative links between neighboring items. A chain of items is formed by tying the items together in linked pairs. For example, "Banana and peach are both yellow, peach and potato are round, potato and meat are served together, meat and milk both come from cows." There is no consistency in the attribute or characteristic by which one link of the chain is joined with the one that precedes and the one that follows.

Key rings. The key-ring complex consists in taking an item and linking all the others to it by choosing attributes that form relations between the central item and each of the others. For example, "Painting—well, one thing is a newspaper has got some painting in it, a book has got some black printing, a radio and a telephone have painting on them and a horn—well, there's a little painting on it, and a bell is also the color of paints." Or, "Germs are in banana, peach, potato, meat, milk, water, and air."

Associations. In the association complex the child links two items and then uses the bond between these items as a nucleus for the addition of other items. For example, "Bell and horn are music things, when you dial a telephone it's music a little." Or, "Bell, horn, telephone, and radio make noises, if you fold back a newspaper, then it will crackle and make a noise."

Multiple groupings. The multiple-grouping complex consists of the formation of several subgroupings. For example, "A telephone is like a radio—I know that. A horn and a bell both make sounds, but I don't know about a newspaper." The list is thus segmented into several groups, and the gap between them is not bridged.

3. *Thematic groupings* are formed on the basis of how the items fit in a sentence or a story or a thema. The construction of thematic groupings, in fact, most often depends on a sentence for tying items together. The sentence carries a story or thematic line: "The little boy was eating a banana on the way to the store to buy some peaches and potatoes."

We can turn now to the patterns of growth observed in the children. To begin with, there is a massive change that takes place between the sixth and nineteenth year (Figure 4). At six, half of the groupings

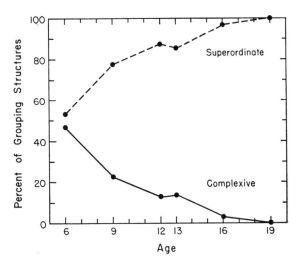

Figure 4. Percent of grouping structures of two types.

made by the children are complexive, half superordinate. By nine, the balance shifts to three-quarters superordinated. And by nineteen, the complexive grouping has virtually disappeared, at least among these subjects and in this culture.

Not only do the younger children use complexive groupings more often, they also fall back on them more readily when the going gets hard. Recall that the items in an array diverged increasingly from the opening pair as successive ones are added to the list. The degree of divergence is an inexact matter, but at the very least it can be said that for virtually anybody, child and adult alike, it is more diffi-cult to form a grouping for the first four or five items in a list than for the first pair. We took advantage of this fact to compare the per-formance of our subjects on the first pair, trio, and quadrad of items (easier items) with performance on five, six, seven, and eight items. The results tell their own story—brave starts and weak finishes by the younger subjects, until finally the task is within reach of the older ones (Figure 5). And when the younger children fall back on com-plexes with the longer lists, they tend to use the less demanding forms such as collections and edge-matchings, whereas the older ones use associations and key rings more often.

There is a striking relation between the syntax and the semantics of the groupings the children made. If the attributes used in grouping

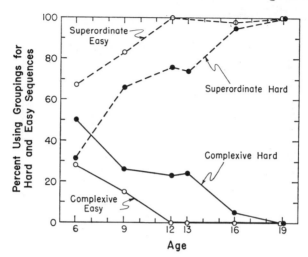

Figure 5. Percent of groupings in easy and hard sequences that are complexive and superordinate in structure.

are perceptible, then the grouping is likely to be complexive. If attributes are functional, on the other hand, the chances are greater that they will be grouped superordinately.

Our excursion into the domain of grouping, using verbal materials as stimuli, leads us to several conclusions. Perhaps the most obvious is that in tasks such as we presented our subjects, growth is reflected by a steady movement from grouping complexively to grouping by superordination. This progress is achieved at the same time that the child stops paying sole attention to the perceptible properties of the objects to be grasped and begins attending more to their functional significance.

We cannot help saying a word of caution. It is evident that the tasks we used were ones that the children were increasingly likely to see as they grew older as "academic," to be dealt with "intellectually," as one deals with such tasks. To a degree, their competence to deal with tasks in this way—consistently, logically, and so on—depends upon their being in the culture, whether in school or in social settings where we demand of older children that they put aside childish ways of thinking. There is little question that our older subjects were also able to be more complexive, though they did not sense this experiment as an appropriate occasion for it. We shall have ample opportunity to explore this question later.

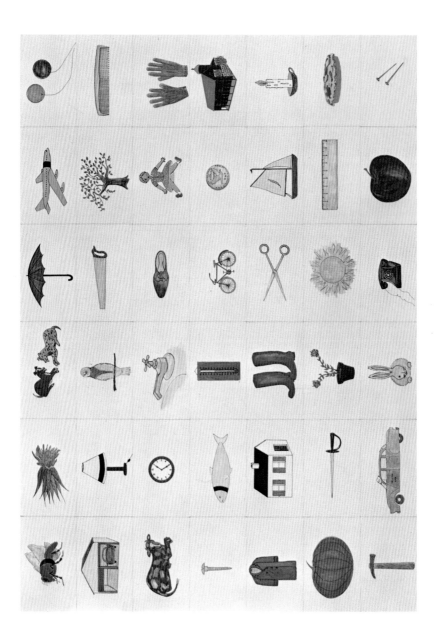

II-6 Pictures used in equivalence task with pictorial material.

We have observed both the "overshoot" of complexive thinking in the younger children and the corresponding "overshoot" of the use of superordinates in somewhat older children. Six-year-olds who attempt to use superordinates in the "easier" first half of the array fall back on complexes in the more difficult portion of the task. Yet by a comparable token, nine– and twelve-year-olds get lost in what we have come to call "hyperordination." Trying to use the superordinate rule, they mire down by grouping highly diverse items under the rubric, "They are all things," and fail to achieve the benefit of the simplicity of such grouping. For "hyperordination" is knowing the form of the behavior but not the substance—as in the pseudoconstraints in Chapter 4.

Obviously, the two approaches to grouping are required in adult functioning, and though in our data we see one replacing the other, the replacement is probably more for public activities than for those done more subjectively. The loose-knit complex, as Wittgenstein and others have noted, is a vehicle for searching out possibilities of kinship. It is also the vehicle of poetry and fantasy. What it lacks in tidiness, it recovers in richness. So too the superordinate category: if its applicability is limited to well-formed problems, at least it is capable of precision and a workable exclusiveness.

Before drawing conclusions, we should examine a variant of the present experiment, lest we be victim of results imposed by our methods. We turn now to a related experiment much like the first, save in two respects: the first experiment used verbal materials, and it forced them in a fixed order on the children. To some extent, these procedures constrained the nature of the response made.

In the second experiment, the stimuli were pictorial, and the subjects could deal with them in their own order.

Experiment 2: Equivalence Formation with Pictures. We presented children from age six to eleven with an array of forty-two water-color drawings. Ninety boys, thirty each from grades 1, 3, 6, of a suburban school near Boston served as subjects, and each was individually tested (mean ages and IQs were 6:3, untested; 8:4, 121; and 11:4, 117, respectively). Their task was to select from this array a group of pictures that "are alike in some way." The drawings represented familiar objects such as a pair of scissors, a doll, a garage, a bee, a pumpkin, various articles of clothing, a sail boat, a taxi, and so forth, and these were placed on a table in front of the child (Figure 6). He was first asked to identify each picture to ensure that he had seen and was familiar with all of them. Whenever he was unable to provide any sort of identification for a picture, he was told what it was.

Then he was asked to choose pictures that were alike in some way— "any way at all in which a group of things is the same"—and to remove them from the array. He could take as many pictures as he wanted. When he had completed his grouping, he was asked to tell how the pictures he selected were alike. The pictures were then replaced in their original positions in the array, and he was asked to form another group. The task was repeated ten times, the child selecting new groups from the full set of pictures each time.

The picture-grouping task differs from the verbal task in several important ways that can be expected to influence the equivalence groups formed. Davidon (1952), in working with college students, has found that the nature of the materials affects the type of concept formed in the following manner:

> When grouping verbal symbols there appears to be a greater tendency to attain concepts based on common *use* than when grouping pictorial symbols (drawings and photographs). And with pictorial symbols, conversely, there is a greater tendency to attain concepts based upon common parts [p. 78].

Since in this task we are dealing with pictures rather than verbal materials, we might expect a greater use of perceptible attributes and a decreased use of functional characteristics. Because the task permits the choice of any number of objects for grouping, it might also permit more pair-formations based on idiosyncrasies shared by members of the pair. Both these characteristics should promote differences between the two procedures.

Consider first the relative use of perceptible and functional attributes as the basis of equivalence in the two tasks. As would be expected from Davidon's study, the picture task elicits a greater use of perceptible and a lesser use of functional attributes as the basis of grouping than did the verbal materials. At age six, there is a significantly greater use of perceptible attributes as the basis of grouping in the picture task. Forty-seven percent of the groupings in the picture task at this age are perceptually based, and 29 percent in the verbal task. By age eleven there is still a difference, but it is not statistically significant (Figure 7).

Although picture materials produce a greater reliance at all ages on perceptible properties as the basis for judging likeness, the six-year-old still bases far more of his groupings on the way things look than do older children. The use of perceptible attributes declines steadily from 47 percent at age six to 27 percent at age eight to 20 percent at age eleven.

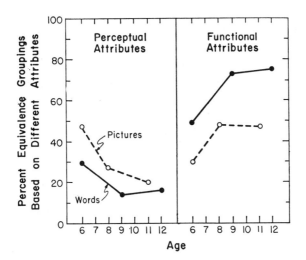

Figure 7. Percent of equivalence groupings based on functional and perceptual attributes in verbal and picture tasks.

What about the use of functional attributes as the basis of grouping? Functional equivalence is used to a significantly greater extent in the verbal task at age six and at age eleven. At age six, 49 percent of the equivalence groupings are functionally based in the verbal task, while only 30 percent are so based in the picture task. At age eleven, the difference is even greater, 75 percent of groupings in the verbal task being based on functional attributes, but 47 percent of the groupings in the picture task are so based.

And so, although there is an increased use of functional attributes as the basis of grouping, from 30 percent at age six to 48 percent at age eight, the use of function is less evident in the picture task than in the verbal task at all ages. It seems likely that in the picture task the child has a powerful alternative to functional grouping, for he can use nominal grouping readily in this array. Indeed, the use of nominally based equivalence increases steadily from 6 percent at age six to 23 percent at age eight, and to 32 percent at age eleven. All the eleven-year-olds use nominal groupings at least once as the basis for equivalence, whereas 83 percent of the eight-year-olds but only 47 percent of the six-year-olds use class names as the basis of equivalence. In the verbal task, in which the items selected were not easily grouped by a conventional name, the use of nominal groupings remained fairly constant at about 10 percent from age six to twelve.

In the picture task, then, growth expresses itself in a greater tendency to use the nominal technique of imposing equivalence. Although the young child knows the conventional groupings—even three-year-olds, when presented with the picture array and asked to pick out all the animals, all the articles of clothing, and so forth, can easily accomplish the task—their self-generated, self-directed use of linguistic terms for categorizing objects demonstrates a gradual course of development.

One wonders about the significance of nominal groupings in the picture series, whether it might not indeed be a verbal method of "pointing" to pictures, a way of signifying them by label in a rather superficial way. "Those are clothes," or "Those are food." It may well be that such superficial word labeling (reminiscent of Sapir's [1921] discussion in the preceding chapter) is tempted by pictures more than by other words. To say of words heard that they "stand for food" seems somehow more banal than saying that some pictures "are food." Perhaps it is regarded by us all as a step ahead to describe a picture with a simple descriptive word, whereas no such sense of progress is felt in substituting one simple descriptive word for others. It may amount to some sort of culturally acknowledged superiority in having something pinned by a word.

As we might bet, the average number of items included in a group by six-year-olds is close to a pair. About 61 percent of all groups formed by six-year-olds consists of pairs; this figure drops to 36 percent for eight-year-olds, and still further to only 25 percent of the groupings of eleven-year-olds. The pairings of six-year-olds are often capable of including "logically" more than two items in the array, but they do not extend to these other items. The young child will form a group consisting of *house* and *barn* "because they have red on them," and yet ignore the red *apple* and red *balloon*. Or he will select just two animals or two foods and fail to include the other animals or foods. Indeed, he may later form another pair on the same basis as an earlier two-item group. This finding suggests a comparable one by Vurpillot and Zoberman (1965) mentioned in the first chapter, concerning the young child's method of searching for similarities. Vurpillot and Zoberman found that, in general, the young child is satisfied with a judgment of similarity when a single feature in two displays is found to correspond. We shall see in the next chapter, moreover, that information is rarely integrated over more than two encounters. In the present instance, the young children simply form "perceptible" pairs, group on the basis of a single attribute, and have done with the task once a pair has been found.

Many of the pair groups formed by the younger children are sentential in nature—the grouping of two items in a sentence—"the *bunny* ate the *carrots*" or "the *bee* stung the *cow*." Such sentential structures, like the edge matching or chain complex, exhibit constraints running sequentially from one item to the next, but they lack the higher level summarizing constraint of the superordinate structure. If additional items are added to a group that begins as a sentential structure, there are few limits to what may be included. For example, "*Bee* can be around *cow, cow* is around a *person, person* has with him *apple, sword, rabbit,* and little *dog* he found, he got a ride back in the *taxi* to the *garage,* the *garage* has the other things (*clock, lamp, plant, thermometer*)."

The use of sentential structures declines from age six on: six-year-olds construct 31 percent of their groupings as sentential structures, eight-year-olds 20 percent, and eleven-year-olds only 8 percent. It would seem that for the young child the sequential form of the sentence is a powerful determinant of connections between things, while for older children other aspects of language become more instrumental in thought—for example, form class. This shift in equivalence is consistent with the transition from the syntagmatic to the paradigmatic responses in word association noted by Ervin (1961) and by Brown and Berko (1960) from grades 1 to 6.

In addition to the formation of sentential pairs at age six, the six-year-olds form complexive structures more often than do older children. Complexive structures decrease from 38 percent at age six, to 18 percent at age eight, to 12 percent at age eleven. All the types of complexive structures noted in the verbal task also occur when the child is free to select the items to be grouped from an array of pictures:

> *Collections:* The grouping of *boat, ruler, quarter, doll, bicycle, scissors, saw, shoe, gloves, barn, candle, pie, nails,* and *taxi* as, "Some are red, some are gold, and some are yellow. One is white, some are brown, and some are blue."
>
> *Edge matchings:* "*Candle* and *clock* are on a table and this (*lamp*) is round and this (*clock*) is."
>
> *Associations:* The grouping of *boots, cow,* and *gloves* as, "These could be leather *gloves* and leather *boots,* and you get leather from *cows*."
>
> *Key rings:* "You build a house with the *hammer, nails, screw,* the *barn* is next to the *house.* By the *house* you have a *tree.* You eat the *carrots, pie, apple, pumpkin* in the *house.* And you have *clock, bird, faucet* in the *house*."

Multiple groupings: Screw, ruler, nails, candle, hammer, taxi, coat, scissors, sword, and *bicycle* are alike because, "They have a part that you get dressed with, or they have holes in them, or you use them for tools, taxi goes with bicycle."

As a corollary to the decrease in sentential and complexive groupings, it comes as no surprise to us that there is also an increase in superordinate constructions from 34 percent at age six to 69 percent at age eight to 85 percent at age eleven. Increasingly with development the child isolates one or more attributes that are common to all the items in the group: "They are all tools," or "You can eat them," or "They can all move," and so on.

With pictures as with words, the child first achieves invariance across a series of items by taking himself as a reference point. Eight-year-olds reflect this self-reference by using "you" and "I" in their responses more than either the younger or older children do. "You use them for tools," or "You wear them," or "I can ride in them" are frequent in their protocols (see Figure 2), but the tendency to use such egocentrism as a crutch is less with pictures than with words.

To summarize: the same pattern of growth emerges whether we use words or pictures as stimuli, and whether the child is given items in a fixed order or chooses his own groups *ad libitum.* Equivalence for the six-year-old reflects a basis in imagery, both in what he uses as a basis for grouping and in how he forms his groups. From age six on, linguistic structures increasingly guide what and how things will be judged alike. With the development of symbolic representation, the child is freed from dependence upon moment-to-moment variation in perceptual vividness and is able to keep the basis of equivalence invariant. A first step away from domination by the perceptually salient comes when the child, at about age nine, takes himself egocentrically as a reference point for establishing equivalence among things. He does this by imposing upon the world what *he* can do to things, producing equivalence by reference to his own actions. In time, he accommodates to more conventional definitions of how things are "alike."

However, it is not entirely a matter of what features of the world serve as a basis for defining how things are alike. There is also the grammar of grouping what is alike and segregating it from the rest of the world. The effort begins with loosely ordered definitions of likeness, ordered sequentially and in a fashion that makes discrimination difficult and combination awkward. Only gradually and by dint of much language development does the child work his way toward true conceptual grouping, based on the rule of the superordinate class, which opens new possibilities for relating and combining and structuring information about the world. By early adolescence the rules are mastered, and then the question remains as to how well the child learns to apply them in a variety of contexts.

We could (and perhaps should) go on at this point to an interpretation of the phenomena reported in the experiments in this chapter. It is better, perhaps, to wait until different aspects of the developments we are studying have been looked at more closely. Yet this much must be said. It is quite clear that the shift from complexive-perceptual definitions of equivalence to ones that are superordinate-functional is *not* a universal property of "growing up." For one thing, we shall see that the "natural" terminus of growth depends to a very considerable extent on the pattern imposed by the culture. The techniques used in this chapter have, in modified form, been used in studies of children in Alaska, Mexico, and Senegal—work reported later in the book— and it is plain that school children in Dakar or Mexico City look very much like the school children of this chapter. But it is equally plain that the village child of rural Mexico and the unschooled Wolof of Senegal seem very different, much more complexive, much more perceptually oriented. Later we shall explore why this may be.

A second consideration has to do with the relation of the two systems of representation and their interaction in growth. We know from the searching studies of Wallach and Kogan (1965) that the two orientations—call them ikonic and symbolic as a shorthand—can be quite independent one of the other. That is to say, one finds children who are clearly proficient both in the kinds of complexive and metaphoric activities of the first mode and in the more abstract activities of the second. In others, the first suffers a kind of replacement by the second, and a different style emerges. All this is within the limits of our own culture.

The need for delaying interpretation is, then, obvious enough. All we need say here is that our middle-class children do show a pattern of growth in which "appropriate" rational classification based on the functional properties of things "replaces" earlier complexive grouping based on the surface properties of events. But such growth is not inevitable, not complete, and not something that invades every corner of the mind.

CHAPTER 4

On Asking Questions

Frederic A. Mosher and Joan Rigney Hornsby

One of the most characteristic features of seeking information is that we must sift alternatives in order to decide what is relevant. Sometimes the alternatives appear "ready-made" and "there," as when we must find out which fuse in a panel of fuses is blown; and sometimes the alternatives do not appear so clearcut, as when we seek out the cause of some mysterious illness. In the latter case we must not only sift alternatives, but in a sense invent them.

In either instance, whether the information to be sifted is there and displayed, or whether it must first be manufactured, there are at least two important aspects of seeking the information to be examined. The first concerns the questions we ask; the second, the manner in which we integrate or compile the answers we receive. The two are not completely independent, though they can be treated separately. Yet we would certainly recognize that *what* we ask and *how* we use answers both depend upon how we organize knowledge; whether for example, we think of the causes of a disease in a list form to be ticked off, or whether we think of a hierarchy with three branches to accommodate bacterial, viral, and toxic agents on one side, and with another branch for stress. In some cases there will be neither a list nor a tree, but only one thing suggesting the next thing, which in turn calls up something else.

If information-seeking reflects the way we organize our thoughts, then we might reasonably expect some drastic changes to occur in the way children at different ages go about putting questions and organizing answers. The "general" question, for example, since it presupposes an ability to equate things in a superordinate category, should by the testimony of Chapter 3 be out of the reach of the

younger child. His approach to interrogation should be consonant with
the "complexive" structures discussed in Chapter 3. And so it should be
with growing up: each emerging form of cognitive organization and
representation should be reflected in the questions a child generates
and in the manner answers are used.

The studies reported in this chapter deal concretely with that part
of cognitive growth which is reflected in seeking information. The
vehicle used is the old parlor game of Twenty Questions, intended
to manifest how children at various ages seek information. Two versions of Twenty Questions were used. In one the children were shown
an array of forty-two pictures of common objects (the array described
in the previous chapter), and their task was to find out which one
of the objects the experimenter had in mind. They could ask questions,
but only in a form that could be answered with a simple "yes" or
"no." In the second version the children were presented with problems
of the form: "A man was driving down the road in his car, the car
went off the road and hit a tree. Find out how this happened." Or,
"A boy leaves school in the middle of the morning. How come?" Again,
they were to find the answers by asking questions which could be
answered by "yes" or "no."

In one game, then, the set of alternatives to be considered is concrete, finite, and given. In the other the child must construct the alternatives to be searched, as well as find the right one among them.
The tasks in either case may be complicated by requiring our subjects
to find the answer by using a few questions as possible—rarely the
"natural" tendency among either children or adults. As we shall see,
our urging economy in the number of questions was hardly successful.
Although the verification in both tasks rested with the experimenter,
the information a child obtained depended on *his* questions and *his*
use of the answers, and not upon the experimenter. Both games, particularly the "open" one, tapped the child's cognitive structure, his
"theory" about the domain with which each game was concerned, and
thus, ultimately, the way he represented the world to himself. The
fact that the child had to take his steps toward solving the problem
overtly and in sequence made this type of game not only useful in
general for studies of problem solving but also strikingly convenient
for sequential analysis.

Previous work by Mosher at the Center for Cognitive Studies reveals
two ideal strategies for playing Twenty Questions.[1] "Strategy" is used

[1] The coding system reported in this paper is a simplified version of the original
and retains the major distinctions made among responses. For the full detail
of the coding system see F. A. Mosher, Strategies in the Acquisition and Use

here in the sense of Bruner, Goodnow, and Austin (1956), as a rule
or plan for choosing steps in problem-solving that strikes a particular
balance among at least three requirements: the degree of certainty
with which a solution can be reached, the speed with which it can
be reached, and the degree of cognitive strain imposed by the plan
employed. The two strategies previously identified for the game
differ in all these respects. The first, called "constraint seeking," is
based on a principle close to a theorem in information theory: assume
that alternative possibilities are all equally likely, try to eliminate exactly half of the alternatives with each question. You then tend to mini-
mize the number of questions needed over a series of games. This is the
idealized statement of the strategy. As seen in practice, the child begins with a general question that groups a large number of specific
possibilities into two domains, in one of which the correct answer
must lie. This guarantees usable information on each question, since
both a positive and a negative response are equally useful to the child,
at least theoretically. He then uses the information gained on each
question to narrow in on the answer, successively constraining the
remaining domain until he can almost derive the correct answer from
the information known without actually asking about it directly. In
the game involving the auto accident, the children using such a strategy
might start with questions of the form, "Did it have anything to do
with the weather? with the car?" and so forth. Then they could proceed to specific questions.

The polar opposite of constraint seeking is called "hypothesis
scanning." A child simply asks a series of questions, each of which
tests a self-sufficient, specific hypothesis that bears no necessary relation to what has gone before. Such sense as there is to the order
of questions asked in this strategy seems to be determined by crude
orders of likelihood, by associative connection, or by "prompts" contained in the immediate environment. A question out of the blue, "Did
the driver get stung in the eye by a bee and lose control and go
off the road into the tree?" would be typical of a scanner's approach,
particularly if it were followed by another about a wasp sting, or
a blinding flash of lightning.

It is evident that each of these approaches involves costs and
benefits for the information seeker. Constraint seeking offers efficiency
in the use of information as well as a fair certainty of success within
a reasonable time. But it does so at the expense of cognitive work, the

of Information. Unpublished doctoral dissertation, Department of Social Relations,
Harvard University, 1963.

work involved in forming a plan for the strategy and in building the conceptual structure required. Hypothesis scanning, on the other hand, is presumably less of a strain in both formulation and use, and it offers, moreover, the chance of a "quick-rich" success that cannot be won with constraint seeking. On balance, of course, such scanning will require a greater number of questions to reach a solution. Finally, scanning does not insure a coverage of the full array of possibilities (when these are not presented before one). For its ease depends upon *not* using a conceptual scheme to organize the full array of alternatives. So the scanner, for all his ease, may fail to reach any answer at all simply by overlooking an alternative.

One other feature differentiates the two approaches, one well-known to information analysts, though it is by no means obvious. Hypothesis scanning lives entirely on positive answers. A "no" to the bee-sting question is useless. In time, the scanner gives up trying to derive information from negative replies. Constraint seeking can use both positive and negative instances—if it did not happen in the night, it *must* have happened during the day—but it is often the case that an earlier habit of ignoring negative instances prevents a child from using information properly, even though he may generate it expertly.

Obviously, the choice between the two strategies is not a free one. Constraint seeking presupposes skills without which its use is simply excluded. To use it, a child must first be able to organize things hierarchically. For it is hierarchy that permits one to narrow down from general to specific questions and to keep track of the ground already covered. In so far as the child organizes things in arbitrary lists or in complexive structures (see Chapter 3), the strategy of constraint will be out of his reach.

With this much behind us, we can turn now to the experiments proper. As in Chapter 3, we shall be comparing children of different ages, working with different kinds of problems, with a view of discerning the pattern of growth.

Experiment 1: Games with Fixed Alternatives. The subjects in this experiment were the same ninety grade-school boys used in Experiment 2 of the preceding chapter, thirty each from Grades 1, 3, and 6. Each child, tested individually, was given two tasks using the forty-two familiar pictures described before (see Figure 6 in Chapter 3). The objects depicted, as already noted, were diverse and lent themselves to a rich variety of groupings—modes of transportation, tools, animals, things with red on them, things you would find in a house, things you can eat, clothing, things with wheels, and so on.

A child was asked first to identify the pictures, to ensure that he was familiar with them, and then he carried out the equivalence groupings described in detail in Chapter 3. He then played two games of Twenty Questions with the object of finding the picture the experimenter had in mind.

The instructions given for the game of Twenty Questions were:

> Now we're going to play some question-asking games. I'm thinking of one of these pictures, and your job is to find out which one it is that I have in mind. To do this you can ask any questions at all that I can answer by saying "yes" or "no," but I can't give any other answer but "yes" or "no." You can have as many questions as you need, but try to find out in as few questions as possible.

The "correct" picture in the first game was a saw. The second game was the same as the first, but this time the child was limited to ten questions. A doll was the correct answer in the second game.

All questions asked were classified as constraints, specific hypotheses, guesses, and pseudoconstraints. A constraint is any question general enough to refer to two or more pictures. It must be of a type such that a "yes" answer cannot solve the problem. Specific hypothesis names a particular object—"Is it the hammer?" Guesses are those specific hypotheses that bear no discernible relation to previous constraint questions. They provide an index of the "unconnectedness" of a subject's search strategy. Pseudoconstraints, like specific hypotheses, refer to only one item in the array. But they are phrased like constraint questions: a single attribute is referred to, but it is one that characterizes only one picture: "Does it have a sail?" or "Does it bark?"—thinly disguised efforts to pinpoint the single sailboat or the single dog in the array. They are form without substance, as though the child had learned how to make the question sound "right" without knowing how to use it appropriately.

Our first-graders went about the game with a strategy of almost pure hypothesis scanning (Figure 1). Only five of the thirty six-year-olds asked any constraint-locating questions at all, and not many at that. All told, then, almost all the questions asked by our youngest subjects were in the form of specific hypothesis. We commented earlier on the possibly revealing nature of guesses in indicating the degree of sequential organization in the search for information. At age six, the strategy of hypothesis scanning is one guess after another—more than nine in ten questions in each of the two games being of this type. By the eighth year, guesses have declined to only a quarter of the questions asked, and by age eleven they constitute only a scattering of temptation unresisted. In striking contrast, twenty-six

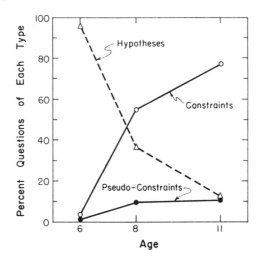

Figure 1. Percent questions of each type asked by children at three ages— unrestricted picture game.

of the thirty eight-year-olds and *all* of the eleven-year-olds asked some constraint questions.

In the second or restricted game, where the children were limited to ten questions, it would seem that constraint-locating questions would have been encouraged, but our limitation produced no increase in constraints at any of the three ages. As likely as not, the younger children, not able to muster constraint-locating strategies to begin with, were unable to do so when the questions were restricted in number. The older children gave the impression that they were already using constraint location to the limit of their capacity, thinking it appropriate at the outset. However, there is at least one striking difference between eight- and eleven-year-olds. It is in "narrowing," as we have come to call it. Narrowing refers to what one can do after having established some prior constraint—particularly whether one asks a *further* constraint question or shifts to hypothesis testing. The older children were more likely to narrow the remaining possibilities with further constraint questions, whereas the eight-year-olds tended to leap immediately to specific hypotheses (Figure 2). One eight-year-old asked first, "Is it a toy?" Receiving a "yes" to this constraining question, he immediately explored the possibilities by asking a series of specific hypothesis questions; "Is it the bicycle? . . . the balloons? . . . the sailboat? . . . the doll?" An eleven-year-old followed his constraint-locating question, "Is it a tool?" with the further constraint, "Can you cut things with it?" Receiving a "yes" to this question as well, he then ventured the hypothesis that it must be the saw.

Apparently the older children consider specific hypotheses inelegant. They prefer constraints to such a degree that sometimes pseudoconstraints replace out-and-out guesses, even when specific hypotheses are more efficient than constraints. A few eleven-year-olds even interpreted the rules of the game as excluding all but a final specific hypothesis, or else asked whether they were allowed any

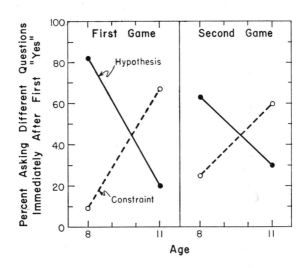

Figure 2. Percent children asking different questions immediately after first "yes" response—picture game.

"guesses." The best exemplification of this point is found in the percent of children who ask any constraint questions before receiving a first "yes" response. Figure 3 indicates that between age six and eleven the proportion goes from approximately "none" to "all."

Finally, the record of success. Six-year-olds take more than twice as many questions to solve the first problem as do eleven-year-olds—an average of twenty-six questions for the sixes, fifteen questions for the eights, and eleven questions for the eleven-year-olds. In the second game, in which the children were limited to ten questions, nearly as many six-year-olds achieved a solution within the limit as did the eight-year-olds, with the eleven-year-olds coming out best: eleven in thirty, twelve in thirty, and sixteen in thirty, respectively. We suspect that the good showing of the sixes may have a little to do with the popularity of the doll and its frequent inclusion in the groupings of the six-year-olds. It made the doll a salient figure and a likely choice in the second game.

Consider now the relation between equivalence grouping and information seeking. Recall that when grouping pictures, the six-year-olds based their equivalence judgments on the intrinsic perceptible features of pictures; the eight-year-olds preferred functional groupings and were often egocentric in their notions of how objects can be used; and eleven-year-olds used more conventional functional and nominal attributes as a basis for judging equivalence. We wondered whether

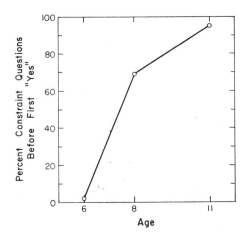

Figure 3. Percent questions asked before first "yes" response that exhibit constraints—picture game.

the attributes preferred by children in their grouping task would also predominate in the games of Twenty Questions. Would six-year-olds ask, in framing constraint questions, "Is it red (rounded, pointed)?" eight-year-olds, "Can I use it for cutting (for transportation)?" and eleven-year-olds, "Does it give protection?" or, "Is it a tool (food, building)?"

To assess the matter, we coded all constraint and pseudoconstraint questions in both games by the identical coding system reported in the preceding chapter, designed to distinguish the different bases of grouping. Alas, only five six-year-olds asked any constraint or pseudo-constraint questions at all, but among them they asked about twenty in the first game and eighteen in the second. Sixteen in the first and ten in the second game were based on intrinsic perceptible attributes. The remaining questions were all based on the position of the item in the array—whether the item was in a particular column or row of the array—what has already been called the extrinsic perceptible qualities of objects, their location. (Despite the potential efficiency of this positioning strategy, only a handful of the older children—six eight-year-olds and just three eleven-year-olds—asked any position questions at all.) In short, the six-year-olds, perceptually oriented in grouping, are similarly perceptual in their approach to information seeking.

Recall that eleven-year-olds more than the others used nominal attributes as a basis for establishing equivalence. Twice as many of the older children used such attributes in their constraints and pseudo-constraints as did the eight-year-olds (Table 1). Again there is a parallel between equivalence grouping and information seeking. But interestingly enough, significantly more eleven-year-olds also ask constraint questions based on perceptible properties than do eight-year-olds. This is not surprising on closer inspection. For with pictures such as ours, "perceptual" questions like these, "Is it mostly grey?" or "Is it something that belongs in a house?" are strikingly effective.

TABLE 1

Number and Percent of Subjects Whose Constraints or Pseudoconstraints Employed Each Type of Attribute—Picture Game

	Game 1				Game 2			
	Age				Age			
	Eight		Eleven		Eight		Eleven	
	Number	Percent	Number	Percent	Number	Percent	Number	Percent
Perceptible intrinsic	10	40	21	70	8	30	13	43
Perceptible extrinsic	3	12	11	37	3	12	10	33
Functional	22	88	24	80	19	73	27	90
Nominal	10	40	24	80	10	38	24	80
Position	5	20	3	10	6	23	3	10
Number of subjects asking constraints or pseudo-constraints	25		30		26		30	

They provide a more symmetrical division of possibilities than do questions about "food," "tools," "animals," or even functional probes such as, "Is it used for transportation?" or "Does it give light?" In short, perceptible attributes are effective, and eleven-year-olds use them.

Indeed, the oldest children are in general more flexible in the kinds of constraints they use, and perhaps it is because their initial approach to the task is better conceived, more designed to divide the domain of possibilities evenly. One measure of this symmetry is the number of items included in the child's first question. That is, if the child asks, "Is it a tool?" how many items in the array are tools? Or, if he asks, "Does the object have some red on it," how many objects fulfill that requirement? In the first game, the opening questions asked by eleven-year-olds included an average of twelve items; those of eight-year-olds only five items, a striking and significant difference. (In the second game, restricted to ten questions, the difference diminishes to insignificance; eight for eleven-year-olds, six for eight-year-olds. Whether it is experience with the game or the more stringent requirements that diminishes the difference is a moot point on which we have no proper evidence.) It may well be that to achieve this greater symmetry of initial approach, the older children simply have to use a wider range of bases for partitioning possibilities. In any case, the eleven-year-old children use a wider variety of attributes than do eight-year-olds. The six-year-olds ask too few constraint questions to assess in this way. In the free game, the older children who asked constraint questions used an average of 2.77 different types of attributes as bases for their questions as compared to 2.00 for the younger. In the second and constrained game, the averages were even more strikingly divergent: 2.63 for the elevens and 1.77 for the eights.

Will a subject who grouped animals or one-eyed things in the equivalence task ask in Twenty Questions whether the right item is an animal, or has one eye? Six-year-olds do not; when they ask constraint questions at all, these are likely to be new ones. But older children carry their past endeavors with them. Take all constraints in the first ten questions asked by a child. Which are based on the same attribute as previous equivalence groupings? Roughly half are. The eight- and eleven-year-olds lean about equally on prior grouping experience, in contrast to the six-year-olds. In sum, then, the older children carry the past into the present not only by the use of constraints, but also by using the contents of the experience through which they have worked.

To sum up the first experiment in a word or two, six-year-olds seek information directly by testing specific hypotheses, eight-year-olds establish some constraints before leaping to hypotheses, while eleven-year-olds postpone specific hypotheses until they have narrowed the possibilities beyond a first set of constraints. The development of strategies for seeking information is toward increasingly connected acts designed to locate relevance by more economical but less direct means. This growth parallels the development of means for establishing equivalence through superordinate categories, but it lags slightly behind that development. Six-year-olds are very perceptual in their approach to constraint location, organizing things as to how they look and where they are. Constraint questions become increasingly functional and nominal with age. What is most interesting is that the oldest children, the eleven-year-olds, are those who use the greatest variety of attributes in establishing information-seeking constraints, fitting their choice better to the requirements of the task before them.

Experiment 2: Games with Unrestricted Alternatives.[2] In our second investigation seventy-seven boys aged six to eleven, drawn from the first, third, and sixth grades, played games of Twenty Questions having to do with cause and effect. The two youngest groups began with a warm-up task:

> We're going to play some question-asking games. In these games I will tell you something that happened and your job will be to find out how it happened, by asking me questions I can answer "yes" or "no." That is, in the first game I tell you that, "A boy goes home from school in the middle of the morning." Then you will find out how this happened by the way I answer questions you ask me about it. But I can only answer "yes" or "no."
> If your question isn't clear or I'm not sure how to answer it, I will say, "I can't answer," and then you will have to rephrase or explain your question or ask a different one. The object of the game is to find the answer in as few questions as possible, though you may ask as many questions as you need to find the answer. If you don't think you can get the answer, it's all right to give up after you've tried, but don't give up unless you have to.

The first game completed (the boy left school in the middle of the morning to go to the dentist), the subjects went on to a second and a third game, on which all the analyses are based. They were asked to find the cause of an auto accident—"A man is driving down the road in his car, the car goes off the road and hits a tree"—the answers for the second game being that it had been raining and the

---

[2] This study was done in collaboration with Betty Burgoon of the Center for Cognitive Studies, Harvard University.

man's car skidded off the slippery road on a curve; and for the third, that the man had been driving home late from work and had fallen asleep at the wheel. The eleven-year-olds were presented the first accident game with the same introduction as was used for the warm-up.

The children were finally asked to describe how they had played the games: did they have a system for getting the answers? did they think any kind of questions were better than others for getting the answer in the fewest questions? We also asked our subjects which question they would rather have answered if they were again at the beginning of a game: "Was there anything wrong with the man?" or, "Did he have a heart attack?"

There are, of course, some crucial differences between the picture problem and the verbal one. The domain of possibilities differs between the two tasks in ways that can be expected to influence how a child (or adult) proceeds. With the pictures the possibilities are there before one. As we have already remarked, it is a far cry from constructing a set of possible solutions for oneself. Generating alternative possibilities imposes a burden. In the picture task, moreover, the children had had prior experience in grouping and regrouping the pictures. There was no such opportunity in the verbal task. That experience, while not affecting the six-year-olds, did influence the older children. It is not quite clear what to expect *ex hypothesi* by way of difference, save that the picture task should be easier for all children and notably easier for the youngest children, who are least able to organize the possibilities present before them, much less those that are part of an abstract domain.

The difference can be sketched very quickly. Recall that in the picture games eight- and eleven-year-olds were quite alike in their capacity to establish constraints. Now, with the verbal game, six- and eight-year-olds are very much more alike in their approach. This time the two younger groups are closer to hypothesis scanning and further from constraint seeking. Eleven-year-olds continue to be constraint seekers. Now the six-year-olds guess about as often as the eight-year-olds. In the picture task the comparable difference was nearly four-fold. As before, eleven-year-olds guess strikingly less than do the younger children (on four in ten chances, as compared to two-thirds of the time for younger groups). One can sense the difference in age by computing the number of children who show any follow-up in the questions they ask—basing later questions upon answers obtained earlier. Figure 4 indicates a steady climb from age six to eleven in this ability, the proportion doubling during this period. Where success is concerned, the expected order occurs. In playing the last game,

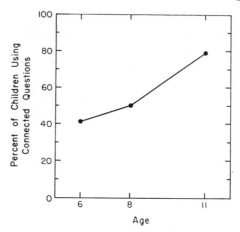

Figure 4. Percent of children using connected questions in Twenty Questions
game—verbal game.

for example, less than ten percent of the six-year-olds got the correct
answer, about a third of the eight-year-olds, and close to two-thirds
of the eleven-year-olds.

The epitome of the difference is provided by the eight-year-olds.
They do strikingly better with pictures than with words. With pictures
they are like eleven-year-olds. With words, they are more like six-year-
olds. It is as if they learn their strategies of information seeking on
picturable and discrete materials first, with recourse to perceptual supports, and then later extend the strategies to nonpicturable and less
formulated material.

The inquiry that followed the games produced interesting
reactions. When the six-year-olds were asked whether they had any
system for getting the answers or for asking questions in the games,
only four of the seventeen responded at all. The rest merely said "No,"
or found it very hard to understand the question. The answers of
those who did respond were hardly descriptive of a "system," though
they were amusing. In response to, "How did you think of the question you asked?" one six-year-old replied: "Well, I just say them in
my mind, and then I start to think about them, as I say them in
my mind, so then I say the words and that's what it is." Or another
young subject: "I think, and I told them." There is no rationale for
the order of questions asked and little sensitivity to the relation of
one question to the next one. The routine sounds rather associative.

Of the twenty-two eight-year-olds, sixteen had something to say about how they worked. Nine of these children said essentially that they tried to ask about the most probable or most "reasonable" or "sensible" possibilities. They said, for example: "Think of the most likely things to happen," or "Think of things that you've seen before, could have happened." Others said they just pictured themselves driving and thought what could have happened. None of the eight-year-olds mentioned the idea of a general question or of narrowing in on the answers. As a group they could be characterized as rank empiricists. Almost all the eleven-year-olds were able to say something about their approach to the game, and of these almost half touched on the principle of asking broad or general questions, many of them in quite explicit terms:

> Well, to eliminate big things quickly—like was there anything wrong with the road—was there anything wrong with the weather—was there anything wrong with the car—was there anything wrong with the person—if there's something wrong with the person, you start from the bottom and go to the top.
> I group like all the things with weather, breaking, then I group them smaller and smaller till I get to the point.

The remaining eleven-year-olds were more like the eight-year-olds, explaining their approach in terms of the likelihood of different possibilities.[3]

Much of the rest of the inquiry serves to reemphasize the development of strategies from one involving discrete questions, each quite unrelated to what went before, each designed to test a self-sufficient, specific hypothesis, to a strategy based upon the derivation of specific hypotheses from previously organized information.

When children are offered a choice between a general and a specific question, if they "were at the beginning of the game and wanted to get an answer in as few questions as possible," only a third of the six-year-olds when given the choice between, "Was there anything wrong with the man?" and, "Did he have a heart attack?" chose the more general question. All the eleven-year-olds did so. Immediately, one senses a puzzle. The eight-year-olds operated like six-year-olds in the game itself, but when given the opportunity of *choosing* between *fixed* alternatives, they behaved like eleven-year-olds. They appeared able to *recognize* a better strategy in the verbal game, but they seemed less able to mount the strategy on their own initiative.

---

[3] The eleven-year-olds had also had more experience with this type of game, though it is doubtful that their greater sophistication comes entirely from that (cf. Mosher, 1963).

When the six-year-olds were asked to explain their choice, half of them justified it in terms of the specific consequences in reality of their chosen alternative, rather than in terms of the work the question would accomplish in the game. For example, the justification of a general choice: "Because if he had a heart attack he'd be dead, but if he was sick you can fix it up, if you take medicine. And for a specific choice: "Well maybe this man was old, and maybe he had trouble with him." What is most important to bear in mind is that no six-year-old explained his choice in terms of its relevance to the requirements of the game.

A third of the eight-year-olds justified their choice of the more general question much as the younger ones did: "If he had had a heart attack, he would have been in a hospital, not driving." But most of the rest who chose the general question did so on the grounds that it helped in the game. For example:

> Well, she could say "yes"—and then you would start giving answers, but if you were saying that, ah, "Did he have a heart attack?" you'd say "no," and you'd guess and guess and guess, and you wouldn't even know that if he might be sick or not.
> Because it if wasn't a heart attack, you'd have to keep on guessing.

A good two-thirds of the eleven-year-olds justified the universal choice of the general question in terms of strategic advantage, and usually in clearer terms than did eight-year-olds. The following is a particularly good answer:

> It's broader; it's an approach question or a clue question; if you answer "no" to the other, then you still have to ask about a lot of other things that could happen to him; you could go on guessing for-ever.

To sum it up, six-year-olds just think of questions to ask; they seem to have little consciousness of the game's requirements save of an answer to be guessed. They make no explicit distinction between general and specific questions. No surprise then that those six-year-olds who were well able to form superordinate groupings in the equivalence task did not use these groupings as aids in playing Twenty Questions.

The eight-year-olds are more aware of the game as a game, recognizing distinctions among questions on the basis of their likelihood of yielding the right answer. They are strongly influenced by empirical probability. Given a choice between a general and a specific question, they justify their choice with some sensitivity to the usefulness and efficiency of inclusive questions.

The eleven-year-olds go beyond the eight-year-olds not only in appreciating the requirements of the game, but also in grasping the importance of narrowing successively in one's approach to an answer.

The pattern that emerges from these studies of information search and usage—whether the domain be limited to an array of pictures spread out before the child or whether it is initially virtually unbounded, as in the "causal" game—is that with development the child builds a more constrained strategy for using information. He is increasingly able to guide his inquiries by what he has found out earlier and to eliminate possibilities by ruling out whole classes of objects or events. In part, this growth of strategies in the use of information is based on the structure provided by the achievement of superordinate-equivalence categories. For, as the child increasingly relies on symbolic representation rather than on representation by action and image—and thus is able to construct groupings of objects and events on the basis of characteristics they have in common—he attains the structure of information necessary to follow through a constraint-seeking strategy, to guide his inquiry by cycles of questioning that narrow from the general to the specific. In contrast, the child relying on enactive and ikonic representation with the consequent complexive nature of his equivalence groupings lacks the prerequisite structure for such a constraint approach, and thus can do little more than use hypothesis scanning in seeking new information.

There is an additional prerequisite, however, for the use of an optimally constrained strategy in the search for information. The child must see the requirements of the task, be able to examine the search for information itself and thus realize that the use of general questions helps achieve a solution. It is striking that the inquiry reveals a heavy preoccupation in younger children with the story quality of the game. They become so involved with the action and themes that they lose touch with the task as given. Indeed, the younger children seem to visualize the scene of the accident in the hope that a cause will appear. Such a representation of the task does not provide the child with a way of "standing outside" his search for information. He is unable to evaluate strategy, unable to plan his course of action even a step or two ahead. It is intriguing that a sense of strategy in playing Twenty Questions appears at the same age, eight years, as the emergence of "self" as a constant reference—the egocentric functionalism in the equivalence tasks described in Chapter 3. Both indicate a newfound freedom from the perceptual and immediate properties of the environment.

The achievement of grouping skills—while providing the necessary basis for asking constraint questions—does not by itself lead directly to the use of constraint strategies for seeking information. We know this from the fact that children who show adequate superordinate grouping may not use these skills in the game. It may well be that what is missing is mastery of hierarchical organization. For Twenty Questions does imply that one can not only sort things into categories, but array the categories into hierarchies. Such structures exist in the syntax of the child's language—as noted in the opening chapter. They do not exist at the semantic level, at least not in a usable fashion. We shall consider this problem again in the final chapter.

One final point about the transition in growth from hypothesis scanning to constraint locating. We have noted that the child goes from a kind of associative guessing at six, to a weighing of likelihoods at eight, to constraint searching at eleven. The comment was made earlier that the youngest children visualized the situation as if to "discover" what happened, waiting for something to come into mind. Weighing probabilities is already one step removed from such direct confrontation. Still another step removed is the establishment of a constraining framework before one ventures into probabilities. The three processes—constraining, assessing, and specifying—fit within each other like Chinese boxes. As soon as one seeks discrimination among a set of specified alternatives, one must assess how likely they are. If one seeks better discernment among a set of likelihoods, then one must know what constrains the occurrence of events. In the final chapter we shall consider what it is that may lead to growth from the "pure" guess to the "probable" guess to the "constrained" guess.

CHAPTER 5

On Perceptual Recognition

Mary C. Potter[1]

Recognition is equivalent, in the formal sense, to the act of categorizing. A recognition task requires that a connection be made between a present experience and the memory of a like experience. One uses the term "category" when the memory takes the form of an abstraction of certain shared characteristics of a number of experiences. Perhaps the most primitive act of categorizing is the infant's recognition of the sameness of an object when it reappears. We know relatively little about the development of categories in early childhood, but it is clear that only by some such process of reduction and summary can the "blooming, buzzing confusion" of James's description be brought under control. It may even be that certain categories come already built into the organism—not, perhaps, the innate ideas of Kant, but rather the squares, the lines, and the like which trigger individual neurons in the visual cortex of Hubel's newborn kittens and monkeys (1963). However a set of categories is built up in infancy, it is of interest to see how the child at later ages applies whatever categories he has to the new events he is asked to recognize.

Two major phases are distinguishable in an act of perceptual recognition: first, the organizing of the incoming stimuli into figure and ground, texture, tridimensionality, and the like; and second, the relating of this organized perception to one or more categories—recognition itself. Under ordinary conditions, recognition is complete in

[1] The help of Jennifer Campbell-Pitt and Jan Bettman in the gathering and analysis of these data is gratefully acknowledged.

103

these two steps, since there is only one way in which the stimulus can be organized into figure and ground, and so forth, and there is a single, readily available category that fits it, with no competing categories. That rectangular dark solid on the desk *is* a book. However, when recognition is made difficult—for example, by brief presentation, reduction in size, removal of pieces of the stimulus, or (as here) defocusing—categories may have to be sought actively. Then the two phases may interact: a tentative identification may effect a reorganization of the initial perception, and, by altering the proximal stimulus in the direction of a better fit with the proposed category may actually prevent correct identification (Bruner and Potter, 1964). The hunter thinks he sees a deer: he can make out the antlers near the dark mass of the body, but he ignores the incongruous contour of the haunch. One hopes the "deer" will shout a greeting before the hunter fires.

Whereas simple perceptual processes are almost fully developed within the first three or four years, the more complex perceptual-cognitive task of recognition might be expected to show changes over a longer period of time. Studies, some of which are found elsewhere in this book (see Chapters 3 and 4), document the differences in cognitive operations among five- or six-year-olds, nine-year-olds, and older subjects that may affect perceptual performance. The younger groups are primarily responsive to the surface perceptual qualities of displays in such tasks as equivalence sorting, concept attainment, and so on. At six a child makes little effort to build items sequentially in a Twenty Questions task; he is unconcerned about the relation between the information now available and the information encountered earlier. These findings suggest that in a recognition task the young child will stay close to the stimulus, with the minimum of interpretation and with little attempt to attain logical coherence in his ideas. The older child should abandon simple responses to visual properties and should move toward the elaboration of hypotheses while increasing his consistency within hypotheses.

METHOD AND PROCEDURE

Ordinary photographs of familiar objects in a natural setting were shown to subjects ranging in age from three to twenty-two. At first, each photograph was seen in a badly out-of-focus version, and then step by step the focus improved. Figure 1 shows one picture in three representative stages of focus, and the other five pictures in full focus. Recognition consisted in identifying the main subject—an object or

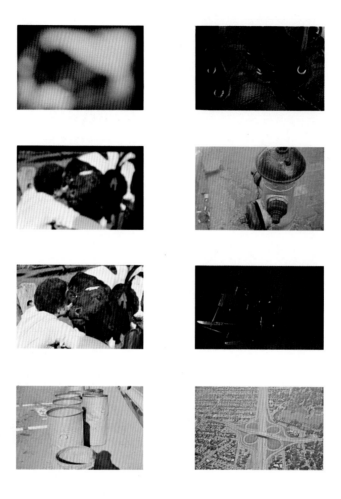

VI-1 Pictures used in experiment.

TABLE 1

Number of Subjects, Mean Age, and Age Range of the Four Groups

	Number		Mean Age	Age Range
	M	F		
Nursery school	8	15	3:11	3: 5– 4: 5
Kindergarten	9	11	5: 6	4:11– 5:10
Third grade	10	10	8: 9	7:11– 9: 4
High school	10	10	16: 9	15: 7–18: 4
College	7	4	19: 4	18: 0–22:10

scene of a type well-known to the children (with the exception of one picture), though the *particular* object and scene was new to them.

The subjects were children from a private nursery school and from the kindergarten, third grade, and high school of a well-regarded public-school system, as well as a group of Harvard and Radcliffe students. The number of subjects in each group of each sex and their average age range are shown in Table 1.

The material to be recognized consisted of color photographs (Kodacolor prints) of common objects, arranged in sets. Each set was composed of from twelve to fourteen pictures of the same object in varying focus, from very blurred to clear. The steps were of roughly equal subjective size; improvement in focus was gradual but discriminable. The prints, about $3 \times 4\frac{1}{2}$ inches in size, were mounted in small photograph albums, one stage of focus on each page. The experimenter sat opposite the subject at a table and turned the page at ten-second intervals; thus, each picture took two minutes or a little more to change from an unrecognizable blur to a perfect focus.

Six different pictures were used—five of objects familiar to children as well as adults—and shown in this order: trashcans on a sidewalk, a person looking across a fence at a cow, a close-up picture of a pair of laced boots, a fire hydrant, and silverware scattered on a rug. The sixth picture was fairly remote from childhood experience: an aerial view of a cloverleaf intersection. All six of these pictures are shown in Figure 1. The instructions read in part as follows:

> . . . Let's look at the first book of pictures. In this book there are a whole lot of pictures of the same thing, and you see if you can figure out what the picture is. The first picture will be very

fuzzy, but you try to guess what it is. After a while the pictures will get clearer, as I turn the pages. You tell me all the time what the picture is about.

For high school and college students these instructions were modified somewhat, though the same meaning was approximated—for example, they were told: "As you are trying to figure out what the picture is, I would like you to tell me all your ideas . . . . even if you feel very uncertain." The instructions were modified in the opposite direction for the three-to-four-year-old group. Subjects at all ages were given neutral prompts ("How about now?" "Tell me anything you can.") whenever twenty seconds or so had elapsed without a remark or whenever they appeared to have ideas they were not reporting. The youngest group was encouraged and prompted more frequently. At all ages some verbal approval was given for any response, ranging from explicit encouragement at age three to a minimal "umm" at high-school age and later. The experimenter made no special comment when correct recognition occurred, but continued through the remaining stages to full focus. The entire session was tape-recorded.

SAMPLE PROTOCOLS

Before presenting quantitative results an illustrative protocol from each age group will be given. The picture in every case is the second one shown, that of a person leaning over a fence to look at a nearby cow, with other cows partly visible in the background (see Figure 1). The picture is predominantly white and brown. The numbers refer to the stages of focus: 13 is full focus. Stages 1, 8, and 13 are shown in Figure 1. Each stage was shown for ten seconds.

A four-year-old:

1. (E: What do you think it could be?) All different colors. It's a picture. (E: It's a picture. yes.) Maybe it could be a little girl before it has long hair.
2. . . . That picture could be a little, a little, a big round orange ball.
3. (E: What do you think it could be?) A bunny rabbop. (E. Keep watching.) Oooh, you know my sister calls rocks and a rabbit a bunny rabbop. (E: Really? Keep watching.)
4. (E: What do you see now?) That has a little eye. I think it's a skunky. (E: Maybe.)
5. It could be. . . . That could be a Indian. . . . I know all the animals.

6. That could be Queeny. Do you know what's Queeny? (E: No.) That's Molly's horse. See, it's a girl horse and she's, she's pretty tall.
7. (E: Well, let's see what's in the picture. Keep watching all the time.) Ooooh, there's a little round nose and mouth. . . . I think it's a face and it's an Indian.
8. Another Indian. . . . Indian. What's in that black books? (E: We'll look at those later.)
9. It's, isn't he a cow. . . .
10. Another cow. (E: And what else?) I don't know. My sister doesn't know all the animals like I do.

A five-year-old:

1. (E: What do you think this picture could be about?) A—some ice cream. (E: Uhmm. Keep watching the picture; don't look at me.)
2. (S mumbles) Some chocolate ice cream, with white ice cream.
3. Somebody sleeping in a bed.
4. Somebody a little clearer, sleeping in a bed.
5. Even a person clearer than the other one, sleeping in a bed. (E: Uhhm. Keep looking.)
6. And now—there's somebody even clearer—sleeping on a bed. (Repeats this again in 7 and 8.)
9. And, er, even another person sleeping on the bed. (E: Uhhm. Anything else?) It might be chocolate ice cream.
10. (E: What do you see now?) A small picture. (E: What's in the picture?) (S sighs:) A bull.
11–13. (Continues to report cow. At 13, E asks: And what else?) I don't know what the white thing is—is it the bed? It might be sheets.

Here is a nine-year-old boy:

1. Oh, that looks like the shadow of a person—like in New York . . . the colored lights, not in focus.
2. But that looks like car lights, and the very lighter the shadow, the people.
3. That looks like other lights, around here, or a car behind that car, over here with its car lights in different colors.
4. Those look like people, and these look like decorations, and the cars, and the cars in back of them and you can see the . . .
5. I see different colors. . . . in the stream of lights here.
6. I see a diff . . . like a little mouth, and very lightly, very very lightly . . . two eyes.
7. In the what I call a person . . . I see darker colors on decorations over here and darker lighting, like the lights of the car.
8, 9, 10: (Continues in the same vein as 7.)
11. Oh, this looks like the face of a bull or something like that.

Here is a sixteen-year-old boy:

1. Looks like—two or three people uh some kind.
2. Seems to be a person here, person here.
3. Could be a person bowling, and the pins are in the right-hand corner and the person in the left.
4. Still looks like a person bowling.
5. It's a man who—who's red-headed.
6. Seems to be some kind of an animal, that he's looking at.
7. Looks to be a—looks like a bull. Looks like a man with red hair looking at a bull—kind of brownish white.
8. Man is wearing white clothes, with red hair.
9. Yeah—it is—it's—man looks to be maybe Spanish or some kind—red hair, looking at a bull fight or something.
10. And the bull seems to be wearing something across his neck, over his neck, some kind. Either that or it's in the background.
11. And the man—he seems to be looking over the fence at him.

Here, finally, is an eighteen-year-old male college student:

1. It's in color too. It looks like two people in fencing outfits, with the white jacket-like things that they wear.
2. And it still looks, er, like that, though the floor has an awful lot on it for two people to be fencing. There's too much going on . . .
3. Ah . . . still don't er . . .
4. Know . . . these, er, look sort of like they might be round chestnuts or something, with these black spherical-looking things.
5. Uh . . . possibly a bowlful of something or other. . . .
6. It's starting to look like a dissection in a biology lab.
7. Oh . . . oh . . . here, well this looks kind of ridiculous, but it looks like a fellow in a white shirt, with red hair is kissing a cow wearing a white nightcap.
8. And, er, I suppose he's looking at a cow in a stall.
9. I'm pretty sure it's a cow. And I think it's a woman not a man, that's looking this cow in the eye.

The findings can be discussed under five headings: Recognition; Nature of the responses; Awareness of recognition; Differences between the sexes; and Organization: the key to differences.

RECOGNITION

Age Differences. The first question is whether subjects of different ages recognize a given picture at the same point of focus. All but one of the pictures can be readily recognized by most children of the ages we studied, if the pictures are first shown in full focus; so ultimate recognizability is not a primary issue. A reliable criterion of recognition was set up for each picture, on the principle that the main object or objects should be correctly reported, whether or not details and background are correct. Since the rate of presentation of the stages of focus was fixed, the results can be given in the form of time required for recognition. The median recognition time in seconds for all pictures is shown in Figure 2 along with the times for the most quickly and most slowly recognized picture for each age group. It is clear that recognition occurs earlier, on the whole, the older the subject, although there is considerable overlap in the distributions. Of twenty-four median comparisons between adjacent groups, all but two are in the direction of greater speed with age; thirteen are highly reliably different. The picture that elicited the greatest age differences in recognition was, as expected, the aerial view of the highway: 71 percent of the four-year-olds and 25 percent of the five-year-olds never reconized it as a road, whereas all college students recognized it by the fifth of the twelve stages of focus. The picture which shows the smallest difference is the silverware; it will

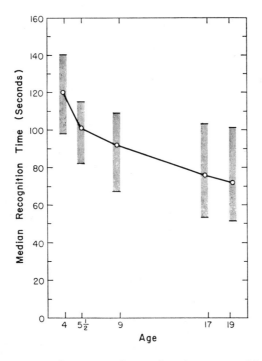

Figure 2. Median time and range for picture recognition.

be discussed presently. Note that the greatest improvement in recognition speed occurs between the ages of four and five-and-a-half, although there is also a marked improvement in the eight years between nine and seventeen.

Some subjects in the three youngest groups never recognized certain pictures, even at full focus, until hints were given, and sometimes not even then. Thirty-four percent of the fours, 13 percent of the fives, and 3 percent of the nines did not recognize spontaneously. The older subjects invariably recognized. In general, the range and variability of recognition points decreased with age. The average range for the six pictures was, in order of increasing age, 57 seconds (the range is constricted because of the cut-off for nonrecognition), 72 seconds, 73 seconds, 62 seconds, and 40 seconds (this group had only eleven subjects, so the range is somewhat restricted as compared with the other groups).

As a check on the fairness of our criteria of recognition, we also scored performance, using minimally stringent criteria: for instance, accepting as recognition the report of any large animal in the case of the cow. The median point of recognition was revised upward on about half the pictures, but the age differences remained equally great. Thus, an inability to give a comprehensive report of recognition is probably not a large factor in the obtained age differences in recognition speed.

Individual Differences. If age differences in recognition speed are appreciable, what of differences between individual subjects of the same age? Do some people consistently recognize faster than others? This question is particularly pertinent if one regards this experiment as a study of the overcoming of ambiguity, or alternatively as a test of flexibility in perception, in line with the interpretations of some previous investigators (Crowell [1961]; Galloway [1946]; Gump [1955]; Wyatt and Campbell [1951]). If recognition is delayed by the difficulty of rejecting a wrong hypothesis, one might perhaps expect marked individual differences in recognition speed of the sort sometimes found in studies of "rigidity."

Kendall's coefficient of concordance, W, was used for the test of individual consistency in recognition speed. At four, $W = 0.37$, (d.f. 22, $p < 0.001$); at five, $W = 0.32$ (d.f. 19, $p < 0.01$); at nine, $W = 0.22$ (d.f. 19, $p < 0.10$); at high-school age, $W = 0.37$ (d.f. 19, $p < 0.001$); and at college age, $W = 0.14$ (d.f. 10, $p > 0.50$). This nonsignificant outcome for Harvard-Radcliffe undergraduates has been obtained repeatedly in a series of basically similar recognition studies. It might be remarked that the high-school subjects covered a wider range of age than did the three younger groups, and that whereas the college group was also quite variable in age, selection procedures are such that the group is comparatively homogeneous in general performance.

Among the four younger groups, then, we do find individual consistency in recognition speed, but it is clear that these individual differences account for only a small portion of the variance. Myriad factors probably determine the exact point of recognition: the recency with which items like those pictures have been seen, the similarity of a particular "generic image" (if memory has such entities) to the object in the picture, and like factors controlling the strength of competing wrong hypotheses.

Reaction Time. Another aspect of recognition speed concerns the rapidity with which the information on each new page is used. A measure of this is the number of seconds after a new page is turned before the subject begins to report recognition, looking only at the particular stage at which recognition occurred in each case. It turns out that the older the subject, the more rapidly does he stabilize his interpretation of a particular stimulus: it takes him about 7.0 seconds at four years, and decreases steadily to 2.5 seconds at college age.

The median times are, in order of increasing age, 7.3 seconds, 4.7 seconds, 3.8 seconds, 2.6 seconds, and 2.5 seconds; the differences appear consistently on all six pictures, with only two reversals out of thirty-six comparisons. Whereas the five-year-old, for example, is almost equally likely to recognize at any point between two and ten seconds, more than half of the college student's recognitions occur in the first three seconds, and only 20 percent occur later than five seconds.

NATURE OF THE RESPONSES

Subjects were encouraged to report their ideas freely as they tried to identify the pictures. What kinds of things are said, and did these vary from age to age? The remarks were chiefly of three kinds: guesses about things in the picture ("it's two people boxing"); descriptions of colors, shapes, and textures ("there are white spots on a dark background"); and remarks indicating disturbance or lack of understanding of the picture ("I can't figure it out"). The guesses were either major hypotheses having to do with the main part of the picture or hypotheses about details, including the background. Repeats of a guess mentioned earlier were counted separately. The average number of remarks of each kind at each ten-second stage is shown in Table 2, and percentages in Table 3.

When considering the results from the four-year-old groups, it must be borne in mind that these subjects were prompted and encouraged much more frequently than were the older groups. The fours often appeared unaware of the requirements of the task, and their reports strayed into conversation about personal experiences and other seeming irrelevancies. Thus the results are not fully comparable with those from the other ages.

It is clear that beyond four years the ages do not differ very greatly in the proportion of each kind of response, although there are distinct age differences, in the total *rate of production*. If we exclude repetitions and irrelevancies, four-year-olds are the least productive, with a remark every fifteen seconds on the average. Five- and nine-year-

TABLE 2

Average Number of Prerecognition Remarks in Each Category
per Ten-Second Stage of Focus (Six Pictures per Subject)

	New Hypotheses		Repeated Hy- potheses	Attri- butes	Dis- turbed Process	Total Remarks
	Major	Detail				
4 years (N = 23) 1893 remarks	.20	.13	.44	.08	.25	1.10
5½ years (N = 20) 1310 remarks	.24	.27	.34	.16	.11	1.12
9 years (N = 20) 954 remarks	.24	.22	.20	.11	.17	.94
17 years (N = 20) 1179 remarks	.31	.33	.24	.25	.28	1.41
College age (N = 11) 839 remarks	.45	.44	.23	.51	.30	1.93

TABLE 3
Percentage of Prerecognition Remarks in Each Category,
Excluding Repeated Hypotheses

| | New Hypotheses | | | Disturbed |
	Major	Detail	Attributes	Process
4 years	30	20	12	38
5½ years	31	35	20	15
9 years	32	29	15	23
17 years	26	28	21	24
College age	27	26	30	17

olds are almost equal in productivity, again excluding repetitions: both groups say something new every thirteen seconds on the average. At seventeen, new comments are made every 8.5 seconds, and at college age, every six seconds, more than twice the productivity of the three youngest groups (Figure 3).[2]

Speed and Fluency. One may ask whether the speed of recognition is a simple function of fluency; the recomputation of recognition using very lax criteria, mentioned earlier, was an attempt to circumvent this problem, and it resulted in no change in the relative standing of the age groups. The fact that nines, who talk rather less than fives, recognize rather sooner, also suggests that it is not a change in verbal facility alone that accounts for the increased speed of recognition with age. And, within each age group, the correlation between talkativeness and recognition speed was negligible.

Since the rate of talking changes with age, whereas the percentage of each general category of response stays fairly constant, at least beyond four, it is of interest to compare the two most and two least talkative subjects at each age to see if they also maintain the same over-all distribution of responses. In fact, they do not. Disentangling the effects of talking and of age, we find that the more talkative subjects (who talk at from four to twelve times the rate of their opposite numbers) make more guesses about details, describe many more of

---

[2] If we consider the total number of remarks of all kinds, only the differences between the college group and each of the other groups are significant. (Mann-Whitney U, two-tailed, between college and fours, has $p < 0.01$; fives, $p < 0.01$; nines, $p < 0.001$; and seventeens, $P < 0.05$). The difference between nine- and seventeen-year-olds approaches significance ($p < 0.12$). There are large and consistent individual differences in talkativeness at all ages.

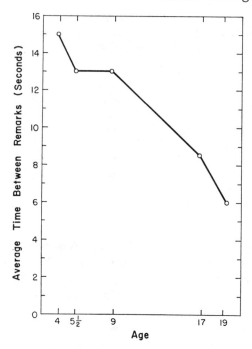

Figure 3. Average time between remarks during recognition process.

the surface attributes of the picture, and are more repetitious—but they make proportionally fewer major hypotheses (although absolutely more), and actually make fewer disturbance remarks than do the least talkative subjects. Increased age is likewise associated with increases in reports of details and attributes, so perhaps this increase is primarily the result of increased fluency. (This probability is borne out by the larger number of details and attributes reported by fives as compared with the less talkative nines.) But increasing age, unlike increasing talkativeness, is associated with an increase in the production of major hypotheses, a steady *reduction* of repetition (from 57 percent of all guesses at age four and 40 percent of guesses at age five, to 20 percent at college age), and an *increase* from age five on in disturbance remarks: these changes we may regard as age differences that are independent of changes in fluency. It is fair to conclude that the apparent stability, over the age range studied, in the percentages of various types of remarks is the outcome of complex age changes sometimes working in opposition.

This analysis is pertinent to a question sometimes raised: does a talker in fact really have many more ideas than a nontalker? The selectivity of the nontalker's remarks suggests that he does not simply have fewer things to say, since in fact he continues to give about as many major guesses as the chronic talker. Presumably he reports major ideas because they represent possible final answers, which other classes of remarks do not. On the other hand, the rate of major hypotheses does increase with age, along with other kinds of talk, suggesting that older children "really" have more ideas. Curiously, the average *number* of major ideas prior to recognition (disregarding the rate) is almost constant at between 2.0 and 2.2 per picture until college age, when it rises to 2.9.

Response Changes in the Course of a Picture. To examine the process of recognition as it occurs through time, one can look at the changes in the categories of response from the first stage through to recognition. For this purpose we can compare responses in the first ten seconds with those in a ten-second stage near the middle of each protocol and in the last ten seconds before recognition occurs. All five ages have in common certain changes through these three phases. The total number of remarks, omitting repetitions, declines somewhat, as we might expect. The proportion of hypotheses goes up, in particular, guesses about details. The report of attributes—color, shapes, and the like—declines. Disturbance remarks also decline, *except* among college students, of which more will be said later. There is no doubt that the increase in number and specificity of contours resulting from the improved focus is associated with an increase in the rate of tentative identifications. Subjects shown each picture, starting midway in the focus series, gave few attribute descriptions but many hypotheses. The general process through the focus stages, common to all ages, involves a shift from an occasional major hypothesis accompanied by noncommittal descriptions of colors and shapes, and by protests of uncertainty, to the building up of further major hypotheses with increasing numbers of details.

The emphasis is characteristically different at each age, however. The four-year-old, like the others, reacts first to the whole picture and gives few details. Later, as the picture becomes clearer, he offers a few guesses about details, but he neglects to revise his major hypothesis, which he simply repeats if he mentions it at all. At five, the performance is similar, except that details are mentioned in considerable quantity after the first major hypothesis. At nine, major hypotheses predominate throughout, with a lesser but continuing flow of detail. The high-school student, after an early major guess, is led on by details which interplay with less frequent major revisions. At college age, details are bunched toward the middle of the prerecognition period, and shortly before recognition the college student turns to new major guesses.

If, as we found, older subjects have more ideas about a picture in a given time, do they also give their first guesses earlier than do younger subjects?

This query about the time of the first guess is pertinent to a body of work (Binder [1958]; Messick and Hills [1960]; Smock [1955, 1957]) on the conditions under which meaning is attributed to ambiguous stimuli. In an experiment also using a series of blurred pictures, Draguns and Multari [1961] found that seven- and eight-year-olds made a guess about the object considerably earlier in the series than did ten- and twelve-year-olds. While our older groups do not overlap with Draguns', it is nonetheless surprising that we find just the opposite: the older groups give their first guess distinctly earlier than the fours, fives, and nines. However, the subjects in the Draguns-Multari study were only allowed one guess, after which the picture series was terminated without correction. Thus, delaying one's guess allowed one to see clearer stages of the picture and, in fact, increased the likelihood of correct identification. In contrast, our subjects were urged to offer guesses as soon as an idea occurred, and were in any event allowed to continue with the picture to complete clarity.

If we take the two findings together, it appears that whereas older children and adults *can* attribute meaning to impoverished stimuli more readily than children can, they are also able to discriminate between these early impressions and a later, more probable guess, and if necessary they can delay guessing until this more probable hypothesis comes to mind. This ability to tell right from wrong will occupy us in the discussion to follow.

AWARENESS OF RECOGNITION

The ability to withhold a response until "you know you're right" appears to increase with age. There are other indicants of a general sharpening with age of one's sensitivity to the fit between a tentative category and the incoming stimuli.

Disturbance and Awareness. Recall the fact that, excepting the four-year-old group, the rate of disturbance remarks ("I don't know," "It's terribly fuzzy") increases with age: a curious finding, since performance is actually improving. If older groups are more conscious of the inadequacies of their prerecognition performance, however, we might expect such a rise.

The percentage of disturbance remarks reaches a peak at high-school age (Table 3). At the younger ages, many remarks in this category are occasioned by the experimenter's prompts. The experimenter asks, "How about now?" and the subject replies, "I don't know." The number of prompts, which were offered when the subject remained silent for about twenty seconds or appeared to need encouragement, decreased from an average of one every thirty-five seconds with five-year-olds to practically none with college students. (The rate of prompting was much higher with the four-year-old group: an average of one every fifteen seconds. This was deemed necessary to keep the subject's attention on the task.) If we omit all disturbance remarks which are replies to such prompts, the increase in disturbance remarks with age (to high school) is more marked: the percentages of all utterances are 5, 14, 18, and 15 in order of increasing age from five to college. (The fours, noncomparable for the reasons mentioned, expressed unprompted disturbance in 11 percent of their utterances.)

Consider the finding mentioned earlier on the rate of disturbance remarks at different points between initial blur and recognition. For fives, nines, and high-school students the percentage of disturbance is at its highest when the picture is very far out of focus, and it declines to less than half this initial level shortly before recognition. In contrast, college students start the picture with the lowest rate of disturbance remarks (14 percent to the five-year-olds' 29 percent and the four-year-olds 53 percent) but they actually increase this percentage as the picture becomes clearer to a final 21 percent (higher than any other group) just before recognition. Thus, though the college student gives a smaller over-all percentage of reports of dissatisfaction than does the high-school student, his reaction is highly sophisticated: it is only in the face of increasing clarity that the adult feels that his failure to recognize is egregious.

The Language of Doubt and Certainty. There are other ways of expressing disturbance when one is trying to recognize a blurred picture. For instance, there is the choice of verb and modifiers when making a guess. An hypothesis may simply be named: "A house." There may be verbal assertion without qualification: "It's a house." Or there are numerous forms in which an element of doubt or noncommitment is expressed: "I think it's a house." "It looks like a house," "A house, I guess." Figure 4 shows the percentage of hypotheses qualified in

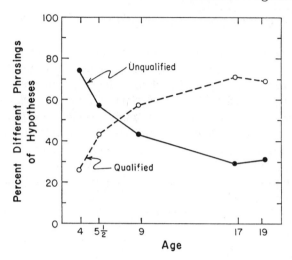

Figure 4. Percent of hypotheses using different phrasings.

some way, compared with hypotheses that are simply named or asserted. The percentage of guesses couched in such qualified terms
rises with age, reaching a peak at high school. L'Abate (1957), who
examined the uncertainty expressions (including both qualifiers and
disturbance remarks as defined here) of children from kindergarten
to the fifth grade in a standard task, likewise found an increasing
percentage of such remarks.

However, these findings might be dismissed as an artifact of the
growing complexity of language with increasing age. A further observation is more interesting: if we look at the form of the first statement
of the correct hypothesis, for example, the first mention of a cow,
we generally find a *drop* in the use of doubt-indicating qualifiers. Significantly, the size of the drop increases with age (from a 3 percent
drop at four to a drop of 40 percent at seventeen and 30 percent among
the college group). Concomitantly, the use of "it is" assertions quad-
ruples with the onset of correct recognition in the older groups,
doubles among the nines, but remains unchanged (at about 12 percent) among the fours and fives. These findings strongly suggest improvement, at least to high-school age, in the ability to discriminate
between an hypothesis fully adequate to the picture and earlier, speculative hypotheses. This interpretation is further confirmed by a count
of exclamations of surprise or confidence: "Oh!" "I know what it is,"
and the classic "Ah ha" and the like. The occurrence of these excla-

mations before recognition is rare in all groups. At the moment of recognition, the four- and five-year-olds are still unlikely to exclaim, but older subjects show a marked increase in exclamations, with the greatest increase at college age, as can be seen in Figure 5.

Looking at the course of doubt-indicating language from the very blurred stage of a given picture to the point of recognition, one finds changes that parallel rather precisely the changes in disturbance remarks already noted. The qualification of guesses decreases as the picture clarifies, *except* among college students, when it increases slightly. Again, although the college student makes no more qualifications over-all, his uncertainty does not, like the high-school student's, diminish with increasing clarity, but remains high until correct recognition.

A Paradox: Talkativeness. It was reported earlier that talkativeness is not correlated with recognition. The remarkable fact is that in certain cases a subject talks as little as one-fourteenth as often as his classmate and yet recognizes about as quickly. One might have expected that unwillingness to hazard guesses would have meant a delay in mentioning the correct guess as well: how does the subject know when to speak and when he can afford to remain silent? For the older subjects, who appear to be aware when they have recognized correctly, there should be no great problem. For the younger groups, part of the answer lies in the fact that silent subjects continue to give a

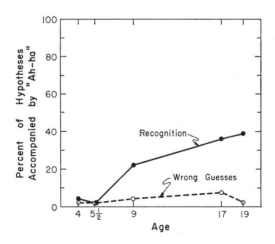

Figure 5. Percent of correct and incorrect guesses accompanied by "Ah-ha" or its equivalent.

relatively large number of major hypotheses. An examination of the data gives a further explanation: at four and also at five the relation in question is in fact curvilinear. Both the high and the low talkers recognize much later, on the average, than do the moderate talkers. From their protocols it looks as though the excessively talkative children are attending primarily to their own responses and only secondarily to the picture—usually their responses are highly stereotyped and are repeated from frame to frame, perhaps with systematic variations stemming chiefly from the nature of the response rather than from the picture. For example, in the picture of the trashcans (see Figure 1), a boy says, "A hammer?" The next frame: "Two hammers?" then "Three hammers?" "Four hammers? . . . . and the picture's getting clearer." Finally, in full focus: "Seven cans—hammers." The correct interpretation of the picture—cans—almost penetrates, but is denied in favor of repetition. (After further conversation the child spontaneously reports "trash barrels.") A child who talks very little also recognizes late, presumably because the correct response is suppressed along with the wrong ones—an outcome consistent with the other evidence that indicates a lack of sharp awareness in younger subjects of the nature of recognition.

The Click of Recognition vs. *Lax Criteria.* The use of expressions of doubt, affirmation, and confidence; the occurrence and distribution of disturbance remarks; and the capacity to withhold a guess until it has a good chance of being correct (whether because of reluctance to talk or, as in the Draguns-Multari study [1961], because of instructions)—one sees in all these the sharpening boundary between uncertainty and certainty, a sharpening that may continue into college age. Adults frequently experience a click of recognition, a startling sense of rightness, which probably results from a sudden, sizable improvement in the fit between the hypothesis and the stimulus.

It is worth mentioning that in some circumstances this sense of rightness can be upset, even in adults. For example, when adults are required for two minutes to look at and guess about a single blurred stage of a picture, and then are shown subsequent stages at a very slow pace, correct recognition, when it comes, is very much more tentative, and a temporary return to a wrong hypothesis is much more likely. Perhaps the necessarily slower accumulation of information under these circumstances approaches the condition of the young child, who exhausts the information in each frame more slowly than adults do, and takes more frames to recognize.

Another facet of the change in the awareness of recognition is the change in the conception of the task. Because of the lack of contrast between an adequate and an inadequate identification of the picture, recognition does not dominate the on-going process in the four- and five-year-old as it increasingly does later. Recognition is often simply another incident (recall that the experimenter makes no signal when a correct identification is made). Recognition occasionally occurs piecemeal at this age: the main part of the picture may be recognized correctly while some other part is totally misinterpreted. The remnants of earlier ideas may be wholly incongruous to an adult: a subject who had recognized one of a pair of boots in a close-up shot persisted in seeing the second boot as a deer. This is a characteristic problem of the five-year-old perceiver: his criteria of fit between hypothesis and stimulus are not very stringent. And where the criterion is lax its fulfilment is neither as rare nor as noticeable as when the criterion is more stringent: hence the lesser awareness that one has recognized.

An an example of the problem of lax criteria, consider Picture 1, trashcans on a curb with the markings of a crosswalk visible in the background (see Figure 1). At about the fourth stage of increasing focus one begins to distinguish a set of greyish or colorless cylindrical objects. These are commonly seen as smallish containers like jars, glasses, or beer cans, although some subjects report other things, like "people" or "candles." The small-container hypothesis appears to be somewhat seductive: those subjects who do *not* offer such a guess recognize earlier, on the average, at every age. Interestingly enough, the five-year-olds had almost as much difficulty with this picture as with the unusual shot of the highway intersection, and in fact six of the twenty subjects failed to recognize it at all until broad hints were given. (Even more four-year-olds failed.) Despite the apparent simplicity and familiarity of this picture, the common wrong hypotheses still fit moderately well at full focus, and the five-year-old, uncritical about such fit, remains satisfied with "glasses" or "cups."

DIFFERENCES BETWEEN THE SEXES

There are few sex differences in any of the measures where they were sought. There are no notable differences in the median recognition point save in two cases: nursery-school and third-grade boys were distinctly more likely to recognize the aerial view of the highway, which can hardly surprise us in view of the excessive interest in transportation seen in young boys. Four-year-old boys say somewhat less than girls, but thereafter boys say somewhat more, with the greatest difference at high-school age. Yet girls make at least as many major guesses as boys. The boys gain their extra responses from attribute descriptions (at nine and seventeen) and from disturbance remarks. Boys in all groups except the fours express disturbance much more commonly (an indication of greater orientation toward achievement in the boys?). L'Abate (1957), in a study of uncertainty expressions (including both disturbance remarks and qualifying terms), found fewer such expressions among girls, a conclusion which parallels this observation. However, there is no sex difference in our groups (from five on) in qualifying expressions associated with hypotheses: girls are just as likely as boys to say "It might be a . . . ."

ORGANIZATION: THE KEY TO DIFFERENCES

Characteristic Changes with Age. Up to this point, in discussing the subjects' responses as they attempt to recognize a blurred picture, we have considered response units as independent entities. However, interesting properties of performance become visible when one looks at the relation between a given response and earlier responses on that picture. To guide this examination, first recall the two basic phases of visual recognition that we have assumed: the organization of the stimulus and its categorization. We shall consider these two processes in much greater detail in the final chapter. For the moment we use them in their intuitive sense—being occupied with sensory properties or features, and being concerned with "what object that is." When recognition is difficult, one or both of these steps occurs more than once: the subject looks, guesses, continues looking, guesses again, and so on. There are four possible basic forms of sequential dependence in this kind of sequence: guesses can depend on prior guesses or prior looking, and the organized look can depend on prior looks or prior guesses.

The nature of the dependence can vary also. Consider the relation between one hypothesis and an earlier hypothesis. The simplest relationship is repetition: H2 is the same as H1. At a more complex level, H1 and H2 could be hypotheses about different parts of the picture that are related to one another logically or probabilistically: for example, a dog would be more likely to be standing on grass than on water. Other possible relationships include phonological connections and associative or thematic connections, which may *not* be logical or probabilistic. Or, of course, there might be no visible association at all. The other three dependencies mentioned can likewise take various forms: repetition, associative connection, and so on.

An important characteristic of performance arises from the joint action of the two potential influences on a guess or look. For example, an hypothesis can be determined by a previous guess (dog → grass) or by the look of the particular part of the picture (green expanse → grass). Each of these influences by itself might lead to other guesses, however; for example, dog → ground or floor; green → water or bushes. But when both "dog" and "green" are taken into account, "grass" is the more likely guess for the background. A two- or three-step process is required to make this integration, in contrast with the single step from guess to guess or look to guess.

The subject's verbalizations as he attempts to recognize are not a perfect reflection of the processes we have described, but they do give some information about these dependencies and their interaction.

Four-year-olds. Responses—and presumably the underlying processes of perception and categorization that they reflect—are fragmented at first. There is a markedly greater restriction of ideas than at any later age. Responses are either nonexistent or highly sterotyped until the stimulus becomes quite definite. The three- or four-year-old shows only the organization of repetition: one response is hit upon and reiterated and is commonly used again on succeeding pictures. If the guess is enlarged upon, the elaboration is likely to be unrelated to the picture:

> (The highway, approaching full focus:) A railroad. (E: A railroad?)
> Yeah, we have some railroads. . . . I have a choochoo train, too.

Typically, the four-year-old mentions only one idea at a time, repeats it, and ultimately switches without comment to a new, unrelated idea. Sometimes, however, two or more ideas may exist in parallel, ideas that are utterly incompatible to an adult. The top of the fire hydrant was seen by one boy as a pumpkin and the lower part as an ice cream cone. One child, looking at the highway, first reported a table, and then added, "People watching" (the rows of suburban houses look like rows of heads). When asked what the people were watching, he said, "The table."

It appeared that for the four-year-old the identity of an object is not easily separated from his own experiences: guesses often take the form of wholesale personal associations to some one dominant feature of the picture. If the child eventually notices that the picture has changed, he is not discomposed, since what occurred a moment ago has no necessary relation in his scheme to what will next occur. No active, directed process seems present with regard either to structuring the formal elements of the picture or to generating appropriate guesses and weeding out ones that do not fit. The child's talk at times seems to be an autonomous process, a linguistic exercise that is only casually referential.

The submersion of the very young child in a world of subjective experiences unclearly differentiated from the objective world can reach autistic lengths, and then the speech of the child is released in a rapid flow. Consider this response to the aerial view of the highway intersection:

> (After a long silence): Oh, hey, this looks like a table . . . Just like a table. Something green (pointing, but unable to identify when asked) . . . It's way in the, W-A-Y. . . . (What's that?) It just looks like where we went, you know, where the mountain is (pointing to the upper right hand corner). We were in Chattanooga. 'Member we saw some cars, looking down on the cars. Just under where we were, remember?

Needless to say, the experimenter had not been on this journey to Lookout Mountain.

Even after the picture is recognized, the child when questioned will sometimes maintain that he still sees the earlier wrong items. If there is any attempt to rationalize disparity, it is primitive: since there is both a boy and clouds, the boy must be outside; if there is a table, but also people watching, then they are watching the table. This is integration virtually by fiat.

Five-year-olds. At five and a half the ability to fit one hypothesis to another and to the changing picture is somewhat more advanced, although some of the same problems exist. There is a lot more talking, and the five-year-old piles up guesses and descriptions a little as if the emerging image were a random collage.

> (The cow.) Spots. And a cloud. . . . That looks like a reindeer. . . . with spots in his eyes and a cloud on his head.

It has already been noted that the more talkative five-year-olds frequently generate autonomous response sequences which follow their own logic independently of what is happening to the stimulus: "One hammer," "two hammers," and so forth. These response sets may be carried over from picture to picture; for example, one child reported "someone taking medicine" as a first response to three consecutive pictures. Thus this age has its own way of meeting the requirement of response-response consistency. This sort of thematic association seems to be responsible for the appearance of many guesses as well as serving as a criterion of their fit to the pictures. On occasion the theme may overwhelm the perceptual process: here is a five-year-old looking at the later stages of the picture of the trashcans. Each "and then" is the start of a new stage of focus:

> Person holding a glass of milk. The milk's on the table. Then somebody's beginning to pick it up. The somebody's right close to the glass of milk. And then she's going to pour some, and then she's all through pouring the milk, and then she's gonna bring it to the people, and then [full focus] the people are all through with that and she brings them back to the kitchen.

The child of five offers fewer change/no-change markers during his report than do older subjects. Although he is highly repetitious, he is less likely to signal continuity by such expressions as "It's still a . . ." or even "Same thing." And when he does change his guess he rarely makes an explicit negation ("It's not a . . . .") of the rejected guess. At all ages explicit negation is uncommon, but there is a consistent increase with age: at five, 1 percent of prerecognition hypotheses are so rejected; at nine, 4 percent; at high-school age, almost 6 percent; and at college age, just over 6 percent.

Just as a theme can run away with the five-year-old's responses, word play may momentarily take control. This boy says, halfway through the picture of the trashcans:

> Cannons? Candles. . . . Same thing . . . cannon . . . candles. Same thing . . . cans and candles . . . and a man. Cans . . . street.

(This phonological play in connection with a visual experience reminds one of Conrad's (1962) finding, that visual stimuli (printed letters) may be systematically confused in memory in terms of similarity in *sound*.)

When the child of five attends to the stimulus, he may simply play with the shapes and colors with little visible attempt to arrive at the perception of real objects:

> Here's the little diamond over here . . . and a little orange and green . . . orange and green are my favorite colors, and that color too.

Even after he offers a specific hypothesis for one part of the picture he continues to report mere shapes and colors in other parts, without distinction between the two levels of report: "A clown and er bricks and a round spot."

There is no ready way of assessing the dependence of figure-ground organization and the like on hypotheses or on prior organization, from these reports. It might be mentioned that there is evidence that younger children are less good at reversing figure and ground (Elkind, Koegler, and Go [1962]) and are more prone to symmetry, structure, and closure in perceptual tasks (Drosler and Kuhn [1960]), than are older children and adults. These findings suggest a rather strong autochthonous process which would lead to conservation of the initial stimulus organization and perhaps to resistance to the influence of hypotheses on organization. Rather than reorganizing the stimulus, the child may simply ignore any lack of fit between hypothesis and stimulus.

There are, then, two sources of guesses for the five-year-old: the picture itself, and his own previous guess. What is missing is the interaction between these sources: he cannot readily take into account *both* his guess about one part of the picture *and* the appearance of another part of the picture. When his guesses about two parts of the picture *are* related, they may share only a common theme or association, and the probabilities of scale and arrangement in space are occasionally ignored. A white rabbit and a gorilla may not only appear in juxtaposition but may even be equal in size.

A count was made of the number of guesses—whether major guesses or details—that are reasonably linked with other hypotheses in terms of likelihood of coappearance. The judgment was subjective, but consistent for the various groups. Examples of links include "An animal—that is his eye" and "It's a seal, and that's the ocean." Guesses that were from the same category (for example, animals) but that would not be expected to appear together were not counted as links. The four-year-olds linked 20 percent of their guesses; the five-year-olds linked 23 percent; the nines, 32 percent; the high-school group, 51 percent; and college students, 37 percent. There is certainly an indication here that the older groups develop and relate hypotheses more systematically than do younger subjects.

The opposite phenomenon was also examined: the occurrence of anomaly or incongruity. Incongruities arose when two items were mentioned which would be very unlikely to appear together, or which were grossly different in scale. Such incongruities were not common at any age, but those that were found did occur chiefly among the five-year-olds. They gave twenty-seven such anomalous responses; the nine-year-olds gave ten; the high-school students, two, and the college students, six (including four from a single subject, who interpreted the instructions to mean that he should free-associate).[3] Just as reason-

---

[3] The four-year-olds rarely held more than one idea at a time, so that the opportunity for incongruity was low, yet sixteen such responses were given.

able links between hypotheses increase with age, incongruities diminish. The slight reversal of both effects at college age reflects the generally more facile and productive performance of this group, in whom the generation of a large number of guesses may momentarily be put ahead of selection from among them.

It was reported before that the five-year-old has unusual difficulty with the picture of trashcans, in part because, with his lax criteria, "glasses" or "cans" fit sufficiently well. His relative inability to relate two hypotheses also works against him in this picture. The street with a crosswalk may be identified, but, as far as he is concerned, glasses can appear on it.

One picture was noted before which the five-year-old recognized almost as early as did the older subjects: the silverware (Figure 1). There was only a five-second difference between the medians of kindergarteners and college students. Unlike the other pictures, this picture is likely to be recognized only if a single small object, one of the utensils, is first identified, independently of one's over-all impression of the picture. No contextual cues are available, since the silverware is uncharacteristically jumbled on a neutral background with unusual lighting. Here piecemeal recognition may actually be an asset: the earliest recognizer in our study was a five-year-old.

In an earlier experiment another instance of this phenomenon was observed, with a picture of a distant seagull flying against a cloudy sky. To recognize the bird it was necessary to look directly at the small area which it occupied in the center of the picture. When the picture was out of focus, this area looked very much like a smudge on the slide. The adults usually reported that they stopped looking at that spot early in viewing, and were often shocked to discover a clear bird there when they happened to look some time later. (We do not, of course, know whether the adults literally did not look at the bird, or whether they selectively did not attend to that spot even when looking at it.) In any event, the median point of their recognition of this picture was later for the adults than for the nine-, six- and even the three-year-olds. In both these pictures a smallish area looked at with an "empty head" was the prerequisite for recognition.

In sum, the five-year-old may reiterate a given hypothesis or perhaps develop a story unrelated to the picture, but he is poor at relating two or more hypotheses in the light of what he sees. A corollary to his lack of ability to link hypotheses is his failure to recognize incongruity in his ideas. It is hard to generate a sense of paradox at an age when probabilities are so dimly perceived.

The observation that young children appear insensitive to incongruity has suggested the hypothesis that pictures that are in fact incongruous might be more readily recognized by children than by adults, who are known to experience great difficulty in recognizing incongruous stimuli (Bruner and Postman [1949]). To test this hypothesis, a pilot study was performed by Modigliani and Rabin (1962). They presented pictures of commonplace scenes and objects either singly or in anomalous montages which combined the salient features of two pictures. The subjects were first-graders and college students. The pictures were shown out of focus at first, and were then brought slowly into focus, while the subject reported his ideas. Each subject was shown two of the single pictures, followed by an incongruous montage of two different single pictures, in a counterbalanced design. The children took longer than the adults to recognize both the single pictures and the montages, but appeared to be relatively less delayed by the montages than were the adults. (An extension of this experiment is being carried out by the author of this chapter.)

An interesting observation was that, whereas adults always reacted strongly when they finally perceived the incongruity, relatively few children expressed any surprise. When questioned, some of them were unable to point out the incongruity, especially if only the *scale* was out of line, as in a picture with the enormous head of a dog set in a living room. These results support our contention that younger children have a relatively weak sense of what goes with what in pictures.

Nine-year-olds. At nine there is again a change. Many of these third-graders were wary and comparatively unresponsive: they gave the impression that they had discovered the possibility of error, but did not know how to avoid it except by remaining silent. The search for internal consistency was present, though not always successful. Although they had not yet mastered the technique of relating things logically, the nine-year-olds were practicing. Here is a boy who recognized the cow and the person in white but could not make out the extra white areas:

> It's like a decoration of lights . . . it's probably at night, and so there will be black in between here to show that that's the night. [Since full focus had been reached, E. said: What if I said that it was daytime?] Well, I don't think it would be because, er, people don't wear white clothes in the daytime. They wear black clothes in the daytime.

This age mentions fewer descriptive attributes than any other does, and those that are mentioned are apt to be associated with object guesses ("something brown . . . in the snow"), whereas at five, color and form reports appeared not to constrain hypotheses. The child of nine, then, is relatively object-centered, less taken with the stimulus properties of the picture, and more concrete: he searches for the main thing in each picture, and is distressed when he cannot find it. He can detect inconsistencies, so he is less likely than are the five-year-olds to pile up a mass of mismatched guesses, but he cannot easily generate consistencies, so he simply offers fewer guesses about details than do the fives.

High-school Students. By sixteen or thereabouts the subject has ready control over all the relationships we have discussed. Some subjects at this age, as at earlier ages, talk very little, and from them we learn little about structure. From the more talkative subject we can draw some conclusions. If he mentions colors, shapes, or textures, they serve either to signal a lack of thingness ("Oh, I just see pink and lavender. . . .") or they lead directly to efforts to make guesses:

> [The picture of silverware:] Oh, I don't know . . . it's more of those circles. It may be earth, because the others [other pictures] aren't that dark. . . . It looks like traffic at night with all the things except that they are not in order . . . an abstract painting of traffic at night with spot lights. . . . No, now doesn't . . . the black things are giving it some sort of shape . . . like stick things. . . .

This protocol also demonstrates the ability of these adolescents to cycle from guess to picture to guess, building up, modifying, perhaps tearing down a hypothetical structure that simultaneously takes into account the probabilities of scale, spatial arrangement, and association, and relates these to the visible attributes of the picture. This active, problem-solving approach is itself, one guesses, often responsible for the temporary stuckness that at times besets adults as well as children; the adult is altogether too good at molding what he sees to fit his current hypothesis. Though uncertain of his early ideas, he struggles to shore them up if possible, and may in the process postpone a switch to the correct guess.

College Students. There is a considerable difference in the tone of the reports from the high-school students and from these intellectually homogeneous and able college students, but the structure of the performance differs little as between the two groups. The college group is more verbal, and unlike the high-school group, had only one subject who was conspicuously quiet. These students were more likely than were younger groups to talk about the process itself and their own reactions, directing themselves to areas of confusion, or evaluating the picture:

> "There's something going there in the background. I can't identify it; it doesn't mean anything to me yet." "Very exciting. It looks

like a dance. . . ." "Reason I'm saying chicken legs is because I've
just finished making chicken soup at home, but I do see chicken legs
all the way through here." "Religious symbols, symbols of food, um,
the dark part is the very interesting part now."

The college students also made explicit mention of the secondary
areas of the picture: they appeared to explore the picture more widely
in early stages than did the high-school and younger groups. For
example, in the picture of the fire hydrant there was a bright area
in one corner, away from the red areas that were part of the hydrant
itself. Prior to recognition, 73 percent of the college students made
some reference to this spot, whereas only 25 percent of the high-school
students mentioned it, 10 percent of the nines, and none of the fives.

The college performance, then, has greater diversity than that of
any younger groups. The college student has larger numbers of major
ideas, many of them cited momentarily and then dropped, but others
taken up and debated at length while search of the picture continues:

> There's a white streak going down the middle of the paper, but
> whether that has any continuity of itself, or whether it's just blurring
> together the light, I don't know. . . . Although there's definitely some-
> thing crossing. Now what would cross? There are also . . . it looks
> sort of like a cloverleaf . . . highway system.

College students mention descriptive attributes ("a white streak")
twice as frequently as do high-school students, and, as can be seen
in the previous example, these reports are closely interwoven with
hypothesis construction.

One might have expected that the peak in reports of these object-
free perceptual attributes would occur at six and younger, when other
studies (see, for example, Chapter 3 in this book) suggest that perceptual qualities are more salient than functional or other more abstract
qualities. In fact, there are few reports of attributes in our youngest
group: already at three and four the world is reported in terms of
objects, not forms and colors. The function, then, of these descriptive
reports is more complex than we anticipated.

If we could isolate those reports of color, form, and the like which
were thought by the subject to be satisfactory answers to our instruction, "What is the picture about?" we would undoubtedly find that
very young children give many more such objectless answers than
older children do. But there are other functions of those descriptive
statements: as mentioned earlier they may serve to fill in an interval
when the subject has no hypothesis or knows that an hypothesis would
be premature. They may also reflect the subject's attempt to inventory

and perhaps reorganize the picture as he generates and tests hypotheses: it is this function that predominates at college age.

At moments, however, the look of the picture overcomes the search for object identity, and (like some five-year-olds) the college student rejoices in the colors and forms:

> Ah, this is all very grey and misty. It looks very mysterious. It's almost a shame it's going to get clearer because it's a frightfully attractive color combination right now.

Altogether, the typical performance of the college student has great virtuosity; if it has a fault, it is that, as in the high-school student's performance, hypotheses are so well-developed that their rejection is at times difficult, and recognition is delayed.

Delay of Recognition. In experiments with adults it was found that seeing a picture first in a blurred stage resulted in a delay of ultimate recognition, beyond the point of clarity normally required for correct recognition (Bruner and Potter [1964]). Do children also show this delay? This question is of interest, because one explanation of the delay effect among adults is that premature hypotheses interfere with correct recognition. If, as we have been suggesting, young children show less effort after continuity as they view the focus series, one might expect them to show less delay. Conflicting with this prediction is the opposite observation, that young children perseverate in their responses under certain conditions, and thus should be especially helped by the removal of misleading material.

To answer this question three further groups of subjects were studied: eleven five-year-olds, eleven nine-year-olds, and sixteen college students. Each was shown the same pictures seen by the regular subjects, but with the early stages of focus omitted (otherwise the procedure was identical). A different starting point for each age group and each picture was chosen in an effort to pick a point at which some regular subjects had recognized (showing that recognition was possible), but one at which most had not recognized. Of the thirteen original focus stages of each picture, about eight were omitted in the youngest group, seven in the next group, and five among the college students.

As had been the case in the earlier study of adults, all groups showed some tendency to recognize more rapidly when the worst blur was omitted. The effect increased with age, from a minimal tendency among the five-year-olds, to a measurable effect at nine, and a strong effect among college students. This shift is particularly noticeable in the picture of the silverware. Recall that this picture is best recognized by picking out one or another small object, and disregarding the impression given by the whole picture: the result was that the young subjects under the usual procedure did as well as the adults. When the silverware is shown in medium blur, however, marked age differences appear: five-year-olds show no change in recognition speed, nine-year-olds do somewhat better, and college students do very significantly better. This is a further confirmation of the hypothesis that delay in recognition results from the carryover of a premature interpretation of the picture. The ability to form stable and lasting interpretations increases with age, and so, likewise, does the deficit that can result if the interpretation is wrong.

Not all pictures were helped by the late-start procedure: on the picture of the trashcans, for example, performance was actually somewhat worse. Recognition has to be won, on this picture, by the checking and rejection of a rather compelling initial wrong impression, an impression that is given by even the intermediate stage of focus. Time, here, is slightly more important than small increments of clarity, whereas for most of the pictures the opposite is true.

Exactly how does the omission of the worst blur help? Apparently by permitting the first impression to be correct: for when the data were examined, it was found that virtually all the improvement was accounted for by recognition during the first, medium-blur frame. If those subjects who do *not* recognize on the first frame are compared with subjects in the regular groups who have also not recognized up to that point, performance is almost identical: if you start off on the wrong foot, you lose all the potential advantage of a late start.

In sum, recognition is impeded by prior commitments among older subjects, whereas young subjects remain relatively free of such pictorial prejudices.[4]

SOME CONCLUSIONS

If a single principle concerning the growth of perceptual recognition with age emerges from this study it is that the "span of integration" increases with age. The span of immediate memory approaches an asymptote by age five and a half, but the range of items which can

---

[4] A study by A. Crowell (personal communication, 1965) has since come to my attention, one which demonstrates that under certain circumstances children of four-and-a-half show as much delay effect as do adults. Line drawings of single, familiar objects were used. This finding is consistent with the interpretation that a child's deficit lies in his inability to interrelate various aspects of a complex picture; with a simple, unitary picture he is on a par with adults.

be integrated by a series of cyclical operations does not. At age four the identity of an object is not fully separated from one's own experiences; this lack of differentiation precludes an active discriminatory matching process. The five-year-old does very well when only one leap from stimulus to hypothesis is required—when there is one simple object to be identified—but he lags further and further behind as more steps are required. The nine-year-old does a good job of fitting together his guesses, but the match between his guesses and the picture is unsubtle, lacking the extra steps required to search out the logical implication between the shapes colors, and textures and the things that these might signify. The high-school student, and still more the college student, shows a more intricate development of major and supporting hypotheses as the picture clarifies, hypotheses that are continually checked against the data of looking.

From the four-year-old's lack of differentiation to the college student's structured integration, there is a familiar theme of development. Differentiation of components in perception takes place, just as it does in motor responses, in language, and in concept formation, until a phase of apparent fragmentation appears. Performance in terms of adult criteria may even worsen as the units of a task are practiced at the expense of the task as a whole. In perceptual recognition of new instances of a familiar category, fragmentation is best seen in the parade of unrelated hypotheses offered by the five-year-old. He has, however, gained on the four-year-old, who sees one undifferentiated thing at a time (although he may talk up a storm). A further step in differentiation is taken by the nine-year-old, who can distinguish more successfully between hypotheses that fit the picture and those that do not. At the same time, the ability to integrate the two dependent variables in recognition—the visual stimulus and the memory store—continues to grow, perhaps reaching a culmination only in adulthood.

The growth of integration makes possible the maximal use of the information in a complex stimulus. An inferential structure can be built up which relates various aspects of a picture to an integrated set of hypotheses. At the same time, this very structure has a conservative effect on the interpretation of the stimulus: it resists change. The increase with age in the span of integration improves the recognition of complex materials, but this gain is offset to some extent by the self-maintaining characteristics of good structures, since on occasion the good structure is in fact wrong.

The account here rendered of the development of recognition has immediate bearing on a host of questions raised in the opening theoretical chapters and in the two preceding reports of experiments on equivalence and information seeking. Is there, for example, any inkling of whether the child's perceptual experience is organized in a fashion to permit its ready translation into a linguistic form? Is the young child's insensitivity to perceptual anomaly and incongruity related in any way to his weakness in being able to spot semantic anomaly in speech samples? Does his near equality with adults in recognizing "simple" pictures that need no integration of features over time (although he is much weaker with complex ones that do) reveal his inability to organize experience hierarchically? Again, is the younger child's inability to cycle easily from "looking" to "guessing" the same sort of failure as in the Twenty Questions game where he deals with information as "sufficient unto the moment thereof?"

These questions are better reserved for the final chapter, when these and other issues still to be raised can be seen in a common perspective.

CHAPTER 6

On Conceptual Strategies

David R. Olson

$\mathbf{M}$ost studies of problem solving in children characterize the behavior of the preschool child as receptive or respondent to stimuli, while the behavior of the older child appears to be determined far more by the plans or hypotheses the child generates, rather than by immediate stimuli. The transition, we have urged, depends upon the development of representational systems. And one of the important aspects of such development is the shift to symbolic or linguistically mediated representation. Luria (1961, p. 22) puts it well: "Once taken into the system of verbally formulated links the stimulus becomes not a mere signal but an item of generalized information, and all subsequent reactions depend more on the system it is taken into than on its physical properties."

In previous chapters it has been suggested that the child's cognitive development involves the successive appearance of more powerful modes of representing experience, beginning with the enactive and later augmented by ikonic and symbolic systems, and that these permit the child to move increasingly beyond the stimulus to the nature of the setting of the stimulus in a broader domain.

Particularly with the development of symbolic representation the child masters "higher order techniques for processing information by consecutive inferential steps that take one beyond what can be pointed at" (Bruner [1964] p. 14). The appearance of such symbolic representation has enormous effects, as we have seen in the preceding chapters, on the way children tackle problems. Indeed, there is interesting evidence presented in passing in those chapters that the strategies employed by children change drastically as the

135

more powerful tools of symbolic representation become available to them.

The present chapter deals directly with the issue of strategies and their development. A decade ago, Bruner, Goodnow, and Austin (1956) first examined the nature of strategies in some detail—the nature of the sequence of decisions made by a subject in attempting to delimit a concept. The solution of concept-attainment problems, it turned out, could be more clearly understood as a systematic sequence of hypotheses than it could in terms of specific, single responses. The three major strategies described in that work were: (1) *simultaneous scanning*, in which subjects attempted to deal with the task of attaining a concept by generating and evaluating all possible hypotheses at once and at each presentation of new information; (2) *successive scanning*, in which subjects worked on a single hypothesis at a time and examined subsequent presentations only in terms of that hypothesis; and (3) a *focusing* strategy, in which subjects dealt not with specific hypothesis but rather with constraints on the features that a correct hypothesis would have to take into account.

When a subject is accumulating information to solve a problem, the questions he asks or the hypotheses he tests are determined by several considerations. Among these are the complexity of the problem, the amount of certainty required, the "pay-off" or cost involved in each question, and, as we have seen in preceding chapters, the person's basic orientation to problem solving.

Surely the child's mode of representation should affect his strategy, that is, the pattern of hypotheses or decisions he makes en route to problem solution. The strategy used by a child who represents his world ikonically should be qualitatively different from that of a child capable of symbolic representation. One would expect, for example, that the more ikonic child would test hypotheses "directly," in the sense of checking whether an instance "pointed" to the correct solution. He would be likely to test one image at a time as to what the correct solution is. As in the Kuhlman (1960) experiments mentioned in the first chapters, we would expect such a child to operate, so to speak, in an "image space" rather than in a conceptual one.

As symbolic representation comes to be handled more competently by the child, we should expect that information would be less tied to specific instances or images, that a "conceptual space" would replace (or augment) the earlier "image space," and that encounters with new instances would be used to decide among alternative hypotheses rather than to check the "correctness" of a single image.

That is all we need consider by way of introduction. The significance of the forms of representation will become more precise in the context of the experiments to be reported.

AN EXPERIMENT

Some ninety-five children served as our subjects, about equally divided into threes, fives, sevens, and nines. About half of them came from the Boston suburban area, the other half from Halifax, Nova Scotia. They were assigned at random to two experimental groups, as will presently be explained. The relevant vital statistics about the children are contained in Table 1.

The task set the children involved determining which one of several alternative patterns on a board was "correct." To understand how "correctness" was defined we must say a word about the apparatus. It was a "bulb board" consisting of five rows and seven columns of red light bulbs, each one-half inch in diameter and set one-half inch apart. The bulbs were mounted on a uniform gray surface. Normally the bulbs were off and in that state were a dark red color. If a bulb were part of a prearranged pattern on the board, it would light up when pressed, and go off again when released. When lit, the bulb was a brilliant "instrument-panel" red. Bulbs that were not part of the prearranged pattern remained dark even when pressed. Manual switches at the rear of the board made it possible to set any pattern desired. Each time a bulb was pressed, the fact was recorded on an Esterline-Angus recorder. Masks could be placed over the bulb board to reduce the size of the matrix of bulbs from 5 by 7 to any alternative numbers of bulbs—in this case to matrices of 5 by 5, 3 by 3, and 1 by 4. A drawing of the apparatus appears in Figure 1.

TABLE 1
Number and Ages of Children in the Experiment

	Free Condition			Constrained Condition		
Age	Number	Mean Age	Standard Deviation, Months	Number	Mean Age	Standard Deviation, Months
3	10	3:10	3	10	3:9	4
5	10	5:3	4	15	5:2	5
7	10	7:7	4	15	7:7	3
9	10	9:3	6	15	9:3	7

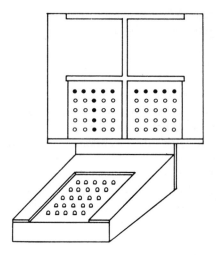

Figure 1. Apparatus used in the experiments.

Each child (they were tested individually) was presented at each trial with one, two, or more alternative models or diagrams mounted above the bulb board. The models contained possible patterns of lighting bulbs on the board. The child's task was to determine which was correct. or, in the case of the single model, whether it was correct. Bright red circular spots corresponded to the bulbs that would light up when pressed; dark gray spots represented the bulbs that would remain unlighted. The dimensions of the models were always identical to those of the bulb board itself. On each trial, only one of the alternative models correctly represented the pattern that would light up when pressed.

The children were introduced to the task by being shown first the correspondence between a single model and the bulb board. Then a series of problems were presented in which two diagrams at a time were mounted in front of the child and he was required to choose, with a minimum number of presses, which of the two models corresponded to the bulb board. They worked at each task until they had solved the problem or until, in the judgment of the experimenter, they were making no progress toward solution. If a child appeared to be guessing or showing signs of doubt, the experimenter reminded the child what the task was and urged him to work for the correct answer. Since our major concern is with the strategies or the sequences of bulbs pressed, the eventual solution of the problems was only indirectly relevant. The atmosphere of the task was to encourage the children to keep trying.

Of the various problems set the children, three have been selected for detailed analysis here to show as clearly as possible the differences between children of different ages. Others will also be treated, but not in such fine detail.

Problem A was given on the 3 by 3 board and involved two alternative models, one resembling an inverted T, the other a single bar across the bottom of the board. The inverted T was always correct. Using X to indicate the illuminated bulbs and O the others, the patterns were as follows (the one on the left being correct):

$$
\begin{array}{ccccc}
O & X & O & \quad & O & O & O \\
O & X & O & \text{and} & O & O & O \\
X & X & X & \quad & X & X & X
\end{array}
$$

Problem B was given on the 5 by 5 board, again with two alternatives. One was an upright T and the other a horizontal row at the top of the board. The latter was always correct.

$$
\begin{array}{ccccc}
X & X & X & X & X \\
O & O & O & O & O \\
O & O & O & O & O \\
O & O & O & O & O \\
O & O & O & O & O
\end{array}
\quad\text{and}\quad
\begin{array}{ccccc}
X & X & X & X & X \\
O & O & X & O & O \\
O & O & X & O & O \\
O & O & X & O & O \\
O & O & X & O & O
\end{array}
$$

Problem C was presented on the 5 by 5 matrix and required the selection of one of three alternatives: an upright T, and inverted T, and a ⊥ which "shared" the midcolumn and one-half the top and bottom rows with the alternative diagrams. This last alternative was the correct one.

$$
\begin{array}{ccccc}
X & X & X & O & O \\
O & O & X & O & O \\
O & O & X & O & O \\
O & O & X & O & O \\
O & O & X & X & X
\end{array}
\quad
\begin{array}{ccccc}
O & O & X & O & O \\
O & O & X & O & O \\
O & O & X & O & O \\
O & O & X & O & O \\
X & X & X & X & X
\end{array}
\quad
\begin{array}{ccccc}
X & X & X & X & X \\
O & O & X & O & O \\
O & O & X & O & O \\
O & O & X & O & O \\
O & O & X & O & O
\end{array}
$$

All three problems involve overlapping patterns. We can distinguish in each problem three kinds of bulbs. There are those that are off the pattern of any of the alternative models; these we shall refer to as "off-pattern" positions; they are redundant, carrying no useful information. Of those positions that fall on the alternative set of patterns, we can distinguish redundant positions that go on for all the alternative models, and informative positions that go on or stay off on only some of the alternative models. In short, then, there are *off-pattern redundant positions, on-pattern redundant positions, and on-pattern informative positions.*

A correct solution to a problem with two alternatives requires a minimum press of one informative bulb, and for a three-alternative problem, a minimum of two informative bulbs.

The same set of problems was presented to all the children. The children were equally divided between two experimental conditions: one did the problems under "free" conditions, the other under "constraint." The children who went "free" were permitted an unrestricted choice of bulbs to solve the problem, provided that "you find the correct answer with as few trials as necessary and that you point to the correct answer as soon as you know it." Children were, in effect, free to use any strategy or appoach they preferred. The "constrained" children were permitted to press only one bulb at a time. After each press the experimenter asked, "Now do you know which of the pictures is the correct one?" If the child did not, the experimenter asked, "Would you like to press one more bulb to find out for sure which is the correct picture?" The procedure was designed, of course, to encourage the most economical or informative strategy of which a child was capable. The "constrained" children were permitted to press one bulb at a time until they had located enough information to solve the problem and had pointed to the correct diagram. In principle, two conditions were employed to determine the difference between what children at various age levels *would* do if left free and what they *could* do when pressed.

THE EMERGENCE OF STRATEGIES

We shall examine the results in two ways. One is in terms of *achievement*—how well the children succeeded in solving the problems, how success relates to age, and so on. Such analyses are based, of course, on grouped data and averages and provide useful if limited information. A second approach emphasizes the *process* of problem solving: the strategies employed by individual children on individual problems. Of necessity, there are aspects of such an analysis that are more "subjective" or arbitrary, for it is not always completely apparent what a child has in mind over a series of presses.

We shall necessarily move back and forth between these two approaches. We begin with an analysis of the bulbs pressed by the children while attempting to solve the problems. Inferences regarding strategies may be drawn from these results. If, for example, the children press bulbs that fall on pattern more often than could be expected by chance, we can infer that the children are at least following the models. The question would be which ones of the on-pattern bulbs do they favor? And in what order? From data such as these, strategies can be reconstructed.

Consider first the primitive approach of the youngest children, the *Search Strategy*. It can be described as a quasi-systematic search of the board for bulbs that will light up. The search of any particular child can be shown to be nonrandom, for not all the bulbs are pressed with equal frequency. Edge bulbs predominate. There are, moreover, two ways to show the systematic search pattern of these children. There is first, the occurrence of runs of from four to over fifteen neighboring bulbs in a sequence that could hardly be random. On Problem B, for example, nineteen out of twenty of the youngest children made such runs ranging from three to twenty-seven consecutive presses, with a median of six per run. If, moreover, the bulbs were being pressed at random, we would not find such a high predominance of corner bulb presses followed by the pressing of an adjacent bulb: in fact, the frequency of such adjacent sequence is wildly beyond chance. Children, in short, even young ones, are poor random generators. But we call their performance "quasi-systematic" because it has nothing to do with the nature of the patterns to be found.

What the three-year-olds are doing is best described as a somewhat orderly search of the board for bulbs that will light. As we shall see, the search is conducted quite independently of the diagrams mounted in front of the child. The plan for gathering information, in sum, does not emerge from the models presented the child. Let it be said at once that the older the child, the less likely he is to use this primitive approach—of which more presently. For the three-year-olds who use the strategy, a successful solution is infrequent, but before that matter can be pursued we had best examine some of the other strategies.

By five years of age, a striking and pervasive change occurs in the children's mode of responding, particularly when their choices are "free." While the younger subjects have searched the board in a manner independent of the alternative models, the five-year-old tried out each model successively, independently of what he had tested before or would test next, and he tried it out in its entirety against the bulb board to see which one matches. We call this the *Successive Pattern-Matching Strategy*. Its salient feature is its almost total concentration

upon on-pattern bulbs, redundant and informative alike. When a
Search Strategy is in force, on-pattern bulbs are pressed no more frequently than off-pattern ones (save for the tendency of some three-
year-olds to return to a row that lights up). In successive matching
(and a still more sophisticated strategy to be described) off-pattern
bulbs are rarely pressed. One would expect by rule of chance that
about a third of the bulbs pressed on Problem A would be on-pattern,
and a bit over a half on Problem B. For children five and over, these
figures are always in excess of eight in ten, and often over nine in
ten (Figure 2).

Another marked change begins around seven. What appears now

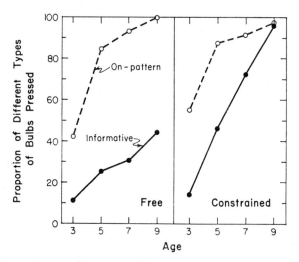

Figure 2. Proportion of different types of bulbs pressed on single problems
(free and constrained).

is the *Information-Selection Strategy*. It develops first in response to
the constraint imposed on bulb-pressing in one of the two conditions.
Recall that the children in this condition are told to select one bulb
that will tell which alternative is correct. Only if he is unable to
choose the correct model with certainty is he permitted his next
choice of a bulb. Information Selection shares with Pattern Matching
a preoccupation with on-pattern bulbs. But increasingly, these are informative on-pattern bulbs. It is not age alone, however, that accounts for this increased power of strategy; rather, it is the response
of older children to the conditions in the constrained procedure. This
is also plain in Figure 2.

The difference between constrained and free conditions is nowhere better illustrated than in the speed with which each condition leads subjects to their first informative bulb. The data are set forth graphically in Figure 3. The two conditions produce virtually no overlap in their distributions of responses.

There is still another fairly direct way of checking on the advent of Information Selection. It is by determining whether a child, once he has pressed his first informative bulb, does in fact now have the information in a form that he can use to solve the problem. The data for both our problems are summarized in Figure 4. In effect, the older the child, the more likely he is to solve the problem directly upon

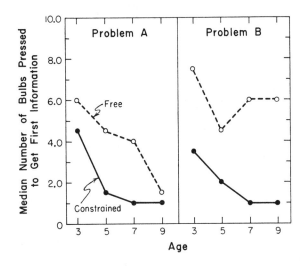

Figure 3. Median number of bulbs pressed to get first information.

achieving the minimum information necessary for that solution. And as before, constraint improves this likelihood strikingly. Note too that, to put it figuratively, a five-year-old operating with constraints imposed will perform in an informationally more efficient fashion than will a seven-year-old operating freely. This suggests (although it is a speculative matter) that perhaps the effect of years is to internalize informational constraints. It may be that at the base of such internalization is the sort of hierarchical structure discussed in Chapter 4 in connection with the use of questions for gathering information.

One final matter before we turn to the detailed analysis of individual performance: the amount of time required by children of differ-

ent ages in choosing bulbs to press. This suggests some interesting
things about the issue of "internal" and "external" constraints. For one
thing, there is not much by way of change in time required choosing
the bulbs as far as the free condition is concerned (Figure 5). It either
declines slightly, or remains rather constant. The sharp change is under
conditions of imposed constraint, in the time needed to choose a next
bulb that may be the last. Between three and five there is almost

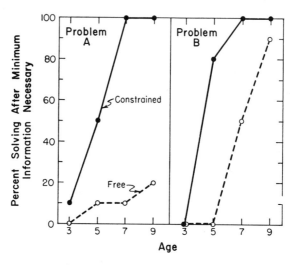

Figure 4. Percent of children solving problems after obtaining the minimum
information necessary for solution.

a tripling in the time taken. But interestingly enough, while the three-
year-old takes just about the same amount of time to choose, whether
free or constrained, the five-year-old requires more than four times
as much time under the constrained condition than when he is free
to choose. The same thing holds for the seven-year-old. By age nine,
however, the difference between constrained and free choice (for this
set of problems) begins to diminish very strikingly. For now the nine-
year-old is already operating with internal constraints, which are thoroughly mastered; these internalized operations ran off as smoothly and
effectively as the externalized ones employed by the "free" nines.

   The three patterns—that of the threes, of the fives and sevens, and
of the nines—provide vignettes of the strategies: Search, Successive
Pattern Matching, and Information Selection. In Search, with no guidance from the alternative models, time is no consideration. One
searches, and the time needed is simply the time to pick a handy

bulb to press. In Pattern Matching, the free condition is simply a matter of choosing bulbs that are on-pattern, and this the fives and sevens have mastered. Constraint forces them to use a strategy which they control rather poorly and do not use habitually. But by age nine Information Selection has become second nature enough, and the times required under both free and constrained conditions are again within a close range.

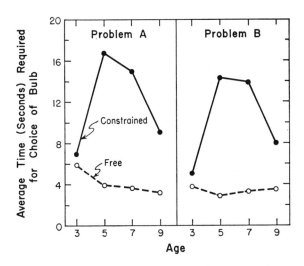

Figure 5. Average time (seconds) required for choice of bulb.

INDIVIDUAL STRATEGIES

Consider the three strategies in detail as we find them, not in "average data," but in the behavior of individual children. Each strategy can be described in terms of certain hallmarks.

Search:
a. bulb presses are independent of the model provided;
b. off-pattern bulbs are as likely to be pressed as on-pattern ones;
c. since no particular bulbs are recognized as informative, this strategy frequently fails to lead to a solution.
Successive Pattern Matching:
a. bulbs are pressed that are part of the pattern suggested by one or both of the models;
b. on-pattern presses are no more likely to be informative than re-

dundant, and the one type is no more likely to come first than the other;

c. subjects begin by pressing bulbs of one pattern, whether or not these bulbs will permit discrimination between diagrams;

d. an attempt is usually made to trace out the entire pattern;

e. if a pattern is tried and found to work it may be selected even without considering the alternative;

f. because the entire pattern is tested, subjects require a larger number of trials to solution;

g. because the problem is externalized, the time required per trial is relatively small.

Information Selection:

a. bulbs on-pattern are pressed more than those off-pattern;

b. on-pattern informative bulbs are pressed earlier and oftener than on-pattern redundant ones;

c. because the problem is internalized, the amount of time required per trial is relatively large.

Using these criteria, we sorted the children into three categories according to their strategies on the two problems: Search, Pattern Matching, and Information Selection. Because eighty-five of our ninety-five subjects followed the same strategy on the two problems (itself a rather striking tribute to their strategic consistency) there was little difficulty in classification. For the others, their entire protocols, involving all problems, were examined by two independent judges using the criteria to determine the prevailing strategy. They agreed 94 percent of the time in classifying one hundred eighty problems done by subjects. In the few cases of disagreement, the protocols were re-examined until an agreement was reached.

The picture that emerges is very much in congruence with what came from the analysis of group data. There are plainly marked and reliable changes that occur with growth (Figure 6). One of the most striking changes takes place between three and five, as we have already noted, and it is closely related to the growth of Pattern Matching. But there are also some striking changes between five and seven, best illustrated by the peaking and decline of Pattern Matching around the fifth year and the surge forward of Information Selection (under constraint) at age seven.

There is a striking oppositeness about Pattern Matching as the strategy of the free-choice condition and of Information Selection under constraint. Among the fives, for example, all those who used Pattern Matching in the free situation succeeded, though it just begins to ap-

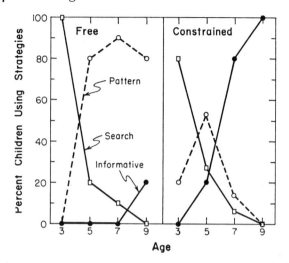

Figure 6. Percent of children using search, pattern, or informative strategies on simple problems.

pear at this age. And among the sevens, when Information Selection makes its first appearance under constrained conditions, all who use it also succeed.

In sum, then, the close study of individual records gives a realistic concreteness to the picture of strategies we have been drawing. The strategies are there; they are programs for finding and using information in certain specified ways: by encounter, by the search for matching images, and by the analysis of information (in the information-theory sense of that word).

STRATEGIES ON A COMPLEX PROBLEM

The performance of children on the more complex problem (Problem C) should provide some indication of the viability of the three strategies. Recall that Problem C presented three alternatives, in which all the models partially overlap one another. At least two decisions in selecting bulbs are needed for a correct solution.

Using the criteria already described, we classified the individual protocols on Problem C according to strategy. Performance on this problem was very similar to that on simpler problems, the only difference being that fewer younger subjects develop Information Selection in response to the constraint condition (Figure 7). In the main, the

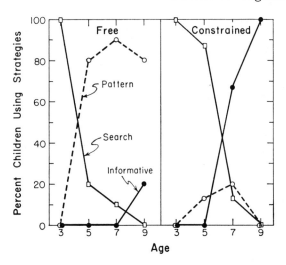

Figure 7. Percent of children using search, pattern, or informative strategies on complex problem.

TABLE 2
Percent of Children Solving Problems and the Median Number of
Bulbs Pressed before Solution

		Problem A		Problem B		Problem C	
Age	Condition	Trials	Percent of Success	Trials	Percent of Success	Trials	Percent of Success
9	free	5.0	100%	6.0	100%	9.5	100%
	constrained	1.0	100%	1.0	100%	2.0	93%
7	free	5.5	100%	9.0	100%	11.5	100%
	constrained	1.0	100%	1.0	100%	4.0	93%
5	free	8.0	100%	11.0	100%	15.0	100%
	constrained	4.0	80%	7.0	70%	...	30%
3	free	...	40%	...	30%	...	0%
	constrained	...	30%	...	20%	...	0%

children do about as well as on the simpler problems—all over five reaching a solution under free conditions, and none under that age. Pattern Matching, interestingly enough, leads to the solution of the complex problem just as well as it did for the simpler problems. But the Information-Selection strategy used under constraint fares less well: at age five only 30 percent reach the solution of the complex problem under constraint, as compared to 70 percent under comparable conditions with the simpler problems (Table 2). Pattern Matching, once developed, seems sufficiently viable to deal with more complex problems. The Information Selection, on the other hand, is somewhat easily swamped by our increasing the number of sequential decisions necessary for solution. This finding suggests in what measure the strategy of Information Selection is not yet consolidated among the middle groups of children.

As might be expected from this result, the complex problem produces much the same kind of on-pattern responding at the different ages (Figure 8), again underlining the viability of Pattern Matching under complex conditions. Again, what suffers is the Information-Selection strategy, and this can be seen on the same figure in the failure of the fives to concentrate their on-pattern choices on the informative bulbs.

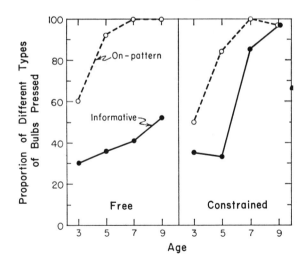

Figure 8. Proportion of different types of bulbs pressed that are "on-pattern" or informative on the complex problem.

The difficulty of Information Selection is illustrated by one child who looked at the three alternative models and selected an informative bulb on the first press. This bulb provided the information that the correct answer must be M1 or M2. He then selected a second informative bulb, this one providing the information that either M2 or M3 was correct. But the child had now forgotten that his first bulb press had already led him to exclude M3. His inability to combine the information from the two presses led him to press four other informative bulbs before he solved the problem. Again, it would seem that the location and utilization of information might best be considered independently. One is struck, moreover, by the self-same difficulty of children working a two-step information problem such as this one, and that of children trying to use the information obtained in playing the game of Twenty Questions. The structure for combining information sequentially is either not yet developed or it is simply not well enough managed.

SOME OBSERVATIONS AND CONCLUSIONS

One is struck, looking at the behavior of our children in the large, by the fact that there is a very large gap between what children conventionally do and what they are capable of doing. Constraining the children to a more careful use of information leads them to far more sophisticated strategies than we would have anticipated from observing their behavior in the absence of this constraint. It is hard to find problems that are impossible for a child, given some coaching and some external aids.

What did the strategies require? The first requisite for the development of any appropriate strategy was the ability to "map" alternative models on the bulb board. Doing this may be more complex than simply seeing the correspondence between a model and the board. Could children have an image of the model that they could impose on the board without verbally encoding it? To some extent, yes, but to a limited degree. If a model is set near the board, those children not capable of mapping will press the bulb closest to a red mark on the model. The result can be a reversal: a red mark at the *bottom* of a model *over* the board may lead a young child to press the nearest bulb at the *top* of the board. Mapping itself is something of a skill, as we know from Piaget's work (1962). But coaching can help the child, though seemingly through the intervention of language. If a three-year-old can be led to say, "These are at the bottom," in describing the model, he can move to the bottom of the bulb board without error. Parts of the model that are easily encoded in terms of "top" or "bottom" or "this side" can then be handled, even if the model is set at some distance from the board. With this aid, the child on occasion can even copy the model, though it has been presented and then removed. It is interesting that children have an easier time finding patterns that are inscribed on the outer border of the bulb board than located in interior columns and rows—suggesting the extent to which they use such landmarks.

It seems, then, that the child must learn some way of abstracting a model of a thing from the real thing—must learn to use a "diagram" to guide his action. Minskava (Luria [1961], note p. 36) has shown that three- and four-year-olds can do tasks requiring the practical manipulation of simple levers to reach a goal inaccessible directly. When the whole system is presented in picture form, however, the children are helpless. And there is ample evidence, too, that diagrams and even pictures require practice before they can be used as substitutes for the "real thing."

A child may grasp correspondence between board and model and yet be unable to press the bulbs depicted in the model. One four-year-old was shown a model having a T-pattern. He correctly identified the places on the model that stood for light and those that did not. Asked to press the bulbs on the board that would light up, he was not guided at all by the model. When the experimenter asked, "Do these come on?" indicating a row on the model, the child would say, "I'll see," and he would press the indicated bulbs. Indeed, we have cases where the child can clearly discriminate whether a model corresponds or does not correspond to the pattern of lights on the bulb board—with all the relevant lights lit up simultaneously or successively. Yet, the child is unable to *reproduce* the pattern depicted on the model. Obviously (as in speech) there is a striking difference between *recognition* and *reproduction*. (Indeed, it is particularly noteworthy with a diagonal pattern which young children cannot reproduce until around the fifth year. The reasons for this lag are currently being studied in detail by the present author.)

So there must obviously be not only the achievement of recognition of correspondence between a model and its referent, but also an achievement of the ability to reproduce. Both of these seem necessary if the child is to go from Search to Pattern Matching. To put it in the language of the opening chapters, there must develop some interplay between the image and the action it must guide and this interaction does not come automatically.

To move on to Information Selection requires, as we have already

seen, a large step forward. Specifically, it involves being able to deal
not with one image at a time, but rather with the properties or
features of several images simultaneously. Such a step corresponds to
the development in the Twenty Questions game when children are
able to ask "indirect" questions about constraints, rather than testing
hypotheses directly. Each depends on two achievements—the first
being the mastery of hierarchical organization, the second being
"feature analysis." Of the first much has already been said. To deal
with a set of patterns "informationally," the child must conceptualize
them in terms of the properties that distinguish between members of
the set. Such a conceptualization is necessarily hierarchical, for information that leads one to accept one subset and reject another then leads
one to the use of a feature to distinguish further among the remaining
alternatives.

To understand the construction of such a hierarchy, one must also
consider the question of "distinctive features." When a child begins
to use Information Selection, he is also beginning to select distinguishing features that can discriminate between a set of alternatives. To construct a hierarchy, he must isolate the defining features
that fit its structure. It is at this point that the child's mental processes
can be said to be guided *not* by individual events but by the ensemble
of possibilities of which they are members. E. R. Gibson (1966) and
Garner (1966) take it for granted that this is characteristic of cognitive
processes generally. We take the position here that it is a mode of
functioning that develops only gradually and only when ikonic representation has been buttressed by the kinds of symbolic processes we
have discussed here. It requires conceptualization of the domain of
alternatives.

A word, too, about the importance of externally imposed constraints
in leading children to improve their strategies, particularly to adopt
Information Selection. It appears that intellectual or informational
efficiency is willingly sacrificed for economy of effort. It is misleading
to assume a close relation between what a child tends to do and what
his mind is capable of. Note, however, that this tendency to economy
leaves adequate reserve for sudden complexities, such as required
in our Problem C, whereas the more efficient but demanding strategy
was easily swamped by added complexity. The mind appears automatically to break the information into "chunks" sized appropriately
to its level of development. Crutchfield's (1964) success in training
children to use information ("clues") suggests, however, that there
are many educational implications of this issue.

Finally, then, the component skills of mapping, locating, and utilizing information change with the growth of the child's powers of representation. It is their orchestration that produces a shift with growth from Search, through Pattern Matching, to Information Selection, a development that bears striking resemblance to performance in earlier experiments—to the hypothesis testing and constraint locating in Twenty Questions, and to the progress from pure guessing, through estimated guessing, to constraint guessing in the perceptual tasks. What is plain, however, is that while the component skills of mapping, locating, and using information are orchestrated, they seem to have an independent course of development that remains to be studied.

CHAPTER 7

On Multiple Ordering

Jerome S. Bruner and Helen J. Kenney[1]

W̶e turn to a problem that is by now familiar
to the reader. It is the question of the means by which the growing
child brings classificatory order into the world around him. The reader
will recall that in Chapter 2, in discussing the growth of symbolic
activity, we commented on the fact that there were certain "innate"
properties of symbolism that expressed themselves with apparently no
preparation in the syntactical structures of the child's language. One
of these is the property of *modification*. It involves, of course, the
formation of an intersect of properties: *hat* plus *green* to make *green
hat*. It is with one aspect of this problem that the present chapter
is concerned: with the way the child learns to grasp such "double
classification."

Many investigators have concerned themselves with this problem,
and for a variety of reasons, diagnostic as well as theoretical. To make
our own purpose clearer we concentrate at the outset on one of these:
the volume on the growth of classification by Inhelder and Piaget
(1964). They see the problem of the development of classification as
involving the formation of logical structures that allow the child to
coordinate the two aspects of classificatory behavior: *extension* by
which the members of a class are specified, and *intension*, by which
the common property defining the members is specified. In their words,

> Now the intension is based on relations of similarity, which means
> that it harks back to sensori-motor assimilations: even at the sensori-
> motor level there is association by similarity; it derives both from
> the perception of common qualities and from an elementary kind of
> abstraction which is intimately bound up with functional ends. On the

[1] We wish to express our thanks to Maxine Barrett Kuhl for her assistance with
these experiments.

154

other hand, the extension of concepts can only be developed with the aid of precise symbolism. Nor is it enough to possess the appropriate verbal signs; they must enter into an adequate system of quantification (p. 283).

This point of view is highly interesting, and their experiments shed some light on the matter. But it is, as noted in the first chapter, an instance of explaining a psychological problem in logical concepts. Their principal concern, and it is a deep and admirable one, is "to know why later forms of classification tend to approximate more and more closely to logico-mathematical structures," and they complain,

> The question of how structures are elaborated is not one with which psychologists in general have been much interested in logic, and this means that they have a tendency to accept what they regard as logically necessary as somehow "given," instead of posing a problem (p. 282).

We are, like Inhelder and Piaget, interested in how the child reaches the point of being able to deal with logical problems, but unlike them, we believe that logical behavior grows out of and is sustained by psychological processes. To define the psychological problem of classification as representing a difficulty in coordinating intensional and extensional definitions of class is to beg the question, it seems to us. What seems more interesting psychologically is their hypothesis about there being some problem in reconciling a sensorimotor or perceptual mode of operating (grouping by similarity) with a symbolic mode (where one has to bear in mind not single instances, but many of them simultaneously, as in extensive definition).

What we shall do in this chapter relates to this last objective, though it differs programmatically. That is to say, we too are interested in the relation of ikonic and symbolic operations, but in a more general way. In the opening chapters the point was made that for language to become an instrument for ordering perception and thought, both these latter processes had first to be ordered in a way that made it possible for the categories or operations of language to "fit" them. In short, there had first to be a symbolic transformation that corresponded to the rules of language. Chapter 6 provided a case in point, in which we observed how the child developed strategies that permitted him to deal simultaneously with an array of objects in terms of their features, rather than with each object or "model" as a percept or image by itself. Once this achievement is secured, the child is enabled to talk and "think with language" about ways of combining and recombining, dividing and subdividing the array. Without that step, all the words in the world are of little use to him, save as descriptors of individual instances.

Our objective, then, is to learn how a child comes to deal with two aspects of a situation at a time, and we have chosen as our instrument an experiment involving the most logically "complex" of classification tasks: the matrix, a task involving the joint ordering of two ordered arrays, the so-called multiplication of classes. We have chosen this task precisely because it entails simpler logical operations, for we believe that it is more likely to reveal the underlying psychological processes that a child depends on to solve the problem (or to fail in his solution in characteristic ways). We shall consider the problem in the abstract here, and in a later chapter try to show that in another cultural setting, some quite different processes might appear in the behavior of the children.

THE TASK

We designed a straightforward problem as our vehicle of study. It consisted of a set of nine clear-plastic beakers, to be arranged in a three-by-three matrix. The beakers varied three degrees in height and three in diameter. They were first laid out before the child on a ruled plaque of cardboard, as in Figure 1.

In order to acquaint the child with the matrix (turning now to

Matrix Procedure

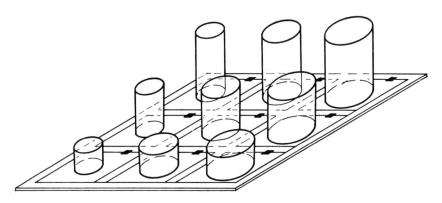

Figure 1. The Matrix.

the procedure proper), we removed first one glass, then two, and then three at a time, and asked the child to replace them. We also asked the child to tell us how the glasses in the columns and rows were alike and how they differed. Then we scrambled the glasses and had the child reconstruct, in effect *reproduce,* the entire arrangement by asking him to build "something like what was there before." After this we scrambled the glasses once more, but this time we placed the glass that was formerly in the southwest corner of the grid in the southeast corner (it was the shortest, thinnest glass) and asked the child again whether he could make something like what was there before, leaving the one glass where we had just put it. In short, we asked him to *transpose* the matrix, a task that could be accomplished only if the underlying rule or ordering principle of the matrix as constituted was understood.

Fifty children served as subjects, ten each of ages three, four, five, six, and seven. The procedure described was supplemented for the two younger age groups. The younger children were usually unable to handle the problems of double classification. After they had tried double classification, a comparable one-dimensional problem was given to them. Four glasses were used, varying in either height *or* diameter only. As with the other case, the task here was successively one of replacing within, then reproducing, and finally transposing the ordered one-dimensional array. A careful measure of the time needed for placing each glass in all the tasks was kept for the two youngest groups.

The gross findings can be quickly told. When asked to replace the glasses taken from the matrix, virtually all the older children (ages five, six, and seven) succeed. It is a different story with the younger ones. All manage to replace one glass correctly, but 30 percent reverse the positions when two glasses are removed, and 55 percent fail when three glasses (the diagonals of the matrix) are involved.

Just as the ability to replace items in the matrix increases with age, so too does the ability to *reproduce* the matrix in its original position after it has been scrambled. But the ability to perform this task lags behind performance on the replacement task at all ages.

Finally, the transposition task with the displaced glass proves most difficult of all. Again it is only among the oldest children that one finds as many with a perfect performance as in the reproduction task. The matter is summed up in Figure 2, where we see the lag graphically.

The data can also be described, perhaps more discriminatingly in

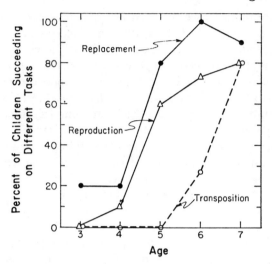

Figure 2. Percent of children succeeding on different tasks.

terms of the percentage of glasses put back on the board in a correct position in each of the three tasks (Figure 3).

Our task now is to account for the difference in performance at each age—why, if you will, one type of task is so much more difficult, or why at a given age a matrix can be "dealt with" in one way but

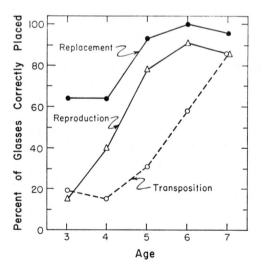

Figure 3. Percent of glasses correctly placed.

not in another, by reproduction but not by transposition, or by replacement and not by reproduction.

HOW MASTERY IS ACHIEVED

An analysis of the three tasks—replacement, reproduction, and transposition—very quickly explains their difference in terms of "perceptual" support. In the replacement task the child fills a perceptual gap. We aid him in doing so in the first replacement task by the very nature of the task—replacing a single beaker in a "hole" in the matrix. Then two glasses are removed, two glasses that are alike in either height or diameter, and the child must replace them. He usually succeeds, even at age three (seven in ten succeed). Failure in the task, rare though it is, comes from an error in matching the beaker to be replaced with the beakers around it. The child, tempted to work with a single dimension, will match the replacement beaker to the height of surrounding glasses, ignoring diameter, though it is the relevant cue. And so he fails, even though he looks steadily at the board and carries out his task with conspicuous diligence.

When he comes to replacing the three beakers in the central diagonal of the matrix, the child's task is made enormously more difficult, given his tendency to look for one-dimensional perceptual guidance. For again he uses the approach of "edge matching," placing each beaker next to one that matches it in a single respect. No surprise then that there is a striking difference in the proportion of successful replacements on the two tasks, the linear and the diagonal (Figure 4). We do not know why the child prefers to be guided by the height of the beakers, but this is usually his tendency, and if one were to judge his performance on whether the matrix was in order on this dimension, the differences between the older and younger children would disappear. What is important, in any case, is that the younger children are very perceptual in their orientation, and very much given to guidance by a single visual feature of the task.

The reproduction task is more difficult. The actual matrix, with all its visual support, is destroyed and scrambled. Now it must be reproduced. Note first that virtually every child who succeeded, in fact, reproduced the matrix in its original orientation with no transposing of dimensions. It was seemingly a copying task, in which the "template" seemed to be a memory image of the original matrix. Indeed, the children appeared to be remembering rather than figuring out. When asked what they were doing, they would often tell you that they were trying to remember where the glasses had been before.

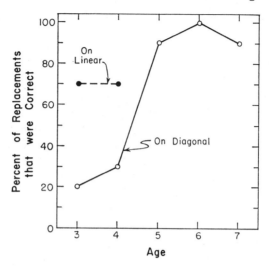

Figure 4. Percent of replacements that were correct.

Transposition is something else. Children below six rather typically begin to perform the task by trying to take the transposed glass from its new position and returning it to "where it belongs." At the very least, success depends upon their holding in mind either some version of the verbal formula—to quote a child, "They get fat in one direction and tall in another"—or what is far less likely, matching the transposed case to one of the eight depictable versions of a three-by-three double-classification matrix. It is interesting that only the oldest group of children were able to perform the task at all well. Indeed, a comparison of the three older groups is revealing. On the reproduction task a majority of the children were able to perform perfectly. But on the transposition task none of the five-year-olds and only a small fraction of the six-year-olds succeeded. Not until the seventh year is the task well within their reach.

It is probably the same image-bound procedure that leads children to success on the reproduction procedure that produces failure in transposition. For again we see the younger children trying to "copy" something they have in mind—an easy road to failure in transposition. Usually they will try to move the single transposed beaker to "where it belongs," i.e., its place in the original matrix. Or, when prevented from moving it, they may simply build the old matrix right around the newly positioned beaker. Another typical procedure is to handle the task by edge matching, placing one beaker at a time, matched in a single characteristic, to a beaker next to it.

SYMBOLIC STRUCTURE IN THE TASK

In the main, the foregoing describes how the children proceeded in these tasks and how well (or poorly) they did. What does this tell us about the organization of experience, how it related to the possible symbolic coding that makes transposition possible? We have some inklings already. For one thing, the younger children seemed to be guided by a rather nondecomposable memory image that guided their reconstruction of the matrix in much the same fashion as children "copied" models on the bulb board in the experiment of the preceding chapter. They put the beakers "where they had been." And, as we have already noted, this procedure failed to achieve transposition.

A second suggestion of the difficulty of younger children comes from some incidental observations. Recall that we asked each child to say how a pair of beakers were alike, and how they differed. No child had any difficulty in saying how two beakers *differed*. But often they had difficulty saying how they were similar. We were astonished that 41 percent of the three-year-olds named a *difference* in height or diameter when we asked them how two beakers placed before them were alike. The proportion drops to half that among the four-year-olds, and is rare after that. But, throughout, the responses to the question on similarity seem somewhat slower coming than the one on difference. This suggests to us that (contrary to Inhelder and Piaget [1947]), relations of similarity are not so easily formed in early life, or if early formed, then surely not easily abstracted from the perceptual whole. This means, in effect, that the young children could not easily hold one aspect of the beakers constant on the basis of similarity, while serializing them on the basis of differences in the other. For a child who cannot do this much easily, the verbal formula: "They get fatter in one direction and taller in the other" is of no more use than a description of a sunset to a sufferer from color blindness.

Indeed, it may well be that one requires a highly differentiated discrimination of similarity *and* difference in order to be able to use a verbal rule such as that just stated. We have checked on this hypothesis as follows. Three "linguistic modes" are used by the children in describing similarities and differences. One is *dimensional,* language being used to describe two ends of a continuum, as in "fat" and "skinny," or "tall" and "short," to use two very

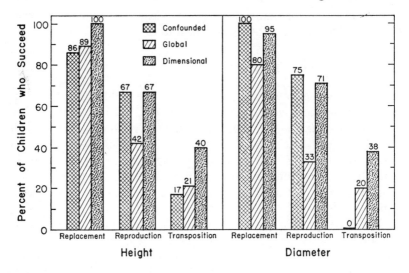

Figure 5. Percent of children who succeed in replacement, reproduction, and transposition using confounded, global, or dimensional language.

common dimensional pairs. A second mode was *global* or un-differentiated, as when "big" and "little" were used to describe differences in either height or diameter. Finally there is *confounding*, in which one end of a continuum is described dimensionally and the other globally, as when a child says of two glasses that one is "tall" and the other "little," and of two others that one is "fat" and the other "little."

The language children use is associated with how well they carry out their tasks. For purposes of analysis we grouped all fifty children studied and examined what kind of linguistic mode they used and how they performed on the three tasks (Figure 5). Global language (associated principally with younger children) appears to diminish the quality of performance on all tasks, whether replacement, reproduction, or transposition. Confounded language has a striking association with failure on the transposition task, i.e., if a child shows confounding, he is almost sure to fail on the task. But also note well that, while dimensional language is a good prognosis of success in the transposition task, it by no means guarantees such success.

One other point about the organization of experience into a form amenable to translation into a verbal rule has to do with temporal integration. Watching the two youngest groups of subjects, one gains the impression that each placement is an act unto itself. In the replacement task involving two beakers, for example, a first beaker is replaced without regard for how the second has to fit in. In a nutshell, a verbal rule would be useless at this age simply because their temporal span does not match the requirement of going beyond the single placement.

To sum up matters at this point: younger children tend to be strongly guided by the perceptual nature of tasks, and by only a single perceptual feature at a time. As they grow older, they seem no less perceptual in their approach to our tasks, but they are now able to deal with several features of a task at once. But while (at age six, for example) they can reproduce complex perceptual displays, they are poorly equipped to do tasks that require a translation of a perceptual array into a verbal formulation of more general type. In a word, these are children who can do the perceptually supported replacement task but fail on reproduction and transposition. There are children who can reproduce but not transpose; and they can virtually always succeed on replacement. Finally, if a child succeeds in transposition, he will almost certainly achieve success in the other tasks. In these thirty children age five and over, there was only one who did not fit this pattern. We shall consider the younger children in this regard later in this chapter.

Another way of summing up matters is to describe the nature of the performance at each age level. A convenient way of doing so is in

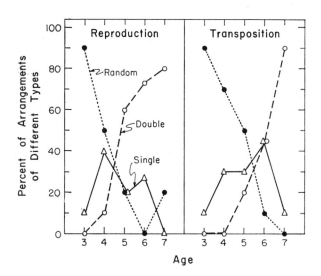

Figure 6. Percent of arrangements of different types.

164 — Studies in Cognitive Growth

terms of whether the arrangements made on the reproduction and transposition tasks achieved double classification, single classification (with ordering of only one variable, usually height), or apparent random ordering. The result of this analysis is presented in Figure 6. The picture is plain enough. Random ordering in response to these tasks starts high and drops to nothing by the sixth or seventh year. Single classification grows rapidly from three to four (for reproduction) and then declines, to be replaced by multiple ordering. The picture is the same for transposition, only delayed. Our supplementary observations of the two younger groups, using one-dimensional arrays, reinforces the finding that children can, by four, handle one-dimensional ordering quite well. But, and it is a big qualification, they cannot handle two dimensions, for the reasons mentioned earlier.

TIME AND TECHNIQUE

We had noted at the outset that children were timed. The results of the analysis of solution time, while not very revealing, can at least be described briefly. The distractibility and special vagary of the three- and four-year-olds were such that the timing of their performance provided little information, save that in general very quick and very slow reactions were usually the wrong ones. If we use the three older groups, the picture is even clearer. Arrangements of the random type are usually the fastest. If we leave these out, there is a negative correlation, indeed −0.7, between the quality of solution offered (as measured on our "scale") and the time required to reach a solution —the better the solution, the longer the time required. Time, then, can be taken as a measure of information processing.

REPRESENTATION OF THE TASK

Consider now how the children of different ages go about their task, particularly with a view toward clarifying the nature of representation. The very young children, the threes and fours, seem to "play their own game," a game consisting primarily in handling the glasses, moving them about on the grid, placing them in the center of the squares, and then looking at what they have done. When replacing glasses in the matrix, for example, they will tell you that the glasses should go where they put them because there were empty spaces for them. The relation of the replaced beakers to the component groups is not appreciated, and similarities among beakers are often attributed to the fact that pairs may be in the center of the squares or simply on the grid itself. Despite our best efforts, the task could not be grasped by our younger subjects, and they were so eager to begin manipulating the beakers, putting them here and there, that they could scarcely wait to begin.

The older children are strikingly different. In the reproduction task (at which most succeed) they uniformly produce a matrix of glasses that is positioned identically to the original display. And even those who do not reproduce the matrix exactly are obviously using the original orientation. Whatever else they may be doing, it is clear that these older children are copying an established image. They tell us that they put the glasses "where they were before." With the transposition task a further difference among the age groups appears. Before the age of six many children attempt to move the transposed glass back to "where it belongs." Failing this, they may try to rebuild the original, by edge-matching one beaker at a time to the transposed glass, working along a single row or column. The five-year-old, so well served by his imagery on the reproduction task, attempts its use again, and is thwarted by the transposition. Knowing how difficult it is to effect transformations on images, we are not surprised by his failure. But he seems to be surprised, often starting confidently and "petering" out. For the age of five seems to be a transitional stage. Imagery, while it cannot readily solve the problem as given, does allow a child to re-establish some of the constituents of the matrix, but imagery cannot handle their relation. It is this, we believe, that leads the five-year-old to start out with such confidence and end in so much confusion.

What makes the difference in the case of the successful six- and seven-year-olds? We believe there is a discontinuity in their handling of the task. The younger children treat the display as a picture or image. The older ones have translated that image into a form that can be subtly encoded into language, and have formulated a set of verbal rules that can guide them in producing transformations that include the required transposition. The two approaches are strikingly different.

We have already mentioned the child who "summed up" the matrix with the phrase, "It gets fatter going one way and taller going the other." This is a nice example, for it lays bare the striking substitutability gained by such a formulation. In the most concrete terms, there are now four ways in which "it" can get "fatter," and once one chooses one of them, there are still two ways left for "it" to get "taller." Imagery now can serve as a check—and it does. Older children often lean back and have a look at the result of their work before being fully satisfied that the reproduction has been accomplished. In the transposition task, the transferred beaker does, of course, reduce the substitutibility to two alternatives, but the crucial matter is not how *much* substitutibility, but rather whether the child's representation of the task permits *any* substitution.

Here is where the cost of imagery is so high. The children who try to "copy" the original as a means of solving the transposition task end in a muddle precisely because they cannot get any match between what they place on the board and what they have in their heads. You will often see a child, relying on such imagery, try first to place a beaker by edge-matching it to one already on the board, and then moving it to where it "should" be in the light of where it had been.

We have already commented on the fact that "having" the correct dimensional language helps the child toward a linguistic formulation of the display, but does not guarantee that he will be able to deal with transposition. Indeed, if the child can deal dimensionally with the language of both height *and* diameter, he is virtually sure to be able to cope with the problem. But "having" vocabulary, even organized in dimensional pairs, is not necessarily the same as using them in organizing experience or in ordering one's intellectual operations. That step, it would seem, requires further exercise. We refer to the fact that the children who fail on transposition can probably exercise the skills needed to succeed on that task—but only on simpler tasks. Analogies probably help very little, but we are reminded of the neophyte skier who can use his skis quite adequately on moderate trails, but does not yet know how to deal with steeper ones. Again, he cannot yet recognize what is demanded by the task.

To sum up, then, a study of how children represent complexly ordered arrays such as a two-dimensional one yields a variety of suggestive conclusions. One of them is that children of three and four generally go about the task with a great burst of manipulation, as if overt trial-and-error will reproduce a scrambled matrix or replace a pair or a trio of missing elements. They seem not yet able to form images or schemata that embody the ordered relation of two dimensions.

By the fifth year the child is able to develop an image of a two-dimensional array, and his efforts to reproduce it are quite effective. Once he must alter that image, however, it is apparent that he can deal with only a single dimension or grouping at a time and cannot relate these groupings to one another in a matrix. Even in the perceptually supported task of replacing beakers in the matrix, children have the most trouble with replacing the diagonal set that varies in two dimensions at once.

Finally, the six- and seven-year-olds achieve the capacity to render the matrix into a verbal or symbolic formula: one that is amenable to order-preserving transformations, including the spatial transposition we have used in this experiment. "Having" the proper language helps the child take this final step, but there is much that is still unexplained as to how the child progresses from merely having to knowing how to use. We incline to the view that what is needed for the child to take that step is organizing experience into a form that allows more complex language to be used as a tool not only for describing it but transforming it.

CHAPTER 8

On Relational Concepts

Jerome S. Bruner and Helen J. Kenney

By now the reader will have become very familiar with two hallmarks of the young child's ideas. In the first place, he is apt to base his notions of the world on some feature to which he can point directly. Necessarily, this leads him in his explanation of things to a heavy reliance upon their color or height or width. It also leads, as we have seen, to certain characteristic strategies in seeking information or in recognizing aspects of his environment—as in tasks described in previous chapters. Extended inferences, indirect information, nonsensory features of things are all eschewed. One further part of this pattern, a second hallmark, is the "one-track" tendency of the young child: his inclination to focus on a single aspect of the situation at a time. Both of these we have characterized as typical of early ikonic functioning.

In the present chapter we concern ourselves with examining some of the consequences of this mode of ikonic functioning for the mastery of ideas that cannot be reduced to fit the young child's mode—ideas that in their very nature cannot be expressed by pointing to a perceptible feature, and certainly not by pointing to a *single* such feature. Chief among such ideas are those that rely upon the grasping of *successive* and *related* items of information, as in the earlier discussion of obtaining information either through verbal questions or by physical search. We have seen how difficult such ideas and strategies are for the young child, and how his eventual grasp of them depends upon the child's shifting to another mode involving symbolic operations and a hierarchic structuring of information. A second and closely related kind of notion is one that depends upon a *relationship between perceptible features* in the world, a relationship that cannot itself be indicated by pointing. One of the most striking examples of such an "indirect idea" is the notion of a ratio—a quantitative relation between two or more features that remains invariant, provided that the relation is constant, and quite regardless of the absolute state of the component features. The idea of a physical proportion is typical of this class of ideas, and it is with this idea that we shall be concerned: with proportion as embodied in the question, which of two containers is fuller or which emptier.

In the case of proportion, looked at formally, there is an especially great difficulty for the child. Take the notion of which of two identical glasses is the fuller: one that is a third full or one that is two-thirds full. To appreciate proportion, one needs first to estimate the volume of the glass that is filled and relate it to total volume, again a ratio. Yet for all that may be said of such ratios, it is plain that in some primitive form the child can deal with "empty" at a very tender age, certainly long before he understands ratios, as when he turns his cup upside down after finishing his milk and proclaims "all gone." Indeed, the child has such a firm grasp of the idea, as we learn from the work of Braine (1963), that he converts it into a generalized pivot word when combinatorial grammar begins and pairs it with a host of other open-class words—*allgone mummy, allgone sticky,* when jam is washed off his hands, and so forth. And all this before the age of three. So, too, with *full,* usually handled by "spill" or "tippy top," and the like, again well before we might expect the child to be trafficking with ratios. However, these are binary terms as the child uses them, and it is plain that the child does not grasp what is meant by *fuller* or *emptier. Full* and *empty* are a pair of names for particular states, much as any other names applied concretely to things or definite states. It is instructive to trace the course of growth of these terms to their more adult usage to see how, in fact, the child gets to concepts that are not defined by ostensive rules.[1]

It is very likely the case that when the child must deal with ideas like *fuller* and *emptier* in a continuous way and not in the very simple binary fashion, he does so only if he can reduce them to the case

---

[1] Of such rules, Körner (1959) says, ". . . all or almost all human beings (after a certain stage in their development) accept what I propose to call 'ostensive rules.' A very simple example of such a rule would be conveyed if anybody said [with appropriate pointing gestures] that this and this and everything like it is to be called 'green,' the term being thereafter referred to as an ostensive predicate, and the particulars to which it is applicable as its bases" (p. 7).

in which "all other things are equal," in which the idea of ratio is replaced by a simpler idea that can in fact be rendered by ostensive definition. That can be done, of course, by reducing the comparison to the case in which the containers whose relative fullness or emptiness must be judged are identical. For then *fuller* can be reduced to deciding which container has, say, the highest water level, and the water level can be easily indicated by the end of a finger.

There must be some critical event along the way that leads the child to go from the partial and restricted idea of fullness to the proper notion of ratio, just as the child was led from the raw operationalism of "spilly" for *full* and "all gone" for *empty* to the continuous idea of a variable water level. It is these matters with which we are now concerned.

AN EXPERIMENT

The basic problem posed for the children in this experiment, on the surface, is a simple one: which of two vessels in a pair is fuller, and then which one is emptier. The experiment itself consists of paired comparisons of glasses that are presented two at a time, filled to varying degrees with ordinary water. In all, one hundred and sixty children served as subjects, forty children in each of the age groups of five, six, and seven, and twenty children each in the age groups of nine and eleven. Originally the study encompassed only the three younger age groups, but, when it became quite clear that by age five, a definite idea of "proportion," albeit an incorrect one, is already present, and that by age seven the children still had not grasped the idea in its proper mathematical sense, the two older groups were included in the study. The order in which the glasses were presented was fixed, as represented in Figure 1.

Note that the task begins with a very easy judgment involving two identical glasses filled to the same proportion. From there on it becomes more complicated by virtue of there being pairs that are made up of glasses of unequal volume and pairs that are equally or unequally full. Let it be noted, for future reference, that any two pairs of glasses can differ or be the same in the following respects:

(pF)   the proportion they are filled;
(pE)   the proportion they are empty;
(L)   their water levels;
(H)   the height of the glasses;
(W)   the diameter of the glasses;

(VF)   the volume of water they contain;

(VE)   the volume of empty space they contain.

Aside from the first two of these measures, which bear a complementary relation to each other, all the other measures are independently variable of one another, as well as independent of the first two indices. That is to say, a glass can have a higher water level than another

Ratio   Procedure

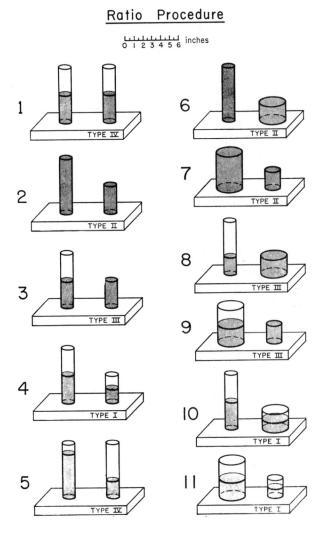

Figure 1. Pairs of beakers used in ratio procedure.

and contain a smaller or larger volume of water or a smaller or larger proportion of filled space, and so forth. And as is evident in the displays, this feature of independent variability was used in constructing the displays. All but the first two ratio measures can be "pointed at" in a single operation.

Not all combinations of features are used in forming the display pairs; rather they are of four types. In Type I (Displays 4, 10, and 11), glasses of unequal volume are partly filled but to an equal proportion. One can arrange the perceptual features of the pairs in such a way as to throw the perceptual factors either for or against a correct ratio judgment. Pair 11, for example, is one in which everything perceptual goes against a judgment of equally full: one of the glasses is taller, has a higher water level, is wider, and has a greater volume of water than the other does.

The Type II displays (Displays 2, 6, and 7 are the examples) have an unequal volume, but both glasses in the pair are filled to the top. Again, it is possible to bias perceptual indices for or against an equal judgment. The Type II displays share some of the properties of the old riddle: whether a pound of lead or a pound of feathers is heavier.

The Type III displays (Displays 3, 8, and 9) again contain pairs of unequal volume, in which one glass is fractionally full, the other completely full.

Finally, Type IV consists of a pair of identical glasses in which the only factor that differs is the water level (Display 5). In all other attributes there is complete equality.

As for the instructions and the tasks given the children, each of the three younger age groups—five, six, and seven—was divided into four even groups of ten children each. A first group was taken through the task in the fixed order, and their job was to say of each display whether the glasses were just as full or whether one glass was fuller than the other, and then to tell why they thought so. A second group went through the fixed order and was asked each time to indicate their judgment of fullness, and then to tell whether the glasses were just as empty, or whether one glass was emptier than the other, giving reasons for their judgments as they went along. A third group went through the same sequence of questions about fullness and emptiness, but was asked in addition whether the water was just as high in each glass or higher in one than in the other. They were asked only for their reasons for their full-and-empty judgments. Finally, one group went through the sequence, and it was asked of each pair which was fuller, which emptier, in which glass the water was higher, which glass was taller, and which glass was wider. Again, only the reasons for the first two judgments about each pair were solicited. The two older groups, ages nine and eleven, were asked only to give and justify judgments of fullness and emptiness, for reasons which will become clear shortly.

The rationale of these rather elaborate questions was this. Would alerting the children to the specific perceptual properties of the displays alter their judgments of proportion? Would any effect upon such judgments be produced by marshaling such perceptual cues as are useful or harmful in reckoning proportionality? Finally, would there be a relation between the child's judgment of fuller and his judgment of emptier? That about sets the procedural stage, and we may turn now to one "failure" in the results before considering in more detail how the children proceeded.

The "failure" was our attempt to produce "linguistic activation." The children who had been alerted, by questioning, to all the features of the display tended to do slightly, consistently, but insignificantly better than the others; but even that small result (even if statistically reliable) may have been due more to "slowing down impulsiveness" than to activation. In this sense, the effect would be as in the experiments with the bulb board; constraints imposed had the principal effect of slowing the child down to a pace at which he could process the information he was generating. Although we do not have evidence enough properly to interpret the ineffectiveness of verbal activation, in the present instance it seems to us to represent the general case. If there is nothing by way of structural experience or action for the verbal activation to relate to, it will simply not activate. In this experiment we were activating the children to attend to the *terms* that go into a ratio. They had no working structure into which to fit those terms. The activation, then, did not work.

THE MAJOR FINDINGS

Four aspects of the findings are of special interest. The first has to do with the bases for judgments of fuller and emptier in children of different ages. This in turn leads to a consideration of the extent to which perceptual factors operate in a judgment that, to be correct, must resist such factors. Then we shall consider the contradiction between one judgment and a next—what it means when a child says of one glass that it is both fuller and emptier than a second. And finally, we can assess more deeply why linguistic activation failed to achieve its expected result.

What is fuller and what emptier? If we consider first the Type I displays, in which glasses of unequal volume are filled an equal proportion, each halfway, and examine the responses to the "full" question, we find that 88 percent of the fives, 89 percent of the sixes, 71 percent of the sevens, 74 percent of the nines, and 31 percent of the elevens say that the taller glass with the higher water level in each pair is fuller. The relevant data are in Figure 2. But now consider the judgments made by the five age groups with respect to which glass in each pair is emptier (Figure 3). Here 66 percent of the fives say that the shorter glass with the lower water level is emptier, while only 43 percent of the sixes, 23 percent of the sevens, 31 percent of the nines, and 8 percent of the elevens make the same judgment. When the children are asked for their stated reasons for judging fullness and emptiness, the sevens and nines take "full" to mean more volume of water and "empty" to mean more volume of space. On the other hand, the younger children point to the level of the water, higher for "fuller" and lower for "emptier." In fact, as we shall see, the young ones take "fuller" to mean bigger in some undifferentiated sense, and "emptier" to mean littler—both referring to the water. To say that they *point* is perhaps too specific. Rather, they *wave* at the water, especially at its upper portion including its specific water level. It is only among the more advanced nines and the elevens that one gets an attempted or successful formulation of the ratio idea in terms of a relation between quantities. The matter wants a still closer analysis, but consider first what happens on the other types of displays.

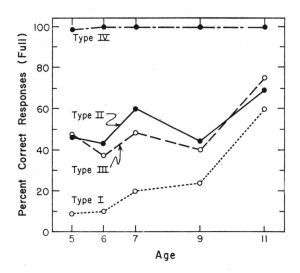

Figure 2. Percent judgments of which of two beakers are fuller that were correct.

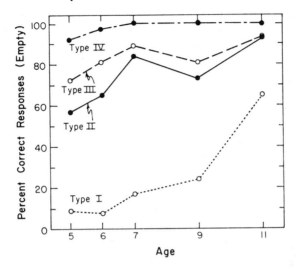

Figure 3. Percent of judgments of which two beakers are emptier that are correct.

Turning now to the Type II displays, in which both glasses are filled to the top, 46 percent of the fives, 43 percent of the sixes, 60 percent of the sevens, 44 percent of the nines, and 69 percent of the elevens make the correct judgment of equality as to fullness. Almost without exception, the erroneous judgment selected the larger glass. Again "fuller" means bigger volume of water, bigger glass, or higher water level. But "emptier" cannot mean "more empty volume" because there is no empty volume in the glasses. Now 86 percent of the seven-year-olds and 93 percent of the elevens call the two glasses equally empty. The younger children, on the other hand, faithful to their criterion that emptiness means littleness, choose the smaller volume of water. Some 41 percent of the five-year-olds call the smaller of the glasses emptier. Again the data are in Figures 2 and 3.

With the Type III displays, an added factor enters. One glass is full to the top, the other fractionally full, but both glasses contain water that is up to the same water level. This display is much easier for all the children. For the "full" judgment, about half of the children under eleven are correct, although the six-year-olds (always more seducible by visual factors than either the fives or sevens are) are slightly less competent at this judgment. Virtually all the errors go in the direction of calling both glasses equally full and of justifying the judgment in terms of an equal water level. With respect to "empty" judgments, this task is much easier than the others, although the older children do better—72 percent correct for the fives, 81 percent for the sixes, 89 percent for the sevens, 81 percent for the nines, and 94 percent for the elevens. Errors in judging emptiness are justified either in terms of "littleness" or of water level—nearly three times as many such errors appear among the youngest children as among the older (Figures 2 and 3).

The Effect of Perceptual Factors. The degree to which perceptual factors contribute to the errors in judgment is, as we have already seen, very considerable. The picture can be drawn more sharply by taking into account how these factors operate. An inspection of the distribution of judgments of "fuller" indicate that three factors predominate either in giving perceptual support to correct judgments, or in misleading the children. The most important is water level: if these levels are equal, children tend to call the displays equal; and if they are unequal, they favor the higher as the fuller. A second factor is the volume of water, particularly if the water levels are equal. Equal volume predisposes to the judgment of equally full, unequal volume leads to a favoring of the greater volume. And finally, and particularly when given no basis for choosing between the first two, "reaching to the top" is a factor. If both beakers contain an equal amount of water, this judgment follows: if one is all full and the other partly so, then the former is favored.

Figure 4 shows the manner in which the three factors operate with respect to the eleven displays, which cues favor and which lead away from a correct judgment. The displays can then be subdivided into those in which all cues favor the correct judgment (1 and 5), those in which most do (6 and 8), those in which they are balanced (2 and 10), those in which most cues mislead (3, 7, and 9), and those in which all mislead. We would expect the number of correct judgments to conform to this order, and this turns out to be the case (Figure 5). It should be the case, further, that the older the child the less likely is it for perceptual factors to dominate his judgment in this way. In general, this also turns out to be the case—notably and reliably so, if we divide the children into those age seven and below and those over seven.

Unfortunately, the experiment is not designed in such a way as to pick up the interaction among the factors—holding constant certain factors while varying others, and so forth—so we must leave these details unexplained.

"Consistency" and "Contradiction." Consider now the relation between a judgment as to which glass is fuller, and one as to which

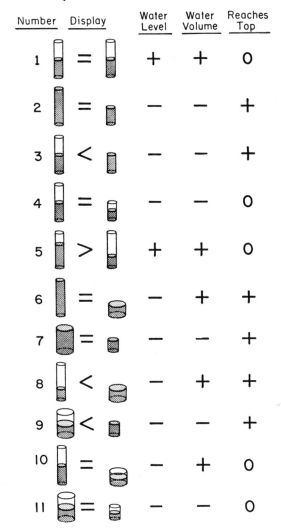

Number	Display	Water Level	Water Volume	Reaches Top
1	=	+	+	0
2	=	−	−	+
3	<	−	−	+
4	=	−	−	0
5	>	+	+	0
6	=	−	+	+
7	=	−	−	+
8	<	−	+	+
9	<	−	−	+
10	=	−	+	0
11	=	−	−	0

Figure 4. Attributes favoring (+), opposing (−), or neutral (0) with respect to correct judgment of the relative fullness of two beakers.

in a pair is emptier. These two judgments can be looked at in several ways. We can ask, first, whether the two judgments are both correct, whether only one is correct, or whether both are wrong. A glance at Figure 6 very quickly reveals that from age five through age nine only about a third of the children get both judgments correct. And, to some small degree, the "emptier" judgments are easier (principally

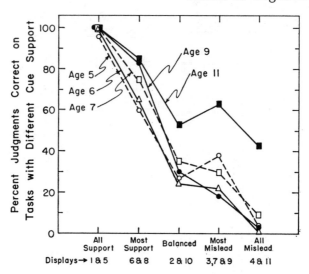

Figure 5. Percent judgments that are correct in tasks with different cue support.

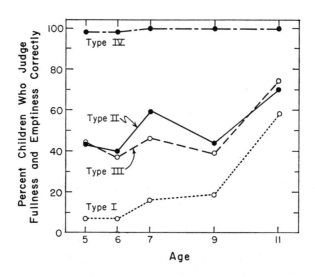

Figure 6. Percent children who judge fullness and emptiness correctly.

because the judgment is so much easier when one beaker is full to the top and the other not). Up to age eleven, the Type I displays (both partly full) are significantly more difficult than either those of Type II or III, and these in turn are more difficult than those of Type IV. At age eleven the difference all but disappears.

Now consider plain and contradictory errors. A contradictory error consists in calling two vessels equally full but one emptier, or the same vessel as both fuller and emptier. A plain error consists in calling one beaker fuller and the other emptier—both incorrectly. The proportion of errors that are contradictory, much to our astonishment, increases with age rather than decreasing, as one might have expected (Figure 7).

On all three types of display significantly more of the errors made by the older children are contradictory, most markedly in Type I and Type II displays, in which the percentages are of the order of 30 percent for the fives, 50 percent for the sixes, 70 percent for the sevens, 55 percent for the nines, and 75 percent for the elevens. Are older children less concerned with consistency? This explanation does not sit well with us, considering what else we know about children and their development. Another appears more reasonable: this holds the contradiction in logic to be a by-product of the way children of different ages apply criteria in judging what is full and empty.

An examination of the basis for judgment in the Type I displays

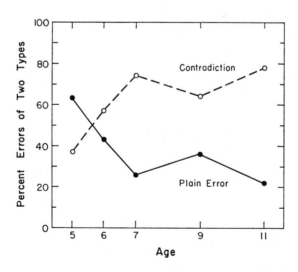

Figure 7. Percent errors of two types.

will make this clear. The correct judgment for these displays is that both glasses are half full and equal. All the children used much the same criteria for judging wrongly that one glass of the pair was fuller—the water level or "more water," criteria based on directly observable indices. Yet note the basis for judging "emptier" at different ages: to the older children who err "emptier" means the glass that has the larger volume of *unfilled* space, just as "fuller" means the glass that has the larger volume of *filled* space. They have developed some appreciation of the complementary relation of filled and empty space which, when consistently applied, leads them into logical contradiction, for, indeed, with this rule they can say serenely that, given a large glass and a small glass, both half full, the glass that is fuller is also emptier. For the larger member of the pair does indeed have the distinction of having both more filled space and more empty space.

The younger children, however, have a much more global approach. The glass that has more water is seen as such, and is usually described as "the water is more" or "bigger water." "Emptier" is judged by the same criterion. An emptier glass is one that has "less water" or "littler water." The younger children, operating with the equation of "littleness" and emptiness, are no more correct, but they end up by being consistent.

The bedevilment of the sevens and nines by their more complex rule of using filled-unfilled space as criteria for judgments of fullness and emptiness is clearly illustrated when they are presented glasses of unequal volume, with each member of the pair filled to the brim. Most of them, about 80 percent, make the correct judgment for "empty"—both are equally empty. But 36 percent of them will say at the same time that the larger vessel is the fuller. The younger children on the same set of displays maintain their seeming logic by judging the larger glass "fuller" and the smaller glass "emptier"—again "big" and "little."

What then accounts for the differences we have found between the younger and older children? We suggest that what is involved is that the children are at differing points en route from the ikonic to symbolic reckoning. The younger child differs from the older child in the number of attributes he attends to in these situations involving fullness and emptiness. It is quite clear that the younger child attends to one—the apparent amount of water; the older to two—the volume of filled space and the volume of empty space. The younger child attempts to apply a single variable to fit a contrast pair. The older child can dissociate the situation into two variables—filled space and empty space—but is not yet able to relate them to a third, the volume of the container itself. To accomplish this, the child must be able to detach himself from perceptual features in order to deal with a relationship. When the child can establish the relationship among all three terms—the amount of water, the amount of empty space, the volume of the container—he has a symbolic concept of proportion. The older child who is able to cope with several cues simultaneously is almost always the one who has some structure into which he can fit them.

There is one more thing to be noted about the handling of the displays by older and younger children. Older children, in justifying their erroneous judgments, tend to be somewhat more pluralistic about the criteria they use. In giving an erroneous judgment that one glass is fuller than another, they are likely to mention not only the amount of water but also the water level, or the height of the glass, or even the width of the glass when appropriate. The younger children, on the other hand, are more likely to have some single attribute as the chosen instrument for justifying a judgment. Older children—at least until age eleven, when they are able to coordinate the crucial relationships and state these economically—are not only considering both filled and empty space in their judgments, but also more attributes in general. We have computed the number of children who named several perceptible attributes as a basis for their "fuller" judgments. For all the Type I, II, and III problems, we find that 7 percent of the fives give multiple reasons on the average problem, 16 percent of the sixes, 22 percent of the sevens, 37 percent of the nines, and 20 percent of the elevens. For "empty" judgments the same trend prevails: multiple bases are given by 4 percent of the five-year-olds, 9 percent of the sixes, 16 per cent of the sevens, 23 percent of the nines, and 8 percent of the elevens. The eleven-year-old, knowing the answer, need not give multiple reasons: he merely remarks on the common fraction. The proportion of children giving multiple bases for their judgments of fullness quintuples between age five and age nine, and triples for their judgments of emptiness.

CONCLUSION

We have examined the manner in which a powerful concept like proportion grows step by step in the child's thinking. What emerges is the importance of his method of dealing with the perceptual features of the task. The child begins with a discrete, almost binary, rendering of the two extreme states, empty and full. He accomplishes this by the use of highly enactive definitions—"empty" is turn-over-able after drinking, perhaps, and "full" is when you are about to spill. This accomplishment comes early in the child's speaking and thinking life. At the next stage, there is a movement toward a perceptual definition of the two terms. "Full" means much water, "empty" means little. At the next stage there is a separation of the attributes used for dealing with this contrast pair. Now "fuller" means much water, and "empty" means much empty space. When the child achieves this new bit of cognitive technology, he is led into what appears to be a contradiction—particularly when he is badgered by the kinds of displays that we have used in this experiment. However, for all the so-called contradiction, the child is progressing to the next level. What seems plain is that his taking the next step does not involve simply attending to more cues but, rather, using a new computing of relationships. To accomplish this he must master what it takes to hold several different things in mind at once. He does it by relating them. What remains is the question of the means by which the child finally succeeds in doing just that. That is the issue of how the child uses his symbolic capacity to form a ratio idea into which previously dominating perceptual cues can be fitted and put to a new use.

CHAPTER 9

On the Conservation
of Liquids

Jerome S. Bruner[1]

Our concern in this chapter (and in the two that follow) is with the growth of the ability to recognize that, though a particular magnitude has changed its appearance, it is still the same magnitude. It is a powerful idea not only in science but also in the conduct of everyday life. We need not pause over its generality in mathematics, in which it plays such a crucial role in the idea of a function, or in physics, in which the conservation theorems are so powerful an extension of the common-sense version. Indeed, much of common sense and all of science would be impossible without conservation.

We are greatly in Piaget and Inhelder's debt (1962) for bringing to the attention of psychology the fact that Western children below a certain age (somewhere around seven) are typically unable to "conserve" a quantity of matter over transformations in its appearance. The classic experiment, repeated many times in Europe and America, is illustrated in Figure 1.

In such an experiment the young child is presented with two beakers and told to pour exactly the same amount of colored water into each beaker. After he has done this to his satisfaction, the water from one of the beakers is poured into another glass of a different shape, and the child is asked if there is still the same amount. If the second beaker is thinner, the child will usually say that there is more water because the water level is higher, while if the second

---
[1] We are greatly indebted to Miss Susan Carey, several of whose ingenious experiments are reported in this chapter. She also helped reanalyze and reformulate several other experiments reported here.

Conservation Tests

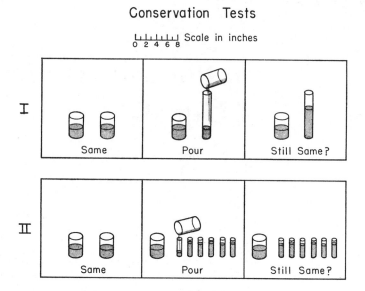

Figure 1. The two tests used in classical conservation experiments.

glass is wider the child will ordinarily respond that there is less water because of the lower level. In the case in which there are six small beakers, he will likely say that the little beakers have more because there are more of them. He seems unable to grasp the invariance of the quantity of water across transformations in its constituent dimensions.

Piaget has interpreted these findings in terms of a logical meta-theory, from which he derives interesting psychological implications. It is the latter that concern us here. His explanation of the phenomena (discussed in general terms in our opening chapter) is that the shift from nonconservation to conservation represents a crucial change-over from a preoperational phase of thinking to the concrete operational phase. What characterizes the shift is that operations on the environment that were before carried out overtly now become internalized. The crucial characteristic of internalized, concrete operations is that they are reversible—in one's head one can not only carry out an operation, but also undo it or reverse it. The achievement of this stage permits the child to perform additional operations, operations conceived by Piaget to be organized in the form of mathematical groupings. One of these groupings involves the multiplying of relations. One such form of the multiplying of relations is called compensation. That is, the child when confronted with a tall, thin beaker and a short, fat one filled with liquid to a lower level supposedly multiplies "greater height" by "lesser width" and comes out with "equal quantity." At an earlier, "less operational" stage, the child knows that the quantities of liquid in the two beakers are equal because of reversibility, the possibility of an inverse operation. At this point he may give as an argument in favor of invariance, something like, "If you were to pour the water back, it would be the same." In summary, one senses in Piaget's writings that at first it is the inverse operation and later the compensation that make conservation possible.

The rather lengthy series of experiments reported in the following pages grew out of our efforts to explore more deeply the psychological factors leading to the growth of the idea of conservation or invariance, for Piaget has principally described the invariance pattern as if it were a series of quasi-inevitable maturational steps involving the unfolding of logical operations. Like others who have followed his lead, we too are in his debt, though in the end we have been led onto other paths and, on some crucial points have been forced to bring his theoretical account into serious question.

Our argument is in sharp contrast to Piaget's. On purely logical grounds, we believe he has missed the heart of conservation. Both inversion and compensation to be effective must rest upon an appreciation of the original equality of the quantities involved. A continued grasp of this initial equality is crucial to both inversion and compensation. Indeed, the inverse operation of "pouring back" is effective for achieving conservation only in so far as it is a path to the original state of equality in the two "standard" beakers (Figure 1). And compensation and inversion, it can be even more forcefully argued, depend on the maintenance of some primitive identity in two "versions" of an event. Such identity can be illustrated by the case in which one uses, say, a single quantity of liquid, first contained in a standard beaker, then poured into another that is taller and thinner. The only "similarity" between the two is achieved through maintenance of their identity. If the child says that the two quantities of liquid are not the "same," (i.e., that what was present before and what is present now are unlike) then he must mean either (a) that they do not look the same; or (b) that they are a different substance. We shall see shortly that, in the overwhelming number of cases, they deny that the liquid is "different" but at the same time claim there is "more water" in one version than another.

Now, Elkind (1965) comments on the fact that Piaget is often misunderstood in his characterization of conservation by virtue of his failure to make clear the difference between the conservation of equivalence and the conservation of identity. While we do not agree with Elkind's treatment of this matter, we agree with his general point that not only are the two concepts different on an abstract level, but each requires a separate form of operational definition. The usual way in which conservation studies are carried out permits no proper inference to be made about the two notions, identity and equivalence. The way experiments are done is as follows, with S being a standard stimulus such as a ball of clay, V being one that is indistinguishable in appearance from the standard, and V^1 being an altered version of V (e.g., V flattened into a pancake form is V^1) and "$=$" is equal in quantity:

	Conservation	*Nonconservation*
Child:	$S = V$	$S = V$
Child:	$S = V^1$	$S \neq V^1$
Experimenter's Inference:	V and V^1 are identical	V and V^1 not identical

From a logical point of view, the inference is completely unjustified. What is necessary is a confrontation of V and V^1 in terms of whether they are the same *substance* or whether something has been changed. Indeed, that is what is needed psychologically as well as logically to separate identity from apparent equivalence.

We shall return to this problem in a moment in reporting a first experiment. But before turning to the empirical case, one last point needs clarification. It is a point that has appeared in the literature on conservation before (cf. Wallach, 1963). What shall we take, if we reject the idea of compensation as central to invariance or conservation, as the mediating factor. Wallach and Sprott (1964) have suggested reversibility, but there is also the logical issue raised above: without some primitive sense of identity, how could reversibility provide a test? We would, as noted above, choose identity as a basic "carrier" of the growth of conservation (a view already suggested by Wohlwill [1959]), and as a guide to the discussion that follows, we sketch out the idea in brief.

We assume, at the outset, that some primitive sense of identity is either innate, or develops well before the child is active in the manipulation of objects. In the first chapter, mention was made of the child's slight startle when an object changed its properties when passed behind a screen (Bower, 1965) and the young child's capacity to recognize objects previously presented underlines this "sense of sameness." William James (1890, Vol. I, p. 459–460) remarks,

This *sense of sameness* is the very keel and backbone of our thinking. . . . We do not care whether there be any *real* sameness in *things* or not, or whether the mind be true or false in its assumptions of it. Our principle only lays it down that the mind makes continual use of the *notion* of sameness, and if deprived of it, would have a different structure from what it has.

He then goes on to his celebrated justification of the sense of identity as the source of the constancy in conceptual thinking, concluding with his famous remark (p. 463), "A polyp would be a conceptual thinker if a feeling of 'Hollo! Thingumbob again!' ever flitted through his mind."

More "complicated" forms of invariance develop when this earliest conception of identity is translated into new terms—terms of action, of imagery, and of symbolism. The question of *how* the progress goes, *how* there is translation of primitive identity into a form that makes it possible to recognize identity across transformations in properties, is a question of the maturing and learning of identity-preserving transformations: that an object is still in existence though out of sight, that it is the same object in new contexts, and so on. Obviously, a great many of these *must* develop in the sphere of perception in order to sustain perceptual constancy—no matter what stance one takes on the issue of the innateness of constancy. And if the child is to learn to manipulate objects and reach for them appropriately, which he does in his first year, he clearly has a motoric representation. Indeed, what is so striking is that it is a Piaget study (his work on the child's "construction of reality," 1954) that best shows how many invariance transformations the child is learning to take in his stride during the first year of life.

We shall return to these issues later. The first experiment to which we turn concerns itself with the relation of equivalence and identity.

IDENTITY AND EQUIVALENCE

This experiment was designed to discover what is implied psychologically by a judgment of identity: does such a judgment in any way affect how one views the equivalence of two quantities—whether they are the same amount? And can training in labeling identity promote the development of judgments of equivalence?

The experiment that concerns us here was designed and conducted by Patricia Nair, who used as her subjects forty five-year-olds drawn from a kindergarten in a Boston suburb. The experiment has been designed in such a way as to highlight the identity of a quantity of water being moved from one vessel to another—an objective served by having the water "owned" by a wooden duck, who "takes the water with him" in moving from one "lake" to another.

The children were equally divided between those who had shown conservation on the classical pretest (Figure 1) and those who had not. Immediately following the pretest, the child was presented with a pair of identical plastic boxes, open at the top, measuring five inches long, three and a half inches wide, and two and a half inches deep. They were equally filled with water, one of them by the experimenter and the other by the child, who was told to match what the experimenter had until he was sure they had the same amount in their "lakes." Then experimenter and subject alike chose a wooden duck to put in their ponds. The child's duck being somewhat crowded, the experimenter then suggested the child move his on to another pond, then another, and finally a third. The child's duck would "have to take his water with him" on these moves. At each move the child was asked two questions: "Is there just as much, more, or not as much water here [pointing to the new container] as here [pointing to the original one]?" and "Is this the same water as the duck had there [pointing back]?" Half the children always were asked the questions in one order, and half in the other—indicating equality and then identity, or identity and then equality.

The first "lake" into which the child's duck moved was identical with the original, and it was put into the experiment to make sure the instructions were understood. The next two "lakes" were larger than the original in both width and length. They were equal in size, though one of them was deeper. They measured seven and a half inches long, five and a half inches wide, and two and a half inches deep in one case, four inches deep in the other. The responses that concern us are all related to a comparison of the "standard" with the two larger "lakes."[2]

There is, first, a somewhat surprising difference between children who demonstrated and those who did not demonstrate conservation in the initial pretest. Their responses to the "training" differed. Take answers to the question whether the transposed water was the "same water." Whereas 36 percent of the responses of the children without conservation were negative, only two percent of the conservers' responses were. In short, a good third of the children without conservation do not use the words "same water" when it has changed containers. Quite in keeping with the pretest, some six in ten answers given

---

[2] Some details of the experiment are omitted in the interest of brevity and because they are not relevant to the issue under discussion.

by children without initial conservation asserted that with a change to a different size of lake, the amount of water was no longer the same. Even 36 percent of the answers of children *with* conservation was of this type. But these are not the main findings, in our opinion. Rather, these have to do with the relation between the two types of response.

In effect, virtually all children who say that the water in the two different-sized lakes is the *same amount*, also say that it is the *same water*. But the reverse does not hold. Many children who assert that it is the "same water" also judge that the two lakes do not contain the "same amount." And finally, as already noted, there is that group among the original nonconservers who hold that the water is neither the same amount nor is it the same water. The relevant data are in Table 1. It seems fair to conclude tentatively that a recognition of identity is a necessary if not a sufficient condition for the recognition of quantitative equivalence.

This view is also supported by the reasons the children give for their judgments of amount. For children showing conservation on the pretest, identity is the dominant reason given for their equality judgments during the "lakes" procedure. Indeed, 50 percent of these children use some variant of "It's the same water" as their main argument for maintaining invariance of amount. The reasons given by the children who do not start out with conservation are in sharp contrast: only 10 percent of this group uses the "sameness" of the water as their

TABLE 1

Percent of Responses Asserting Amount of Water Was the Same (Equivalence) and that the Water Was the Same (Identity) When Moved from One Container to Another

	Pretest Status	
Training Responses	Conservation	Nonconservation
Equivalence & identity	63%	29%
Equivalence & nonidentity	1%	0
Nonequivalence & identity	35%	35%
Nonequivalence & nonidentity	1%	36%
	100%	100%
Number of responses	80	80
Number of children	20	20

main justification for equality judgments. Their reasons are most usually some variant of "I poured it" or "The duck took it with him."

Moreover, the experience of being asked the identity question, "Is
it still the same water?" has a striking effect in producing conservation
on the posttest: 65 percent of the children who did not conserve quantity on the pretest now give conservation responses. This compares
very favorably with various kinds of training procedures to be reported later in this chapter. The order of the identity and equivalence
questions is unimportant as far as posttest conservation is concerned.
All that matters is that the question of identity be highlighted.

But now consider for a moment the immediate effect of the order
of questions on how children respond *during* the "lakes" procedure.
Take first the children who showed conservation on the pretest. If
one begins with an identity question first, then eight times out of
ten the equivalence question that follows will be answerd correctly.
It is striking, however, if the equivalence question is asked first, that
only half of the children answer it correctly. For children *with* conservation a "reminder" about identity seems to help get them over
the hump of recognizing that not only is it the same water they are
dealing with, but also the same *amount* of water. The identity element
appears to be part of the system for them.

Contrast this now with the picture for the children who show no
conservation on the pretest. (We must first eliminate from consideration the third of them who answer the identity question in the negative.) On taking the remainder, it is apparent that "preactivation" by
a question about identity does not help them at all—indeed, it hurts
them. Only a third who have been given the identity question first
follow it up by saying that the transposed water is the same amount.
This is in marked contrast to the *six* in ten who call the water equal
in quantity when asked without "identity preactivation." The figures
just discussed are found in Table 2.

TABLE 2
Percent of Children Who Say Both "Same Water" and "Same Amount"

| | Pretest Status | |
	Conservation	Nonconservation
Identity question first	78%	20%
Equivalence question first	50%	60%

How do we explain these findings? Recall first that *order* of asking the question about identity and equivalence did not affect the considerable improvement of the nonconserving children on the posttest. What we are puzzling over is why asking the identity question first hinders the nonconserver in his response to the equivalence question, whereas it helps the conserver. Our hunch has to do with a matter considered in Chapter 7, a matter that also relates to how a child "translates" his primitive and immediate sense of identity into more indirect forms. Recall the discussion about the young child's difficulty with the distinction between how things are alike and how they are different. We rather suspect that when a young child is asked whether the water is the same water in the two lakes he is answering that they are the same in some global sense. Ask him a second question, whether they are the same amount, and he is primed to tell you of their difference. This is further reinforced by the preconservation child's poor grasp of the idea of "amount." Now, with equivalence asked *first*, the children asked whether x is the same (x being amount) reply in terms of the sameness of the water—it was taken there by the duck. When the next question comes, "same water," they answer it in effect the same way: "Yes, it is the same water." In a word, the nonconservation children simply do not have the notions of identity and equivalence clearly distinguished and certainly do not have them in a common system of reckoning. Yet, even the small amount of practice involved does lead to striking improvement on the posttest—an improvement that may come from the confrontation with tasks that involve making a distinction that conflicts with their earlier amorphous conception of "sameness."

We can only conclude that for children with conservation already established, identity is "in the system." Conservation responses and nonperceptual reasons are stimulated by "reminding" the child first about identity. Identity is present in most children who do *not* have the idea of conservation, but it obviously is not integrated with a notion like invariance of amount. Prodding the child to consider the identity of two things seems to lead him to be more perceptual and *less* conservational in the immediate context. Remember, however, that this same prodding ultimately succeeded in pushing him on to conservation judgments.

Before leaving this experiment, let us look at a point relevant to our next attempt to create instructional conditions favorable to the development of conservation. Which children are not helped in performing the posttest by identity training? In six out of seven cases these are children who were focusing on a *single perceptual* feature of the displays. A perceptual reason is one that deals with the appearance of the water, "lake," and so forth. In contrast, the children who were helped are much more likely to utilize *several* perceptual features of the situation in their arguments. We mention this result to suggest that perhaps, as in the previous studies reported in these pages, general intellectual growth may depend to some extent on sheer "channel capacity," the ability to register on several aspects of the situation simultaneously.

Obviously, no firm or strong conclusion can come from one experiment of this kind. We only want to underline the point that the process of translating "primitive" identity into a more conceptually refined form goes through a stage in which there is little explicit distinction made between identity and equivalence. A grasp of a "linguistic" version of the former seems to be a necessary but not sufficient condition for understanding the latter. Yet "forcing" the distinction on the child often has the effect of leading him to make the distinction on a new task. Once the distinction has been made, then the child is able to relate the two into a system in which he can say, for example: "They are the same water, but they do not look the same." Finally, this can be translated into the linguistic equivalent: "They are the same amount."

We turn now to an experiment precisely of this order.

PERCEPTUAL SCREENING

This experiment grew out of a set of observations made informally by Bruner, Inhelder, and Bovet in 1962, working on techniques that might be used to help the child grasp the idea of the invariance of quantity. At that time it was apparent that at least two sources of difficulty had to be overcome if a child were to comprehend the idea of conservation. The first might best be called "perceptual seduction." Children before age six almost always judge an amount of fluid in terms of a single, directly estimable property of a display, one to which they can readily point—usually the height of the water. The "lakes" procedure illustrated that point nicely. Since amount—like ratio as treated in the preceding chapter—is a relation between at least two attributes, height, width, and so forth, the preference for a single, vivid attribute leads the child away from an appreciation of invariance in so far as the preferred attribute of water level changes with any transformation in the diameter of the container.

A second source of interference was the child's seeming "insensitivity" to conflict and contradiction in his own behavior. In a word, he could at one moment say that one beaker had the same amount of water as another, and then turn round immediately and say that the same water, now in another beaker, was less. It was as if there were an absence of temporal integration, as in the studies reported in Chapter 4, in which children were unable to tie together into a workable whole the information gathered from a sequence of questions.

It seemed plain that the children who had not yet achieved conservation would need help that would shield them from the bias of perceptual immediacy, that would not only permit them to take two things into account at once, but would also permit them to recognize a conflict between them. We can restate the matter in the theoretical schema that has been set forth in these pages as follows. The children of the ages with which we had been working (four through eight) are, as we have seen, highly dependent upon the perceptual properties of events and upon images that represent these events ikonically. They are in process of developing symbolic techniques of representation that permit them to recognize properties and relations that transcend particular, "point-at-able" instances. If they could be shielded from a quick, misleading ikonic rendering of the situation—shielded in a fashion that would permit them to represent the situation in language *before* they could see it—perhaps the language would serve as a guide for organizing their perceptions in a new way. The linguistic rendering might serve, if not as an organizer, then as a source of conflict with the perceptual rendering. What was needed, in brief, was a perceptual shield and a linguistic operation performed while the shield was in place.

This was the rationale of the experiment carried out by Françoise Frank. Forty children participated, equally divided between ages four, five, six, and seven. They came from a surburban school near Boston and were quite unexceptional with respect to intelligence (all of them operating at about the appropriate grade level). All the children were given the standard conservation pretest described in Figure 1.

The experiment was as follows: four pairs of beakers were used, each pair containing the standard beaker and one other, as indicated in Figure 2.

In Part I of the experiment, the standard beaker, half full of colored water, and one empty comparison beaker at a time were shown to the subject and then placed behind a screen twelve inches wide and five inches high, so that only the tops of the beakers showed. The water was poured from the standard to the comparison beaker, the subject was asked whether there was still the same amount of water, and he was asked the reasons for his answer. The screen was never

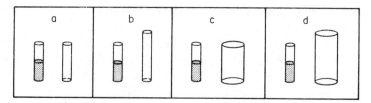

Figure 2. Pairs of beakers used in screening experiments.

taken away, so the child never saw the level of the water in the second beaker. The beaker pairs were always presented in the order Pair a, b, c, d.

In Part II of the experiment, the beakers were presented to the subject in pairs again, and in the same order as before. This time, however, the screen was not used and the subject was asked to predict whether there would still be the same amount of water if it were poured from the standard beaker to the comparison. He was also asked to indicate with his finger the level to which the water would come in the second beaker if it were poured. Again, his reasons were asked. The water was never poured, so the child did not see the level of the water in the second beaker.

In Part III, the beakers were presented in the same pairs before a screen. The child was asked to draw a line on the screen that corresponded to the level of the water in the standard beaker. Then, as in Part I, the pair of beakers was placed behind the screen, the water poured from the standard to the comparison beaker, and the child asked if there was still the same amount of water. He was also asked to draw a second line that predicted the level of water in the second beaker, using the line he had already drawn as a reference. Then the screen was taken away. For the first time in the screening procedure the child saw the level of the water in the comparison beaker. He was asked at this point to *judge* whether there was still the same amount of water as there had been before pouring. Again, his reasons for all his answers were asked.

Finally, there was a posttest, repeating the standard pretest shown in Figure 1. The screening procedure dealt entirely with the comparison of a standard beaker and one other that was either equal in diameter or wider, while both pretest and posttest involved the comparison of a standard with others that were narrower or more numerous. So there was no *specific* training for the posttest. Figure 3 presents the

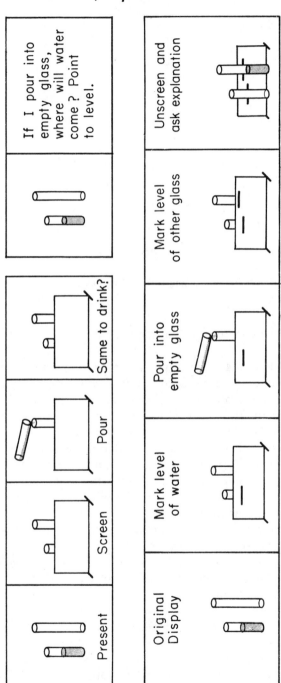

Figure 3. Three screening procedures: The unmarked screening procedure (Part I) is at the upper left, the water-level guessing procedure (Part II) is at the upper right, and the screening-marking procedure (Part III) is across the bottom of the figure.

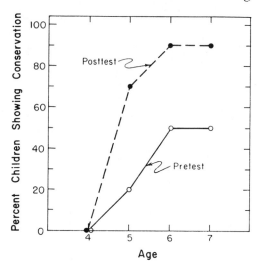

Figure 4. Percent of children showing conservation before and after screening.

three parts of the experiment, illustrated by a single pair of beakers in each part.

A glimpse of Figure 4 makes it plain that the training has a marked effect on all but the four-year-olds. Indeed, the proportion of five-year-olds achieving conservation after training more than trebles—from 20 percent to 70 percent. Sixes and sevens also show a striking rise, nearly doubling their achievement of conservation.

Closer inspection of what is happening during the "training" is provided first by Figure 5. Its story is quickly told. The presence of the screen leads, almost universally (in all save the fours), to the judgment that there is the same amount in the wider glass after pouring. The screen "forces" judgments to be based on an identity argument. "It's only the same water," or "You only poured it," are the two most frequent justifications for the judgment of equality.

However, with the removal of the screen in Part III of the experiment, a striking thing happens. Virtually all of the four-year-olds, who had given a conservation judgment when the screen was present, regress to nonconservation. They cannot resist the visual presence of the beakers. "There is more because it is higher"—the old refrain returns. Not so the others, however. They are able to resist, and the tenor of their comments and justifications is highly revealing. These most often constituted some variant of the statement of one five-year-old. "Well, it looks like more to drink, but it is only the same, because it is the same water and it was only poured from there to there." These reasons reveal a conflict between identity of substance and change of appearance, but the identity schema wins out.

There are several very telling clues as to what is going on to change the judgments of the children. For easy reference to these, the data are summed up in Table 3.

In Part II (no screen, no pouring), one may note first that almost all the children show conservation; but correct judgments of amount mean different things to the younger children than they do to the older children. This is shown by their height predictions on Pairs c and d, in which the comparison beaker is wider than the standard. At age four only 10 percent realize that the water level will go down. Age five does better, 40 percent realizing that the level will go down, and from 70 to 90 percent of the older children predict the level correctly. Of the four- and five-year-olds who make errors in water-level predictions on these two displays, almost all say that the level will be the same in the second beaker. They base their judgments on the notion that nothing will be changed—it is the same water; there would be the same amount—the level would be the same. The older children, on the other hand, predict correctly that the level will go down, al-

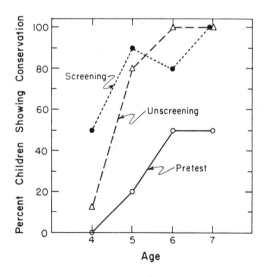

Figure 5. Percent of children showing conservation at different points in the screening procedure.

TABLE 3

Percentage of Children Giving Correct Amount Predictions (AP),
Level Predictions (LP), and Amount Judgments (AJ) on Three
"Screening" Procedures.*

	Display a	Display b	Display c	Display d

Part I	AP	AP	AP	AP
Age 4	90 %	70 %	90 %	80 %
Age 5	100 %	90 %	70 %	100 %
Age 6	90 %	100 %	100 %	100 %
Age 7	90 %	80 %	90 %	90 %

Part II	AP	LP	AP	LP	AP	LP	AP	LP
Age 4	100 %	100 %	90 %	60 %	90 %	10 %	90 %	10 %
Age 5	100 %	100 %	90 %	80 %	90 %	40 %	90 %	40 %
Age 6	100 %	100 %	100 %	80 %	100 %	80 %	100 %	80 %
Age 7	100 %	100 %	100 %	80 %	100 %	90 %	100 %	70 %

Part III	AP	AJ	LP	AP	AJ	LP	AP	AJ	LP	AP	AJ	LP
Age 4	100 %	100 %	80 %	100 %	100 %	60 %	50 %	11 %	30 %	20 %	0 %	80 %
Age 5	90 %	90 %	70 %	90 %	90 %	30 %	90 %	80 %	70 %	80 %	80 %	90 %
Age 6	100 %	100 %	90 %	100 %	100 %	20 %	80 %	100 %	100 %	100 %	100 %	100 %
Age 7	100 %	100 %	100 %	100 %	100 %	30 %	100 %	100 %	100 %	100 %	100 %	100 %

* Ten children were tested for each condition save for AJ in Display C where the number of four-year-olds dropped to nine. One child refused to judge.

though they too give correct predictions of the amount. The young child's correct judgment of amount is still corrrelated with an imagined perceptual equality; but the screening procedure has helped the older child to separate perceptual evidence from judgments about the amount of water. This is the big step forward—the newly achieved capacity to make a judgment on something other than an immediate accessible ground such as water level.

Some of the difficulties involved in this dissociation of judgment from direct perceptual report can be found in the handling of Pair b, two beakers of the same diameter, the standard one being six inches high and the comparison one eight inches. Consider the responses to this pair in Part III of the experiment. All the children predicted that there would be the same *amount* in the taller beaker after pouring. But interestingly enough, on this display the younger children were "better" in their prediction of *water level* in the taller beaker. Sixty percent of the youngest group were right, but with the three oldest groups the correct prediction of level hovered between 20 and 30 percent!

The older children make two different kinds of mistakes. One is a misuse of the principle of compensation. They say that the level will be lower in the taller glass because the glass is "taller" or "bigger." Here again is a tendency to equate all larger magnitudes as being from one pool of "bigness." But note that the error is along the way toward achieving a sense of the relationship between two variables, height and width. The second error is based on a misuse of the idea of a ratio (a matter encountered in Chapter 8). The children say that the water level will be higher because the glass is taller, or, as one child put it, the level would be twice as high because the glass was twice as tall. Again, there is a beginning grasp of a relational concept with all that means in the achievement of freedom from direct perceptual indicia.

It was no surprise, then, that in the two oldest groups the children who had shown conservation on the pretest were the very ones who had committed these errors on this tell-tale display. Indeed, nine in ten children showing conservation on the pretest made one or another of these errors with this pair of beakers, while only one-half of the children without conservation did. The result suggests again that there are indeed characteristic "errors of growth," as in the instance of "self-contradiction" among the older children en route to grasping the idea of ratio.

The reasons given by the children during the pretest, screening, and posttest yield interesting leads. More than 95 percent of all the reasons given fall into one of the following categories. (We are considering now only the pairs of beakers, Pairs c and d, that differ in width, for they are the only two that are relevant to the issue of conservation.)

Perceptual. Reasons pertaining to the size or the shape of the bottle or to the appearance of the liquid itself. Some examples commonly heard are: "There is less to drink (or more) because the glass is bigger"; or "There is less to drink because the water is lower."

Identity. Reasons mentioning the identity of the water itself or of the amount of water. In this class are statements like: "It is the same water," or "You just poured it," or "If it were still in the first glass, there wouldn't be anything different," or "You haven't added or subtracted any from the water."

Conflict. Reasons that imply a conflict or a resolution of conflict. "It just looks less because it is fat." Or simply, "It goes down because it is wider." Although these answers deal with perceptual properties, they are quite different from those in the "perceptual" class because they do not directly answer the question, "How do you know there is the same amount of water?" These children interpret the question as asking them to account for the fact that they said it is the same amount of water yet it looks less.

TABLE 4
Percent of Reasons Given by Children of Different Ages in Support of
Judgments of Conservation and of Nonconservation

Reasons	Ages Four and Five	Ages Six and Seven	Conservation Responses	Nonconservation Responses
Perceptual	48%	16%	6%	100%
Identity	46%	57%	49%	0
Conflict	6%	27%	45%	0
Number of reasons	31	59	67	23

In Table 4 are set forth the reasons given by children of different ages and with different achievement. Older children give more identity and conflict reasons than do younger, and what is even more clear-cut is that *all* nonconservation responses are backed by perceptual reasons, but that virtually no conservation responses are at all.

These results suggest indeed that there is a critical step forward when the child learns to use less direct perceptual cues to define the semantics of "amount to drink," and even more interesting, that the child can be helped to leap this gap by being screened from perception of the displays and encouraged to encode his judgments and reasons during this screening, in language that highlights continuity—that is, in the language of identity. Having gone through this training, the child is now sensitized to the conflict that can exist between "appearance" and "reality." "Appearance" is defined by ikonic representation, "reality" by symbolic.

What then of the role of reversibility and compensation? There are some puzzles here that turn up in the reasons children give. To be sure, reversibility and compensation are all represented in the reasons children give for conservation. But consider some reasons that children give for nonconservation, for the belief that there is a different amount of water when it is poured from a standard beaker into one that is taller and thinner (as in Figure 1). In the following five protocols the child's remarks are in italics. They all involve the use of reversibility or compensation—to support nonconservation.

Lisa. Age 4:0. Water is poured. Is there still the same? *Shakes head no.* Who has more? *You.* Why? *You put it in a thinner glass.* Will they be the same or different when I pour it back? *Same, 'cause you have a fat glass.*

Carol. Age 5:3. (Water is poured.) Is there still the same to drink? *No.* Why not? *Because it is higher.* Who has more to drink? *You.* How come I have more to drink? *There is not enough room (points to width of comparison beaker).* (While E is pouring) what will happen now? *You will get the same amount.*

Bruce. Age 5:0. (E pours.) Do we both have the same to drink? *You have a little more because that's a little skinnier.* Does that mean I actually have more to drink? *No, that's a bigger glass.* So do I have more? *Yes, because the glass is bigger.* Is it really more or does it just look like more? *It looks like more and it is really more.* What will happen when I pour it back? *It will be the same.*

Emily. Age 5:0. (Water is poured.) Do we have the same amount still? *No.* Who has more? *(Indicates comparison beaker.)* Why? *That's littler (pointing to standard.) That one is fat (standard) and that one is skinny (comparison).* And what will happen if I pour it back? *That one (standard) is still smaller.*

Roderick. Age 5:3. (Water is poured.) Do we still have just as much? *No.* Who has more? *(Points to taller, thinner beaker.)* Why? *Because it is thinner and then because you poured some extra juice into the other. This is a mixed up game for me.* (E starts all over, equalizing standard beakers.) (*Roderick is sure that they are the same.*) (E pours.) Same? *Yes. I think it has more because it is thinner. That's it.* And if I pour it back? *Both the same.*

Reversibility and compensation could not by themselves be *producing* conservation, bringing it into being. They are too often encountered in instances in which the child has not achieved conservation. There is a very nice example of this point in the data of this experiment, at least with respect to compensation. It is provided by a comparison of the four-year-olds in two parts of the experiment. Recall that these children begin with no conservation on the pretest and end with none on the posttest, though during training it is not unusual for them to give a conservation response when the screen is in place to shield them from the "evidence of their senses." There are two "conservation" pairs in the training series—the first is the standard beaker paired with a beaker of the same height but much wider. The second is the standard and a much wider beaker that is also taller. In Part II of the experiment the children are asked to say simply whether, if water is poured from the standard into the comparison, it will be the same amount to drink or different. They are also asked to point to where the water would rise in the comparison beaker if poured into it. Now, consider only the reaction to the last pair—the standard beaker and the one that is wider and taller. In Part II of the experiment 90 percent of the children said that there would be the same amount to drink if it were poured. But only 10 percent were correct about the height

the water would reach in the comparison beaker. Now we come to
Part III with the same beakers, now behind a screen. But note. Before
the children see the pair of a standard and a wider, taller comparison
beaker, they have been exposed to the *unscreening* of the pair made
up of a standard, and a wider, equally high, comparison beaker. They
have noted in that pair that the water is *lower,* when poured into the
comparison beaker. What do they make of it when they come to the
last pair?

Their predictions are impeccable from the point of view of "perceptual logic." Now, only 20 percent say there will be the same amount
to drink in the comparison glass, but 80 percent are correct about
where the water will come to. They learn, yes, but what they learn
is where the water level will be. Rather than the learning having
helped them toward conservation, it has had just the reverse effect.
If the water level turns out to be lower, they argue, then the amount
to drink will be less! This is our first clue that children can have
compensation without conservation. The next experiment is designed
to examine this matter more closely.

COMPENSATION AND REVERSIBILITY AS FACTORS

In this trial experiment, devised by Susan Carey, nineteen four-
and five-year-olds were our subjects, and all of them were found on
a standard pretest (Figure 1) not to have achieved conservation. The
experiment consisted of five "tests." Before the child, there was placed
a partly filled standard beaker, and next to it an empty, identical
beaker: "his glass." He was then shown a series of five pairs of beakers
with the instruction to choose that one in each pair that would give
him just the amount of water necessary for his glass to match the
experimenter's glass. The correct choice was always of the type that
would be responded to in a "nonconservation" fashion—for example,
it would be a wider beaker with a lower water level or a narrower
one with a higher water level. The displays are contained in Figure
6.

Without burdening the reader with details, the results of the experiment can be very quickly told. Half of the fours' choices and half of
the fives' were correct. The reasons given for choices, asked before
they were permitted to check by pouring, were of three types: compensation arguments, given by about a third; global arguments based on
the theme, "They just look the same"; and appeals to the experience,
"It worked before." The latter two types of reason were given about
equally.

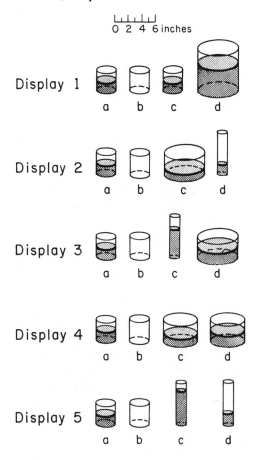

Figure 6. Displays for compensation in action.

The children finally were given a posttest. The four-year-olds continued to show no conservation. Only two of the fives moved to conservation—not unimportant, but also not the heart of the matter.

What are we to make of this rough-and-ready experiment? It is in need of repetition and more careful control, to be sure, but it is worth reporting for several reasons—not the least of which is to suggest a less verbal way of carrying out conservation studies more in the manner of Braine (1959), Wohlwill (1960), and Wohlwill and Lowe (1962). The fact that use of action-oriented procedures produces earlier instances of conservation is not to be dismissed by noting only that "one or two years can be cut off the particular age norms noted by Piaget" (Wallach, 1963). For as we shall see in following chapters, cultural differences not only alter the norms (as Wallach notes in his review) but may in fact alter the mode by which children reckon invariance.

One possible complaint can be quickly dismissed. It can be argued that the children chose the correct beaker on only half of the opportunities presented them. Is that not simply a chance performance? The answer is that given the conventional verbal procedures *all* of their responses were indicative of nonconservation. If we take that as the null hypothesis, then statistically as well as logically their performance in the "action task" is significantly different. But what was most striking was the argument-by-appeal-to-compensation of a third of the children in making their choice of a beaker to match the target beaker (Figure 6).

The experiment needs redoing, certainly, and the issue of "action" orientation *versus* "descriptive" orientation wants closer inspection. For very young children have learned to *do* things in a fashion that takes account of invariance in size, shape, weight, etc. across transformation in their appearance. In effect it may well be that identity is well translated into an action supporting representation years before the child can succeed on tasks such as we give them.

As for reversibility as a possible factor in "producing" conservation, it has logical difficulties, as William James (1890) noted in the quotation already cited. But there is also a puzzling empirical finding to add—one that only confirms what many investigators have already observed. After we gave these nonconserving four- and five-year-olds the standard conservation task (Figure 1), as pre- and posttest, they were asked, "What will happen when the juice is poured back into there (the empty standard beaker) from here (the full thin beaker)?"

Twenty-seven answers indicated that the amount would be the same as before.
Seven answers indicated it would still be more than before.
Four times the children said they didn't know.

What to make of these answers?

I suggest again that there is a problem of a match between the child's language and his way of organizing the experience to which the language must be applied. "Same" and "more" do not have the same senses (semantic markers) as they do in adult speech and are obviously not being fitted to the adult selection requirements demanded by the sentence. "This beaker has more now than before and when it is poured back it will have the same as it did before." It is, if you will, another instance of the failure of the young child to recognize the difference between an anomalous sentence and one that is not anomalous (McNeill, 1966). But the source of the difficulty comes not exclusively from the slow pace of learning to match semantic markers to selection requirements (see Chapter 2). It comes also from the fact that the child does not have the structure built for dealing with perceived identity in a way appropriate for using language in this complicated way. We know from the preceding study by Nair that he knows the water is the same water: the identity is grasped. But the four- and five-year-old has plainly *not* differentiated the idea of identity into a form that contains a base (what the water *really* is) and a surface (what it *looks* like) or into a metric (amount) and continuity (its perduring sameness). In effect, he is operating (as in the Twenty Questions game; in the recognition of pictures with the bulb board; and in the other experiments mentioned) with one "moment" or one event at a time, each event constituting the basis of a single sentence. He can say in *this* situation "now A is more than B" and in the next say that B is bigger than C, but then fail completely in seeing a relation of A and C (e.g., Donaldson, 1963). Since each situation is self-contained, save for the important, undifferentiated identity that characterizes the child's experience, language obviously does not help him "put things together," nor is it adequate as a medium for communicating to an adult what the child experiences.

In time, when the child develops the sort of hierarchical structures that permit him to organize a series of experiences into variants of a base form, he will easily master the task just as he has already mastered the task of realizing that the object before him is the same object as one that a moment ago was out of view. And as the child proceeds further, he then finds means for verifying and checking and extending his simple conception of identity: through an appeal to reversibility, through compensation, through measure, and so forth.

CONFLICT BETWEEN MODES

In Chapter 2 and in the discussions following it reference has been made several times to the role of conflict between representations as a condition for promoting cognitive growth. A good instance is provided by the disparity between the perceptual appearance of beakers in the conservation experiment and their symbolic rendering; ending with the child coming to terms with the idea of "how things look" in contrast to "how things really"—almost the notion of the difference between a surface and base structure or, if one can use another linguistic example, the difference between a set of allomorphs and the morpheme they constitute.

Yet it is not the case that the growing organism is sensitive to all forms of presumably growth-promoting conflicts. Conflicts must, to be successful in leading to a step ahead, mesh into a way of reacting that is already established. The screen worked strikingly well as a conflict-inducing device. The two following chapters describe failures of the same technique, for it did *not* mesh into the established way of reacting. And we have had other failures in inducing conflict. Perhaps a word about a few of them might be suggestive.

One effort involved the standard conservation pretest. In one version we let the child do all the pouring, in another, we ourselves did it.[3] The procedure produced no difference, save perhaps one, some confusion. The children poured, then the children looked. The two acts seemed quite autonomous. Confusion arose when the children became so absorbed in the pouring that they forgot what the initial level was, or, as with the four-year-olds, they became so preoccupied with the delight of pouring that they would lose from mind the object of the activity. Yet there are circumstances in which *just* such a procedure can produce the necessary conflict, as we shall see in the next two chapters.

Another experiment by the same team presented a matrix of beakers to the five- or six-year-old child so that there would be simultaneously present not only the beakers used in conservation but also the so-called system of compensations. For the beakers varied in height and diameter. The children started with the water in the standard beaker and, for training, poured it from one beaker to the next. They learned "empirically" that in thinner beakers water goes up and in wider ones it goes down—as in the screening experiment. But these five- and six-year-olds (many of whom "knew" which way the water would go) fell right back into nonconservation when they were given the test involving the standard beakers and the six small ones (Figure 1). A few fluctuating subjects changed, but that is about all. "Intraperceptually," if the word is permitted, it seems extremely difficult to develop a conflict. Again, it looks as if amount were defined by level, and that compensation may be used with equal effectiveness to explain a change in level or an invariance in amount. Here psychology appears to follow logic, as Piaget has suggested, for compensation, strictly speaking, explains the appearance of the water—it is independent of

---

[3] The observations were carried out on American children by Bruner, Inhelder, and Bovet.

the amount. And this is precisely the way in which children first learn it, as this experiment and the one by Carey clearly illustrate.

Surely, then, it would be of great interest to inquire in the most general terms which kinds of conflicts serve to provoke the accommodations involved in cognitive growth. We turn to this problem in a somewhat different form in the chapter that follows.[4]

---

[4] See also the discussion in a highly relevant paper by Inhelder, Bovet, Sinclair, and Smock (1966), that treats in a most thoughtful way many of the issues discussed in the preceding pages as well as in the next chapter.

CHAPTER 10

On the Conservation
of Solids

Anne McKinnon Sonstroem[1]

In this chapter we continue our scrutiny of
the concept of identity and its relation to conservation—as well as the
role of compensation, reversibility, and reciprocity in these matters.
The ground is to some degree already familiar from the preceding
chapter, but not completely so by any means; for not only does the
change of materials from liquid to solid make a difference, but certain
dilemmas concerning instruction and training also intrude. We shall
proceed by setting forth the problem in a Piagetian framework to see
how well it fits the requirements of our inquiry. Then, with the experiment in hand, we shall explore an alternative viewpoint that is, we
believe, freer of the weaknesses that beset the first approach.

According to Piaget, cognition at all developmental levels consists
of actions performed by the person. At early levels of development
the actions or operations are overt and physical. As the child matures,
action becomes increasingly internalized until covert actions—that is,
verbal, symbolic, formal "operations"—dominate his processes of cognition. Although Piaget's principle of internalization is used thus *generally* to describe the trend of cognitive development from early life to
adulthood, the theory also implies that in the mastery of *specific* cognitive forms the principle of internalization of actions is likewise applicable. At least some of Piaget's students see in the principle of internalization of actions an implication for education. For example, Flavell
suggests that, according to the theory, the best way to teach a child

---

[1] The experiment reported in this chapter was undertaken as part of a doctoral
dissertation in the Department of Social Relations at Harvard (cf. Sonstroem,
1966).

some general principle or rule is to begin with action. "That is, the child should first work with the principle in the most concrete and action-oriented context possible; he should be allowed to manipulate objects himself and 'see' the principle in his own actions" (Flavell [1963] pp. 83–84).

The first hypothesis that this study proposes to test is precisely this notion that a child's physical performance of the appropriate mental operations facilitates his acquisition of a particular cognitive form—in the present case, conservation of amount. To carry out such a test, we must first determine what mental operations are the appropriate ones, and then translate them into physical manipulations that a child can perform in a training situation.

We have chosen to study the operations of *inversion* and *compensation,* because they have been repeatedly suggested by Piaget and others as the operations a child must acquire in order to achieve conservation. What is meant by these two operations? *Inversion* is a simple "returning to the starting point," by "undoing" the operation that has just been performed. The term, applied specifically to conservation of amount, means simply the understanding that one can change an altered shape of a piece of material back into its original shape by reversing or undoing one's actions, and that the amount of material will then be the same at it was in the beginning. The use of the operation of inversion is implied in the answer of the child who says, when asked to judge the relative amounts of clay in a ball and a sausage (made from a ball declared by the child a moment before to be the "same" as the other ball), "They are the same because you can make the sausage back into a ball again and they will be the same."

Compensation refers to the "logical multiplication of relations." Unlike the operation of inversion, there is no literal undoing or reversing of one's actions in the compensation operation. Rather, the operation of compensation depends on an understanding of the reciprocity of two relevant dimensions, for example, length l, and width w. Reciprocity refers to the fact that as l declines, w must increase in order to maintain a constant amount, k: i.e., $l \times w = k$. Again, using the conservation problem to illustrate the operation, we see that compensation refers to the apprehension that, as a ball of clay changes in one dimension, these changes must be compensated for or canceled by changes in another dimension (for example, as it gets longer, it must also get less thick). Thus compensation would be implied in the answer of a child if he were to say, when asked to judge the relative amounts of clay in the ball and the sausage, "'They are the same because the sausage is *longer,* but the ball is *fatter.*" It is obvious that clay presents special difficulties in using the operation of compensation in order to come up with a conservation judgment. Unlike water poured from a fat beaker to a thin one, clay may change in many more aspects than two when changed from a ball to another shape. In short, the *l*'s and *w*'s of our equation are not so obviously and easily "given," but must rather be "selected out" in some way for consideration from a number of possibilities. This problem will concern us shortly.

These two operations, inversion and compensation, may not be so different as they seem. It is obvious in the first place that both of them depend heavily on the idea of *identity,* another important term in Piaget's system. "Identity" means just what it says, that is, it refers to what does not change in a situation. In logical terms, the identity transformation is a transformation that changes nothing in the proposition on which it is performed. Thus the transformations, or operations, of both inversion and compensation achieve the same end as the identity transformation, but by different routes. Whereas the identity transformation never changes a situation in the first place, the operations of inversion and compensation are both applied only after changes have occurred, with the aim of *restoring* the initial situation. Inversion accomplishes this, as we have seen, by literally "undoing" the transformations responsible for the change; and compensation accomplishes it by counterposing the reciprocals of such transformations in order to "neutralize" their effect. Thus both inversion and compensation yield identity. And because they do so *logically,* Piaget apparently expects them to do so *psychologically.* In other words, he implies that if the child can perform the mental operations of inversion and compensation in the conservation problem, he necessarily discovers identity—or "sameness-of-matter," which is what we mean by conservation. Whether or not logical sequences are thus repeated in psychological sequences, as Piaget implies, is a matter for debate; but for the moment we shall let Piaget's formulations stand unchallenged.

When we attempt to translate the *mental* operations of inversion and compensation into *physical* operations that a child can perform in a training situation, we run into an interesting problem that makes their similarity apparent in yet another way. Consider, then, how the two mental operations might be "acted out." Inversion is easy enough: begin with two equal quantities of clay, each in the shape of a ball. The child need only take one of the two balls, change it into a sausage (or another shape), then change it back into a ball again. It is compensation, however, that presents the problem: there is simply no "physical" way to express the notion of compensating dimensions when a clay ball changes shape. The only thing one can do is somehow to highlight or make salient the compensating dimensions as one is physically changing the shape, and the highlighting itself cannot be accomplished physically. Nor, of course, can the *reciprocity* between the dimensions be accomplished physically. It seems then that compensation cannot be acted out without adding to certain physical operations the use of some kind of labeling procedure to make salient the compensating attributes and thus encourage a schematization of their reciprocal relationship. Although the operation of compensation could not really be acted out on *any* material without these extra processes of labeling and schematization, they are especially necessary with clay because, as we have already noted, its compensating attributes are not so easily "given." Thus, to act out compensation in our problem situation, one can only change the ball into a sausage and back into a ball again *while noting that,* as the ball gains in "length" to become a sausage, there is a corresponding loss in "thickness" (or whatever we decide to highlight); and that the length gives way to thickness as the sausage becomes a ball again.

It is striking that this acted-out version of compensation can employ only the same physical actions that are also employed in the acting out of inversion. Because the actions are the same, the only difference between these two operations is that the one involves labeling and schematization, while the other does not. Inversion is simply inversion, but compensation is inversion with a focus on a relationship. Thus if we are wondering about the differential effects of the physical performances of the operations of inversion and compensation, what we are really wondering about is the effect of the labeling and the schematization that it should entail. That the addition of labeling to the physical operations of inversion introduces a qualitative difference of some importance is a point we shall discuss shortly.

First, however, let us consider what constitutes appropriate control groups for the groups of subjects to be trained on the two operations we have described, before we move from our initial Piagetian hypothesis to other ones. Instead of receiving no training at all, the control groups should receive everything in the way of training that the experimental groups do, *except* the opportunity to act out for themselves the operation under investigation. Our control groups, then, will be groups of subjects who watch another person (the experimenter) perform the same operations that the experimental groups perform. The subjects in the control groups will then receive the same visual input, the same verbal information, the same period of directed attention, and so forth, as the experimental groups. We can therefore be sure that whatever increment in learning the experimental groups show over the control groups is due solely to individual manipulation.

Our first divergence from a purely Piagetian design was the decision to include a screening variable in our experiment. A screening technique for use in the water-pouring problem was developed by Frank (see Chapter 9 of this book) and was highly successful in inducing conservation in her group of children. Because her procedure was so successful, we hoped to maximize whatever effects our training produced by the addition of this variable to our design. There was also, of course, the added advantage of being able to compare the effects of screening when clay is the material with those found when water is used. The effect of a screen is to hide from the child the misleading perceptual cues on which judgments of nonconservation are based. When the child is thus "saved" from his perceptual or ikonic representation of the problem, he is forced to rely on other, more symbolic means for reaching his judgments.

The three variables we shall be studying, then, are manipulation, symbolic labeling, and screening. These three variables are combined into the general experimental design diagramed as follows. Each cell represents a training condition, to be described in the next section and the number of children who underwent each procedure is appropriately noted.

	Manipulation		No Manipulation	
	Screening	No Screening	Screening	No Screening
Labeling ("Compensation")	11	10	10	10
No Labeling ("Inversion")	10	10	10	10

We have delayed until now the consideration of an important issue, namely, the role of labeling, because it is more easily discussed when we know how it combines with the other variables to be studied. We have already suggested that to combine labeling with other forms of training produces a real qualitative change in the training. Because this is a matter of some moment, theoretically as well as procedurally, let us consider the training combinations to see how this is true. Take, for example, the training procedure in which both manipulation and screening are provided but labeling has not yet been added. Both manipulation and screening are calculated to facilitate learning, as we have seen, for the misleading perceptual cues are withheld, and the subject is instead allowed to act out the operation of inversion. So far we are dealing with two levels of representation, the perceptual or ikonic and the motoric or enactive. But what happens when we introduce labeling? We introduce, as it were, a "third dimension." That is, the addition of labeling puts us into yet another level of representation, the linguistic or symbolic, and this level is qualitatively very different from the other two. We need not go into the details of the "design features" of this mode of representation that make it so qualitatively different and so much more powerful than the other two modes, for these have been explicated in the introductory chapters of this book. Here let us only note what we are doing when we bring labeling to the training scene: we are arousing the subject's linguistic-symbolic processes, and by so doing we are expanding his "encoding potential" to a degree impossible to attain with merely perceptual or motor cues, no matter how many perceptual or motor cues we can activate. Thus, when we introduce labeling we are introducing a qualitative change, not just an additive one. It is a *different* message that labeling makes possible, not just *more* of a message. For these reasons, we must predict that all our "compensation" training procedures will produce more learning than their "inversion" counterparts.

The foregoing considerations plunge us finally into some issues that can no longer be avoided. Although this study began, as we stated in the beginning, with only Piagetian formulations, we have been led into other domains even in our initial attempt to translate his formulations into a general experimental design. In Piaget's logical scheme of things, for example, there is no real basis for a prediction that compensation training should produce conservation more readily than inversion training, since both yield identity. If either, perhaps inversion should be favored, because its route to identity is more direct. Yet we have predicted that compensation training—inversion plus labeling—will be more effective in inducing conservation. Such a prediction (as also our prediction concerning the effectiveness of a screening procedure) relies heavily on the notions of cognitive development set forth earlier in this book. Let us then pause here, even before we must account for results, to contrast briefly Harvard's notions with those of Geneva, since both have influenced our experimental design and our predictions.

At the Institute in Geneva, cognitive development is seen as almost purely a matter of maturation, maturation that takes place by a process of internalization of logical forms; logic, first expressed motorially, is gradually internalized until it can be used symbolically—at which time physical action becomes no longer necessary for thought. It is this notion on which we have founded our first hypothesis that a physical acting out of the logical operations of inversion and compensation will produce conservation. At the Cognitive Center at Harvard, cognitive development is conceived more in terms of the internalization of technologies from the culture, language being the most effective technology available. Hence our prediction with respect to the effectiveness of adding the labeling factor to simple inversion actions. Harvard also stresses the differences in the ways the world can be represented: enactively, ikonically, and symbolically. Although there is a developmental sequence in terms of which—or more properly, how many—of these modes are available to a person, all three remain "in the system" throughout life, and there is always interaction among them. By recognizing the ikonic mode of representing reality and thus bringing into cognition the role of imagery—a factor which Piaget tends to ignore—Harvard casts a somewhat different light on the conservation problem. It becomes possible to view the lack of conservation as a misleading ikonic representation, rather than as merely the absence of the appropriate logical forms (as Piaget leads us to believe). Hence the value of a screening procedure to knock out the ikonic mode and allow for other more appropriate ones that may also be available.

Finally, let us summarize our predictions about the effects of our three variables before moving on to the details of the study:

1. Subjects who themselves perform the physical operations of inversion and compensation on the clay will learn conservation more readily than subjects who only watch the experimenter perform these operations.
2. Subjects who are provided with verbal labels for compensating attributes will learn conservation more readily than subjects for whom no such labels are provided.
3. Subjects who are allowed screening will learn more readily than those for whom no screening is provided.

THE EXPERIMENT

The general outline of the experiment was that usually followed in conservation training experiment: a pretest, to select subjects who did not have conservation, was followed by a series of training trials and by a posttest identical to the pretest except for item content. Each subject was run individually, in a single session that lasted from thirty to forty-five minutes. All subjects were first-grade children from the public school system of Worchester, Massachusetts. Because the study was conducted toward the end of the school year, the median age was approximately seven years. Children of this age are usually at least on the verge of acquiring conservation naturally, and this fact may have been true of these children when they were subjected to the training conditions. Nevertheless, because we are interested in the *differences* in the degrees of learning produced under our different training conditions rather than in the absolute degree of learning we were able to induce, we need not be concerned with the possible objection that the children almost had the concept anyway. The only criterion for inclusion in our sample was that a child not show conservation on the pretest. Our final sample consisted of eighty-one subjects. Sexes and ages were distributed as evenly as possible among the eight training conditions to be described. There were ten subjects in every condition but one, which had eleven.

Because our use of clay leads to a somewhat different procedure from that used in the water-pouring experiments, which are more familiar, it may be helpful to describe the pretest and training conditions in some detail.

Pretest and Posttest: The child was shown two balls of plasticine and asked if they had the same amount of clay. If the child thought the balls were unequal, they were made the "same" for him by whatever operations he suggested. It is interesting that the children did not always suggest adding or removing pieces of clay to make the balls equal, but often suggested such operations as "roll one of them up," "squash one down a little," and so forth. (We might add here, in advance of discussing the other results, that the kinds of operations a child suggested in the pretest were unrelated to whether or not he learned conservation during the trials.) When the child stated that the two balls were the "same," the experimenter changed one of them into a "hot dog" while the child watched. Finally the child was asked whether the ball and the hot dog had the same amount of clay, or whether one had more. If he asserted that they were the same and explained his answer adequately, he was dropped from the study. All these children were retained in the study who gave nonconservation answers of the usual kind (for example, "The hot dog has more because it's the longest," or "The ball has more because it's round," and so forth). Those children were also retained who first gave a conservation answer, only to reject it immediately for a nonconservation one when they were questioned about it. The latter case usually occurred when the child sounded quite unsure of his first answer, and the experimenter altered the pieces a second time in order to question the child again. These children were also challenged in the posttest, and learning was not scored unless the child this time maintained his conservation answer in the face of challenge.

The posttest was identical to the pretest, except that the experimenter made a "snake" or a "jump-rope," which was much longer than the pretest hot dog.

Training: The training consisted of a series of "trials" in which one of two balls of clay (declared by the child to be the "same") was changed into a new shape, and then back into a ball again. After each such alteration the child was asked which one had more clay or whether they had the same amount, and the reason for his answer. The child was allowed to choose the new shape he wanted made from one of the balls on each trial. Each such trial was duplicated: first one ball was converted to the new shape and the child's judgment solicited; then it was converted back into a ball and the child's judgment solicited again. This process was then exactly repeated with the other ball. In effect, then, the child was asked to judge amount when the ball was changed to a new shape, when it was converted back to a ball, when the other ball was changed to the same shape, and when it was turned back into a ball. A "trial" consisted of this changing of one ball into a new shape, changing it back, changing the other ball, and changing it back. Each child had four such training trials, except for those children who had received unscreened inversion training. In this case five trials were used instead of four in order to equalize the number of times the child was asked to judge amount. This addition was necessary because in all the training conditions except these an additional judgment had to be solicited from the child at the end of the trial in order to ensure that the balls were perceived as equal for the next trial.

To describe the training procedures for the eight different conditions, we shall consider each variable separately:

1. *Manipulation:* Subjects given manipulation training were allowed to manipulate and shape the clay themselves, while the others only watched the experimenter manipulate it. The same actions, however, were performed under both conditions.

2. *Screening:* Two small plastic bowls were used in screening training. In each trial one of the balls of clay was hidden under one of the bowls while the other ball was being made into something else.

As soon as the alteration was complete, the altered piece of clay was also hidden, under the other bowl, and the subject was asked to judge the relative amounts of clay in each. The altered piece was removed from its hiding place for its reversal back into a ball; thus the second time the subject was asked to judge amount he could see one of the balls but could not see the other one (the standard). When the standard was uncovered the subject had to judge amount a third time to ensure that the next trial could begin with the balls the "same."

3. *Labeling:* The difference between the training procedure that employed labeling and those that did not can be described best by way of illustration. For example, in manipulation training with no screening the procedure was as follows when there was no labeling:

> After the subject had made a pencil (or whatever he chose) from one of the balls and had judged their relative amounts, the experimenter said to him, "O.K., now will you please take that pencil you made and make it back into a ball again, *just like it was before* (the italicized phrase was always emphasized). As the child made the pencil back into a ball, the experimenter asked him several times, "Is it just like it was before yet?" When the child asserted that it was just like it was before, he was asked to judge the relative amounts of the two pieces again.

The identical procedure for training, but with labeling added, was as follows:

> After the subject had made a pencil, he was asked, "Which one is the longest?" If he indicated that the pencil was the longer, the experimenter then said, "Now tell me which one is the fattest?" If the child indicated the ball, the experimenter said, "O.K., the pencil is *longest*, but the ball is the *fattest;* now tell me, does one of them have more clay than the other or do they have the same?" After the child had given his judgment, the experimenter said, "O.K., you told me the pencil is the longest and the ball is the fattest. Now I want you to take this long pencil and make it just as fat as the ball for me." As the child rolled the pencil back into a ball (which he usually did to make it just as fat), the experimenter asked him several times, "Is it as fat yet?" and "Is it still longer?" When the child asserted that it was just as fat, he was asked to judge the relative amounts of the two pieces again. In the second half of these trials, when the subject made a pencil from the other ball, he was asked to "make the fat ball just as long as the pencil," instead of the other way around as in the first half.

We should note about the labeling trials that in every instance the experimenter sought to find two labels for the compensating attributes that clearly had meaning for the child. For example, if the child showed any hesitation or uncertainty in responding to the questions about the attributes, or if he indicated the same piece of clay for both attributes, the experimenter would try some more labels or chat with the child about the two pieces of clay until she picked up some of his own labels. This was necessary only very occasionally because labels like "longest," "fattest," "the most spread out," and so forth, were almost universally understood and responded to appropriately by the children.

RESULTS

Thirty-five of our eighty-one subjects learned conservation, according to our criterion for learning (Table 1). The criterion is simply that a child who gave a nonconservation answer on the pretest shifted to a conservation answer on the posttest. But did manipulation, labeling, and screening have anything to do with a child's learning, and if so, in what ways?

First let us consider screening. Training with screening here had virtually no effect on learning (Figure 1). We cannot be entirely surprised at this finding when we consider our screening procedure more carefully. That our procedure constitutes screening in the same way as Frank defines it in her water-pouring experiment is questionable because the child here sees far more than the transferring action that he sees in the water-pouring. In fact, the only thing screened for him here is the *simultaneous* perception of the two pieces of clay and the perceptual comparing that such simultaneity allows. He sees the

TABLE 1
Number of Subjects Who Learned Conservation from Pre- to Posttest
in Each Training Condition

Condition	Learned	Did Not Learn	Totals
I. Labeling and manipulation, screened	8	3	11
II. Labeling and manipulation, unscreened	8	2	10
III. Labeling and no manipulation, screened	6	4	10
IV. Labeling and no manipulation, unscreened	2	8	10
V. No labeling and manipulation, screened	4	6	10
VI. No labeling and manipulation, unscreened	2	8	10
VII. No labeling and no manipulation, screened	1	9	10
VIII. No labeling and no manipulation, unscreened	4	6	10
	35	46	81

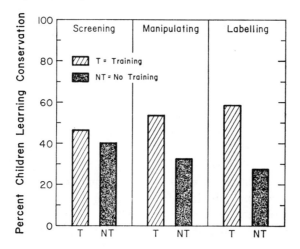

Figure 1. Percent of children who learned conservation with three main training procedures.

shapes of the clay pieces, albeit separately, whereas Frank's children never see either of the water levels they are comparing. Although our procedure was based somewhat on the assumption that such simultaneous comparison was the crucial perceptual factor in what Frank had screened out, we were primarily forced into this procedure because we were working with clay instead of water. It is impossible to design a screening procedure that allows the subject to see his (or the experimenter's) manipulations of the clay without also seeing the effects of such manipulation. Hence the most we can conclude from comparing our lack of success with screening with Frank's success is that the perceptual cues that constitute the stumbling block to conservation are more complex than those provided by simultaneous perception. Screening out simultaneous perceptual cues is not enough to induce conservation; as long as the child has been able to see, even separately, the disparate shapes, he remains "hung up" on the perceptual cues and makes the wrong judgments. Perhaps, when he is making his judgments about the amounts of the unseen shapes, he is doing so by some process of simultanization of the images he has already formed of the objects. He is comparing his images, rather than his percepts, and the images are as interfering with symbolic processes as the percepts.

The results of manipulation training are much more impressive. Twenty-two of forty-one children learned conservation when they were allowed to manipulate the clay themselves, whereas only thirteen of forty learned when they could merely watch the experimenter's manipulations (Figure 1). This finding is striking, for it demonstrates clearly that action makes a difference in learning.

However, does manipulation *always* make a difference, and if not, when? A consideration of the different effects of manipulation training when combined with the labeling-training procedures reveals some startling facts. When labels are provided, manipulation makes a big difference: sixteen of twenty-one subjects learned conservation when manipulation was allowed, whereas the ratio is reversed and only eight of twenty learned it when no manipulation was allowed. But when labels are *not* provided, the manipulation effect drops out entirely: the ratios are almost identical, with six of twenty subjects learning with manipulation and five of twenty learning without it (Table 2 and Figure 2). Allowing a child to manipulate the clay augments the learning of conservation *only* when verbal labels for compensating attributes are also provided for him. In such cases, however, the influence is a tremendous one. Indeed, it is strong enough to give us an over-all significant effect for manipulation even when the cases of labeling and no labeling are combined for analysis.

The results of training with labels are even more impressive. Twenty-four of forty-one children learned conservation when their training tasks were structured with verbal labels for compensating attributes, whereas only eleven of forty learned when no such labels were provided (Figure 1). Thus labeling, like manipulation, makes an important difference in whether or not a child learns conservation.

We must ask here, however, as we did about manipulation, whether labeling *always* makes a difference and if not, when. When we consider the different effects of training with labels when it is combined

TABLE 2
Number of Children Who Learned Conservation in Conditions under Which Labeling and Manipulation Variables are Combined.

	Labels with Manipulation	Labels with No Manipulation	No Labels with Manipulation	No Labels with No Manipulation
Learned	16	8	6	5
Did not learn	5	12	14	15
Totals	21	20	20	20

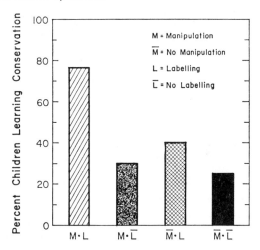

Figure 2. Percent of children who learned conservation in conditions where labeling and manipulation variables are combined.

with the manipulative-training procedures, we again see a striking relationship. When the subject is manipulating the clay, labeling makes a big difference: sixteen of twenty-one manipulating subjects learn conservation when labels are provided, whereas the ratio is reversed and only six of twenty learn it when no labels are provided. But when the subject is *not* manipulating the clay, labeling makes no appreciable difference: the ratios are about the same with eight of twenty subjects learning with labels and five of twenty learning without labels (Table 2 and Figure 2). Thus, providing a child with labels for compensating attributes helps him to learn conservation *only* when he is also manipulating the clay himself. Yet the influence of labeling in these cases is strong enough to yield an over-all significant effect for labeling even when cases of manipulation and no manipulation are combined for anlaysis.

Let us sum up our results before considering their implications. Screening had no effect on the learning of conservation, probably because our procedure did not allow us to screen out enough perceptual cues. Manipulation and labeling, on the other hand, were highly successful in inducing conservation; but—and this is the most interesting fact of all—*each of these worked only when the other was also present.* Thus manipulation without labeling was virtually ineffective, and the same was true of labeling without manipulation; but *together* they produced a remarkably high degree of learning among children.

What can we make of our results? Consider first our original Piagetian formulations. Our basic early hypothesis was that, if the mental operations necessary for conservation are translated into physical operations that a child can perform on the materials of the problem, the physical "practice" of such operations will facilitate the internalization of the concept. As we shall see, there are several factors that make us question the value of this original formulation.

The sheer physical performance of the operation of simple inversion without verbal labeling of relevant attributes does not facilitate learning (Figure 2)—though Piaget implies that the operation of inversion makes conservation possible. A tentative conclusion and one that does not yet reject our basic hypothesis, is simply that we have "actionized" the wrong operation, that the achievement of conservation does not depend in any simple sense upon the logical operation of inversion as such. Such a conclusion is supported somewhat by the experiments reported in Chapter 9.

Now consider the significance of our success with labeling *cum* manipulation. At first glance it seems that we have some support for the Piagetian hypothesis, and that all we need stipulate in order to accept it is that compensation, rather than inversion, must be the crucial operation involved in the acquisition of conservation. But two considerations force us to reject this view. The first is, again, the work reported in Chapter 9, which demonstrates that compensation, like inversion, is not sufficient to produce conservation; that compensation may be grasped by children who have not yet mastered conservation. But more important is a second consideration: the reasons our children gave in support of their judgments once they had acquired conservation. Of all the children who learned conservation in any of the conditions, there were only two who gave a compensation reason to justify their judgments, and only one of these received labeling training. In fact, most of the explanations that children gave after labeling training invoked the principle of inversion or something like it ("It's the same because, when you rolled them up, they looked the same" is a typical example), although several other kinds of reasons were also offered. It looks as though the labeling of relevant attributes does something other than focus the child's attention on the compensatory relation of those attributes.

In short, the kind of training we give seems to bear no relation to the kinds of reasoning the child uses to justify conservation once he acquires it, despite the fact that it *is* related to whether or not he acquires it. He may "have" the cognitive tools of inversion and even those of compensation without "knowing" conservation, as Carey has demonstrated (Chapter 9). And when he acquires conservation, no matter under what kind of training, he may use either of these tools to support his new knowledge, or he may not even rely on them at all. Surely, then, we have to reject as inadequate the view that the children who were required both to label and to manipulate materials learned conservation because they first learned the principle of compensation at the level of physical action and were therefore enabled to internalize it as a mental tool with which to grasp conservation. Indeed, we would again question seriously the more general Piagetian view that a cognitive achievement like conservation is the result of the internalization of actions and their conversion into operations governed by certain *logical* "rules." First of all, we find too little evidence for logical rules as such in the answers that children give. But what is more important, the general Piagetian view leaves out of account the *psychological* processes involved in achieving some particular form of cognitive mastery—such as the idea of conservation.

Consider our results now, within the theoretical framework developed in this book. The conservation problem has been cast in somewhat the following terms: the young child, relying on his usual ikonic mode of representing events, makes the judgments he does in the conservation situation because it is a situation in which perceptual cues are dominant. The teaching problem, then, is to lead the child to represent events before him in other ways, ways that will conflict with his perceptual rendering to the extent that he will reject it in favor of the more compelling alternatives. Such a rejection, the argument might run, constitutes at least a tacit acceptance on the child's part of the imperfect correlation between appearance and reality, and he is therefore less likely in the future to take appearance, without questioning it, as an adequate representation of reality.

What our experiment did precisely, by the use of manipulation and labeling, was to offer the child ways of representing the conservation problem that conflicted with the ikonic. By offering him manipulation, we were encouraging enactive representation; and by offering him verbal labels for compensating attributes, we were encouraging symbolic representation. In short, he was made to cognize the clay "physically" and verbally, instead of only perceptually.

The interesting fact is, however, that neither of these new modes of representation *alone* was able to induce enough conflict to produce appreciable learning. This is not really surprising when we consider how compelling were the perceptual cues in the situation, and how strongly the child of six or seven has learned to rely on his perceptual processes for representing his world. Would it not perhaps be asking too much of enactive representation—developmentally prior to ikonic representation and not so salient to the child as it once was before he came into the world of imagery—to undo entirely what ikonic representation is doing? An enactive message, "It *feels* the same" (as one child told us), pitted against a most compelling "But it *looks* different," may have a poor chance of survival in the ikonic child. The same thing is perhaps true with respect to a verbal message by itself. But when both enactive and verbal messages are saying "same" and perception alone is signaling a difference, the two win out over the one. Thus it is only when we marshal both enactive and symbolic forces against the ikonic that the ikonic finally gives way. It is when the child is both saying and doing that he learns not to believe fully what he is seeing. Except for the interaction among different modes of representation, learning could not occur.

An interesting question, one that we can only raise here and leave open for future inquiry, is just how labeling works. The verbal labels must in effect be giving the child a "conservation" message in the symbolic medium. But the form this message takes is not nearly so obvious to us as the ikonic message, "It looks different," or even the enactive message, "It feels the same," or (perhaps also) "I can make it the same." Because the child usually does not use the labels we give him in his explanations of conservation, it is difficult to determine by what process the "message" gets to its destination. As we have seen, the process does *not* seem to be a matter of activating the logical operation of compensation, which is then used to deduce conservation. It would be worth while to investigate whether words which do not specifically label the compensating attributes would work as well as these labels have. Perhaps the process is simply a matter of providing the child with many different words with which to describe the same clay, thus forcing him to think of the clay in many different ways. Certainly, once he can think of the same clay in a multiplicity of shapes, he is well on the way to conservation.

Perhaps the psychology of conservation (in contrast to its so-called logic) is a recognition that the same thing can take many guises and still be the same thing. One can achieve the insight enactively—by using the same stick in different ways for different ends—or symbolically, by the powerful devices of periphrases and relabeling. It is perception and imagery that most succumb to the error of taking a change in appearance to signal a change in identity.

CHAPTER 11

On Culture and Conservation

Patricia Marks Greenfield[1]

Both too much and too little have been said about "primitive mind"—too much in that the descriptions given us by anthropologists have been for the most part rather global generalizations based on inference from language, myth, ritual, and social life. Such accounts are not founded upon the observation of "mind in action," upon an analysis of behavior in concrete situations. So, we know very little indeed about "primitive minds" at work, and their operation remains largely to be explored. In fact, it is not unreasonable to ask in what sense the label "primitive" is even applicable to the thinking of non-Western peoples.

What has been implicit in the work of such anthropologists as Boas,

[1] I am grateful to M. Papa Diaw of the American Cultural Center, Dakar, for his generous Wolof lessons. I am also indebted to Dr. and Mrs. Robert Lagacé of the Yale Human Relations Area Files, who helped me to continue in their village of Taiba N'Diaye. M. Abdoulaye Sar assisted in the village, and Mlle. Secundine Sané served as recorder throughout all the experiments. M. Abdoulaye M'Bodj, Instituteur à la Direction des Inspections du premier et du deuxième Degré at the Senegalese Ministry of Education, deserves appreciation for making it possible for me to work in the elementary schools. I would also like to thank Mr. H. Hoffman and Mr. Thomas Zalla, of the American Peace Corps in Senegal for their kind help.

The research was carried on under the auspices of the Institut d'Etudes pédagogiques of the University of Dakar, Senegal. Mme. Simone Valantin of the Institut and M. Serge Sauvageot of the Institut français de l'Afrique noir (IFAN) were of particular help. A grant from the Ford Foundation made the work possible. The research here reported is also reported in a doctoral dissertation submitted to the Department of Social Relations at Harvard (cf. Greenfield, 1966).

Durkheim, Mauss, Mead, and Whorf is the assumption that different modes of thinking are characteristic of different cultures. It is a bold hypothesis that variations in cognitive functioning are formed by cultural influences. Unfortunately, from the point of view of testing the hypothesis, the study of intellectual development has been confined almost entirely to members of our own Western societies. Our richest picture of cognitive development, that drawn by Jean Piaget, is based entirely on experiments in which age alone is varied. In his view, cognitive maturation is made to appear like a biologically determined and universal sequence. While Piaget admits that environmental influences play a role, the admission is *pro forma*, and inventive experiments remain confined to American and European children, usually middle class children at that. Where Piaget's work has been extended to non-Western societies, the emphasis has been almost entirely quantitative. Such work has been confined largely to timetable studies, to the time "lag" in the development of "foreign" children in contrast to children in Geneva or Pittsburgh or London (Flavell [1963]). Qualitative differences between Western thinking and that of traditional societies have rarely been explored. Psychologists, when they have gone abroad, have usually approached their work in other cultures as though they were dealing with familiar phenomena, present in greater or lesser quantity (usually lesser). Hence the equation of "primitive" adult with "civilized" child.

Cambridge has steadily disagreed with Geneva on the fundamental "how" of intellectual growth. Our own work has emphasized the role of internalized, culturally transmitted technologies. One way of exploring this role is to establish the manner in which an enriched (or impoverished) environment affects growth. This approach uses instruction in its broadest sense as its instrument of exploration. A second approach is to study development in societies in which the culturally given "technologies" are radically different from our own, with the hope of finding and analyzing differences in cognitive functioning. This is the major strategy of the research reported in this chapter, though we shall at the same time study the effect of instruction on children in the different cultures.

The experiments to be described were done in Senegal, the westernmost tip of former French West Africa. The subjects were Wolof, members of the country's dominant ethnic group. The Wolofs, who are Moslem, constitute over one-third of Senegal's total population of 2,300,000. The basic experiment was the familiar one developed by Piaget to study the conservation of quantity and is described in

Chapter 9. It consisted in equating the quantity of water in two identical beakers, then pouring the contents of one beaker into one of a different size and inquiring whether the amount of water is now the same. Particulars will be set forth in a later section. For theoretical purposes the experiments could have been done almost anywhere. Many other preliterate traditional societies would provide as dramatic a contrast with our own milieu as this one did.

The Wolof group was selected from those found in Senegal largely because its children are to be found not only in the French-style schools of Dakar, the cosmopolitan capital city, but also out in the bush, sometimes receiving the beginnings of a French education, more often not.

The children were constituted into nine groups, the better to discern the effect of cultural differences: three degrees of urbanization and education were represented, with three age levels within each. As in all underdeveloped countries, the contrast between urban and rural life is enormous in Senegal, independent only since 1960. In the city one finds the accoutrements of Western industrial life; in the rural village, no matter how close, there is virtually none. School itself represents a new world of French culture and the written word, a world in almost dizzying contrast to the oral traditions of traditional West African society.

The cultural milieu of our first group, the rural unschooled children, had neither schools nor urban influence. Their setting was Taiba N'Diaye, a traditional Wolof village of about a thousand people. Its economy, like that of the whole country, is based on oil-producing peanut cultivation, although millet is grown for local consumption. Still, undernourishment is the general rule. Socially, residentially, and economically, the village is divided into fifty-nine compounds, each surrounded by a wooden palisade and inhabited by an extended family unit. Within each compound are several small, round, thatched huts inhabited by various members of a patrilocal family.

The village, located in the Cayar region of Senegal, is fifty miles by a good road from the country's coastal capital. It is found in the midst of bush, Senegal's dominant rural landscape. Flat expanses of grass are broken only by scattered baobab trees. The grass is mostly brown and dead during the cool, dry season (November through June). The landscape returns to green after the first rain, when the year's cultivation begins. The two sharply divided seasons are typical of the subtropical climate which covers most of the country.

Although the village has an elementary school, the children of our first group had never attended it. As already noted, they were subdivided into three ages: six to seven, eight to nine, and eleven to thirteen (seventeen, twenty, and twelve children respectively). Our age data are, alas, approximate. African children, especially in the bush, have only the vaguest idea of how old they are in terms of years; and parents stop counting age after a child receives his Moslem baptism, which happens on the eighth day after birth. Fortunately for us, however, the French government a number of years ago instituted civil status for all with its prerequisite census, a source from which reasonable age estimates can be obtained for children born since 1950. Any child not on the census rolls of Taiba N'Diaye was automatically eliminated from the study. Still, the census is far from perfect, and it is probably more accurate to say that our age data are accurate on the average, rather than in the particular case.

The cultural setting of the second major group—rural school children—was identical with that of the first with respect to the rural Wolof milieu in which its members lived. In fact, many of the children came from the same village of Taiba N'Diaye, and in at least ten cases from the same families. These children, however, unlike the first, were receiving a French-style education. Taiba N'Diaye's own school provided the two oldest groups of children, who were in the third and sixth grades. These groups (twenty and twenty-four children respectively) matched the two oldest unschooled rural groups. To find a group corresponding to the youngest unschooled children, it was necessary to go to a very similar Wolof village nearby where the school included a first-grade class. Twenty-three first-grade children from Méouane participated in the experiment.

Finally, the cultural milieu of the third group was characterized by the presence of both aspects of Western culture, urban setting and schooling. This group came from Dakar, the cosmopolitan capital of Senegal and the former capital of French West Africa. The children in this group came from three of the city's public schools. As with the rural-school children, the Dakar group was selected from the first, third, and sixth grades. Thus the two school groups were matched exactly with respect to the number of years of schooling as well as approximate age. Grade level and age are only roughly correlated in Senegal because of the vagaries which result from attempting the relatively sudden conversion to literacy of an entire population. For this reason, the ages of the school groups were more variable than those of the unschooled groups, and at least some of the school groups had a slightly higher average age. (There were twenty-three first-grade children, twenty-two third-grade, and twenty sixth-grade.)

According to a Wolof informant, children in the bush are *not* chosen to go to school on the basis of their intelligence. In fact, if a child shows promise at the Koranic school to which all boys and girls are first sent, he may be kept there and never sent to the national school. Such a selection factor would preclude an imbalance of native intelligence in favor of the school group. In general, certain families elect to send their children to school. If one child is sent, all usually go, except that girls, in line with the Moslem attitude toward women, are often not sent to school at all. Thus, there is no reason to believe that the rural children in school and out were not equivalent with respect to native endowment, and we can confidently attribute differences between the two groups to the school experience itself. Traditionally, school attendance has been linked with caste membership, with low-caste members of the society being the most willing to give their children a French education. In this village, however, school attendance was not related to caste.

The academic program is based on a French model and, as in France, is under the central control of the Ministry of Education. Indeed, the curriculum is specified in such minute detail by a booklet entitled *L'Education sénégalaise* that, for all practical purposes, our two school groups were having the same educational experience; and consequently the differences between the two groups must therefore be attributed to other distinguishing features of urban and rural milieu.

The school children went through the experiments individually at their school. Though every effort was made to hold things constant from school to school, there were some inevitable and considerable variations. In one city school the principal occupied the office adjoining the room in which the experiments were being carried out, and his callers periodically passed through the room, unannounced except by the long compulsory series of Wolof salutations. In the bush schools, at the other extreme, privacy was fairly complete, but the exigencies of space were such that the experimenting was done outdoors rather than in. Sampling in general was systematic. In a given school class every *n*th child would be taken from the roll in order to arrive at a sample size close to the target of twenty children per subgroup.

The unschooled bush children were examined at the author's compound in the village, one much like all the others. Its combined dining-room-and-kitchen building served as the experimental room, and a rough thatched shelter in the middle of the compound provided a "waiting room" for the next subject, who was usually accompanied by a good number of curious children from his own extended family. While an

official document from the Minister of Education aided us in securing
school children as subjects, it was necessary to obtain permission from
every family head individually so that the children under his juris-
diction might participate. Although none refused, there was an initial suspicion that an attempt was being made to conscript their children into school. For these children, the sampling unit was the resi-
dential compound, and the selection of children within a compound
was made on a systematic basis from among those enumerated in the
census rolls.

The experimental situation, in so far as it consists of an interview
of one child by one adult, is unheard of in the traditional culture,
where almost everything occurs in groups, and adults command
rather than seek the opinions of children. The children, nevertheless,
whether attending school or not, seemed at home with the tasks, and
many seemed to be enjoying themselves thoroughly. Although they
talked much less than Western children do and restricted themselves
to answering questions, their patience was monumental and, correlatively, their attention span seemed to surpass by far that of American
children.

The author carried out all the experiments in the Wolof language.
A young Senegalese girl served as recorder, taking verbatim
transcripts of the children's responses in a highly individualized phonetic system, for Wolof is an oral language and the recorder was not
a linguist.

The exact conservation task was based on the most unambiguous
translation of the American and Swiss procedure as could be formulated in Wolof. Although the school children were at various stages
in learning French, the language of all formal instruction, the use
of French in the experiments would have annulled their value by destroying the comparability of the groups. Among the subgroups of
the school sample, for instance, the developmental progress between
the first and sixth grades which is simply due to an increased ability
to understand and express oneself in French would be indistinguishable from that due to an actual shift in modes of thought. Moreover,
the school groups responding in French would in no way be comparable either to their unschooled Senegalese comrades or to their
European counterparts, both of whom would have the advantage of
being interrogated in their native tongue. At least one previous study
of conservation in Africa suffered from this methodological flaw
(Flavell [1963]).

In the basic conservation task (pretest, Figure 1) a child was
presented with two identical beakers partly filled with water.

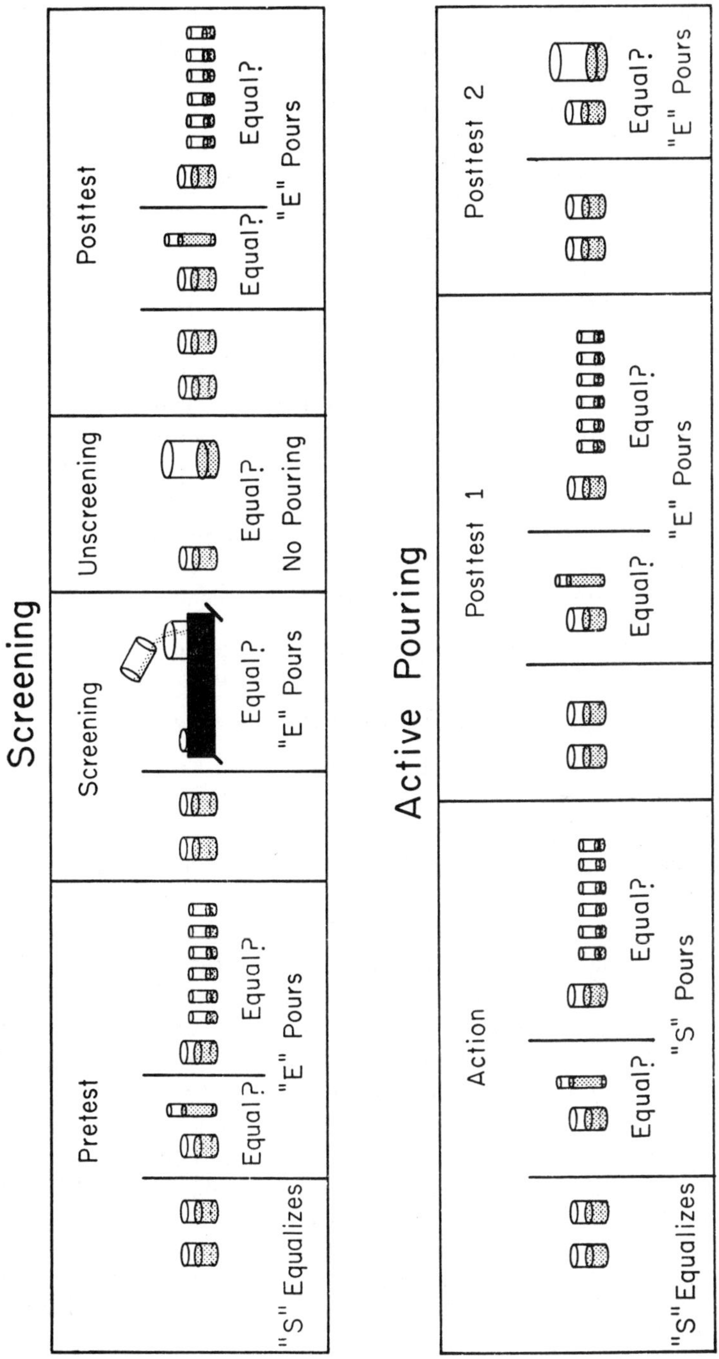

Figure 1. Procedures used in experiments.

The child equalized the water levels of the two beakers. The water of one of the beakers was subsequently transferred to a second longer, thinner beaker, causing the water level to rise, of course. The child was then asked whether the two beakers still had the same amount of water. In the second part of the experiment six shorter, thinner beakers replaced the long, thin one, and this time the water was divided among the six. The child compared the water in the original beaker with the total contents of the six small ones and judged whether or not the amounts were equal.

A major linguistic difficulty that had to be overcome was the inherent ambiguity in the Wolof language surrounding the two words for "equal" (*tolo* and *yem*). Both have the double sense of equal level and equal amount. Since the correct solution of the conservation problem depends on recognizing the distinction between these two "equalities," the cognitive implications of this linguistic difficulty are substantial.

Adult Wolofs agreed, however, that the version finally used referred unambiguously to the quantity rather than the level of water. In Wolof, the key conservation question was asked this way:

> Ndah sa verre bi ak suma verre bi nyo yemle ndoh; wala suma verre bi mo upa ndoh; wala sa verre bi mo upa ndoh?

A literal translation into English yields the following:

> Does this glass of yours and this glass of mine have equal water; or does this glass of mine have more water; or does this glass of yours have more water?

An interesting problem arose when it came to asking the unschooled children to justify their answers to this question. A previous experiment had shown that whereas the question, "Why do you *think* or *say* that thus and such is true?" would meet with uncomprehending silence, the question, "Why *is* thus and such true?" could often be answered quite easily. So the question asked of American children,"Why do you *think* this glass has more (or equal) water?" was modified to, "Why *does* this glass have more (or equal) water?"[2] It would seem that the unschooled Wolof children are lacking in Western self-consciousness: they do not distinguish between their own thought or a statement about something and the thing itself. Thought and the object of thought seem to be one. Consequently, the idea

---

[2] The question actually asked was, "Lu tah nyo yem?" (literally, "What reason they are equal?") or "Lu tah bi mo upa bi?" ("What reason this one has more than his one?")

of explaining a *statement* is meaningless; it is the external event that is to be explained. The relativistic notion that events can vary according to the point of view may therefore be absent to a greater degree than in Western culture.

THE PATTERN OF CONSERVATION

The development of the conservation of a continuous quantity, as a maturational achievement, is said by Piaget to be but one manifestation of more general and fundamental changes that occur in the course of cognitive growth. The first question we must ask is whether conservation does in fact develop among the Senegalese and whether this development relates to chronological age.

The achievement of conservation was said to be present when a child gave equality responses to both quantity comparisons with the standard beaker, that involving the long, thin beaker and that involving the six small beakers. A child who changed his mind was given credit for his final answer. The data on conservation are presented graphically in Figure 2. The most striking thing here is the one point at which conservation *ceases*, for all practical purposes, to be related to age. The oldest unschooled bush children (eleven- to thirteen-year-olds) show no significant increase in conservation over the eight- and

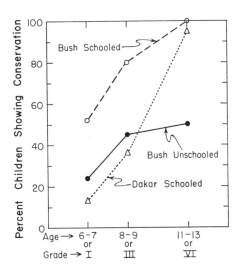

Figure 2. Percent of children of different backgrounds and ages exhibiting conservation of a continuous quantity.

nine-year-olds. Only half of the unschooled bush children attain conservation at this late age. It is possible, of course, that development is simply slower without school, so that an adult group might manifest 100 percent conservation behavior. Other results, however, obtained both from these subjects and from subjects in other cultures do not make it seem likely. A study of conceptualizing was done with unschooled adults (see Chapter 13) when we found that eleven- to thirteen-year-old children had responded in essentially the same manner as the eight- and nine-year-old group. No further changes in the pattern of conceptual thought were observed in the adults, save for a decrease in the variability of response from subject to subject. That experiment and this one suggest that, without school, intellectual development, defined as *any* qualitative change, ceases shortly after age nine. An investigator in Niger has made the same observation among unschooled African children on a completely different type of activity—drawing.[3] And another investigator who worked with conservation tasks (albeit different ones) found no difference between minimally schooled Chinese adolescent boys and a matched group of adults in Hong Kong in the percentage of subjects with conservation Goodnow (1962). It would appear at first glance that the technologies and skills absorbed from the school experience may indeed strongly affect the question of whether some children in Senegal (and perhaps elsewhere) even achieve conservation of a continuous quantity.

In contrast, the school children of bush and town yield the familiar developmental sequence, with conservation virtually always attained by the sixth grade. Note one point. The interviews were all in Wolof, as mentioned; but schooling is in French. It is interesting that the skills being learned in French do in fact carry over into thinking and speaking in Wolof. Bush school children, indeed, are almost indistinguishable from American or Swiss children. The studies reported elsewhere in this book, using much the same procedure as was used in Senegal, report conservation in half the children at ages six and seven (first and second grade) among American children. Other investigators have reported 75 percent conservation behavior at age eight (third grade) (Flavell, 1963). Bush school children show 52 percent conservation in the first grade (probably an average age of eight) and 80 percent in the third grade (average age between nine and ten). In terms of grade level, the Senegalese figures are close to being identical to the Western ones, although the Wolof children are behind in terms of chronological age. The parallel findings certainly cast

---

[3] Evelyn Pierre, personal communication.

strong doubts on any simple maturational notion of development. Rural Wolof children exposed to a certain set of cultural influences, namely, the school, differ more from other rural Wolof children raised without school than they do from European children. As the two groups of Wolof children are from the same gene pool, whereas the Europeans represent a nonoverlapping gene pool, this finding casts deep doubt on any biological-genetic point of view.

As for the performance of the Dakar school children, it is markedly inferior to that of the bush children in terms of the proportion of children showing conservation, until the sixth grade, when the two school groups are virtually indistinguishable in this respect and the unschooled group falls dramatically behind. We could attribute this difference to the globally disrupting effect of urbanization. Yet a look at the reasoning behind the children's amount judgments indicates that such an explanation is not only too general to have much explanatory value, but is also untrue. In any case, we cannot talk about these children's lives as being "disrupted" by urban influences, for the overwhelming majority were born in Dakar and have been children of the city from the start. So let us go on to the children's reasoning, which is in any case more interesting than the percent attaining conservation at each age.

There are basically three types of justification. These can be ordered according to how much they reflect *directly perceptible* features of the current situation. First, *perceptual* reasons do so to the highest degree. This class of reason refers to the features of the display in front of the child; it includes any description of the beakers and their contents. Perceptual reasons can be classified according to analyticity and complexity. In addition, one type of perceptual reason expresses a conflict between the appearance ("It looks like more") and the reality ("But it's really the same") of the situation. This type of reason occurred in the conservation responses of American children (Chapter 9), but did not manifest itself in the African protocols. If any conflict between the "appearance" and "reality" of the situation exists for these African children, it is expressed in different ways. In fact, previous pilot work at the Institut d'Etudes Pédagogiques at the University of Dakar had indicated that there is no conventional way of translating into Wolof the question oriented towards an appearance-reality conflict—"Is the water in the second glass 'really' different or does it 'just look' different?"—and that when the translation is made the children do not understand what it means.

Second, *direct-action* reasons refer to the act of pouring the water from one of the standard beakers into a test beaker (or beakers). Note that these reasons are still rather closely tied to the situation, for the act actually takes place in the experiment and is the most recently observed physical action. Nevertheless, a direct-action reason can also be considered a Piagetian operation. Piaget states that an operation is an action that is both *internal* and *reversible*. We shall keep only the former part of the definition, leaving the latter for empirical investigation and later discussion. Still, it is an open question whether the direct action has in fact been internalized. If so it has been retained *exactly as it happened*.

The third category of reasons is called *transformational*. These reasons go beyond the "givens" of the present situation and represent a transformation of that situation in the child's head. For this reason they are truly "operational" in Piaget's sense, for they are by definition the products of *internalized* (or mental) *action*. In the present experiment, the transformations utilized in reasoning were of two main sorts: action and identity. The action transformations were sometimes inverse, also called negative or reverse ("If you were to pour it back . . ."), sometimes correlative ("If you were to pour the other one . . ."). These action transformations will be called *indirect-action* reasons, so as to emphasize the fact that they are not directly observed in the experiment. Note that the correlative action creates a *hypothetical* state of equality in the two sets of test beakers (for example, two long, thin beakers) while the inverse action recreates the *initial* state of equality in the two standard beakers. The inverse thus reestablishes the original state produced by the first equalizing operation. Reference to the original state of the system, in this case the state of equality in the two standard beakers, constitutes the third and most important type of transformation argument, the *identity* reason (for example, "This one '[full standard beaker] and this one [empty standard beaker] had equal water"). Identity is the "null" transformation: nothing is changed. Logically, the identity argument is the most basic, because it is in fact the initial equalizing operation that determines the correct answer to the conservation problem. But logical primacy cannot be automatically equated with psychological primacy, as Piaget is wont to do; therefore let us examine the psychological status of the identity argument.

In America, younger children rely much more heavily on perceptual reasons than do older children. This is also dramatically the case among the Wolof school children (Figure 3). Indeed, we find a drop from 79 percent perceptual reasons in the first grade of the bush school and 63 percent in the first grade of the Dakar school to 27 percent in both sixth grades. But the unschooled bush children, iden-

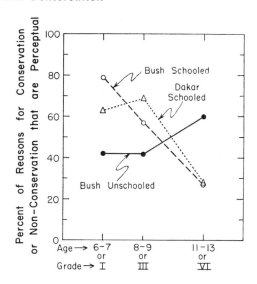

Figure 3. Percent of reasons for conservation or nonconservation that are perceptual.

tical to the bush school children in every respect save one, use *more* perceptual reasons as they grow older. Yet note that the unschooled children start out less perceptually oriented than those in school. It seems, then, that the *first* effect of schooling is to increase their analytic attention to the perceptible features of situations such as our experiment, and that this effect is then followed by a systematic and drastic reduction in the importance of such features. This result finds an interesting parallel in the American children, who, in developing the relational idea of a proportion (Chapter 8), first become *more* perceptual with age, in the sense of learning to utilize more than one perceptible attribute at a time. Only after this stage do they unify these attributes by means of the "fraction" schema. This simpler, more symbolic "theory" in turn eliminates the need for the plural perceptual reasons out of which it arose.

Let us now look at reasons in relation to conservation judgments. Do Wolof children fail to conserve for the same reasons as Western children, and do they attain conservation by the same paths? In most cases the Wolof children use a transformational or direct-action reason as the basis for justifying conservation, just as American children do (Chapter 9). However, direct action assumes greater importance in the conservation reasoning of these children than it did in the American children's proconservation arguments. Price-Williams (1961), working with Tiv children in Nigeria, also found that justifications for equality judgments were in terms of action. The over-all totals of the reasons used by all one hundred eighty-one children studied were:

40 percent based on perceptible features,
16 percent based on direct action,
44 percent based on transformation (identity and indirect action).

In support of nonconservation, they were:

78 percent based on perceptible features,
20 percent based on direct action,
2 percent are transformations.[4]

These figures indicate that transformation reasons are a sufficient, if not a necessary, condition for conservation. A closer look at the actual transformation arguments reveals that 95 percent of them contain a reference to the identity "transformation." Therefore, we may conclude that the identity argument is not only *logically* but also *psychologically* sufficient for a conservation judgment. On the other hand, the psychological results do not confirm the logical idea that an identity reason is also *necessary* to conservation of amount.

As for reversibility, that is, the possibility of inverse action, it is secondary to the identity element in two ways. First, it usually does not appear as a reason in isolation, but is accompanied by an identity argument (for example, "If you were to pour this water [long, thin beaker], here this one [full standard beaker] and this one [empty standard beaker] would be equal"), whereas identity alone often appears as an argument for conservation. Thus, it would seem that identity is a necessary condition for the use of reversible action as a conservation argument. One could say that reversibility without identity yields the kind of result obtained by Carey (Chapter 9): a change in level obtained by pouring the liquid into a beaker of a different shape is seen as reversible; but, although the young child may realize that the change is temporary, it is no less "real" to him, for the change in level implies a correlative change in quantity. In brief, Carey finds reversibility without conservation.

Second, it is *identity* rather than *reverse* transformations that cause direct-action reasons to be associated with an "operational" or correct

---

[4] Seventy-eight percent of the children contributed two reasons, corresponding to the two parts of the conservation task. Only three out of the one hundred eighty-one children gave as many as four reasons, the maximum number possible.

solution to the conservation problem. In other words, direct-action reasons are *always* in support of conservation when they contain an identity element. When they do not, they frequently support an incorrect judgment. Reverse action, in contrast, is rarely even associated with direct-action reasons. In consequence, it seems more accurate to say that it is identity, and not reversibility, that turns actions into operations, at least in the conservation situation.

One final observation concerning the role of identity in conservation. As action reasons become more operational, both in the sense of supporting conservation judgments and in the sense of being more internal (that is, indirect), identity arguments increase in a rather dramatic correlation (Table 1). Thus identity would seem to be an accurate index of operationality defined according to these two Piagetian criteria.

Before leaving the discussion of reasons in support of conservation judgments, we must point out an interesting difference between American and Wolof justifications. The older American children participating in Frank's screening experiment sometimes spontaneously remark upon the *necessity* of equality (e.g., "It must be the same"). There is not one instance of such an appeal to necessity among all the Wolof children, although the language does contain the requisite vocabulary.

Turning now from equality to inequality judgments, we see that the general picture of nonconservation reasoning is also very similar to that found in the United States, for the overwhelming conservation block is a perceptual one. The Wolofs deviate from the American pattern in one major respect, however: there is a significant minority (20 percent) of inequality judgments that are supported by *direct action* reasons. That is, Wolof children often say things like, "There is more in this glass because you poured it." American children only use such reasons to support a conservation position, although Piaget (1952) reports one instance of an action reason for a nonconservation

TABLE 1
Percentage of Action Reasons That Include a Reference
to the Identity Justification

	Direct-Action Reasons for Nonconservation	Direct-Action Reasons for Conservation	Indirect-Action Reasons for Conservation
Reference to identity	0%	47%	75%
Number of reasons	19	75	20

response in a four-year-old. This seemingly bizarre reasoning did not come as a complete surprise, since pretests conducted in the Senegalese bush in 1963 by Bruner and Valantin had underlined the importance of definition by action. They had found that one glass would be called "the same" as another by virtue of the fact that each had "been poured into." But here was something different: inequality based on an action.

It could not be simply a matter of equating actions rather than amounts of water, for different children gave the same action answer in the same situation, sometimes to justify a judgment of equality and sometimes to justify a verdict of inequality. A control procedure also cast doubt on the idea that equality would be based on identical actions when the quantities of water were different. More likely, the children are utilizing *action* reasons to explain a *perceptual* discrepancy between the appearance of the water in the two glasses. The contrast between the initial appearance of equal quantities of water and the later appearance of inequality is perhaps resolved by recourse to the experimenter's action. It is that form of "magical" thinking in which natural phenomena are explained by attributing special powers to intervening human agents.

School suppresses such thinking with astonishing absoluteness. There is *not one instance* of such reasoning among the children who have been in school seven months or more. Urban life itself exerts no influence in this direction, for among the first-graders in Dakar (who had completed no more than four months of school at the time of the experiment) one finds the most "magical" reasoning of all—80 percent of these children's action reasons are of this type.[5] So, Wolof children who have not been to school differ from American children in the reason why they do not have conservation. Their reasons reflect less "perceptual seduction" than "seduction by the experimenter's actions."

As just described, direct actions are less likely than indirect actions to bear the mark of an operation (internalization), for their origin is to be found in external physical action. And note that it is also *direct-* rather than *indirect*-action reasons that are used by the unschooled children to support inequality judgments. This finding is in line with Piaget's general point that conservation demands internalized operations.

---

[5] These children had had less schooling than the first grade bush children, as they had to wait several months for their parents to construct a classroom. In fact, the few months of schooling they had received were probably ineffectual because of conditions of extreme overcrowding and disorganization.

In Senegal, as in the United States, perceptual reasons support both conservation and nonconservation judgments. Although perceptual reasons are relatively infrequent among both the youngest unschooled children and the oldest school children, the former group uses them to support *nonconservation,* the latter, *conservation.* Can we then find an observable difference between the two types of perceptual reason, a difference that will set off the thinking of Senegalese children who have conservation from those who do not? It would seem so. When perceptual reasons reflect attention to *several* perceptible aspects of the conservation situation, they are likely to back up a conservation position; when they indicate that the child is centering on only one aspect of the situation, they are likely to go along with nonconservation. However, the two perceptible aspects do not have to be the two dimensions of height and width that Piaget claims are of crucial importance to conservation through compensation. In fact, a reference to the *same* dimension of two *beakers* is more effective than a reference to two *dimensions* of one or two beakers.

Returning now to the city-school children, we must note that it is precisely in this respect that the younger city-school children fall behind the rural groups. That is, their transformation reasons are associated with conservation about as often as in the bush. But many more of their perceptual reasons are reasons *against* conservation. It turns out that, correlatively, the city children are much less inclined to focus on more than one aspect of the situation when they give perceptual reasons; they more often think in terms of *one* attribute of *one* of the beakers, never mentioning other attributes of the same beaker or the other beakers involved in the experiment. Nor are they inclined to relate two features of the displays even implicitly through the use of a comparative descriptive word—for example, "thinner," "taller." The importance of getting away from a single salient perceptible cue if an American child is to develop conservation was also commented upon in Chapter 9. Thus, the rural-urban difference in the percentage of younger children showing conservation is *not general,* but is concentrated among those children who give perceptual reasons.

Exposure to the more diverse sensory impressions of the city seems not to make children more perceptual; quite the opposite—their perceptual impressions of the experiment (as reflected in their reasons for judgment) were *less* diverse, *more* restricted to a single impression. We may hypothesize, however, that linguistic conditions produce this poverty of perceptual description in city children. Wolof as spoken in Dakar has become much simplified, owing to its status as the African *lingua franca* there. And, indeed, the descriptive language of the city children was less varied than that of their rural counterparts, particularly the school children. The importance of symbolic coding in fostering a conflict was discussed in the preceding chapter.

A SCREEN AGAINST PERCEPTIBLE CUES

One of the strategies for discerning what produces a particular reaction is to try to alter it. In the screening studies carried out with American children (Chapter 9), it was argued that conservation depends for its attainment on the development of a sense of conflict between how things appeared and how they "really were." If such were the case, the argument continued, one should hasten conservation by shielding the child from initial exposure to the perceptible inequalities by carrying out the pouring with beakers behind a screen. This is to say, one would first show the identical beakers with an equal amount of water in them. Then the contents of one of the beakers would be poured into a taller, wider beaker—with all beakers covered almost to their tops by an opaque screen. This procedure worked in the United States and, indeed, it succeeded strikingly in getting the children to say that the same amount of water was present in both beakers, not only while the screen was in place but also after it was removed. The screen was a success, pedagogically.

Would the same procedure prove successful among children whose language indicates little concern with noting and reconciling self-consciously the differences between appearance and reality? It would seem unlikely. In any case, a screening procedure similar to that used in Massachusetts was employed in Senegal (see Figure 1), including a request for the reasons for amount judgments both before and after the removal of the screen (see pp. 193 ff).

As for gross results, only 30 percent of the eighty-one Wolof children who did not have conservation on the pretest discussed before showed an improved performance on the posttest, in contrast to 61 percent improvement among comparable American children. These results are in terms of shifts among three categories of response: (1) *conservation,* which means an equality reaction on both parts of the pretest; (2) *fluctuation,* or giving a conservation response to one part of the pretest and a nonconservation response to the other; and (3) *nonconservation,* with inequality answers on both parts of the pretest.

While screening was not totally ineffective with the Wolof children, the effect was trivial on closer inspection. For it turned out to be nothing more than a threshold phenomenon. What screening did was to induce cónservation in those children who were already on the verge of conservation, as indicated by their fluctuation on the pretest. Those who had shown no previous signs of conservation were helped little. The change wrought in the fluctuating subjects was virtually the same as with American children: in Massachusetts 65 percent of such subjects were moved to conservation, as compared with 55 percent in Senegal. In addition, 73 percent of the American children who had shown no conservation on the pretest showed improvement (either to fluctuation or conservation) on the posttest. In Senegal, only 13 percent of the comparable group of thirty-eight Wolof children improved on the posttest; and only one of them moved all the way from nonconservation to conservation. In sharp contrast, 36 percent of the children giving nonconservation judgments in Massachusetts moved all the way to conservation on the posttest as a result of screening. In short, if a Senegalese child was not already uncertain on the pretest, he was not likely to be helped by the screening procedure. The same was not true of the American children. The data are summed up in Table 2.

It would be helpful to relate that one could easily tell on the basis of the reasons proffered during the pretest which fluctuating subjects would be moved toward conservation by screening. Alas, the number of subjects shrinks as one seeks to isolate justification patterns. However, some suggestive results can be given. The first is that, if the subjects show any tendency to justify incorrect judgments in the lan-

TABLE 2

Percentage of American and Senegalese Children Who Showed
Various Degrees of Improvement from Pretest to Posttest as a
Result of Screening Experience

	Pretest			
Posttest	No Conservation		Fluctuation	
	United States	Senegal	United States	Senegal
No conservation	27 %	87 %	12%	7%
Fluctuation	37	10	23	38
Conservation	36	3	65	55
	100%	100%	100%	100%
Number of children	11	38	17	42

guage of identity, they are certain to be in the conservation group after screening. At the other extreme, those fluctuating subjects who show any sign of action-magic in their justification are almost sure not to benefit from screening. Finally, fluctuating subjects who use any form of perceptual analysis to back up incorrect quantity judgments are more likely to benefit from the screen than those who use non-analytic perceptual arguments in the same situation. Perceptual analysis involves any effort to describe particular attributes of the water or of the beakers.

In the main, however, we are prepared to believe that screening was of very little help to those who had not yet achieved conservation and that the help it afforded the fluctuaters was nonspecific, the result of an opportunity to practice. It is doubtful whether much is due to special features of the screening technique itself. Other findings support this conclusion. For example, screening does not affect the reasons given by Wolof children without conservation either after unscreening or in the later posttest. Most notably, *perceptual* reasons are not reduced one whit, *even during the time that the water level is hidden by the screen.* In Massachusetts, on the other hand, there is a sharp decline in perceptual reasons with the introduction of the screen (in all age groups) and a further decline in perceptual reasons on the posttest (among all but the youngest group).

What is there in Wolof thinking that renders screening so ineffective as an instructional technique? Certainly, it would appear that school children, particularly Dakar school children, have perceptual barriers to conservation just as American children do. It might be that the screen does indeed shield them from a quick misleading ikonic rendering of the situation (Chapter 9, p. 199), but that the symbolic representation substituted for the perceptual image and designed to serve as a guide for organizing their perceptions in a new way (Chapter 9, p. 201) actually organizes these perceptions by means of a conceptual framework foreign to their thinking. This important pedagogical point will be more fully documented following the presentation of some additional relevant data.

As for the Wolof children who do not go to school, it is not so difficult to understand the failure of the screen as an instructional technique, for perceptual difficulties did not seem to be their problem in the first place. They do not justify nonconservation by a perceptual rationale. Action reasons more often serve that purpose. In this group, moreover, perceptual reasons do not decrease as conservation increases with age. Quite the contrary: an increase in perceptual reasons is associated with an increase in conservation. So it seems reasonable to suppose that a procedure designed to eliminate reasons based on perceptible cues would not be particularly relevant for this group. Consequently, a second training technique, specially planned to combat "magical" thinking about action, was developed for unschooled children. The results of this second experiment should also bear upon the question of whether screening was in fact relevant to the difficulties of our group of unschooled children. Consider this second training technique before we draw any final conclusions about the children's reaction to screening itself.

COMBATING ACTION-MAGIC

In this version of the conservation procedure, everything remained basically the same with one exception: the child did all the pouring himself. The rationale was this: the child, while perfectly willing to attribute "magical" powers to an authority figure like the experimenter, would not attribute any special powers to himself. A discrepancy in the apparent amount of water was not so likely to be rationalized as having been produced by adult magical power. Any child, moreover, is bound to have more accurate cause-effect notions with regard to his own action than with regard to the actions of others. The child with little experience in manipulating environmental objects—as would be truer of children in the passive Wolof culture than of children in America—might also be more prone to attribute puzzling changes to extrinsic powers. Experience in producing effects on the physical world might combat this tendency.

As before, the child began by equalizing the water levels in the two standard beakers, pouring into one to match the other. Then, unlike the first procedure, the experimenter told the subject to pour the water from one of the beakers into the long, thin beaker used in the first experiment (Figure 1). He was then asked if the two beakers contained the same amount of water and why. The wording of the two questions was exactly the same as in the previous experiment. After giving his explanation, the child was told to pour the water back into the standard beaker and finally to distribute the water among the six small beakers. Once again, he was asked if the standard beaker and the six small ones contained the same quantity of water and why. The rest of the experiment consisted of two posttests, with the experimenter pouring, to see whether conservation would carry over to the standard situation. The first posttest, exactly like the posttest of the screening experiment, used the same tall, thin beaker and the six small beakers into which the child poured in the first part of the present experiment. The second posttest substituted a new beaker, the tall, wide one. In this way there was an opportunity to observe whether conservation would prevail in a situation the child had not met while pouring the water himself. (The sequence of events is made clear in the bottom half of Figure 1.)

This "active" version of the conservation experiment can be considered both as a test of conservation and as a training technique for the traditional conservation task. As there was no pretest, we can first of all ask whether the conservation rate and the reasoning when the child pours differ from when the experimenter pours. A comparison with the pretest of the screening experiment yields this information. In the second place, we may ask whether this procedure is effective as a training technique. A comparison of the posttest results of the two training experiments answers this question. A different group of rural unschooled children participated in this experiment, but the two groups were comparable and from the same village. Essentially the same selection procedures were used, but the children doing the "active" version of the conservation test represented only half of the village's extended family units, rather than all of them, as in the first experiment. All the children from a given family who were going to participate in either conservation experiment did so at the same time, so that any contaminating communication was kept to a minimum. Because of the smaller sample in this experiment, the two oldest groups had to be lumped together for purposes of analysis. The formation of a single group of eight- to ten-year-olds seemed perfectly justified by the homogeneity of the pretest conservation results from the two oldest unschooled groups (discussed before) in the screening experiment. There were nine six- and seven-year-olds and eleven eight- and ten-year-olds.

That pouring makes a difference to the unschooled children is evident. Among the younger ones, two-thirds of the group who transfer the water themselves have conservation; only a quarter of the other group had conservation when the experimenter poured. In the older group, the contrast is equally dramatic: 82 percent of those who do the pouring themselves show conservation, as compared with slightly less than half of the group placed in the standard testing situation. So much for the pretest.

The "do-it-yourself" procedure has surprisingly strong effects on later behavior as well. Recall that there are two posttests to compare, each corresponding to a posttest on the screening procedure. The first posttest is comparable to the unscreening. This one is carried out with the same beaker as was used in the "do-it-yourself" condition—the taller, thinner one and the six small ones. The second posttest involves, as in the screening posttest, a change to a different beaker. The two procedures are compared in Figure 4. As far as the older children are concerned, it turns out that it does not matter which posttest we compare. Active participation by the child is superior to screening as a pedagogical experience. In the older group, all the children show conservation in both posttests. Screening had produced it in only two-thirds of the older children, according to posttest figures.

Among the younger subjects, there is a little backsliding on the first posttest, and no difference between the effectiveness of screening and pouring as training techniques. The young unschooled bush children show an effect comparable to that in the youngest group of American children who succeed under optimal training conditions with screening, but who cannot withstand the misleading cues in the posttest. But on the second posttest, eight of nine of the bush youngsters regain conservation, a proportion considerably higher than the half who had shown it after screening in the earlier study of unschooled children in Taiba N'Diaye. This increase is mostly due to the greater difficulty of maintaining conservation when the water is divided among several beakers, a task that was included on the

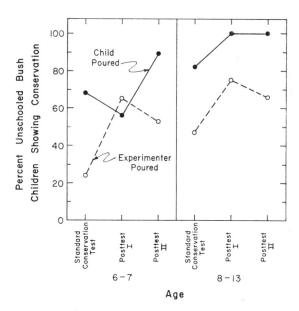

Figure 4. Percent of bush unschooled children showing conservation after pouring and screening.

first posttest, but not on the second. The reasons for the greater difficulty of this task will be taken up later.

Could the rather dramatic effects of "doing it yourself" be the potentially universal result of activity *per se*, or do they occur because this training technique undermines the "magical" mode of causal thinking peculiar to unschooled bush children? Or might the superiority of "pouring" over screening stem from a procedural artifact—in other words, the children who poured had no pretest on which it was easy to err, and thus they had no "commitment" to an incorrect solution. To test these two possibilities, an additional control experiment was run with some Dakar school children attending a girls' school. Although the other groups tested had included boys, this aspect seems unimportant, since no consistent sex differences had shown up in the first conservation experiment in Dakar.

The control experiment comprised two conditions—a "pouring" condition and a "screening" condition. There was no pretest under either condition. Fifteen Wolof children from the first and third grades took part in the pouring experiments, seventeen in the screening experiment. The screening experiment was exactly like that already described, minus the pretest. The pouring experiment was like the first one, except that the six small beakers were completely eliminated.

First screening. The proportion of children showing conservation (41 percent) when the screen separated subject from beaker was between that obtained on the *pretest* of the previous experiment and that obtained while the screen was in place during the same experiment. But the posttest result was clearly inferior to that produced by the first screening experiment. This suggests again that screening itself is not effective, but rather that it permits a repetition of the conservation tasks. The control experiment, lacking a pretest, permitted less repetition and produced inferior results. We may also eliminate the issue concerning the effect of initial error on the pretest, leading to an interfering commitment that diminishes the effects of training. Initial error does not reduce the effect of screening: the screen promotes conservation no better, even when it is the child's first experience with the conservation problem.

The results of the pouring experiment do indeed suggest that the effectiveness of the "active" form of the conservation task is based on its "antimagic" capability. Pouring does not work at all among the city-school children who do not have the "magical" thinking that the procedure was designed to combat. Only one child showed conservation under this condition, a performance that is even markedly inferior to the level of the Dakar school children operating under standard conditions in the first experiment. It may well be that pouring for the city children may have an interfering effect, but time did not permit a fuller examination of the matter.

The success of an instructional method in one group of children and its failure in another strengthens our conviction that differently enculturated children have basically different schemata for approaching conservation, schemata which go beyond mere verbal differences. Indeed, the variation from group to group in response to "screening" and "pouring" indicates the presence of greater subcultural differences in thinking than might have been concluded from the differences in the verbal reasons they gave in defense of their judgments. For example, more than half of the nonconservation reasons given by the two older unschooled bush groups in the pretest of the screening experiment were perceptual rather than action ("magical"); yet the act of pouring was followed by conservation in all of a matched group of rural subjects. In contrast, there is no reason to think that any subject in Dakar was moved from nonconservation to conservation as a result of transferring the water from beaker to beaker, though the verbal justifications of these children were also highly perceptual.

Price-Williams' (1961) study of conservation of both continuous and discontinuous quantities among unschooled Tiv children in Nigeria gives further indication of the importance of active manipulation. This investigator found that 100 percent of the Tiv children had achieved both types of conservation by age eight, in sharp contrast to our upper limit of 50 percent with much older children. However, his description of the children's behavior during the experiments indicates that the Tiv culture is quite different from the Wolof one in promoting an active manipulative approach to the physical world. Price-Williams describes the children's behavior like this:

> These children would spontaneously actually perform the operation themselves. . . . Furthermore, they would reverse the sequence of operations, by, for example, pouring back the earth from second container to the first (Price-Williams, 1961, p. 302).

Such self-initiated action was *never* observed among unschooled Wolof children, and it may well be the key to the great disparity between the two cultures in spontaneous conservation results.

How shall we know directly that the unschooled child's act of pouring infirms his "magical thinking? If such were the case, a child's reasons for his judgments should reflect it. They should differ according to whether the experimenter or the child pours. We have, after all, drawn conclusions about the ineffectiveness of screening on the grounds that the children's reasons were the same before and after the procedure. And indeed, we find that when the child pours, his reasons are dramatically different from those he gives when an adult does. Magical-action reasons, which constituted a quarter of all reasons when an adult pours, are nonexistent when the unschooled older children themselves pour. Responses like, "The water is not the same because you poured it," disappear. In the younger group, action reasons drop from 42 percent with an adult pouring to 8 percent when the children pour. What emerges in place of action justifications are identity reasons. The child who pours on his own now uses his initial equalizing operation as the basis for his justification of conservation. "I made them the same." In the oldest group we find that identity reasons account for 64 percent of all justification when the child does the pouring. When the experimenter pours, only 20 percent of all reasons are based exclusively on a return to the initial situation of equality ("logical identity"). In the younger group comparable figures are 50 percent and 4 percent. There is an interesting difference between the reasoning of older and of younger children. Among the younger ones, the proportion of perceptual reasons stays the same, no matter who pours. Identity reasons replace magical-action reasons when the child pours. In the older group, perceptual reasons as well as action reasons decline when the child takes over the pouring.

How, finally, shall we explain the fact that among the Wolof children who have not been to school, those who pour the water from beaker to beaker have conservation, while those who only watch the experimenter pour do not. Why is this the case? Two possibly related reasons suggest themselves. One stresses motoric experience and its resultant sensory feedback, the other the removal from the task of a powerful authority figure. If the effect were due to feedback from the action of pouring, one would hardly expect action reasons (which refer to this new experience of transferring the water) to decrease. In fact, they do decrease, and drastically. Our view, rather, is that the intervention of an authority figure in the standard experiment attracts attention; whatever that person does is important, even if irrelevant to the solution of the problem. The attention of the child is drawn away from his own action and from the intrinsic nature of the task itself. The child, in a way, is trying to solve the experimenter rather than the problem. Only when the authority figure withdraws does the child turn fully to the logically essential parts of the action, beginning with equalizing the water and carrying through to a recognition that the initial act establishes an identity throughout.

Once again identity—a return to the beginning—turns out to be not only the logical but also the psychological heart of conservation. It seems as though identity may be the "invariant" in conservation itself. At least, identity appears to be as necessary to the attainment of conservation for these unschooled Wolof children as it was for American children (Chapter 9). But if the psychological "essence" of conservation begins to take on an aspect of universality, the techniques by which it can be implanted are not, as these experiments show. Indeed, the variation in successful instructional methods from group to group is nothing more than a sharply focused reflection of the diversity of preconservation schemata that we have been describing.

Lest it appear that action alone plays a part in the preconservation schema that is corrected by "pouring," we might consider a very revealing observation. It was often the case that a child, when asked to match the amount of water that the experimenter had poured into one standard beaker, would pour *all* the water from the pitcher into the second standard beaker, although the pitcher contained too much. The reason for his mistake seemed to be that he had initially watched the experimenter pour *all* the water from her pitcher into the first standard beaker and that he was doing likewise. Yet he was perfectly capable of realizing afterwards that he had poured too much and of correcting his mistake. The child was not merely matching the perceptual end state, as he was asked to do, nor was he matching only the action of pouring. What he was doing was making an erroneous causal connection between the two, just as in the experiment proper. He was assuming that, if he performed exactly the same action as the experimenter, the end result would also be the same.

Piaget would say something like this: "Actions are still not dissociated from the objects upon which they bear. He does not yet apprehend interrelations among objects *per se;* what are grouped are the action-object amalgams" (Flavell, 1963, pp. 137–138). Although this description fits, Piaget uses it to refer to the development of the sensori-motor state that takes place before age two and limits it to the child's representation of his own actions. Thus Piaget's child, in this instance, is said to organize his world in terms of practical space, a space that cannot be represented by symbolic means. But our Wolof children can, and certainly do, represent their world symbolically and in a very complicated language indeed! It makes much more sense to think in terms of an interaction between levels of representation, as these have been discussed throughout these pages. In the present case, we have a symbolic means of coding (language); but in terms of content, i.e., what is coded, the representation does not go much beyond the capacities of the enactive mode—sensori-motor phenomena (actions) are represented by symbolic means. These sensori-motor phenomena differ from concrete operations, for they are not reversible. What this group of Wolof children is coding in language is a sequence of acts in the order they occur; the transformational possibilities of language are not utilized, and we are left with the symbolic analogue of an action sequence.

Consider now whether the unschooled children's lack of response to the screen bears out this view of the achievement of conservation. To do so, we must first look at the school children. The school children, recall, differed from the unschooled young Wolofs and, as we noted, were much closer in their conservation responses to American children than to their own countrymen. Yet they did not learn conservation from the screening procedure, as American children had. We have delayed a closer look at the failure of screening until now. At this point, however, it becomes especially appropriate.

When the screen is put in place before the American children, 82 percent of them agree that the hidden beakers contain equal water. In Senegal 62 percent of the unschooled rural children respond in this way, 67 percent of the rural school children, but only 42 percent of the city children. Why is this the case, if the school children are most like American children in their approach? In fact, it turns out that in certain respects they are even more perceptual than American children, particularly the Dakar children, and far more so than the unschooled bush children. With the beakers hidden behind the screen, they persist in wondering about where the water level is. American children almost always give their judgments when the screen is in place with not an apparent thought for the water levels. Not so the Dakar children, of whom several had to be eliminated because they peeked behind the screen—behavior never encountered in America. The Dakar children often predicted the water level by the compensation principle and then gave the judgment of inequality on that basis.

What happens when the screen is removed? The results are exactly what would be predicted from the preceding analysis of the reasoning in different groups (Table 3; Figure 4). Unschooled children, using action cues more than the school groups, are not affected by the new perceptible cues revealed when the screen is taken away. Conservation responses are more frequent without the screen than they were with it, in sharp contrast to the response of the three school groups (bush, Dakar, and American), in which removing the screen results in a sharp decline of conservation answers. Note that unscreen-

TABLE 3

Percent of Children with No Conservation on Pretest Who Give
Conservation Responses During and After Screening

	Cambridge	Bush No School	Bush School	Dakar School
Screen present	82%	62%	67%	42%
Unscreening	61%	69%	33%	16%
Posttest	54%	38%	33%	19%
Number of children	28	29	15	31

ing involves no new "pouring" cues which might lead the rural children astray. It is just such cues that make the second part of the
standard conservation situation—where the water is divided among
the six small beakers—more difficult for this group of children than
the first part, as has been mentioned before. When the water is poured
into the six small beakers, it is particularly easy to explain the perceptual discrepancy by action inequality. The child is presented with
an action contrast of six pouring motions to one. For children sensitive
to action, this inequality situation must be much more compelling than
the one in which water is poured once into the standard beaker and
once into a beaker of a different shape.

As for the posttest, the school children who survived unscreening
also survive the posttest, the unschooled children less well. It may
well be that the unschooled children, given their tendency to
action-magic, more easily fall prey in the posttest to all the pouring
done by the experimenter, whereas perceptible cues, the nemesis of
the school children, are no more misleading than on the previous
unscreening condition.

SOME CONCLUSIONS

We have covered much ground and examined in fine detail the
responses and reasons of our Senegalese children. Several points stand-
out consistently.

The first is that there is a wider gap between unschooled and
schooled Wolof children from the same rural village than between
rural and urban school children. By the eleventh or twelfth year virtually all the school children have achieved conservation. Only about
half of those not in school have done so.

The school children, moreover, show the typical early reliance on perceptible cues in justifying their judgments and a later decline in such judgments. In contrast, unschooled children in the bush show a gradual rise in perceptual reasons over the same age span.

Screening the children from perceptible cues has a relatively minor effect on children who have not yet started to fluctuate. It has its effect principally by virtue of giving the fluctuaters a chance to practice. In general, screening has a minor pedagogical effect in contrast to its effect in hastening conservation in American children.

A principal difficulty with the unschooled Wolof children was their tendency to "explain" the changed (to them) amount of water in terms of action-magic—it was different because the experimenter had poured it. The specific cure for this was having the children pour for themselves. But it is noteworthy that such a do-it-yourself expedient helped the unschooled children and not the school children, who were much less given to such reasoning.

In fact, the most characteristic thing about the unschooled children is the extent to which action is crucial to their representation of the world and the degree to which symbolic representation is, for them, a sequential account of a train of actions. What is striking about the African child who is exposed to Western education is the degree to which he rapidly becomes perceptualized, almost overperceptualized. This is so much the case that the interposition of a screen between him and the "misleading" beakers of liquid, rather than freeing him to carry on a symbolic equation of the liquid, only tempts him to look behind the screen to see how it looks.

Conservation, it would seem, depends for its development on the presence of a sense of identity, the idea of a potential return to an initial state, in this case, the state of equality. It is identity which must be used to integrate the other cues provided by the situation. The American child often does so through an "appearance-reality" schema which allows him to deal *simultaneously* with the "appearance" of level and the "reality" of identical substance. When the definition of equal quantity shifts from the former to the latter, conservation is achieved.

The Senegalese child, however, cannot use the idea of identity to integrate conflicting cues through cross-classification of the situation according to both "appearance" and "reality." To him this distinction does not exist, and one has more than a little difficulty even communicating the contrast in the Wolof language. When American children use identity as a justification for an equality judgment, they often say, "It's the same water," or "It *looks* like more but really is the same." They make identity a *present* phenomenon. But the Wolof child says, "This one and this one [the two standard beakers] are [or were] equal." Note that one of these is now empty. Therefore he expresses identity through describing a past state rather than a present one; this is identity by recapitulation. The conflict for the Wolof child is between the initial and the later appearances of the water. It is resolved by the recognition of the identity of something observed a moment ago and something observed now. It is perhaps for this reason that the reference to two beakers is the most effective single type of perceptual reason with respect to conservation, for it is the standard beaker that provides a tie with the "past" equality of the initial situation. Similarly, the "action" experiment perhaps integrates conflicting cues by providing continuity of action between the past and the present.

It follows that a training technique for the "perceptually seduced" school children of Senegal would also be one that stresses a continuity of past and present, promoting an easier integration of the two, and one that draws particular attention to the past and its crucial equality cues.

If these experiments indicate one thing of special importance, it is the way in which different modes of thought can lead to the same results. It has too often been assumed that different intellectual means must of necessity lead to different cognitive ends. This might occur in the case of problems which have no objectively definable "right" answer. But where there are action constraints and consequences for behavior (as with the phenomena of conservation), a disparity in results is not necessarily the case. We have shown how an identity schema is as crucial to conservation in Senegal as in the United States but that it can develop by different means. Senegalese children do not utilize the language of identity ("same") or the classification of the present situation according to both appearance and reality to express identity. Both these modes of expression when employed by American children make the equality of the past simultaneous with the present inequality of appearance. The Wolof children, by contrast, achieve conservation by establishing identity between the *successive* states of past and present. Their link might be either the continuity of action from one part of the experiment to another, or the constant appearance of the standard beakers.

It is obvious that in order to survive all peoples must somehow come to terms with a few basic laws of the physical world, despite profound differences in "world view." Certainly, the conservation of a continuous quantity across transformations of appearance is one of these basic facts. Nevertheless, certain ways of thinking may be more powerful than others as a means to the discovery of *new* laws, laws which may be "optional" to survival under certain conditions. Thus Newtonian thinking is fine for some purposes, but Einstein can do the same thing and more. Consequently, it is well to bear in mind that intellectually too there is more than one way to skin a cat—regardless of whether all ways are equally effective for skinning twenty cats, or for that matter, dogs.

CHAPTER 12

On Culture and Equivalence: I

Michael Maccoby and Nancy Modiano[1]

The study reported in this chapter has been undertaken to examine how general is the account of the growth in equivalence transformation found in the work of Olver and Hornsby, reported in Chapter 3. Beyond that objective there is yet another. Surely the manner in which a child goes about abstracting equivalence should reflect the nature of his society. In most instances the equivalences imposed on one's environment have much wider limits of option than, say, such things as physical judgments do; for example, do two containers hold the same amount to drink? Whether objects are considered as food, for example, does not depend on their nutritional value alone, but also on custom and dietary taboo. To the Christian, beef and pork are two meats, different in taste but equivalent in function and formal classification. But Orthodox Jews and Moslems would not group the two as food, nor would they meet the Hindus' equivalence requirements. In these instances, cultural training puts an affective brake on functional and formal equivalence.

Nor should the matter be restricted to determination by cultural *content*—whether in a semantic sense two things are conventionally grouped or not. One might expect that certain cultural traits would extend to the kinds of attributes preferred for equivalence grouping or, indeed, the kind of grouping rules employed. It is surely reasonable to expect, for example, that a "rational" or technically sophisti-

---

[1] We would like to thank Ing. Sergio Beltran of the Centro de Calculo Electronico of the National Autonomous University of Mexico and Dr. Nathan Jaspen of New York University for their generous assistance.

cated culture would place an early and strong emphasis upon the use of functional and formal categories, the better to acculturate its young to the requirements of a technology they would be called on to master.

The first opportunity to explore cultural differences in this kind of activity grew out of broader studies being undertaken in rural Mexico; studies that aimed at elucidating the character structure of Mexican villagers (Maccoby, Modiano, Galvan, 1963). At that time we undertook a pilot study (using the Olver-Hornsby procedure for studying equivalence) to compare North American suburban children with their rural Mexican counterparts.

The task assigned the children was much like that developed by Olver (1961). Items were presented in a series and, as each item was shown, the child was asked to tell in what way it was different from the proceeding items and in what way the items were alike. Each item was presented on a small white card which was read by the investigator. Once an item was presented, it was placed in front of the child so that all previous items in the array could be seen at once. The array used by Olver for the North American children she studied was the familiar one: *banana, peach, potato, meat, milk, water, air, germs, stones*. For the Mexican children, *naranja* was substituted for peach, *frijol* for potato, and *lumbre* for germs. In the testing procedure, the first two items (banana and peach) were shown, and the child was asked, "How are banana and peach alike?" After he answered, the next item, potato, was given with the question, "How-is potato different from banana and peach?" And then, "How are banana, peach, and potato all alike?" The parallel procedure in Mexico continued in this way, with the exception of the final item, stones, when the child was asked to tell only the difference.

The child's responses in both settings were scored in terms of five main classes, which describe the kind of attributes he used in order to group or differentiate objects: (1) perceptible characteristics, either intrinsic, such as shape, color, size, or extrinsic, such as the position of the object in time and space; (2) functions of the object, either what it can do (intrinsic functions) or what one can do with it (extrinsic functions); (3) moral or affective labels, indicating that an object is good or bad, liked or disliked; (4) nominal characteristics, abstractions learned by the child, such as the fact that an object is a liquid or a solid, a fruit, or a food; and (5) a grouping not by attribute but by decree; the child merely states, for example, "All these are similar." In the Mexican scoring we noted separately whether or not a child employed a particular form of grouping in his attempt at differéntiation (analysis) or synthesis. We also judged his analysis or synthesis as successful or not on the basis of (1) the understandable differences in six out of seven cases, and (2) the synthesis of at least those items having to do with ingestion.

The Mexican children numbered fifty-seven, from age five to seventeen, living in a *mestizo* village in rural Mexico with a population of some eight hundred people. These children are compared with fifty American children from age six to seventeen, drawn from a suburban metropolitan school near Boston, the sample of children reported in the first study of Chapter 3.

This comparison was undertaken as a pilot study, and it is here reported as a preliminary to the main investigation that will concern us in this chapter—a comparison of rural and urban children in Mexico, where considerations of language could be held constant. Yet it is instructive as just that, for it raises many interesting questions. To begin with, the youngest children of both cultures, from age six to eight, are more similar than any other parallel age groups in their responses to the task. Both Mexican and North American children of this age group are able to differentiate between objects, but they show little or no ability to synthesize. Of ten North American children from age six to eight, six were able to analyze well, but only one could synthesize; of twenty-three Mexican children, 52 percent scored well on analysis, and 13 percent on synthesis. In both samples, the children employed mainly perceptible attributes such as color and form in order to separate objects (80 percent of the Mexicans, 90 percent of the North Americans). It appears as though they were examining the things in their minds and describing the variations they saw. However, purely perceptible attributes do not serve well for synthesizing a diverse array of objects. To do this the child must be able to employ more abstract concepts.

Even in children of six or seven we can note some important differences between the two samples. The North American children tend to use formal, nominal categories. They are more likely to analyze in terms of what one can do with objects (70 percent of the North Americans versus 26 percent of the Mexicans).

These differences, though they have little effect on the relative performances of the younger children, are the seeds of much greater differences to come. At ages nine and ten, while performance at the task of analysis was still similar (seven out of ten North Americans and 63 percent of nineteen Mexican children could analyze successfully), half of the North American children could synthesize well in comparison to only one of the nineteen Mexicans.

The reason for this disparity is not difficult to see. The American children are learning to handle abstract concepts of use, such as the idea that a group of objects all "are necessary for human life." Such concepts in themselves are a synthesis between the child's interest in both the use and "goodness" or "badness" of the objects. The six-year-old may decree that germs are bad; his older brother is more likely to state that they are bad because they cause sickness and so harm people. Similarly, an eight-year-old may say that banana, peach, potato, meat, milk, water, and air are good for you and that these are foods one eats; while the ten or eleven-year-old would more likely comment that these things are necessary for the maintenance of life, thus implying both use and an objective moral standard.

The Mexican child, rather than move in this direction, continues to employ concrete attributes. His perceptual observations become finer and finer. He may note, for example, that a banana and a bean are both crescent-shaped like the moon, or that one fruit tastes both better and more mealy than another, and so forth. He also becomes more and more concerned with the concrete use of objects, such as different ways to cook or eat them. However, he does not employ abstract concepts and, if he gets stuck in trying to explain why a group of things are similar, he is likely to declare them similar or not simply by decree, and leave it at that. This trend showed no relationship with the children's intelligence, as measured both by the block form of Raven's Matrices, and by the Draw-A-Man Test. Nor was there any significant difference between the performances of boys and girls, the girls scoring slightly higher, in accordance with their more rapid rate of maturation.

These differences in style are remarkably consistent in both groups. Even at the age of sixteen or seventeen the Mexican adolescent seldom abstracts, even formally, while the North American develops increasing facility with abstract functions and formal equivalencies, whether at the expense of perceptible and concrete qualities or not.

In general terms, we would contrast the development of North American and Mexican children as follows: the North American child starts out by seeing objects in terms of perceptible and concrete characteristics, but he soon begins to consider them in the light of what he can do with them. Also, he starts to pay attention to abstract qualities and to similarities between objects. At first he may note the "goodness" or "badness" of things, repeating culturally determined labels; but later, as he reasons more, the good objects are those useful to man. By the age of eleven or twelve, seven of ten North American children, in contrast to none of ten Mexicans, employed concepts such as these. At best the North American child develops an interest in theory, in the abstract equivalencies and differences among objects. At worst he merely manipulates things in a formal and increasingly reductionist manner. In fact, a few of the older children completely lose the ability to analyze, because the concrete attributes of objects have become buried beneath formal and abstract notions.

In contrast, the Mexican child of six or eight is far more similar to his older brothers in terms of intellectual approach. Both are most concerned with concrete perceptible attributes. The difference is that the older child looks more closely at the object and begins to consider more concrete ways to use it. At best he demonstrates a rich interest in, and relation to, the object as an individual thing; he expresses and describes his experience, although he has no interest in theory or abstraction. At worst he merely perceives in terms of concrete but narrow attributes, and when he is in doubt he arbitrarily declares that objects are similar or different by decree.

The American child is taught to abstract, to manipulate concepts, to control things. He is a member of a culture that prides itself on its power over nature. Almost as soon as he learns what things are, he is taught what he can do with them and where they can be found. One American child saw the similarity between banana, peach, potato, meat, and milk, as all very common things which you might easily get at the supermarket. On the other hand, the child from rural Mexico has little or no contact with so large a commercial enterprise as a supermarket. His experience is rather one in which he plants the beans, sees them grow, harvests, and then eats them. His experience is with nature, and it continues for as long as he remains in a farming community. He is more passive than the North American, and his education is more authoritarian, so that, as we have observed in this village, children often isolate the school experience from the rest of life. Actually, no relationship could be established between success at analysis or synthesis and academic achievement. Those children who judge things to be similar or different by decree may be reflecting the attitudes of the adults in their lives; things are so because a parent or possibly a teacher has said so.

On a more general cultural level, the schools are in themselves reflections of larger cultural traits. In a highly industrial and diversified economy such as that of the United States, abstraction is a necessity. Time and money must be equated. Children must at an early age learn the "values" of things, not just whether they taste good or are pleasing, but in terms of money. For the rural Mexican money is less important. He often barters things as needed, or produces his own food, shelter, and clothing. In his mind, time has little relation to money. We are now investigating these differences more rigorously with a test we have constructed, in order to learn more exactly the villagers' ideas of time and value.

Looked at from the point of view of the general theory of development set forth in this book, the relativity of culture depends on the extent to which any culture shapes skills and preferences beyond the first stages of enactive representation. American and Mexican six-year-olds are not strikingly different in their emphasis on perceptible properties, but with growth, the Mexican child moves toward greater perceptual subtlety, and the North American toward more abstraction. Before this divergence occurs, the principal impact of either culture is probably affective, reflecting child-rearing practices and the like. Only when the child is capable of sufficient mastery of the symbolic forms of his culture can there be a divergence to the fullest limit. In this case, the divergence of the two cultures consists of quite different conceptions of man and society and their reciprocal relations.

A CLOSER LOOK AT DIFFERENCE

A comparison of rural Mexican and North American suburban children, while dramatic enough, involves too many things such as language, technology, culture, and so on. The second part of the present study, then, concentrates on a limited comparison of rural and urban Mexican children and seeks to discern in what measure urban culture makes its impact on the growth of intellect.

The sample included fifty-two children from the village already mentioned and one hundred two children from a housing development in Mexico City. Within each population, two age groups were tested, children from eight to ten and from twelve to thirteen. In the city this included a complete third-grade class (forty-nine children), and a sixth-grade class (fifty-three children). In the village there was a wide variation in the ages of children within specific grades, so the children chosen by random means were not necessarily in the same grade at school. Table 1 contains the vital statistics.

The same list as had been used with the rural Mexican group was used for both these groups to test for equivalence. In the village, the children were tested individually with the items printed on cards and read out by the tester. The child's responses were taken down verbatim. In the city, the test was group-administered, with the tester reading out the items and the child writing down his responses.

The bases on which the equivalence and difference judgments were

TABLE 1
Composition of Sample

	Age Eight through Ten			Age Twelve and Thirteen		
	Boys	Girls	Total	Boys	Girls	Total
Village	18	15	33	9	10	19
Mexico City	27	26	53	24	25	49

made were classified within the categories mentioned earlier in this chapter (p. 258). As before, we also noted the differences and the equivalence responses separately. The protocols were also classified in terms of success and failure in both the equivalence and the differentiation tasks. Success on the differentiation task was considered to be achieved if six out of seven possible differences given were comprehensible. For the equivalence task, a successful performance constituted getting all the food words plus *air* and *water* into a group. The criteria for success at the equivalence task are similar to those used in Chapter 3 in classifying superordinate-groupings structures, except that sometimes we allowed complexive groupings which were logical and not too all-inclusive. The scoring for success at formulating differences was less problematic, since any attribute that distinguishes the new attribute from the others was considered adequate, even if the other items were defined only by exclusion (for example, "This is red and one of the others are red."[2]

By about age nine, the difference is plain. More than twice as many urban as rural children succeed at the equivalence task. By twelve, the difference has become fourfold (Table 2 and Figure 1).

We are struck by how much closer Mexico City is to Boston than to a *mestizo* village. Data on the younger groups mentioned in the pilot study are also included. One might well assume that, had we selected a group of six-year-olds in Mexico City, they would have

---

[2] As a reliability check on the food list, the children were also given another array of concepts including: *horse* and *cow, chicken, lion, snake, mosquito, man, tree,* and *mountain.* An analysis of the attributes used showed no significant differences between the reactions to the two tests as measured by the use of perceptible, functional, and formal attributes. The two lists appear only slightly different in difficulty. For example, of the total village sample 51 percent passed the equivalence test on the food list and 48 percent on the animal list. Of the urban sample, 73 percent were scored as passing on the food list and 67 percent on the animal list.

TABLE 2
Percent of Children Succeeding on Equivalence and Difference Tasks

Age

	6–7	8–10	12–13
Equivalence			
Mexican village	13*	16	26
Mexico City	...	44	82
Boston suburb**	10	60	80
Difference			
Mexican village	52*	84	95
Mexico City	...	79	96
Boston suburb**	60	70	80

* This group includes twenty-three children.
** Each American group comprises ten children.

been much like the others. While the urban sample shows a superiority in formulating equivalences, the two groups are similar in their abilty to describe differences. Indeed, at age nine the village children show a slight though nonsignificant superiority.

What causes this difference in the ability to formulate equivalences? Note what kinds of attributes are demanded by the task. While successful equivalence must relate the items of the list, it must not be senselessly inclusive ("All these things are found in the world") or so arbitrary as to contain no principle of including anything more ("I like all these things"). Equivalence on the basis of such shared perceptible attributes as color and shape is easy enough up to a point, but the more a list becomes thus diverse, the more this method becomes powerless to cope, and, as we have seen in Chapter 3, it leads to the kind of complexive groupings that can easily become arbitrary or overinclusive. Adequate superordinate groupings call for the use of functional and formal attributes.

Though functional extrinsic attributes ("I can eat all of these") are more powerful than perceptible ones for formulating equivalence, they too break down on items such as *air* and *fire*. The same is true of such nominal classifications as "foods" or "solids." Some children who seem particularly wedded to formal classification turn to part-whole equivalence when the simple nominal classification no longer serves. Thus they may say that all the other objects contain air. However, many children would reject such a solution as inelegant, and they would seek a more powerful conceptualization, one which would serve

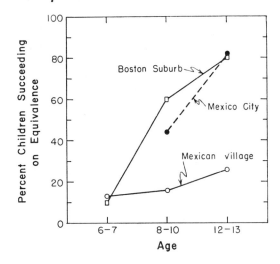

Figure 1. Percent children succeeding on equivalence.

for the inclusion of new items and imply a deeper understanding of the relationship among the concepts, beyond the mere fact that they can be arbitrarily acted on. The child might, for example, describe the array of items as being "necessary for life" or "used by man to stay alive." To be able to make such a classification, the child must go beyond both sensory impressions (perceptual attributes) or his own personal experience (extrinsic functional) to a general, abstract, and theoretical statement which in fact represents a new capacity in grasping truth. The children who remain on a concrete level of equivalence classifications, whether perceptual or functional, succeed less often in uniting the items, whereas those able to make more abstract or generalized classifications are more likely to find similarities.

A comparison of the urban and village children in Figure 2 reveals how few village children use either nominal or intrinsic functional bases in the equivalence task. Even the older village children continue using perceptible or extrinsic functional attributes. In contrast, urban children are already on their way toward functionalism and formalism by the ninth year.

The over-all picture is quickly summarized. Village children show a strong increase in extrinsic functional grouping and in nominal ones, as well as a small increase in the use of perceptible bases. City children show a sharp drop in the use of perceptual attributes and a sharp rise in both intrinsic functional and nominal groupings. The

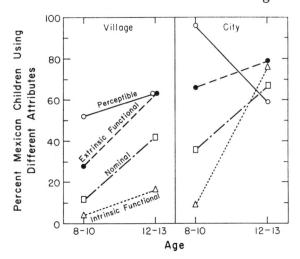

Figure 2. Percent Mexican children using different attributes.

rural child at age twelve is perceptually oriented or, when functional, very concretely so. He asks what something is used for without regard to its abstract properties. The urban child is more sophisticated linguistically, more abstract. Consider now the attributes used by children in characterizing differences (Table 3).

The differences between the younger children of village and city virtually disappears as one shifts from equivalence judgments to judgments of difference. By age twelve, however, there is a striking contrast: again the village children fall far behind in the two more abstract bases for grouping—nominal and intrinsic functional. And the falling behind is highly reliable statistically.

There is still a puzzle encountered in comparing Figure 2 and Table 3. There are rural children who, on the task of finding differences, use attributes that they then do not use in formulating equivalence. For example, 64 percent of rural children from age eight to ten use extrinsic functional attributes to characterize differences, but only 28 percent use them in formulating equivalence. Or, at age twelve, the difference on the same attribute is 84 percent and 63 percent. In other words, there appears to be a group of village children who have the ability to use attributes but resist using them for the equivalence task. Formulating equivalence judgments may depend more on cultural traits than on individual capabilities.

TABLE 3
Percent of Children Who Use Various Attributes in Formulating Differences

Age

	Eight to Ten		Twelve and Thirteen	
	Village	City	Village	City
Perceptible	92	94	90	80
Extrinsic functional	64	68	84	85
Nominal	8	21	26	71
Intrinsic functional	0	9	5	47

In a word, then, there is indeed a patterning of growth going on in the child between eight and twelve with respect to his approach or resistance to equivalence judgments, his preference for attributes, and the manner of specialization in his use of mind. The perceptual, concrete, difference-sensitive, organically oriented, village child is by age twelve in sharp contrast to the more abstract, functional, similarity-sensitive, cosmopolitan city child of the same age.

SOME INFERENCES ABOUT INTELLIGENCE

Unfortunately, growth data are not available on the children with respect to intelligence and other characteristics. But the older group of children were tested for intelligence by using the relatively language-free Raven's Progressive Matrices Test. Intelligence, though related to school achievement ($r = 0.50$, $p < 0.01$) was unrelated to success in the equivalence task or in the use of attributes. Incidentally, success on the equivalence task proved to be unrelated to school achievements (a type of achievement based more on a child's ability to memorize and obey authority than to think).

It would seem, and strikingly so, that we are dealing here with a matter of culturally derived preference, preference which through habit becomes finally a personal style. It is reasonable to suppose that within the context of a cultural style one can find variations in the effectiveness with which a child operates. It is doubtful, however, whether the kinds of intelligence tests now available are designed to elucidate such matters.

CULTURE AND ABSTRACTION

A city child coming from an industrial society starts by dealing with objects in terms of their perceptible, concrete characteristics. He soon comes to consider them in the light of what he can do with them. In time, he is led to more abstract formulations as to how things are, how they are alike and how different. Some go so far that they lose the sense of the concreteness of things and become buried in a dry nominalism. They are like people who see a painting immediately in terms of its style, period, and influences, but with no sense of its uniqueness.

Peasant children do not change that much. They are much more similar to their older brothers: they both look. The older one looks at things more closely and considers more concrete ways to use them. While the older peasant child can say how things are alike, he feels more at home with their differences, for that is where reality lies for him. He does not think in generalities. At his best he shows a rich interest in and relation to individual people, individual objects, or particular events. At his poorest he sees only the concrete and the particular and walls himself off from anything beyond immediate experience.

Essentially, such cognitive styles reflect the demands of a culture. The modern industrialized world demands abstractions by its very arrangements, its stimuli, its contrasts, its laws of justice and exchange. What is demanded of the peasant, on the other hand, is that he pay attention to his crops, the weather, and the particular people around him.

The culture is reflected in its institutions—school, family, or work group. The child in an urban school is more likely to learn to manipulate concepts, to use his knowledge beyond school. In an industrialized society, when a child learns what things are, he is taught what he can do with them and where they can be found. In a peasant village, schooling does not get you a better job or even necessarily make you a better farmer. Some boys who do best at school lack the money to continue their education. The urban child can both live at home and advance to higher schools.

The villager tends to be more concrete and more authoritarian in moral outlook. His values are traditional and conservative, and economic scarcity reinforces moral realism. Traditional authoritarianism is rooted in work relations and in the family, where children are taught to obey without question. Unlike the urban world, the small village offers no alternatives to the influence of the family. Even those games by which an industrial society teaches reciprocity and abstract rules of justice are not played within the village (Maccoby, Modiano and Lander, 1964). Observers have noted that many a villager who migrates to the city feels freer when liberated from the restraints of village life (Lewis, 1959).

If the peasant child is not dulled by village life, he will experience the uniqueness of events, objects, and people. But as the city child grows older, he may end by exchanging a spontaneous, less alienated relationship to the world for a more sophisticated outlook which concentrates on using, exchanging, or cataloguing. What industrialized, urban man gains in an increased ability to formulate, to reason, and to code the ever more numerous bits of complex information he acquires, he may lose in a decreased sensitivity to people and events.

CHAPTER 13

On Culture and
Equivalence: II

*Patricia M. Greenfield, Lee C. Reich, and
Rose R. Olver*

$\mathbf{T}$he very idea of culture recognizes a selectivity and an orchestration in the use of human capacities, and it would seem likely that with each unique cultural pattern would go a certain set of biases in representing the world. In some settings survival may depend on skills in exploiting the immediate "natural" environment, resulting in the elaboration of supporting enactive and ikonic representation. Other, more technically elaborated cultures may be more specialized in symbolic representation, giving more emphasis to the manipulation of such arbitrary systems as machines, money, and the like. The cognitive growth of the child should reflect the emphases evolved by his culture, yet obviously there are "universals" in cognitive development that derive from shared human potentialities and communalities in the human plight. It is anything but clear how these two sides interact.

At a fundamental level, cultural biases ought to affect what is called alike and different, for the act of rendering dissimilar things equivalent yields the categories with which each culture and individual cuts up its world. Equivalence judgments become the stuff of cultural world view.

The Mexican children of the preceding chapter offer some insights into the relationship between culture and equivalence. Their behavior leads to the conclusion that urban culture breeds categories whose structure and content are characterized by abstractness, in the sense that they transcend the particular attributes of individual category members. However, it is still uncertain whether *all* rural traditional milieus may be lumped together against *all* modern urban milieus with respect to the types of equivalence judgments fostered by each. The studies to be reported here serve to test the generality of the urban-rural contrast in cognitive styles described in the last chapter. They do so by extending the study of equivalence grouping to two very different corners of the earth, Alaska and Senegal.

The results of Reich's work among the Alaskan Eskimos and Greenfield's studies of the Wolofs in Senegal should not only elucidate this matter; they should also begin to solve an additional puzzle: *which* factors embedded in a given cultural milieu make a difference in the development of cognitive equivalences? And what aspects of equivalence judgments are touched by these influences? Finally, these studies can tell us something about the psychological nature of equivalence groupings themselves, for instance, about the relation between grouping structure and grouping content.

Our comparative test will be facilitated if we start with the Eskimos, for Reich's study utilizes virtually the same procedure used in the Mexican work reported in the last chapter and in Olver's American experiment reported in Chapter 3.

THE ESKIMOS

One possible beginning would be a detailed anthropological description of the Alaskan Eskimo's cultural background. However, most of the relevant features for cognitive growth are unsure. In fact, the similarity of results in Mexico City and Boston, Massachusetts, and the dissimilarity of both from a small Mexican village give us reason to suspect that modern urban environments everywhere may produce a certain style of equivalence judgments, and that this influence may transcend national and other differences in cultural content. Therefore, the most relevant question we can ask is, to what extent have the Eskimos made the transition from their traditional rural society to the modern urban milieu of Anchorage, where this study was conducted?

Since the first contact with white explorers and whaling ships in the nineteenth century, there has been a gradual disintegration of traditional Eskimo ways of life and an acculturation into the world of the white American, still only partially accomplished. World War II resulted in an accelerated rate of change for the Eskimo, as for all Alaska, so that the Eskimos of today are increasingly oriented toward the white American economy and institutions. Their aspirations toward fuller participation in the white society are frustrated, however, by a lack of adequate training and education, and by a shortage of jobs. They are exposed to disappointment and prejudice at a time when many of the traditional sources of individual security and social cohesion have disappeared.

The children who participated in this study, then, have a real Eskimo heritage, though they are in a transitional phase of acculturation. Their grandparents lived most of their lives in Eskimo villages, engaged in the traditional subsistence activities. Their parents were born in villages, spoke Eskimo as their native language, though all were subject to the upheavals of the past twenty years that led families to move to larger towns and even to cities like Anchorage in the hope of participating in the greater abundance they see existing in the white American society. Although most of the children studied were born in a village, their reference culture, like that of their parents, is the white American one. Most telling in this regard is the fact that all the children feel pressured to speak English and to get as much education as possible—the two best avenues to fuller participation in the white American society in the eyes of the Eskimo.

In fact, the white and Eskimo children who participated in the study had identical or very similar educational backgrounds, at least in terms of curriculum and standards of performance. The sixteen white children attended a public elementary school serving a lower-middle-class neighborhood in Anchorage. The twenty Eskimo children came from two sources: half were pupils in the same Anchorage elementary school that the white children attended; the other half were patients in the Alaska Native Health Service Hospital in Anchorage and were enrolled in the elementary division of the hospital school.

The Eskimo children were separated into a younger and an older group, with age ten as the dividing line. Matching white groups posed a problem. The Eskimo children in a given school grade are on the average older than the white children in that grade; and although the majority of the latter will fall within a two-year age span, the Eskimo children will vary considerably more in age. We chose to follow the pattern in the Alaskan schools. The Eskimo children in both the younger and older groups are on the average older than the white children with whom they will be compared. Although the grade placement for each of the matching groups is roughly equivalent, the age range is greater for the Eskimo children in both groups. In short, the younger Eskimo group averages 9.7 years as compared to 8.5 years for the younger white children; 12.0 and 10.6 are the comparable ages for the Eskimo and white older children. The mean grade placement for both younger groups is around 2.5; for the older children, 4.3.[1]

A comparison of the children's performance on the Goldstein-Scheerer Cube Test supports the division of the children into these four groups. This test is primarily a nonverbal task requiring an analysis of spatial relationships. The child must copy a design with four blocks. He is shown from one to four representations of each design, each successive representation giving greater assistance with the analysis and reconstruction of the pattern the child is to form with the blocks. The child is given a score of four if he correctly constructs the design when shown the first representation—a small-scale version of the pattern; a score of three if he achieves the pattern when shown the second representation—the same size as the first but with the addition of black lines indicating the division of the four blocks that compose the design; a score of two for correct construction given the third representation—a scale representation of the design; and a score of one, if correct construction is achieved with the fourth representation—a scale version with lines dividing the pattern. Ten designs are presented to each child; this procedure allows for a "perfect" score of forty points.

The performances of the two younger groups and of the two older were almost identical—around twenty-eight for the former, and just thirty-five for the latter. In terms of at least one highly respected test of nonverbal intelligence, our younger and older pairs of groups are properly equated.

THE EXPERIMENT PROPER

All the children were given the task of telling how different objects are alike. The testing procedure was a modification of the equivalence task described in Chapters 3 and 12, which used objects commonplace on the Alaskan scene. The child was first presented with a pair, for example, gloves and *mukluks*,[2] and asked, "How are gloves and *mukluks* alike?" Then another object, a parka, was added to the array and the child was asked, "How is parka different from gloves and *mukluks?*" and then, "How are gloves, mukluks, and parka all alike?" This procedure was continued until eight items in the array were

---

[1] For details see Lee C. Reich, A Cross-Cultural Study of Cognitive Functioning. Doctoral dissertation, Harvard University, (in preparation).

[2] *Mukluks* are Eskimo boots made of furs and skins, widely used by residents of Alaska.

presented. A contrasting item was given at the end of the array, and the child was asked only how it differed from all the others. Two arrays were used:

Apple-orange, potato, meat, milk, water, air, germs, (stone).
Gloves-mukluks, sweater, parka, blanket, stove, fire, sun, (ice).

To ensure that the words had the same meanings for all the children and to achieve a standardized translation by the interpreter, appropriate objects were presented for the first six items in the array and were named as the questions were asked. The objects remained on the table as successive items were introduced. The child was free to handle them and to point and demonstrate his meaning as he wished. No attempt was made to represent the last items in each array (air and germs, fire and sun).

An initial attempt was made to administer one array to each Eskimo child through an interpreter speaking the dialect of the child's village, in order to compare the performance of Eskimo children when using English and when using their native language. But the majority of the Eskimo children showed a striking inability or reluctance to speak Eskimo. Although all the children included in the study were of full Eskimo descent, as nearly as could be determined, half denied that they spoke Eskimo and maintained that they understood "only a little bit" when their parents spoke Eskimo to friends and relatives. Other children were shy and disconcerted by the request to speak Eskimo to the interpreter. If a child was either unable or unwilling to respond in Eskimo, the entire series was presented in English, as it was for all the white subjects. The responses of the few Eskimo children who would respond to the task in Eskimo are included in the following analyses, since the comparison of their performance on the arrays administered in English and on those in Eskimo showed no difference.

For children in modern urban settings—notably near Boston and in Mexico City—the development of equivalence groupings involves a change in both structure and content. According to the findings reported in Chapters 3 and 12, the young child forms complexive groupings that need share no common attribute. The conceptual content of his groupings tends to be perceptual; similarities are based on visible or tangible attributes like color or shape. The older urban child constructs superordinate groupings whose members have one or more attributes in common, whereas the grouping strategy of the rural Mexican child hardly changes as he grows older. The older urban American and Mexican children switch from groupings based on perceptual attributes to those based on the functional or nominal properties of things, whereas the rural children, who start out less perceptually oriented than the urban, develop in the opposite direction, toward more (and better) perceptual observations on which to base equivalence judgments.

If this dichotomy between modern urban and traditional rural is a useful one, then we would expect not only our white but also our Eskimo children to follow the urban pattern. In order to test this hypothesis, the children's answers were categorized roughly as before (Chapters 3 and 12). The main types of grouping structure were (1) *superordinate,* explicitly based on one or more attributes common to all the items included, and (2) *complexive,* based on several different attributes, none common to all items. For a detailed description of the subtypes of superordinate structure, see page 74. It suffices for the analysis of the present data to describe the various forms of complexive grouping.

Collections. In a collection, the items are grouped according to contrasting attributes. A different attribute is mentioned for each item, although there may be some implicit relationship among the attributes selected. For example, an eight-year-old said, "An orange has spots all over it and it's orange. An apple is green, and sometimes it turns red, and a potato is kinda brownish."

Edge Matchings. Edge matching may be described as a chain of linked pairs. One item is related to another, the second is then related to a third on the basis of a different attribute, and so on. An eight-year-old Eskimo said, "Orange and apple are alike 'cause they're fruits. The potato and the orange have these little dents [pointing]. The fish and potato are brown. The milk is like the potato because the inside of the potato is white. The milk and water are alike because they are like drinking stuff." There is little consistency in the attributes through which the pairs are linked.

Key Rings. In a key ring one item is taken as a nucleus, and the grouping is formed by relating the other items to it. One child used this construction. "You get to put water in there [pointing to the can of condensed milk] to make milk and you got to wash them [all the other items]."

Associations. In an association two or more items are linked, and their relationship is extended to include other items in the group. "You eat them. You eat the water when you stir it in something. Like you put water in pancakes or something and the water dissolves."

Multiple Groupings. In a multiple grouping two or more subgroupings are formed. One Eskimo child handled apple, orange, potato, and fish by saying, "These two are round [apple and orange] and these two aren't." When milk, water, and air had been added to the array, she grouped them by saying, "You can't see the air and those all have colors."

The conceptual content of the groupings was divided according to the type of attribute on which the equivalence judgment was based. As in Chapters 3 and 12, attributes were classified as perceptible, functional, or nominal. All answers fell into the following categories:

Perceptible. The items are grouped on the basis of phenomenal qualities. Three kinds of intrinsic qualities accounted for most of the "perceptible" responses:

1. **Color**
   Specific: "They are red."
   General: "They have colors."

2. **Shape.**
   Geometric: "They are round."
   Size: "This is almost as big as these."

3. **Material.**
   General: "These are fur."
   Detail: "They have seeds."

There were also a few responses based on perceptible attributes extrinsic to the object, such as location in time or space.

Functional. Equivalence is based on the use or function of the items, either what they do or what can be done to them. Reference in the first or second person to someone performing or receiving an action signals the presence of a *personal* functional attribute. "We eat them," or "They help us grow," or "They keep your body warm" are all examples of personal functional reasons. When no reference is made to personal involvement in the action, or when the reference is in the third person, the attribute is considered an *impersonal* functional one; for example, "They grow," or "They keep people from starving," or "They can be eaten."

Nominal. The items are grouped by using the conventional name that exists in the language. ("The apple and the orange are both fruit.") Note that this type of grouping gives no additional information about the items; it tells only what other things are potential members of the group. It is thus partially redundant. Nominal groupings, however, are usually implicitly functional insofar as common names generally reflect the common uses of objects.

EQUIVALENCE IN ANCHORAGE

In terms of structure, the developmental trends of Eskimo and white children are alike: the proportion of superordinate groupings increases and that of complexes decreases with age (Figure 1). The older children of both groups not only form significantly fewer complexes, but also such complexes as remain tend to be the varieties that involve the connection of longer strings of items, such as associations and multiple groups. Collections, involving as many attributes as items, and edge matchings consisting of overlapping pairs, are formed by the younger children of both cultural groups, but not at all by the older white children and rarely by older Eskimos. These trends are in perfect accord with the pattern found in Brookline, Massachusetts (Chapter 3), in Mexico City and to a lesser extent in a small Mestizo village (Chapter 12).

If we turn from developmental trends to absolute proportions, a quantitative difference between the two Anchorage groups emerges. Superordinates at both age levels are significantly less frequent for the Eskimos than for the white children. This result is not astonishing if these children are in fact breaking away from a traditional milieu that emphasizes concrete uniqueness at the expense of abstract equivalence. Figure 1 indicates that the Eskimos may attain the same level of superordination, but later.

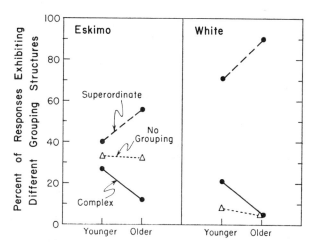

Figure 1. Percent of responses exhibiting different grouping structures given by Alaskan children.

There is one additional difference in the patterning of Eskimo and white groupings with respect to structure. The Eskimos often see neither a complexive nor a superordinate connection among the items; rather they see no connection at all. The resulting refusals to group (Figure 1) often included a specific reference to the differences among the items. For example, one Eskimo boy said, "The same about them is nothing. They have another taste. The milk has a different taste from the orange, the apple, potato, and fish. That's all." The opposition between difference and equivalence was sometimes directly manifest in a type of response employing hypothetical similarities. A good example of these "if" responses is the reasoning of the boy who pointed to the apple and said, "If they both [apple and orange] had this color, they would have been the same." When the potato was added to the array he said, "The only way they could be alike is if this [potato] was a fruit." The impression gained from reading these protocols is that these children do not readily change their point of view in order to resolve a contrast into a similarity. They contrast items within an attribute dimension but do not move to a more general level or shift to another attribute. In the "if" responses the children seemed to be groping toward a superordinate structure but could not quite bring it off technically. They transformed one object to negate the contrast rather than selecting a new single attribute as a basis for equivalence. Among the Eskimo this maneuver was unique to the few who were high in no-grouping responses of all sorts, and it was never used by a white child, either in Anchorage or in Brookline.

One of the problems Eskimo children face in acquiring the techniques of equivalence grouping is overcoming the embeddedness of objects in a particular setting in order first to abstract one attribute and then shift to another point of view. Thus, to an extent, the Eskimos appear to share with the village Mexicans of the previous chapter a remnant of a traditional heritage with its emphasis on the concrete individuality of things.

This picture of the structure of equivalence in Alaska hides one fact: that the Eskimos did not answer or said that they did not know the answer much more frequently than did the white children. The Eskimo children often seemed to withdraw from the situation; and a study of Eskimo culture indicates that passive retreat into silence is the standard way of dealing with tense or unpleasant situations and is consequently a characteristic Eskimo reponse to threatening interactions with the white world. Nevertheless, all the indications were that this response was specific to the task and *not* a reaction to the general testing situation with its unfamiliar white tester, for the Eskimo children had done as well on the Goldstein-Scheerer test as the white children. It would appear that certain Eskimo children have particular difficulty in acquiring the techniques of verbal abstraction valued by the white culture. Their responses illustrate tendencies that perhaps influence the cognitive development of other Eskimo children as well.

Turning now to the content of equivalence groupings, we see that both white and Eskimo children follow the pattern first observed in Brookline, Massachusetts, and later in Mexico City: there is an increasing tendency to pose a similarity judgment on a common function served by objects or on the way they are classified in language (Table 1). The main difference between the Alaskan groups in the developmental picture presented in Table 1 is that the drop in perceptible attributes occurs later for the Eskimo than for the white children. Olver's Brookline data, plus the results in Anchorage, indicate that the sharp drop in the use of perceptible attributes comes in the second or third grade for most American children, in the fifth grade for Eskimo children. Nevertheless, the final proportions of perceptible, functional, and nominal attributes are approximately equal for both groups of children.

The decline in the use of perceptible attributes by Eskimo children is because of a diminution in color reasons. Seven in ten of the younger Eskimos made at least one grouping based on color. No older Eskimos made such groupings, and only a single child in the other groups did so. Yet form and material were used about equally often by all four groups of children. There is evidence that color is especially preferred by the younger Eskimo children, at least in terms of their verbal reasons. They produce two unique responses: grouping items simply because "they have colors" and using "if" responses focused on color, such as, "If this had white, they'd all be the same color.

TABLE 1

Percentage of Reasons of Different Types Given by Alaskan Children

| | Eskimo | | White | |
	Younger	Older	Younger	Older
Perceptible	50%	10%	20%	14%
Functional	34%	71%	73%	77%
Nominal	4%	5%	7%	9%
Refusal to group	11%	14%	1%	0%
Number of reasons	105	111	104	107

Neither the generalized color response nor the "if" color responses have been observed, even in younger white children in Anchorage or in the Olver and Hornsby study (Chapter 3) in the United States.

As the Eskimo children grow older, they seem less caught by the vivid colors of objects, although they continue to notice them and may group on the basis of other perceptible attributes such as form and material. Likely as not, the white children go through the same sequence, but earlier. This conjecture is consistent with other studies dealing with use of perceptible attributes—color, form, and material. Brian and Goodenough (1929) report that children from ages three to six prefer color over form, but that form responses increase with age. And Hornsby (Rigney, 1962) finds that although first-grade children use form almost as often as color, their color groupings drop out by the third grade and form groupings persist until the sixth grade.

Why do younger Eskimos use color at an age when the white children by and large no longer do so? It may be, as Bruner suggests, that color requires fewer transformations than shape for the following reason: (Rigney, 1962, p. 72):

> In forming color equivalence groupings, the subject need attend to only a single dimension—that of hue. Form, however, permits of variation along a multitude of dimensions—height, length, width, number of sides, curvature, regularity or irregularity and so on.

In terms of the number of possible dimensions, function would be closer to shape than to color. In this view, the special status of color would derive from its psychological (if not physical) unidimensionality and the consequent fact that it requires a single step—selection of hue—to be utilized as an equivalence base in this experiment.

The utility of ordering kinds of attributes in terms of the complexity of the transformations they require is borne out by the results of another investigation done by Reich with the same groups of Eskimo and white children. This experiment suggests, however, that transformational complexity affects verbal equivalence more than nonverbal grouping behavior, at least in certain situations. Children were given an "animal sorting task" in which they were to pick out from an array of forty-four animals "those that go together" and then to explain the reason for their groupings. The species represented incuded dogs, cows, lions, seals, bears, sheep, chickens, and whales. Possibilities existed for within-species groupings as well as for more inclusive groups based on habitat or function. Eskimo and white children, regardless of age, do not differ in their nonverbal response to this array. Animals of a single species were almost always placed together. Size or content of the children's groupings did not differ. However, equivalence rules verbalized by the younger Eskimos stand in marked contrast to the reasons for grouping given by the other children. When the older Eskimo and white children gave reasons they named the animals, saying, for example, "These are cows." Although the younger Eskimos could also identify the animals on request, when giving reasons they described physical properties of the items they had grouped, saying, for example, "They are red," or "They have the same black fins," or "They are standing up." As true criteria these perceptible attributes would have dictated the inclusion into the group of other animals, but such cross-species groupings based on essentially irrelevant perceptible attributes were extremely rare. In effect, the younger Eskimos were "explaining" their groupings in terms of prominent attributes rather than formulating an equivalence rule that summarized the similarities within the group as well as distinguishing it from others.

If we judge from the results of the first experiment, the explicit formulation of such an equivalence rule was beyond the means of the younger children, for the verbalization of a nominal grouping rule requires a symbolic transformation—the step from criterial attribute or attributes to class name. As far as behavioral sorting is concerned however, the array was ideally suited to species grouping, for each species was embedded in the most relevant possible context—animals of *other* species. If it is true that for members of traditional societies concept formation proceeds by differences more than by similarities, then species concepts would be formulated in terms of features that distinguish a given species from other species. No transformation from criterial attributes to class name is necessary if grouping proceeds by differentiation among classes on the same level of generaility and not by superordinate generalization. However, when a concept is defined in terms of what it is *not*—that is, its contrast set—rather than in positive terms, it can be brought into play only in a particular context.

The importance of this point will become even more salient when we look at concept formation in Senegal. When the shift from perceptible to functional attributes does come for Eskimo children, the form it assumes is different than for other American children, whether in Anchorage or Brookline. They do not express the function of things in terms of their personal interaction with them nearly so often as do most American children (Table 2). Eskimo children are more likely to refer to function in an impersonal manner, saying for example, "They are to eat," rather than "We eat them." This result had

TABLE 2
Percentage of Functional Attributes that are Personal and Impersonal

| | Eskimo | | White | |
	Younger	Older	Younger	Older
Personal	38%	41%	85%	78%
Impersonal	62%	59%	15%	22%
Number of functional attributes	38	79	76	82

been expected in the light of an analysis of Eskimo culture, for, despite an emphasis on self-reliance, its value system contains ideals of cooperation and the subordination of the individual to the group.

Recall that according to Olver and Hornsby's suggestion in Chapter 3, one's self forms the stable reference point that promotes the change from a complexive grouping structure based on shifting attributes to a superordinate structure based on a single constant attribute. Thus, egocentric functionalism was seen as prerequisite to both superordinate structure and impersonal functionalism. But the development of the Eskimo children indicates that the structure of equivalence groupings is independent of its egocentric content and that egocentrism is not the universal stage postulated by Western psychologists such as Piaget (1930) and Vygotsky (1962).

On the other hand, one tentative conclusion is that specific cultural content has its largest effect on the most specific aspects of grouping strategies. Thus the *type* of structure and the type of attribute are not affected by a specific cultural value, but such a value may determine the form a given type of attribute will take.

Thus, in the example at hand, the ideal relation between individual and group seems to determine whether functional attributes will have a predominantly personal or impersonal content. Another result substantiates this same conclusion: the functional responses of the Eskimo and the white children to the array of ingestible objects varied in content according to the relevant life experiences presumably undergone by each group. The white children refer to health, whereas the Eskimo children are concerned with survival. The white children see the objects as being alike because, "They help us grow," or, "They are good for you." The Eskimos group the items because, "They keep people from starving," "They are all for our existence," or "They keep us living."

In sum, let it be noted that, in Anchorage, the over-all development of equivalence for Eskimo children and for white children is quite similar. With growth both groups of children show a decrease in complexive grouping and an increase in superordinate constructions. This change in grouping structure involves, for both cultural groups, a corresponding change in attention from perceptible to functional properties. How this transition occurs differs in the two cultures. The Eskimo children go beyond immediate perceptual vividness to the objects themselves, their uses and functions, without intervening themselves for reference in the manner of the white children. In each case the pattern is consonant with the cultures in which the children have grown up.

EQUIVALENCE GROUPING IN SENEGAL

The conservation results obtained with Wolof children in Senegal and presented in Chapter 11 would lead one to expect that the cultural variation thus far observed among school children in the United States, Mexico, and Alaska would be overshadowed in magnitude by those obtained from children who have not attended school. If the rural-urban difference can be conceived as variation along an abstract-concrete dimension, then the relevance of school in an oral culture becomes impressively clear. At least one psychologist (Vygotsky, 1961) has noted that the written word *ipso facto* presents a new and higher level of abstraction over the spoken word, abstract in the sense of being removed from the bit of concrete reality to which it points. The spoken word stands for something; the written word stands for the spoken word that stands for something. The anthropologist Malinowski (1930) has pointed out that written language is more abstract than oral language in yet another respect: its meaning is comparatively self-contained, independent of the situational context to which it refers. Bruner (1965) extends this kind of analysis to the intrinsic nature of "learning in school" [p. 1009]:

> The change in the instruction of children in more complex societies is twofold. First of all, there is knowledge and skill in the culture far in excess of what any one individual knows. And so increasingly, there develops an economical technique of instructing the young based heavily on *telling* out of context rather than *showing* in context. . . . School imposes indirect demands that may be one of the most important departures from indigenous practice. It takes learning, as we have noted, out of the context of immediate action just by dint of putting it into a school. In school, moreover, one must "follow the lesson," which means one must learn to follow either the abstraction of written speech—abstract in the sense that it is divorced from the concrete situation to which the speech might originally have been

related—or the abstraction of language delivered orally but out of the context of an on-going action. Both of these are highly abstract uses of language.

Let us start, then, with an experiment carried out only with children who had not gone to school, children possessing an exclusively oral tradition (except for rudiments of Arabic culture transmitted by the Moslem religious school.) These Senegalese children came from the same Wolof bush village of Taiba N'Diaye as the participants in the conservation studies of Chapter 11. Thirty children participated in the experiment. There were ten six- and seven-year-olds, ten eight-year-olds, six ten-year-olds, and four fourteen- to sixteen-year-olds.

The experiment was analogous to Hornsby's free grouping experiment (Chapter 3). Ten objects found in the African market in Dakar were laid out on a table. Each child was asked to indicate those that were alike. He was then asked to give a reason for his choice. The exact instructions literally translated were:

> Won ma yi chi niro. (Show me those in here that are alike).
> Lu nyu niro? ([In] what are they alike?)

The array included four articles of clothing, four round objects, and four red things, so groupings by function, form, and color were possible. There was a sandal, a blouse, a pair of shorts, and a scarf—all to wear. The round objects consisted of an onion, a ball of indigo dye, a glass bead, and a rubber ball. Finally, the ball, the scarf, a plastic drinking cup, and a pencil were all predominantly red.

Naturally, a child could also make groupings unforeseen by the experimenter. The attribute bases for such groups could be discerned through an examination of the child's reasons. Indeed, this experiment allows us to look at equivalence grouping as manifest in both linguistic and nonlinguistic behavior. That is, we compare the child's reasons for grouping and his selection of objects.

Not all arrays of equivalent things reflect a superordinate or "true" concept. Superordinate groupings result from correctly applying a rule. This rule states the criterial attribute(s) that distinguish members of the group from certain other things in the domain. In logical terms, this rule defines the *intensive* properties of a class. If the concept is truly abstract, in the sense that the defining property is superordinate to and removed from its exemplars, irrelevant attributes of particular objects will not affect the grouping. Objects will be classed solely according to the stated criterial attribute. In line with ideas presented by Brown (1958) and Bruner, Goodnow, and Austin, (1956), we may say that the presence of a "true" or superordinate concept is indicated by the correct recognition of its particular instances. The universe of such instances constitutes the *extension* of a concept. As Inhelder and Piaget (1964) point out, intension logically implies extension, and vice versa. This is so because a statement of criterial attributes defines, *deductively*, the universe of exemplars, whereas the enumeration of the universe implies its common properties through induction. In a "true" concept, then, intension (criterial properties) and extension (domain of exemplars) are perfectly coordinated, so that one defines the other (Inhelder and Piaget, 1964).

Let us now look at our results with unschooled Wolof children in terms of these criteria of superordinate structure, criteria derived directly from the definition of superordinate employed in Chapters 3, 12, and the earlier part of this chapter. Recall that the experimental array comprised three groups of four objects each. One group could be generated by the application of a color rule, the second by a shape rule, and the third by a function rule. How many children chose as if following one or another of these rules, grouping, say, all the red objects, all the round objects, or all the articles of clothing? The number of times a superordinate rule is fulfilled increases steadily with age (Figure 2) much as in Hornsbys free grouping experiment (Chapter 3). As in that experiment, this growth parallels a shift away from choosing pairs of objects as groups. Among the youngest children, 60 percent formed pairs; in the oldest group, they were nonexistent.

Can unschooled children say what the attribute is that they are

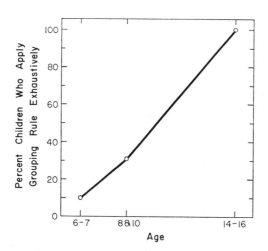

Figure 2. Percentage of bush unschooled children who apply grouping rule exhaustively.

using? In fact, a majority of children at every age are quite capable of expressing attributes relevant to the objects chosen. There are none of the shifting attributes that characterize the complexive structures described by Hornsby in a similar free grouping task. No matter how many objects are chosen, the number of attributes specified never exceeds one. Thus Wolof children attain the superordinate ideal of a single common attribute earlier than do the Massachusetts school children seen by Hornsby! However, this precocious development of structure goes hand in hand with a premature closure of content. For all practical purposes children at all ages base their groupings exclusively on the attribute of color. The percentage of subjects using color attributes as a basis for grouping were, respectively:

> 70% of six- and seven-year-olds
> 40% of eight-year-olds
> 80% of ten- to sixteen-year-olds.

The only other type of attribute to be named with any frequency by these children is typified by the following reason: "They have the same manufacture." This justification seemed to mean that the objects so grouped were man-made, as opposed to the natural objects in the array like the onion and possibly the ball of indigo dye. In all the instances where this type of reason was offered, however, all or most of the objects chosen were in fact red.

The change in grouping structure with age consists primarily, then, in learning to apply the color rule systematically. In fact, the exhaustive groupings chronicled in Figure 2 always consisted of red objects, never round objects or things to wear. To put it another way, extensive properties are developing until they meet intensive definition, thus achieving the status of a "true" superordinate.

These results lead to the tentative, if astonishing, conclusion that Vygotsky's complexive stage may not be a "natural" maturational development, but rather an "error of growth" brought forth by the demands of certain environments, notably the school. It may be that such environments demand the diversification of classificatory bases and that initially this multiplicity of types of attribute entails that inefficient grouping structure called complexive. The complex may thus be a necessary step preliminary to the ultimate accomplishment of equivalence groupings based on a *variety* of criterial attributes.

An affective attribute served as a basis for grouping only once: its form was, "They are pretty." It has often been claimed by psychologists as well as by anthropologists (e.g., Werner, 1948; Durkheim and Mauss, 1963) that traditional peoples use irrational affective reactions as a conceptual link between things. These results indicate that this is not necessarily the case. Indeed, it is possible that a bit of Western individualism might be requisite to using a personal feeling as a classificatory basis. This conclusion is harmonious with the Eskimo children's reticence about putting personal reference into their reasons. Although Hornsby's Massachusetts children do not base groupings on affective ties any more frequently than did these Wolof children, they do frequently utilize their own reactions as links between things through the medium of egocentric reasons, in which the child relates the items to his personal world. At an earlier stage, these American children often use sentential or thematic forms of grouping in which items are linked in highly personal and imaginative, if not logical, ways, (Rigney, 1962). Neither thematic nor egocentric reasons are ever offered by these unschooled Wolof children. In sum, the content of the unschooled Wolof children's reasons is no more affective and much less personal than that of American children.

We have already assessed the extensive aspect of grouping structure in terms of nonverbal criteria, and we have seen that as these unschooled Wolof children grow older, they act more and more as if they were applying a superordinate rule. Consider now another criterion of superordinate structure, one that yields a verbal index of extension parallel to our nonverbal one. In order to receive credit for linguistic superordination the child must explicitly state that there is an attribute common to each member of the group. Superordinates may be either general (e.g., "They are round,") or itemized (e.g., "This one is round; this one is round; this one is round."). The fulfillment of this criterion means (1) that the extension of a grouping has been symbolized by verbal means and (2) that its intensive properties have been stated to remain constant throughout its membership. Because in our present experiment the vast majority of children at all ages conform to the second criterion, the symbolic expression of extensive properties is the only variable tapped by count of superordinate language structure. In contrast to our nonverbal measure, however, this is a purely formal index of extension, for it is independent of the particular objects chosen, of the attribute stated, and of the fit between criterion and objects. Unlike our operational index, this formal measure of extensive superordinate structure does not show an increase with age. The percentage of reasons[3] expressed in superordinate language structure was as follows:

50 percent of six- and seven-year-olds
40 percent of eight-year-olds

[3] No child contributed more than one reason. Ninety percent or the 30 children in the experiment did supply a justification for their grouping.

67 percent of ten-year-olds
25 percent of fourteen- to sixteen-year-olds.

This finding is of special interest in light of the fact that certainly the Eskimo and other American children, and very likely the Mexican children as well, did show an increase in the frequency of this superordinate linguistic structure.

At a concrete level of description, what this difference in the development of grouping structure means is that, whereas the older American child would typically select all items sharing attribute X and would say either, "They are all X," or "This is X; this is X; this is X" the older unschooled Wolof child would also pick all the X items, but would give a one-word reason, "X" or "X-ness," leaving the enumeration of the objects sharing attribute X to be communicated by his previous nonverbal behavior. This difference in the forms of superordination is precisely what our initial analysis of the role of the school would have led us to expect. In the context of the grouping situation, an explicit statement of the criterial attribute plus a choice of all those objects containing the attribute provide a logically perfect definition of the concept in terms of the correspondence of intensive and extensive properties. An explicit statement of the link between attribute and each object selected is unnecessary. In the absence of the stimulus situation, however, the extensive definition must be formulated verbally. This is exactly what the school experience forces on all pupils—the ability to operate intellectually *in the absence of a concrete situational context.* One might say that classification among children who do not go to school remains partially enactive rather than becoming totally symbolized in words. This, however, would distort the situation; for the unschooled bush children learn to symbolize all that information not carried by the situation but needed to define the concept. They easily express their criterial attribute; it is only that they do not symbolize when the information would be redundant. Thus they select objects to form a group and state the criterial attribute. More inspection tells one whether or not all the items share the attribute; it is superfluous to say so.

Unfortunately, this one experiment is not sufficient to demonstrate that the school is the critical factor separating these results from those obtained in Massachusetts and Alaska. Many other variables like culture and language were radically different from the other experiments. Therefore, let us turn to another grouping experiment. Its design was such that the effects due entirely to schooling could be isolated. This was possible because the participants included groups of bush school children whose background differs from that of the unschooled children only in terms of formal education. In fact, this experiment utilized the same groups of Wolof children who participated in the main conservation study of Chapter 11. Consequently, three degrees of urbanization and education were represented, and the effects not only of school but also of the city could be assessed, while native language and ethnic background were held constant.

More precisely, the Wolof children who participated in this study came from three milieus:

Neither Schooling nor Urban Influence. The setting was again Taiba N'Diaye, a traditional Wolof village of about a thousand people. Children at three age levels participated in the study. There were twenty-two six- and seven-year-olds, twenty eight- and nine-year-olds, and eleven eleven-, twelve-, and thirteen-year-olds. A group of five adults were included later.

The Same Traditional Rural Milieu Plus Schooling. Most of the third and sixth-grade children lived in the same village, but unlike the first group they attended the village school. The first-grade children attended a school in Méouane, a similar Wolof village. These three grades approximated on the average the age levels of the three groups from the first milieu. Twenty-four first-grade children, twenty-two third-grade children, and eleven sixth-grade children were questioned in Wolof, their native language. Twelve sixth-grade children went through the experiment in French, the language they were speaking and studying in school.

Schooling Plus Urban Influence. These children attended public school in Dakar. There were groups from the first, third, and sixth grades. The curricula were in principle identical with those followed in the bush schools. The experiment was conducted in Wolof with twenty-three first-grade children, twenty-two third-grade children, and twenty sixth-grade children. Another group of twenty sixth-grade children did the experiment in French. Almost all these children participated in the screening experiment of Chapter 11.

The materials consisted of three sets of three pictures each. In each set it was possible to form a pair based on the color, form, or function of the objects pictured. The three sets, displayed successively, were so arranged that no type of pair appeared twice in the same position. The children were asked to show the experimenter the two pictures out of each set of three that were most alike. They were then asked the reason for their choice.

As in the conservation experiment reported in Chapter 9, the unschooled children did not respond to the question, "Why *do you say* these two are most alike?" but had to be asked, "Why *are* they most alike?" (This question was also used in the first grouping experiment reported.) Evidently they did not distinguish between an opinion and the object of an opinion. Thus they failed implicitly to acknowledge the possibility of other points of view or of opinions about similarities and differences. Perhaps this singleness of point of view is related to the use of only a single attribute—color—noted in the last experiment.

The three picture displays and their presumptive attributes are represented in Figure 3. The color pairs consist of two drawings that have one dominant color in common but are otherwise in different colors. The shape pairs are an approximate match with respect to the dominant outline.

Before the experiment the children played with some toys, tiny models of household objects. They "showed" the experimenter "what you do" with various objects until they seemed sufficiently relaxed

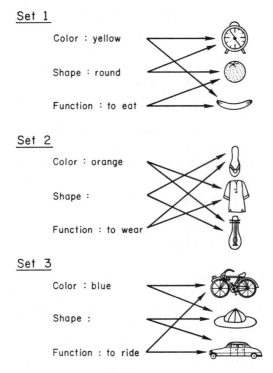

Figure 3. The three picture displays with their attributes. *Set 1*—clock, orange, banana; *Set 2*—sandal, *bubu* (Wolof robe), guitar; *Set 3*—bicycle, helmet, car.

to begin. After the first run-through of the experiment proper, the three displays were exhibited a second time with instructions to show the experimenter "two others" that were alike in each threesome. Again the question "Why?" was asked. At the end, the children were requested to identify the pictures. (Pretests had been conducted in order to ensure that the objects pictured would be equally familiar in urban and rural environments). The children also named the various colors that appeared in the pictures.

All the results that follow are based on the first-choice grouping for each set of pictures (unless otherwise stated). Thus, on the average, each child contributed three groupings and three reasons to the data. Only thirty-one out of the total 212 subjects gave fewer than three reasons.

Let us first look at the difference that school makes with respect to grouping structure, in order to see whether the results of the first experiment are confirmed under more carefully controlled conditions of comparison.

Because the nature of this grouping task was limited to the formation of pairs, we cannot use exactly the same measure of the extension rule of a superordinate concept. But let us go back to the definition of a superordinate rule. For one thing, it is supposed to distinguish members of a group from nonmembers—in this case, the selected pair from the remaining picture. Many of the children justified their choices on the basis of the color white. The background color white was actually present on all three pictures of each set. Obviously, then, "whiteness" did not constitute satisfactory grounds for forming a pair. One would have to include all three pictures in order for the extension of the group to correspond to its intensive definition. Therefore, if the color white was used to justify the inclusion of a pair of pictures, some "noisy" attributes must have entered into the selection, and a rule clearly not "superordinate" must have been used. With age this response pattern disappears in both groups of bush children, declining from a maximum of 16 percent of all reasons given by the youngest unschooled children and 10 percent of those given by the youngest school children. In Dakar this kind of reason never was observed. Olver and Hornsby identified a parallel (although more sophisticated) strategy of illogical overgeneralization in Massachusetts—"hyperordination." It reaches its maximum at a later moment in development but also finally drops out with age.

Another major nonsuperordinate strategy also declines with age among all Wolof children—object naming. Thus automobile and hat would be paired because, "This is an automobile, this is a hat."

Clearly, there is no single and superordinate criterion. Object naming, absent in the first experiment, where it was not a matter of dealing with problematical pictures, is the closest the unschooled children come to forming complexive groupings. Such a complex would be in the nature of a collection. This kind of reason constitutes between 11 and 16 percent of all reasons given by the youngest children. It disappears by the sixth grade among school children and by adulthood among unschooled Wolofs. We take these findings as indices of the growth of superordinate rules with age, school or no school.

Unschooled children, including the oldest among them, could not identify the pictures as well as even the first-grade school children of both bush and city. This relative failure to recognize pictures, despite familiarity with the objects pictured, is interesting in itself. An analysis of the relative difficulty of the various drawings indicates that it is in large measure the two-dimensional conventions for representing three dimensions that are unfamiliar and cause difficulty. One striking aspect of picture recognition is the speed with which school produces an effect. On the average, children who have been attending a bush school for only a few months fail to recognize only 1.8 out of nine pictures. In sharp contrast, the unschooled children of similar age average almost twice as many errors. Errors do not, moreover, decrease at all in the oldest unschooled group. Remember that all these children inhabit the same milieu, except for school, so that their familiarity with the objects pictured is precisely the same.

It may be that this failure to recognize the pictures is related to a change in the usual figure-ground organization. The entire card may be seen as "figure," causing the white background to become relatively salient and to be used as an attribute for grouping. It is interesting that the city children, the only ones who would have had an opportunity to see drawings before starting school, never use the background as a basis for grouping, even in the first grade. Note also that, whereas the first-grade bush school children have a modal recognition rate of eight out of nine, and progress to nine out of nine by third grade, the modal number of pictures to be identified in the city is nine from the first grade on. These findings suggest that for city children learning about looking at drawings takes place before they start school.

As for superordinate language structures, the results (Figure 4) are clear for the school children. First, note that in Dakar the pattern described by Olver holds: superordinate structure increases sharply in frequency as children move from the first to the third to the sixth grade. The rural school children follow the same pattern: superordina-

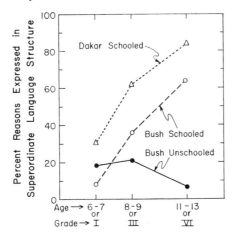

Figure 4. Percentage of grouping reasons expressed in superordinate language structure.

tion increases with age, although the absolute proportion is less at all ages. The developmental pattern of the rural children who have not gone to school is what we found before. For this last group of children superordinates start out in a proportion roughly the same as that of the school children, but do not increase with age.

As in Mexico, groups inhabiting different milieus start out alike and become more different with age. Only the unschooled adult group yields ambiguous results; there is a sudden rise in superordinate grammatical frames to 40 percent of all reasons. The results from this one group are less to be trusted than the others, however, for its members, by force of circumstance, were self-selected. In fact, further analysis indicates that the five adults in this group used more than twice as many French words as any other unschooled group. The possible importance of this fact for an explicit verbalization of extensive grouping structure will be clear in a moment. The adult group also differed from the others in that it was composed entirely of men.

Up to now we have been lumping together both types of superordinate language structures, the general ("They are X" or "These X") and the itemized ("This one is X; this one is X, etc.," or "This X; this X, etc."). The general type of structure is of special interest, nevertheless, because it is farther removed from the situation at hand. A statement of the form, "They are all X," can apply to a group composed of any number of objects. It implies that every object shares

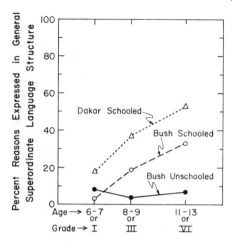

Figure 5. Percentage of grouping reasons expressed in general superordinate
language structure.

the attribute. In contrast, an itemized statement applies to a group
of a certain number of items. One must know how many objects
were in the group before knowing whether the grouping was based
on a principle superordinate to all the individual items. This type
of superordinate is less abstract in that it does not transcend the
individual members of the group. Figure 5 shows that the general
type of superordinate structure becomes more frequent among the
school children as they grow older. Again, the unschooled children
are at the same point at age six or seven but do not change in this
respect with age. Note that only one group, that of the oldest city
school children, reaches a point at which the general type of superordinate frame accounts for more than 50 percent of their grouping
reasons.

Let us now switch from the structure to the content of these children's equivalence groupings. The attributes used by the Wolof school
children as the basis for their groupings are precisely what we would
expect on the basis of our American, Mexican, and Alaskan results.
City school children show developmental trends in the direction of
more functional and nominal concepts as they progress from the first
to the third to the sixth grades (Figure 6). Bush school children,
on the other hand, show practically no development of functional
groupings, and nominal groupings are nonexistent. As in the rural
Mexican village, the proportion of perceptual groupings increases
with age, from 70 percent to 84 percent.

If, however, we break down the perceptible attributes into color and form, it becomes clear that talking about an increase in perceptual groupings masks what is really happening—color pairs are decreasing as form pairs increase (Figure 6). This decrease in the use of color is similar to the pattern found by Hornsby in Massachusetts children and by Reich in Eskimo children.

In order to put these results into perspective, let us turn to the unschooled children. Here the pattern is dramatically opposite and exactly what we found before: color groups increase with age; the use of form and functional attributes is virtually nonexistent at any age; nominal attributes are completely nonexistent (Figure 6). This holds true whether we look for consistent pairing strategies or for explicit grouping criteria. The frequency of noncolor pairs never rises above chance. Note that an adult group has been added to our usual groups of children in order to find out whether color really is the end point in the development of the conceptual content of Wolof

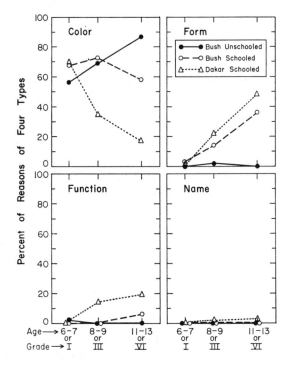

Figure 6. Percentage of grouping reasons of four types: color, form, function, and name.

equivalence groups, at least under arbitrary experimental conditions. The only difference between children and adults, however, is that the adults are better at doing the same thing. They are "better" in two main ways at making color groups. First, they are more consistent in their use of color both in grouping and in explaining. Thus all their pairs are color pairs and all their reasons refer to color. This "improvement" could also be considered an increase in intellectual rigidity and a decrease in group variability. Such a uniformity of response contrasts sharply with the end result of the schooling process, as we have seen. If anything, as school children grow older they agree less with one another on the kind of attributes to be used for grouping. This state of affairs seems as it should be. After all, there is no "right" answer; and it is generally to be hoped that school broadens rather than narrows the options of cognitive functioning.

The other way in which adults are "better" at making color groups is that their choice of pictures is perfectly correlated with their color reasons, a condition that does not hold for the children. This state of affairs reflects the gradual elimination of the use of "white" and "black," color attributes that do not distinguish any pair of pictures from the remaining one. It also reflects the elimination of perceptual errors in color matching. These errors will be taken up later as they relate to the linguistic structuring of color peculiar to the Wolof language. In any case we have here a similarity with rural Mexican children: conceptual development is in the direction of finer and finer perceptual discriminations.

Lest it be thought that unschooled Wolofs merely prefer color but are able to use other types of attributes, the second run-through of the experiment refutes this argument. The types of attribute do not change a whit, even though a different pair of pictures must be chosen. Also, these children failed to make a single functional grouping, despite the fact that they were given some practice in identifying functional attributes in the preliminary play phase. Although the school curriculum does contain specific training in the classification of various objects according to different attributes, the fact remains that without this or some other aspect of the school experience this cognitive ability fails to develop among Wolof children. Furthermore, the first functional groupings made by the school children occasionally manifest a shifting complexive nature, taking the form of a collection of dissimilar functions. Finally, in this second experiment "collections" of different colors occurred three times among the unschooled children. This phenomenon was not observed at all in the object-grouping experiment, where the children were more at home with the array of stimuli. All the indications are that these complexes represent a more elementary way of grouping with a *particular* kind of attribute. Thus, at the age where the unschooled children's color complexes have all but disappeared, the first functional complex is formed by the school children and the school children, presumably earlier at home with color and shape than with function, form fewer perceptual complexes than functional ones. In short, the unschooled children seem to lack even the complexive precursor of more mature functional groupings.

Price-Williams (1962), working with Tiv chidren in Nigeria, found a very different pattern of concept formation. According to his results, school does not affect the kinds of attributes used to classify an array of plants; both school children and those who had not been to school classified the items into edible and inedible groups. Thus unschooled children clearly used a functional grouping rule. Perhaps this difference between the Tiv and the Wolof is a function of the appropriateness of the contrast set utilized in the experimental situation. One may recall that an appropriate contrast set allowed younger Eskimo children to make species groupings in the animal sorting task even though they could not verbalize this classificatory principle. Things may be alike because they are different from some other specifiable thing or things as well as because they share a common feature; but groupings formed in this way are in a sense more discriminations than generalizations. In Price-Williams' experiment, edible plants were placed in their appropriate context: they occurred in an array of different kinds of plants. The Senegalese procedures, by contrast, utilized totally arbitrary contexts. For example, things to eat were contrasted with a clock in the first set of pictures. In order to make a functional grouping in this situation, one would have to define the concept more in terms of a higher-order similarity than in opposition to a category on the same level of generality. When this kind of thinking occurs, the conceptual content of a grouping begins to be independent of the context in which it is placed. The "appropriate" context for a difference, unlike a similarity, is always clearly present in the form of the contrast case. Consequently, it is not surprising that Mexican children often could not see functional similarities among an isolated group of things, although they could formulate functional differences for the very same items. The important role of the contrast case in concept formation is also emphasized by Wallach (1958) in his treatment of psychological similarity.

To sum up what has emerged so far concerning the relations of school and city to the development of the structure and content of concepts: the explicit symbolic representation of the extensive structural properties of superordinates seems to depend on school for its developmental elaboration, whereas grouping operations that are clearly superordinate, given the action context in which they occur, increase with age in all the Wolof milieus sampled. In terms of content, bush children who do not go to school end up with nothing but color-oriented concepts; all school children move away from an initial reliance on color, the bush children mainly toward form, the city children towards form and function.

Certain facts concerning the relation between the structure and content of equivalence groupings begin to emerge. Contrary to Olver and Hornsby's original conclusion (Chapter 3), structures that are clearly superordinate, given the context in which they are formed, do not depend on a changeover from "shifting" perceptible to "stable" functional attributes. For one thing, the perceptible attributes of the unschooled Wolof child, unlike those of Western children, are not shifting at all but are quite extraordinarily fixed. If, however, we are to talk about the representation of a superordinate structure that can stand somewhat out of the context in which it was formed, then we still find that its growth is associated with a shift away from at least certain kinds of perceptible attribute and towards conceptual content that can be utilized in a variety of contexts.

LANGUAGE AND EQUIVALENCE

If at this point we pursue the interpretation of results further, we are restricted to considering the general factors of school and urban environment, when in fact we have information on another cultural variable that is often supposed to be crucial in cognitive development—language. Language at the highest level of generality can be divided into two components, a semantic and a syntactic. Most experiments attempting to relate language to thought have emphasized the semantic side, in the style of Benjamin Lee Whorf (1956). Here the linguistic variable is the richness of the lexicon available in a language for representing a given domain. Implicitly, but not explicitly, these experiments deal with the vocabulary of any one language *at a single level of generality*—its words rather than any structural relation among them.

In the view of linguistic relativity developed by Whorf as early as 1935, language is seen as a system of categories that both incorporates and perpetuates a particular world view. On the lexical level, every language codes certain domains of experience in more detail than others. It has been suggested that when a given language symbolizes a phenomenon in a single word, it is readily available as a classifying principle to speakers of that language. Although any familiar experience can be coded in any language through the simple expedient of a periphrase, experiences that must be expressed in this way are supposed to be less available to speakers of the language (Brown, 1958). The Wolof-French bilingualism in Senegal and the design of our experimental procedure enabled us to try out this view with respect to the principles of classification, that is, the types of attribute used in equivalence grouping by monolingual Wolof, bilingual Wolof, and monolingual French children.

A second kind of semantic variable is more structural. It deals with the *number of levels of generality* that can be encoded by the lexicon of a given language for a particular domain. The relation of this kind of semantic variable to concept formation was also investigated.

Finally, there are the syntactic properties of language to relate to the logical structure of thought. Hitherto the crosscultural study of the relation between syntax and thought has been sorely neglected, although a recent paper (McNeill, 1965) suggests that there is reason to believe that the lexical encoding of events is only a special (and perhaps trivial) case of grammatical encoding. Sapir (1921) may have been the earliest to think explicitly and clearly about the manner in which syntax can shape thought (see Chapter 2). Our research makes a first attempt to relate grammatical and conceptual structure.

For purposes of comparison with the monolingual and bilingual Wolof children, groups of nursery-school, kindergarten, first-grade, and sixth-grade children from predominantly French schools in Dakar were included in the experiment. These children all spoke French as their first language and the great majority were French nationals whose families were living in Dakar. In order to examine the interaction of systems of linguistic categorization as it occurs in bilingual children, the same experiment was done in French with additional groups of sixth-grade Wolof children. These sixth-graders were matched with those who had been through the experiment in Wolof.

Consider first the Whorfian-type of hypotheses that would be derived from a comparison of the Wolof and French lexicons. Only words at a single level of generality—the most specific—will be considered at this point. In Wolof it is impossible to make explicit the three color groupings possible in the picture-grouping experiment without the use of French words. Specifically, in the last set of three pictures, the French word *bleu* (blue) must be used if one is to specify the basis of grouping by naming the color. In the second set, the use of color involves contrasting a pair of predominantly orange pictures with a predominantly red one. The Wolof language codes both colors with a single word (*honka*), so that verbalizing the basis of the grouping by means of the Wolof word would not be as satisfactory as using the French word *orange*, for it would not contrast the pair with the third member of the set. For the first set of three pictures, Wolof does as well with coding the relevant colors as French, although yellow, the color involved in forming the color pair, is not as codable by Wolof according to the criterion (suggested by Brown [1958]) of agreement between speakers of the language. In fact, the same word is sometimes used to name both yellow and orange, the "contrasting" color of the third picture in the triad. This description of the lexical situation is based both on preliminary linguistic investigation and on the actual results of the experiment under consideration.

Let us pass over a comparison of the coding of shapes by the French and Wolof languages, for the relative strength of the two languages is much less clear, and this comparison is not necessary for present purposes. With regard to functional grouping, both easily find ways of saying, "These things are to eat, to wear, to ride in." One cannot say that Wolof is superior to French in this regard, but unlike the color case, it is not clearly inferior in its ability to code at least those aspects of function demanded by the functional groups in this experiment.

From this description of the two languages, one would at the very least expect monlingual (unschooled) Wolofs to be more functionally oriented in the content of their groupings than bilinguals (schooled Wolofs) and that both these groups would form more functional groups than would monolingual French children in a situation of forced choice, where one type of attribute must be used at the expense of others.

We have already seen that the experimental results in no way justify this kind of Whorfian thinking; in fact, the results are unambiguously opposite: our monolingual Wolofs (the bush unschooled groups) are incapable both of operationally forming functional pairs (above a chance level of frequency) and of verbally expressing the functional basis of such groups.

It only remains to present the results from the monolingual French children to complete this picture (Figure 7). Indeed, their perfor-

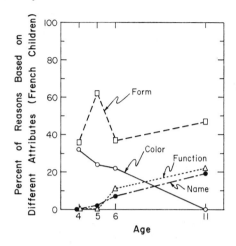

Figure 7. Percentage of grouping reasons based on different attributes (French children).

mance is in line with our modern-urban-versus-traditional-rural hypothesis, and it appears unrelated to lexical considerations. Far from being more color-oriented than the Wolofs, they are much less so from the very outset. The preceding lexical analysis is offered, however, because it is of importance to discard this type of linguistic thinking once and for all.

We have seen that lexical structure does not determine the class of attribute or domain that is selected as a basis for equivalence. Once a domain is selected, however, we may still ask whether lexical structure is related to the particular conceptual cuts that are made within that domain. For example, the Wolofs have few color words, yet this fact does not stop monolingual Wolofs from relying almost exclusively upon color in the formation of equivalence groups. Does this scarcity of words, however, cause them to make less accurate distinctions when they make their color classifications?

It is quite a straightforward matter to identify errors in color discrimination that can be directly related to lexical structuring. For example, the second set of pictures consists of two predominantly orange pictures and one predominantly red one. The orange colors are in fact identical. An error was counted when a child who claimed to be grouping according to color would select one orange and one red picture as being *most* similar. This choice was clearly wrong

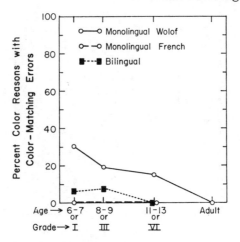

Figure 8. Percentage of monolingual Wolof, monolingual French, and bilingual children showing color-matching errors.

from an objective point of view, for he could have chosen the two orange ones that were of identical color.[4] Similar errors occurred with the other sets of pictures. In the first set, an orange and a yellow picture would be paired instead of the two yellow ones, and the child would say it was because they were "yellow." In the third set of pictures a different type of perceptual error occurred. Instead of matching the two blue pictures for their color, some children would pair a red one with another one containing a little bit of maroon. In Wolof blue is very codable, but it is the French word *bleu* that is universally used, even by unschooled bush people! On the other hand, both red and maroon are coded by the same word, *honka*.

If these errors of discrimination are due to lexical coding, Wolof monolinguals should make them most frequently, Wolof bilinguals next most frequently, and French monolinguals not at all. Figure 8 presents the frequency of the errors among those children who say they are grouping by color. The results are exactly as predicted. At every age bilinguals commit these errors less frequently than do Wolof monolinguals, and they never occur among French monolinguals of similar age. (It must be mentioned, however, that the third type

_____

[4] Note that this is nonlinguistic evidence of the influence of language on thought and so avoids the circularity of the original demonstrations by Whorf. In other words, just calling both orange and red by a single name would not in itself constitute evidence that the two colors would be more poorly discriminated than if there were a separate word for each.

of error described above did occur once among the French preschool children.)

One characteristic of these errors is that by absolute standards they are infrequent, even in those groups of children where they occur most often. There are never more than three color discrimination errors in any single group af children. These relatively rare mistakes are not a major conceptual feature in the total context of Wolof equivalence grouping. We begin to wonder whether the lexical features of language should be assigned as large a role in thought as has been claimed by Whorf and even others who have spoken of covariation rather than determinism.

Of great theoretical interest is the fact that these perceptual errors decrease with age until at last they are completely eliminated in all groups. It appears that age brings increasingly accurate perceptual discriminations. This would appear to be a universal trend (cf., Chapter 12), even when the lexicon of a culture hinders rather than facilitates such discrimination. We may conclude that with age the constraints of reality increasingly overcome language if one opposes the other.

Thus the role of language in terms of specific lexical considerations does not appear to be great, although its domain of operation now seems fairly clear. Factors other than the lexicon determine the bases or dimensions of equivalence, but a specific lexicon may influence the "band width" of the individual categories that constitute a given dimension.

Let us turn now from the role of labels *per se* to the role of a set of hierarchically organized labels, that is, to the role of lexical richness defined in structural terms. There has been much controversy about the place of superordinate words in conceptual thought. The Wolof language, in contrast to French (and to English), has neither the word "color" nor the word "shape." It is clear from the results reported above that the lack of the word "color" does not hinder color groupings from being formed. Does the absence of the general word, however, mean that the Wolofs have no general concept of color? And if not, of what consequence is this seemingly grievous deficit?

First, it is clear that the use of these general words increases with age among the children who attend school. Only 35 percent of the Wolof first-graders employ superordinate words, in sharp contrast to 68 percent of those Wolof sixth-graders questioned in Wolof and 81 percent of those questioned in French. This sort of finding is in itself nothing new; the same trend has been observed before in the development of children's vocabularies (Brown, 1958). It becomes interesting only when one realizes that such a development only takes place among the unschooled Wolofs to the extent that French words are assimilated into their language, for these words do not exist in Wolof (at least in the perceptual domains relevant to the conceptual content of this experiment). Among the schooled Wolofs, moreover, this development of superordinate words means that French words such as *couleur* (color) and *forme* (form) are being introduced into a Wolof narrative.

But these results still do not answer the question of whether this lexical development (or its absence) has extralinguistic consequences. Consider, therefore, the following diagram:

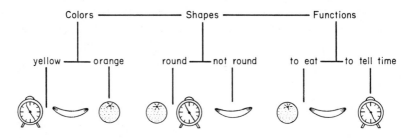

Figure 9. Possible hierarchical organization of first set of pictures.

If this hierarchical organization corresponds to the type of structure generated by the subject in order to deal with the task, then his use of the superordinate words "color" or "shape" should indicate that the person is at the top of the hierarchy and has access to the entire hierarchy. One would predict, then, that he would be able to supply more than one kind of attribute if pressed. For he is plainly contrasting, say, color with shape or with use. By the same reasoning his use of shape names or color names alone (e.g., "round," "yellow") would mean that he was operating one level lower in the hierarchy. He would be "cut off" from the top of the hierarchy and its connections with other branches. He would therefore be less likely to operate in branches other than the one in which he was. A concept (a consciously or explicitly recognized concept) is defined as much by what it excludes as by what it includes, that is, by its contrast class. The concept of color, therefore, comes into being with the appearance of an opposing idea: and this opposing concept cannot exist on the level of specific color names: "round" is related only to other shapes, "yellow" only to other colors.

If this reasoning is correct, then one would expect that, if a subject ever used an abstract word like "color" or "shape," he would vary his choice of grouping attributes when asked to make a first and second choice of pairs for each of the three sets of pictures. But if he used only a concrete word like "yellow," then one would expect him to form nothing but color groupings in all six tasks. The results presented in Figure 10 do indeed indicate that there is an important association between the use of superordinate words like "color" and "shape" and the number of different types of attribute used for grouping. The results are presented separately for each school group, so it is clear that this relationship holds when all other factors such as their knowledge of French and their school grade are held constant. Thus if a Wolof child uses a superordinate word, his chances of grouping by a variety of attributes are twice as great as those of a child who utilizes no superordinate vocabulary. One is reminded that when a Wolof child uses the word "color," it is the French word that he is introducing into a Wolof linguistic context.

The relationship becomes very weak when the experiment is done in French with Wolof sixth-graders: when the children use superordinate words, 65 percent of them use more than one type of attribute; when they do not use any of these words, 50 percent of them use more than one attribute. The difference is comparatively small. The adverse effect on this relationship of doing the experiment in French with Wolof sixth-graders becomes especially interesting when we com-

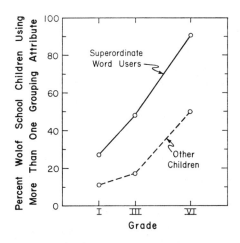

Figure 10. Percentage of Wolof school children using more than one grouping attribute.

pare the results obtained with the French children, who also did the experiment in French. We see from Table 3 that the relationship between the use of superordinate words and the ability to shift from one kind of grouping attribute to another is stronger than that obtained not only with the Wolof school children doing the experiment in French, but also with those doing it in Wolof. If a French child uses the abstract top-of-the-hierarchy labels, he is almost certain to vary his basis of grouping at least once. The contrast between the two groups reveals that access to the pure conceptual hierarchy as diagramed is indicated by the use of abstract terms only if the linguistic terms have been thoroughly mastered in all their semantic implications. When the procedure is such that the Wolof children are obliged to speak French, their use of superordinate language seems to have a forced character and indicates little about hierarchical structure and where they are in that structure. Table 3 shows that general superordinate words more frequently imply a corresponding hierarchical structure when the French superordinates are spontaneous interjections in a Wolof context.

The reasons for color preference among the unschooled Wolofs will be discussed shortly. What needs emphasis at this point is that the basis of equivalence is not an either/or phenomenon, as so much experimentation has assumed. It is, rather, a matter of adding new bases to old and of *integrating them in a hierarchically organized structure*. Everybody is more or less limited in the range of classificatory bases available to him. It is not that one person uses color and another, shape. Rather, one can use color, the other can use shape *and* color. It is the structure of the lexicon and not simply its list of terms that is crucial.

Superordinate class words are not just a luxury for people who do not have to deal with concrete phenomena, as Roger Brown (1958) hypothesizes. In a way quite different from that envisaged by Whorf in the lexical version of his hypothesis, we seem to have found an important correspondence between linguistic and conceptual structure. It relates, however, not to words in isolation but to their depth of hierarchical embedding both in the language and in thought. This correspondence has to do not with quantitative richness of vocabulary in different domains or with "accessibility" but with the presence or absence of words of a higher order that can be used to integrate different domains of words and objects into hierarchical structures. No matter how rich the vocabulary available to describe a given domain, it is of limited use as an instrument of thought if it is not organized into a hierarchy that can be activated as a whole.

Let us consider now the grammatical aspect of language and its relation to conceptual thought. Our focus switches from semantics to syntactics on the linguistic side, and from content to structure on the conceptual side. Remember that superordinate structure is not the same as the use of a general or superordinate word. The attribute that organizes a superordinate group may be general or specific, but it must be shared by every member of the group in question. Superordinate language structure, moreover, demands that the connection between attribute and group members be explicitly stated. Thus "They are all the same color" would have the same structural status as "They are all red." In terms of this structural criterion we have seen that all the children studied in Senegal conform to the usual developmental trend except the unschooled Wolof group. At this point a set of purely grammatical criteria will be introduced in order to test connections between conceptual and grammatical organization.

On the grammatical side, three stages of symbolic reference may be distinguished. The first is the ostensive mode: mere pointing at the object of reference. The second, the labeling mode, involves a verbal tag. The simplest type of label does nothing more than symbolize the pointing operation in a word—"this," "here." The next type of label is one step removed from this operation: it specifies what is being pointed at; "yellow" and "round" are examples of this way of labeling. The third mode is sentential placement. Here the label is integrated into a complete sentence; for example, "This is yellow," or "This is round." In the present experiment these three modes were defined as follows and the definitions applied to grouping reasons:

1. *Pointing*—no verbal response.
2. *Labeling*—tag only; no verb in utterance. Either or both types of label described above could be used. For example, "This," "Yellow," and "This yellow" would all fall in this category.
3. *Sentential placement*—complete sentence. Such a sentence would consist of one or both types of label described above plus a verb. "They are long" and "This one is round" are examples of reasons in the sentential mode.

The results of this analysis are presented in Table 4. Among French monolinguals, pointing is nonexistent even among first-graders. The ostensive mode, however, occupies a definite position in the reasons of all the youngest Wolof groups, especially the unschooled, but disappears in all groups with advancing age. The other differences set the unschooled children apart from all the school children. In the unschooled groups labeling increases with age. The use of the sentential mode stays at a constantly low level, although there is some

TABLE 3
Percentage of Children Using and Not Using Superordinate Words in Grouping Who Employ One or More Than One Basis for Grouping

	Superordinate Word Users		Other Children	
	Wolof in Wolof	French in French	Wolof in Wolof	French in French
Use one attribute	24 42%	2 9%	49 80%	12 75%
More than one attribute	33 58%	19 91%	12 20%	4 25%
	100%	100%	100%	100%
Number	57	21	61	16

TABLE 4
Percentage of Reasons Couched in Different Grammatical Modes

	Monolingual Wolof				Bilingual Wolof				Monolingual French	
	6–7	8–9	11–13	Adult	Gr. I	Gr. III	Gr. VI (in Wolof)	Gr. VI (in French)	Gr. I	Gr. VI
Pointing	24%	21%	0%	0	7%	2%	0%	0%	0%	0%
Labeling	64	58	90	62	86	57	31	4	33	12
Sentential	12	21	10	38	7	42	69	96	67	88
	100%	100%	100%	100%	100%	100%	100%	100%	100%	100%
No. of reasons	50	48	30	13	119	129	93	96	46	59

rise in the adult group. By contrast, in all the school groups, both
Wolof-French bilingual and French monolingual, labeling gives way
to sentential placement with age and increased schooling. The most
dramatic contrast is between Wolof school children and those not
in school, with virtually no overlap in the distributions of the oldest
children. Some ninety-seven percent of the eleven- to thirteen-year-old
monolinguals' reasons are simple labels; ninety percent of the reasons
formulated by the Wolof sixth-graders doing the experiment in French
take the form of complete sentences.

Similarly, Deutsch (1965) finds that lower-class New York children,
although weak in some usages of language, succeed perfectly well
in utilizing its labeling function. And John (1963) shows that these
lower-class children can label the elements in a picture as well as
middle-class children, but they cannot integrate the labels into a co-
herent verbal description nearly so well. This is just one of a number
of the parallel differences between schooled and unschooled Wolof
children and between lower-class (or "culturally deprived") and middle-class children that were noted.

These results, using purely grammatical criteria, reveal larger differences between the groups who know French and those who do not
than did the first, more semantic verbal measure of grouping structure.
Is there, however, any direct relation between grammatical and conceptual structure? According to theory a child can frame an explicit
superordinate structure (general or itemized) in either the labeling
or sentential mode. An example of a general superordinate language
structure in the labeling mode would be "These—round." Expressed
sententially, this structure would be "These" (or "They") are round."
An itemized superordinate in labeling form might be "This—round;
this—round." An example of the same structure expressed in the sentential mode would be "This" (or "It") is round; "This" (or "It")
is round." Obviously, a limitless variety of nonsuperordinate structures
may be expressed either as labels or as complete sentences. It is
valid, then, to ask whether the use of a particular mode of reference
is associated with a particular conceptual structure. The answer is
a strong affirmative for both schooled and unschooled Wolof children.
When a school child frames a reason in the sentential mode, the
probability that he will form a superordinate structure of either type
is on the average almost three times as great as when he uses simple
labeling. For an unschooled child, this same probability of a superordinate structure is almost six times as great when his reasons are
sentences rather than labels.

For a school child, moreover, the probability that a superordinate structure will be in a general (rather than an itemized) form is more than four times as great when a grouping reason is expressed in the sentential mode. In the unschooled groups, the number of reasons falling into these categories is very small. If, however, all four unschooled groups are combined, the relationship does hold: superordinate reasons expressed as labels take the general form about half as often as do those expressed as complete sentences.

All these findings concerning the relations between linguistic and conceptual variables contribute important modifications to the picture of culture and equivalence that emerged from the last section. At that point, large differences in conceptual development seemed due to schooling (rather than to the degree of urbanization or to Wolof culture in general). Now, however, schooling has essentially been held constant, whereas linguistic factors have been varied. The positive results produced by this strategy lead to the hypothesis that the school is acting on grouping operations through the training embodied in the written language. This hypothesis has a good theoretical basis. The written language, as Vygotsky (1961) points out, provides an occasion in which one must deploy language out of the immediate referential context. Writing virtually forces a 'remoteness of reference on the language user; consequently he cannot use simple pointing as an aid, nor can be count on a labeling that depends on the present context to make clear what his label refers to. Writing, then, is a training in the use of linguistic contexts that are independent of the immediate referents. Thus the embedding of a label in a sentence structure indicates that it is less tied to its situational context and more related to its linguistic context. The implications of this fact for the manipulation of concepts are great: linguistic contexts can be turned upside-down more easily than real ones can. Indeed, the linguistic independence of context achieved by certain grammatical modes appears to favor the development of the more self-contained, superordinate structure used by the school children.

For that matter, all of the semantic and syntactic features that have been discussed in relation to concept formation—a rich and hierarchically organized vocabulary, as well as the syntactical embedding of labels—become necessary when one must communicate out of the context of immediate reference. It is precisely in this respect that written language differs from the spoken. The school itself provides an opportunity to use language out of context—even spoken language—for to a very high degree, what one talks about there are things not immediately present. Thus we make no claims that the French language is unique in being able to produce the conceptual effects described above. According to our interpretation, any written language used out of a concrete context should produce these same cognitive results.

The linguistic variables enumerated above are linked in the behavior of these subjects with an earlier accuracy in perceptual discriminations, a more diversified conceptual content in terms of classificatory bases, and a structural representation that is relatively generalized and self-contained (that is, possessing a communication value outside the situation in which it takes form). Thus far the evidence is purely correlational, however. To what extent is language a causative agent in the language–thought relations under discussion? A comparison of the performances of the Wolof sixth-graders doing the picture-grouping experiment in French with those of their classmates who were given the same experiment in Wolof should reveal what effects of school are directly related to the influence of the French language.[5]

We cannot judge whether conducting the experiment in French rather than in Wolof would promote an even earlier accuracy in color discrimination, as no younger children took the experiment in French. But we can test the effect of using French on the growth of superordinate language structures and on the diversification of content, the conceptual variables that correlate with the use of sentences and abstract words. But these conceptual features also correlate with the amount of schooling, as the last section (pp. 283 ff.) made clear. Now we will make sure that the learning of a second (written and spoken) language is the key factor in schooling, as far as forming concepts is concerned. Does instruction in spoken and written French make the difference?

It turns out that all the trends in content (Figure 11) and structure (Figure 12) related to schooling (and described in the last section) are intensified when the experiment is done in French. This generalization holds for both bush and city children. Thus color is less used by the sixth-grade children who are interrogated in French than by those of the same class and school being questioned in Wolof. Correlatively, shape and function are more frequently used when the sixth-graders speak French (in the latter case only among children in the city). As for nominal classes, French appears to make their use not only increase among the city children but also appear for the very first time among the bush children. The effect of French appears even larger with respect to structure, if we look at the general type

---

[5] The effect of inserting French words in a Wolof or French context was explored in connection with superordinate terms, but this is a somewhat different problem.

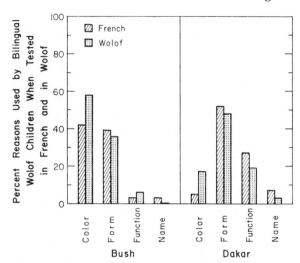

Figure 11. Percentage of four types of grouping reason used by bilingual Wolof children when tested in French and Wolof.

of superordinate linguistic structure (Figure 12). (In contrast, the use of the French language is not associated with a greater frequency of itemized superordinate frames.) This difference between results when the same experiment is done in Wolof and in French may also indicate that what is learned in one language is less than perfectly "translatable" into another.

As for the French children, the two categories of attribute that show a developmental increase are exactly as in the United States and Mexico: functional and nominal. Let us now compare these French children with their Wolof counterparts in Dakar (Figure 7). These two groups of children are following identical curricula in school, and they are both from the same city. The only difference is in the depth and extent of the French language and culture that they command. It is notable that there is no difference between the Wolof and French children in the development of functional attributes; even from a quantitative viewpoint, the final result is almost precisely the same. The French children show considerably more development of nominal equivalence, however. In the context of so much over-all similarity, this difference assumes a special significance, for the creation of a nominal class is unique in requiring a symbolic transformation that makes the leap from a criterial attribute to class name. This leap is symbolic and redundant; it adds no new information about the stimuli not carried by a functional reason. It makes sense that a purely linguistic response (that is, one without referential implications) should be most susceptible to linguistic differences between groups. This point becomes even more intriguing when we consider that the most "universal" or primary grouping attribute, color, is the one requiring the least symbolic transformation in order to be represented—namely, pointing. In fact, nothing but this action of pointing is required to communicate a color similarity. And recall that the unschooled children did point more often in our experiment. Color differs even from form in this respect, for an image is needed to simultanize the continuous tracing action necessary to represent shape.

In terms of the general type of superordinate grammatical frame, there is no difference between the sixth-grade Wolof children using French and the French children. By the sixth grade sixty-four percent of the French children's reasons fall in this category, exactly the proportion observed among the sixth-grade bush children questioned in French (Figure 12). These French children, however, form far fewer of the itemized type of frame (twelve percent of all reasons) than the Wolof children doing the experiment in French either in the bush (twenty-five percent of all reasons) or in Dakar (twenty-two percent). And their total proportion of superordinates is correspondingly less. Evidently, speaking French hinders itemized superordinates

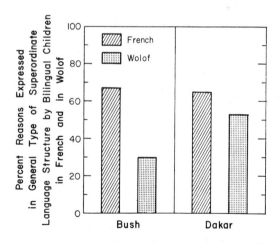

Figure 12. Percentage of grouping reasons expressed in general type of superordinate language structure by bilingual Wolof children when tested in French and Wolof.

while it facilitates general ones, for sixth-grade Wolof children doing the experiment in Wolof form more of these (31 percent of all reasons in both groups) than do any of the groups questioned in French. Thus the use of the French language per se (that is, when all other variables are held constant) augments the frequency of only the most abstract type of structure. Furthermore, the use (rather than the amount of knowledge) seems to be the crucial variable, for the Wolof bilinguals speaking French fare as well in this respect as do the French monolinguals.

Let us take up this same matter in terms of grammatical mode of reference. Table 4 indicates that complete sentences are formulated more readily in French than in Wolof, when there is precisely the same situational context.

Moreover, the use rather than the knowledge of French appears to be the relevant variable, for Wolof bilinguals are highly similar to French monolinguals as far as frequency of using the sentential mode is concerned. But what is the relationship between using French, grammatical mode of reference, and conceptual structure? Labeling reasons are scarce among the Wolof children questioned in French (Table 4), but it is probably meaningful that not a single one expresses a superordinate language structure. In sharp contrast, eighty-two percent of the reasons expressed in the sentential mode have a superordinate structure. Taking these sentential superordinates alone, we find that seventy-four percent of them are in general form—virtually the same proportion as found among the sixth-grade children questioned in Wolof when they use the sentential mode. This similarity introduces the interesting possibility that French augments the production of general superordinates by causing labels to be embedded in sentential structures. Thus the differences in the frequency of general superordinate linguistic structures between the bilingual groups using Wolof and those using French disappear, if one considers only those reasons that are couched in sentential form.

CONCLUSION

What has been found in this chapter supports the picture that emerged from a comparison of urban and rural children in Mexico— but it also goes beyond it. For in Senegal, we have discovered a difference between rural children and urban children which parallels that found in Mexico; and, besides, city-living Eskimos are much like urban children studied elsewhere. But though the rural-urban difference is small, it is similar in nature to a larger difference that separates children who have been to school and those who have not. The difference in both cases is most compactly described as a difference between abstractness and concreteness. We believe that the difference between the city child and the rural child derives from a differential exposure to problem solving and communication in situations that are not supported by context—as is the case with, for example, most reading and writing, the use of monetary exchange, and schooling. Rural life, it appears, is somewhat less conducive to the development of abstraction.

But what is most striking is the extension of this difference when we compare schooled and unschooled children. Schooling appears to be the single most powerful factor we have found in the stimulation of abstraction.

Our Eskimo data indicate that the "egocentric functionalism" of Western children is not a necessary stage in the development of the idea of equivalence. Similarly, the sorting behavior of unschooled Wolof children reveals that a supposedly "universal" stage in conceptual development, complexive grouping, is less than universal and may be produced by school learning. Complexive grouping may be the first result of the development of a semantic hierarchy of greater depth that permits more flexibility with respect to the bases used in making equivalence judgments. Complexive structure is thus probably more closely linked with the semantic or content side of grouping than with the syntactic side. In fact, neither complexes nor functional attributes are a necessary preliminary to the systematic application of a superordinate rule. What is of such great interest to us is that unschooled children, because they show so little variability in their equivalence behavior (things are always alike in terms of shared color), need not develop explicit forms of superordinate grouping. School children, newly equipped with an enriched hierarchy of possibilities for grouping, must become explicit if they are not to be confused by the changing possibilities that present themselves for forming equivalence groups.

Bush children who do not go to school rely on color attributes at every stage of development; school children, in contrast, move away from an initial reliance on color—the bush children mainly toward form, the city children toward form and function. Thus the school appears to favor the growth of a certain type of perceptual equivalence, namely, equivalence based on form. This result is analogous to the finding in Chapter 11 that the first result of schooling is to "perceptualize" a child's approach to conservation. It must be stressed, however, that in both conservation and concept formation this perceptual development is basically a conceptual one. Likely as not, this development is also closely tied to language. By conceptual we mean that school is teaching European habits of perceptual *analysis*. An analysis into parts is plainly crucial to concepts based on the multidimensional attribute of form, whereas unitary global perception could suffice for color grouping. Similarly, the breaking up of innate shape constancies into their component parts of retinal image and angle of view is basic if one is to understand two-dimensional conventions for three-dimensional representation. And we have seen that schooling is required for recognizing objects represented in this way, although not necessarily for dealing with less analytic pictorial representations.

Because the Senegalese school is barely richer in perceptual stimuli than is the world outside, we must look elsewhere for an explanation of the effect of schooling on perceptual analysis. In Chapter 2, (p. 40) it was suggested that because one of the universal design features of language is discreteness, that is, a discontinuity of material on all levels from sound to meaning, "analysis and synthesis are literally *forced* upon anyone who would speak human language. Language, then, breaks up the natural unity of the perceptual world—or at least imposes another structure on it." But there is more to the matter than just being a language speaker—all children are that. Where there is difference is in how language is used and what opportunities are provided for different uses. Here again, school is important. For it is the school children who have the greater opportunity to practice language in contexts that do not carry the meaning for them automatically, who are forced thereby to use sentences to the full. They are the ones who, moreover, are led by the nature of school lessons to translate their experience and actions into words and sentences that will satisfy a teacher—and thereby learn to reorganize experience and action to conform to the requirements of language. Even in conservation experiments (Chapter 11), furthermore, children who did not show conservation were in fact responding to perceptual inequalities, but it was mainly the school children among them who could isolate particular perceptible features and describe them in language.

Now, if perceptual analysis is necessary, then language is crucial as an analytic tool. Where perceptual analysis is not necessary, as in color perception, language is much less important. This formulation is quite different from the Whorfian notion of perception that places the whole burden of explanation on lexical representation and none on the domain being represented. Thus we have seen that color categorizations may be made precisely because they do not demand any linguistic representation at all, whereas nominal classification develops last because it is totally dependent on symbolic representation and transformation. A lexicon at the lowest level of generality is therefore superfluous in determining the content domain of equivalence groupings. But it can affect the perceptual analysis of a given domain, that is, the way in which the domain is subdivided into categories. The fineness of lexical coding can in this way affect the accuracy of perceptual discriminations, at least in children, as our data on color-matching errors indicate.

Language can also act as a synthetic device, once it has broken up the world into pieces. Whereas a lexicon at a single level of generality analyzes a given domain into component parts, a lexicon at higher levels synthesizes various domains into unified hierarchical structures.

Not only do linguistic representations have the properties of analysis and synthesis, they also have a potential for self-containment and isolation from context. As with analysis and synthesis, however, this property is not always exploited to the fullest in linguistic performance and therefore cannot be utilized for the symbolic manipulation of experience. It is this feature of linguistic performance that the Senegalese school seems to develop and utilize for the growth of superordinate conceptual structures that are both generalized and context-independent. One must bear in mind that both unschooled Wolofs and those who have had schooling have the linguistic *competence* to form sentences, but their *performances* with respect to this variable are quite different. What makes the difference is that the school children are trained not only in the context-free use of language, but in the written form of language, and in a second language at that—French, which probably has more "abstract" capacity inherent in it than Wolof. At least, bilingual Wolof children perform more abstractly in French than in their native tongue.

In the end we place great stress on the role of linguistic variables in conceptual growth, at the same time rejecting almost completely Whorf's simple notions about the relation between language and reality.

Looking at cross-cultural differences and cognitive growth from another point of view, Heinz Werner (1948) remarked that:

> Development among primitive people is characterized on the one hand by precocity and, on the other, by a relatively early arrest of the process of intellectual growth (p. 27).

This is an accurate formulation with respect to the difference between the performance of school children and those who have not

been to a Western-style school in the present experiments. The unschooled children early hit on stable rules of color equivalence. School
children are perfectly capable of grouping according to color, but
they go on to other things. Their progress is therefore sometimes
marred by "errors of growth." In conservation behavior, too, we saw
this "early arrest of the process of intellectual growth" in the
unschooled children. And so the differences between those in school
and those out increase with age. This has also been a persistent observation concerning the differences between "culturally deprived" and
other American children (Deutsch, 1965; John, 1963). Thus it seems
that the conceptual development of lower-class American children
resembles that of the unschooled Wolof children in this regard. If
so, then early intellectual stabilization signifies that full cognitive skill
is not being attained. In short, it appears that some environments
"push" cognitive growth *longer* than do others.

   With respect to the growth of representation, what turns out to
be virtually impossible for the unschooled Wolofs are cognitive ac-
complishments that can be carried out *only* by symbolic means, for
instance, nominal equivalence and superordinate language structures.
To at least some degree school alters both the ikonic and enactive
modes of representation by insisting that they be placed in some
confrontation with the symbolic mode. So it may be that modern
technical societies demand of their members a fundamental cognitive
change as their capacities change with biological growth; whereas
traditional nontechnical societies demand only the perfection and
elaboration of first ways of looking at the world.

CHAPTER 14

An Overview

Jerome S. Bruner

We come finally to some closing observations that may bring our enterprise into proper perspective. Our objective has not been to constructed a "finished" theory of cognitive growth or to attain a set of final conclusions concerning the growth of mind. Rather, we have set out to forge a working point of view about growth and to test it in the light of systematic observations of children growing up in different settings.

We have, I believe, achieved this objective. For those who find labels useful the view of growth set forth in the preceding thirteen chapters may be called *instrumental conceptualism*. In brief, it is a view that is organized around two central tenets concerning the nature of knowing. The first is that our knowledge of the world is based on a constructed model of reality, a model that can only partially and intermittently be tested against input. Much of the structure of our cognitive models is quite remote from any direct test, and that rests on what might be called an axiomatic base—our ideas of cause and effect, of the continuity of space and time, of invariances in experience, and so on. It seems not unlikely (no stronger phrase than that is justified) that some of this axiomatic structure informing our models of reality is already given in the innate nature of our three techniques for representing or "modeling" reality: action, imagery, and symbolism. That is, the physical requirements of adaptive action "force" us to conceive of the world in a particular way, a way that is constrained by the nature of our own neuromuscular system. So, too, are we constrained by the primitive properties of visual, auditory, and haptic space in our effort to represent our knowledge in terms of imagery. Finally, our representation of reality in terms of language or symbolism is similarly constrained by what again

319

seem to be our native endowment for mastering particular symbolic systems, systems premised on rules of hierarchy, predication, causation, modification, and so forth (See Chapter 2).

If the first central tenet of instrumental conceptualism is our idea of the model or representation and its constraints (the conceptualist side of the matter), the second is that our models develop as a function of the uses to which they have been put first by the culture and then by any of its members who must bend knowledge to their own uses. As we have commented many times before, models are first adopted from the culture and are then adapted to individual use. Our instrumentalism is inherent in this double emphasis on the role of use. We are well aware, I think, of the fact that one cannot separate (except analytically) *cultural* instrumentalism and *individual* instrumentalism. That is, the language, the values, the ways of looking and thinking that characterize a culture have evolved by virtue of the way a culture has coped with its circumstances over a period of time, usually a very long period. At the same time, the form of the language-in-use, of the values-in-use as expressed in an individual's life, reflects his mode of coping with reality within the wide or narrow constraints imposed by the culture.

There is likely no better example of this last point than one that appears in the chapter immediately preceding. Data are reported there that in effect reject the lexical form of the Whorfian hypothesis. That is, we see that, although Wolof as a language is highly restricted in comparison with French in the number of color words it contains (especially in its more superordinate color words), nonetheless Wolof speakers have a far greater tendency to group objects in terms of their color likeness than do French speakers, or even Wolof-French bilinguals. Indeed, this difference holds true in spite of the fact that color discrimination appears to be grosser among the unschooled Wolof monolinguals, whose errors reflect the gross color lexicon of their language. Obviously, Wolof as a language has not responded to this color-grouping preference of its speakers, probably because color indication is so firmly imbedded in the context of action and is so easily supported by pointing. So, in a deep sense, the adaptation of a culture to historical circumstances and the adaptation of individuals to the circumstances of their lives must be considered as separate, though often they may seem to be inextricably intertwined.

Our point of departure is, then, a human organism with capacities for representing the world in three modes, each of which is constrained by the inherent nature of the human capacities supporting it. Man is seen to grow by the process of internalizing the ways of acting, imaging, and symbolizing that "exist" in his culture, ways that amplify his powers. He then develops these powers in a fashion that reflects the uses to which he puts his own life. The development of those powers, it seems to me, will depend massively on three imbedded predicaments. The first has to do with the supply of "amplifiers" that a culture has in stock—images, skills, conceptions, and the rest.[1] The second consideration is the nature of the life led by an individual, the demands placed on him. The third (and most specialized) consideration is the extent to which the individual is incited to explore the sources of the concordance or discordance among his three modes of knowing—action, image, and symbol.

Relatively little is known about the first two of these—the culture's intellectual amplification supplies and the demands that are placed on an individual. We know that cultures vary widely in respect to the manner in which they empower their members with skills, images, and values. But it is not plain how the empowering occurs. It does not suffice to point merely to the *existence* of skills in a culture as a cultural tradition. The presence of abstract mathematics in Western culture may affect everybody in that culture, but it surely does not affect them all in the same way, the knowledgeable and ignorant alike. Again, we do not have much knowledge of how a culture demands cognitive response from its members. There is clearly a different set of demands made on members of a subsistence culture and members of a technical culture dominated by a market economy. Sahlins (1966) puts the matter well with respect to the "pressure" for planfulness.

What has become much plainer to us in the course of our work is that there are important institutions and pressures that develop within societies of the technical type, which lead to the demand for confirmation between the three modes of knowing. Whenever learning occurs outside the context it will be used, outside the range of events that are directly supportive in a perceptual way or indirectly available for pointing, then language enters as a means of conveying the content

---

[1] It is always difficult for the psychologist to think of anything "existing" in a culture—or however one wishes to express the presence of traits and skills transcending any one individual's life or even the span of a generation. Psychology is in the main acultural and ahistorical in its theories. Kroeber's (1948) early emphasis on the superorganic, Lévi-Strauss's (1963) insistence on structure in culture, and I. A. Richards' (1966) recent criticism of the structural linguist's unwillingness to recognize that a history is reflected in a language—all these are matters that are vaguely embarrassing to the working psychologist, in spite of our lip service to such ideas as "culture-and-personality." We are, alas, wedded to the idea that human reality exists within the limiting boundary of the human skin!

of experience and of action. Under these circumstances, there is more often than not a requirement of developing correspondence between what we do, what we see, and what we say. It is this correspondence that is most strikingly involved in reading and writing, in "school learning," and in other abstract pursuits. The confrontation may not always work its way to correspondence, to be sure. It is interesting that Whorf's first observations as a fire-inspector (1956) were of instances where language had come to provide a reality that dominated and shaped men's experience and action.

In the course of earlier chapters we have commented on a phenomenon called "growth errors," where a child becomes more mistaken about some matter as he grows older before he finally comes to understand it. The conspicuous case was in Chapter 8, when we dealt with the ratio problem, with contradictory errors increasing with age before abating altogether. A growth error is precisely the first unsuccessful stage of trying to achieve correspondence or concordance between systems of representation. It may well be that a certain tolerance is needed in an educational system to appreciate the benign nature of such errors!

Several general issues have preoccupied us in our experiments: the growth of rules of equivalence, the development of "efficient" information searching, and the establishment of invariance as a tool in thinking. With respect to equivalence, we began by noting the progress of Western children from initial reliance in their judgments on the surface sensory properties of events as a basis for judging equivalence, to a later reliance on the common uses to which objects can be put, and finally to the common linguistic classifiability of objects. Hand in hand with this change there is also a shift from complexive rules of equivalence to rules based on superordinate class inclusion. The picture we have obtained is much like that found among urban Russian children a quarter of a century earlier by Vygotsky, although our conclusion represents a considerable theoretical extension of his views. One novel element has been added: the importance of "egocentric functionalism" in helping the Western child to achieve a freedom from his early preoccupation with the more superficial and vivid attributes of things. The Western child passes through a phase in which he groups things as equivalent in terms of what he arbitrarily can do with or to them, until finally he is able to recognize the appropriate uses he can make of things.

These findings are "true" and "important" in the conventional sense. Yet when one goes to a strikingly different culture, by comparing the behavior of Wolof or Eskimo or rural Mexican children, our Western picture turns out to be culture-bound—indeed, any particular pattern of growth one ever finds must be in some important measure culture-bound. However, to say some feature of human development is culture-bound is not to dismiss it but only to recognize that growth itself is culture-bound. Eskimo children, though raised in Western schools, have shown no egocentric functionalism. Wolof children do not grow less perceptual in their choice of grouping attributes. Indeed the unschooled Wolof child comes to terms with the idea of equivalence in a fashion that is his own, not something that is "more" or "less" of some undimensional universal pattern.

The Wolof child who has been to school, however, shows a pattern of intellectual growth that is strikingly similar to patterns familiar in Western society. He early shows the effect of learning to use language outside a context in which his reference is supported either by pointing or by the structure of the situation. The Wolof school child is much more akin to the American school child as far as ideas of equivalence are concerned, closer than he is to his unschooled cousin in the next village. The difference lies, at the very least, in the extent to which and the manner in which children learn to use language as an implement of thought. Even more important, there is a prior stage, at which the child must reorganize his way of viewing and imaging things, in order to use language to describe what he knows. School forces him to rely on linguistic encoding as a way of communicating, because by its remoteness from direct action it robs him of contextual and ostensive reference as a mode of carrying meaning. In the sense intended by Lantz (1963) and by Lantz and Stefflre (1964), codability is a question not only of making the classification of things easy for ourselves, but also making it easy for others to know what we have in mind.

With respect to information seeking, we have a variety of observations that fit into a common pattern. Studies of information seeking that use the game of Twenty Questions (Chapter 4), investigations of perceptual recognition (Chapter 5), and experiments on how children search for hidden patterns (Chapter 6) all indicate that the mode of search changes in a rather regular way with growth (at least in Western culture, for our observations are limited to American children). At first the child deals with single features of a problem, one at a time, "on the plain" rather than in hierarchies, whether it is a causal force to be ascertained by questions, a picture to be recognized, or a hidden pattern to be found. He operates with images, seeking to match what is before him with some specification in his head. In time the child is able to deal with several alternatives simultaneously, hierarchically, and with the inclusive inferences made possible by a hierarchical structure. From then on, as information analysis rather than image-matching comes into play, the child grows in a regular fashion toward a lesser dependence upon redundancy. Ingenious studies by Wohlwill (1962) and Gollin (1965) have illustrated how the child's development then proceeds in the direction of much more efficient information processing. Eleanor Gibson (1966) quite rightly signals this increased informational efficiency as a hallmark of perceptual development.

I have no reason to doubt that at some level of perception this kind of growth is probably universal—at least where the perception of ordinary objects is concerned, objects one uses as tools or as consumables of one kind or another. No review of the meager literature on cross-cultural studies of perception would contradict it (cf. Greenfield & Bruner, 1966). What differs from culture to culture (and within subcultures) is the extent to which ranges of alternatives are fitted together into superordinate or hierarchical structures, so that a given percept is created as one of only a few alternatives or one of many. The hypothesis I would like to set forth is that there is a greater push toward hierarchical connections in technical cultures than in those that are less technical. The hypothesis is based on the assumption that there are fewer compelling reasons in a less technical society for connecting events to anything beyond their immediate contextual settings, such as money value, abstract cause-and-effect relations, or the intricate uniform timing of work periods. In the sense used by Miller, Pribram, and Galanter (1960), hierarchically organized plans need not be so elaborately formulated in a folk society. All this leads me to suspect that in less complex societies perception is likely to be more *ad hoc*, more given to filling the magic seven slots (Miller, 1956) with the particularities of a certain object or event than with a domain of the alternative events that might have occurred.

Finally, a word about invariance or conservation of various forms of quantity across transformations in their appearance is in order. Enough has been said in Chapters 8 through 11 that little is needed here to make our general point clear. That very young children in our own society, children who do not exhibit ordinary Geneva "conservation" (see Chapter 9) are capable of actions premised on conservation, we know from experiments already reported. When it comes to pouring the appropriate amounts of water into beakers, the features that confuse the child when he must "tell" rather than "do," provide him with little impediment.[2] What seems to vary from culture to culture is not the ability correctly to pour uncertain quantities of water into beakers or to shape clods of clay to appropriate equalities. Rather, it is the translation of the primitive idea of the identity of a substance into a visual form, or into a linguistic form, or both. As we have seen, the many unschooled Wolof children do not grow up to achieve "verbal" conservation. Even in their teens they will still *tell* you that there is more to drink in the taller, thinner jars. But, pragmatically, they are quite adequate in handling liquids in the life around them.

Our discoveries on the nature of conservation and on the use of invariance as a tool of thought should not have surprised us. For, in fact, our studies of equivalence rules deal with the same cognitive fabric as conservation. Learning to recognize the underlying respect in which two quantities are alike (though they appear different) is the same task as learning how a bell and a horn are alike—or a man and an animal. It is interesting that studies of both types have yielded not only comparable results during development, but comparable changes in pattern across cultures.

In the end, we are increasingly struck with what occurs in a highly evolved technical society. It is not that one sees "better" or represents what one has learned in habit patterns "better," or even talks or thinks in language "better." Rather, what seems to be the case is that there is an insistence on mapping each of these systems into another, with a resulting increase of the translatability between each of them. We tend to reject those acts that do not lend themselves to a linguistic rendering or accountability, and perhaps to rule out of imagery those features of experience that have no enactive counterpart or words or sentences that render them communicable.

Robert Leeper (1965) has written a brilliant and timely piece on the perceptual representation of emotions and motives. His paper came to my attention late in the day as far as this book is concerned. He conceives of motives and emotions as making themselves felt through their participation in cognitive organization. I believe that, where the emphasis of a technical society is on objects and acts in their abstract and linguistic connection, we may be missing the conditions for satisfying those human needs that are not related to objects,

---

[2] Since the writing of Chapter 9, there has been a beginning of more systematic studies on conservation-in-action—in which the child has the task of choosing a full beaker to pour into an empty one in order to have it come out equal to a third identical one that is partly filled. It is now quite plain that conservation-in-action occurs far earlier than does conservation as a linguistic judgment.

to instrumental acts, or to abstract hierarchies. Since we have often remarked in these pages on the increased instrumental power that comes from "forcing" a confrontation between the three systems of representing reality, it is a proper precaution to comment on the potential dangers of insisting that our acts and images should conform to the austere hierarchies of lexicon and grammar. The functional adequacy of the hunter-gatherer mentioned earlier, or the organic quality of design in folk societies noted by Alexander (1964), may require that there be not only some means by which we may achieve a unity of representation, but also one that leaves room for mute emotions and inexplicable motives, without our labeling them as "sick." This much can serve as something of a concluding *caveat* to those who would read an unqualified progress in our account of the nature of cognitive growth as we find it in our society and (increasingly, with the expansion of Western technical life) as we will find it throughout the world.

But lest we conclude on a note that seems either to celebrate the noble savage or to look darkly at the intellectual future of man, we should state one final conclusion that is crucial. Insofar as man's powers are expressed and amplified through the instruments of culture, the limits to which he can attain excellence of intellect must surely be as wide as are the culture's combined capabilities. We do not know in any deep sense as yet how we shall, in the future, better empower men. Insofar as the sciences of knowing can throw light on the growth of mind, the efficacy of the culture in fulfilling its responsibility to the individual can likely be increased to levels higher than ever before imagined.

References

Alexander, C.: 1964. *Notes on the synthesis of form.* Cambridge, Mass.: Harvard Univer. Press.

Attneave, F.: 1954. Some informational aspects of visual perception. *Psychol. Rev.,* **61,** 183–193.

Binder, A.: 1958. Personality variables and recognition response level. *J. abnorm. soc. Psychol.,* **57,** 136–142.

Bower, T. G. R.: 1965. Perception in infancy. Paper read at Center for Cognitive Studies Colloquium, Harvard Univer., Cambridge, Mass.

Braine, M. D. S.: 1959. The ontogeny of certain logical operations: Piaget's formulation examined by nonverbal methods. *Psychol. Monogr.,* **73,** No. 5 (Whole No. 475).

Braine, M. D. S.: 1963a. On learning the grammatical order of words. *Psychol. Rev.,* **70,** 323–348.

Braine, M. D. S.: 1963b. The ontogeny of English phrase structure: the first phase. *Language,* **39,** 1–13.

Brian, R., & Goodenough, F. L.: 1929. The relative potency of color and form perception at various ages. *J. exp. Psychol.,* **12,** 197–213.

Brown, R. W.: 1956. Language and categories. Appendix in J. S. Bruner, Jacqueline J. Goodnow, & G. A. Austin, *A study of thinking.* New York: Wiley.

Brown, R. W.: 1958. *Words and things.* Glencoe, Ill.: Free Press.

Brown, R. W.: 1966. Personal communication.

Brown, R. W., & Bellugi, Ursula: 1964. Three processes in the child's acquisition of syntax. *Harvard educ. Rev.,* **34,** 133–151.

Brown, R. W., & Berko, Jean.: 1960. Word association and the acquisition of grammar. *Child Develpm.,* **31,** 1–14.

Brown, R. W., & Fraser, C.: 1964. The acquisition of syntax. In Ursula Bellugi & R. W. Brown (Eds.), The acquisition of language. *Monogr. Soc. Res. Child Develpm.,* **29,** 43–79.

Brown, R. W., Fraser, C., & Bellugi, Ursula.: 1964. Explorations in grammar evaluation. In Ursula Bellugi & R. W. Brown (Eds.), The acquisition of language. *Monogr. Soc. Res. Child Develpm.,* **29,** 79–92.

Bruner, J. S.: 1959. A psychologist's viewpoint. Review of Bärbel Inhelder & J. Piaget's *The growth of logical thinking. Brit. J. Psychol.,* **50,** 363–370.

Bruner, J. S.: 1960. *The process of education.* Cambridge, Mass.: Harvard Univer. Press.

Bruner, J. S.: 1964. The course of cognitive growth. *Amer. Psychologist,* **19,** 1–15.

Bruner, J. S.: 1965. The growth of mind. *Amer. Psychologist,* **20,** 1007–1017.

Bruner, J. S.: 1966. *Toward a Theory of Instruction.* Cambridge, Mass.: Harvard Univer. Press.

Bruner, J. S., & Goodman, Cecile C.: 1947. Value and need as organizing factors in perception. *J. abnorm. soc. Psychol.,* **42,** 33–44.

Bruner, J. S., Goodnow, Jacqueline J., & Austin, G. A.: 1956. A study of thinking. New York: Wiley.
Bruner, J. S., Busiek, R. D., & Minturn, A. L.: 1952. Assimilation in the immediate reproduction of visually perceived figures. J. exp. Psychol., 43, 151–155.
Bruner, J. S., & Postman, L.: 1949. On the perception of incongruity: a paradigm. J. Pers., 18, 206–223.
Bruner, J. S., & Potter, Mary C.: 1964. Interference in visual recognition. Science, 144, 424–425.
Bruner, J. S., & Tajfel, H.: 1961. Cognitive risk and environmental change. J. abnorm. soc. Psychol., 62, 231–241.
Bühler, K.: 1930. The mental development of the child. New York: Harcourt, Brace.
Carmichael, L., Hogan, H. P., & Walter, A. A.: 1932. An experimental study of the effect of language on the reproduction of visually perceived form. J. exp. Psychol., 15, 73–86.
Chomsky, N.: 1957. Syntactic structures. S'Gravenhage, Netherlands: Mouton.
Chomsky, N.: 1965. Aspects of the theory of syntax. Cambridge, Mass.: MIT Press.
Crowell, A.: 1961. Decision sequences in perception. Unpublished doctoral dissertation, McGill Univer.
Crutchfield, R.: 1964. Instructing children in creative thinking. Paper read at 72nd Annual Convention, Amer. Psychol. Assoc., Los Angeles, California.
Davidon, R. S.: 1952. The effects of symbols, shift, and manipulation upon the number of concepts obtained. J. exp. Psychol., 44, 70–80.
de Saussure, F.: 1916. Cours de linguistique générale. Paris: Payot.
De Soto, C.: 1965. Reasoning and spatial representations. Paper read at Center for Cognitive Studies Colloquium, Harvard Univer., Cambridge.
Deutsch, M.: 1965. The role of social class in language development and cognition. Amer. J. Orthopsychiat., 35, 78–88.
Donaldson, Margaret.: 1963. A study of children's thinking. London: Tavistock.
Draguns, J. G., & Multari, G.: 1961. Recognition of perceptually ambiguous stimuli in grade school children. Child Develpm., 32, 541–550.
Drake, Diana.: 1964. Annual Report, Center for Cognitive Studies, Harvard Univer.
Drosler, J., & Kuhn, W. F.: 1960. Ein experimenteller Vergleich der visuellen Wahrnehmung von Kindern, Schizophrenen and Alkoholikern mit der tachistoskipischen Wahrnehmung normaler Erwachsener. XVIth Int. Congress of Psychol. Bonn: German Society of Psychol., I, 1-2.
Durkheim, E., & Mauss, M.: 1963. Primitive classification. Chicago: Univer. of Chicago Press.
Elkind, D.: 1965. Piaget's conservation problems. Mimeo., Child Study Center, Univer. of Denver.
Elkind, D., Koegler, R. R., & Go, Elsie.: 1962. Effects of perceptual training at three age levels. Science, 137, 755–756.
Elkind, D., Koegler, R. R., & Go, Elsie.: 1964. Studies in perceptual development. II. Whole-part perception. Child Develpm., 35, 81–90.
Emerson, L. L.: 1931. The effect of bodily orientation upon the young child's memory for position of objects. Child Develpm., 2, 125–142.
Ervin, Susan M.: 1961. Changes with age in the verbal determinants of word-association. Amer. J. Psychol., 74, 361–372.

Ervin-Tripp, Susan M., & Slobin, D. I.: 1966. Psycholinguistics. *Annu. Rev. Psychol.*, 17, 435–474.

Fantz, R. L.: 1965. Ontogeny of perception. In A. M. Schrier, H. F. Harlow, & F. Stollnitz (Eds.), *Behavior of nonhuman primates.* New York: Academic Press. Pp. 365–403.

Flavell, J. H.: 1963. *The developmental psychology of Jean Piaget.* Princeton: Van Nostrand.

Fortes, M.: 1938. Social and psychological aspects of education in Taleland. Supplement to *Africa*, 2, No. 4. Also Memorandum XVII of the *Int. Inst. African Languages & Cultures.* London: Oxford Univer. Press.

Galloway, D.: 1946. An experimental investigation of structural lag in perception. Unpublished doctoral dissertation, Univer. of California, Berkeley.

Garner, W. R.: 1966. To perceive is to know. *Amer. Psychologist,* 21, 11–19.

Gellermann, L. W.: 1933. Form discrimination in chimpanzees and two-year-old children: I. Form (triangularity) *per se. J. genet. Psychol.,* 42, 3–27.

Ghent, Lila.: 1956. Perception of overlapping and embedded figures by children of different ages. *Amer. J. Psychol.,* 69, 575–587.

Gibson, Eleanor J.: 1966. Perceptual development and the reduction of uncertainty. Paper read at Int. Congress of Psychol., Moscow, U.S.S.R.

Gibson, Eleanor J., & Olum, Vivian.: 1960. Experimental methods of studying perception in children. In P. H. Mussen (Ed.), *Handbook of research methods in child development.* New York: Wiley.

Gibson, J. J.: 1941. A critical review of the concept of set in contemporary experimental psychology. *Psychol. Bull.,* 38, 781–817.

Gilson, E.: 1959. *Painting and reality.* New York: Meridian.

Gollin, E.: 1965. A developmental approach to learning and cognition. In *Advances in child development and behavior.* Vol. 2. New York: Academic Press. Pp. 159–185.

Gombrich, E. H.: 1960. *Art and illusion.* New York: Pantheon.

Goodman, N.: 1951. *The structure of appearance.* Cambridge: Harvard Univer. Press.

Goodnow, Jacqueline J.: 1962. A test of milieu differences with some of Piaget's tasks. *Psychol. Monogr.,* 76, No. 36 (Whole No. 555).

Greenberg, J. H. (Ed.): 1963. *Universals of language.* Cambridge, Mass.: MIT Press.

Greenfield, Patricia M.: 1966. Culture, concepts and conservation: a comparative study of cognitive development in Senegal. Unpublished doctoral dissertation, Harvard Univer.

Greenfield, Patricia M., & Bruner, J. S.: 1966. Culture and cognitive growth. *Intl. J. of Psychol.,* in press.

Group on Educational Technology and Training: 1961. *Report to the Secretary of State.* In W. Y. Elliott (Ed.) *Education and training in developing countries: the role of U.S. foreign aid.* New York: Praeger, 1966.

Gump, P.: 1955. Relation of efficiency of recognition to personality variables. Unpublished doctoral dissertation, Univer. of Colorado.

Hallowell, A. I.: 1955. *Culture and experience.* Philadelphia: Univer. of Pennsylvania Press.

Hanfmann, Eugenia, Rickers-Oviankina, Maria, & Goldstein, K.: 1944. Case Lanuti: Extreme concretization of behavior due to damage of the brain cortex. *Psychol. Monogr.,* 57, No. 4 (Whole No. 264).

Held, R.: 1963. Motor-sensory feedback and the geometry of visual space. *Science,* 141, 722–723.

Held, R.: 1965. Plasticity in sensory-motor systems. *Scientific Amer.,* 213, No. 5, 84–94.

Held, R., & Hein, A.: 1963. Movement-produced stimulation in the development of visually guided behavior. *J. comp. physiol. Psychol.,* 56, 872–876.

Hemmendinger, L.: 1953. Perceptual organization and development as reflected in the structure of Rorschach test responses. *J. proj. Tech.,* 17, 162–170.

Herman, D. T., Lawless, R. H., & Marshall, R. W.: 1957. Variables in the effect of language on the reproduction of visually perceived forms. *Percept. mot. Skills,* 7, Monogr. Suppl. 2, 171–186.

Hockett, C. D.: 1960. The origin of speech. *Scientific Amer.,* 203, No. 3, 88–96.

Hubel, D.: 1963. The visual cortex of the brain. *Scientific Amer.,* 209, 54–62.

Hunt, J. McV.: 1965. Intrinsic motivation and its role in psychological development. In *Nebraska Symposium on Motivation 1965.* Lincoln: Univer. of Nebraska. Pp. 189–282.

Inhelder, Bärbel, Bovet, M., Sinclair, H., & Smock, C. D.: 1966. On cognitive development. *Amer. Psychologist,* 21, 160–164.

Inhelder, Bärbel, & Piaget, J.: 1958. *The growth of logical thinking from childhood to adolescence.* New York: Basic Books.

Inhelder, Bärbel, & Piaget, J.: 1964. *The early growth of logic in the child.* New York: Harper.

Jakobson, R.: 1956. Two aspects of language and two types of aphasic disturbances, Part II. In R. Jakobson & M. Halle, *Fundamentals of language.* S'Gravenhage, Netherlands: Mouton.

James, W.: 1890. *Principles of psychology.* New York: Henry Holt.

John, V.: 1963. The intellectual development of slum children: some preliminary findings. *Amer. J. Orthopsychiat.,* 33, 813–822.

Kagan, J.: 1966. Personal communication.

Kagan, J., Moss, H. A., & Sigel, I. E.: 1963. Psychological significance of styles of conceptualization. In J. C. Wright & J. Kagan (Eds.), Basic cognitive processes in children. *Monogr. Soc. Res. Child Develpm.,* 28, 73–118.

Katz, J. J.: 1966. *Philosophy of language.* New York: Harper.

Katz, J. J., & Fodor, J. A.: 1963. The structure of a semantic theory. *Language,* 39, 170–210.

Kessen, W.: 1962. "Stage" and "structure" in the study of children. In W. Kessen & Clementina Kuhlman (Eds.), Thought in the young child. *Monogr. Soc. Res. Child Develpm.,* 27, 65–82.

Kessen, W.: 1965. Looking at looking in the human newborn. Paper given at Center for Cognitive Studies Colloquium, Harvard Univer.

Kogan, N., & Wallach, M. A.: 1964. *Risk-taking: a study in cognition and personality.* New York: Holt, Rinehart & Winston.

Körner, S.: 1959. *Conceptual thinking.* New York: Dover.

Kroeber, A. L.: 1948. *Anthropology: race, language, culture, psychology, prehistory.* (Rev. ed.) New York: Harcourt, Brace.

Kroeber, A. L., & Kluckhohn, C.: 1952. Culture: a critical review of concepts and definitions. *Papers of the Peabody Museum of American Archaeology and Ethnology.* Vol. XLVII. Cambridge, Mass.: The Peabody Museum.

Kuhlman, Clementina.: 1960. Visual imagery in children. Unpublished doctoral dissertation, Harvard Univer.

LaBarre, W.: 1954. *The human animal.* Chicago: Univer. of Chicago Press.

L'Abate, L.: 1957. Sanford's uncertainty hypothesis in children. *Etc. Rev. gen. Semant.,* 14, 210–221.

Lantz, D. L.: 1963. Color naming and color recognition: a study in the psychology of language. Unpublished doctoral dissertation, Harvard Univer.

Lantz, D. L., & Stefflre, V.: 1964. Language and cognition revisited. *J. abnorm. soc. Psychol.,* 69, 472–481.

Lashley, K. S.: 1951. The problem of serial order in behavior. In L. A. Jeffress (Ed.), *Cerebral mechanisms in behavior: the Hixon symposium.* New York: Wiley.

Lawrence, D. H.: 1949. Acquired distinctiveness of cues: I. Transfer between discriminations on the basis of familiarity with the stimulus. *J. exp. Psychol.,* 39, 770–784.

Lawrence, D. H.: 1950. Acquired distinctiveness of cues: II. Selective association in a constant stimulus situation. *J. exp. Psychol.,* 40, 175–188.

Leeper, R. W.: 1963. Learning and the fields of perception, motivation, and personality. In S. Koch (Ed.), *Psychology: a study of a science.* Vol. 5. New York: McGraw Hill.

Leeper, R. W.: 1965. Some needed developments in the motivational theory of emotions. In *Nebraska Symposium on Motivation, 1965.* Lincoln: Univer. of Nebraska Press.

Le Gros Clark, W. E.: 1963. *The antecedents of man.* New York: Harper.

Leopold, W. F.: 1949. Speech development of a bilingual child: a linguist's record. Vol. III. Grammar and general problems in the first two years. Evanston, Ill.: Northwestern Univer. Press.

Lévi-Strauss, C.: 1963. *Structural anthropology.* New York: Basic Books.

Lewis, O.: 1959. *Five families.* New York: Basic Books.

Luria, A. R.: 1961. *The role of speech in the regulation of normal and abnormal behavior.* New York: Pergamon.

Maccoby, M., Modiano, Nancy, & Galvan, I.: 1963. Culture and abstraction. *VIIth Congresso Intramericano de Psicologia.* Mexico D. F., Sociedad Interamericana de Psicologia.

Maccoby, M., Modiano, Nancy, & Lander, Patricia.: 1964. Games and social character in a Mexican village. *Psychiatry,* 27, 150–162.

Malinowski, B.: 1930. The problem of meaning in primitive languages. In C. K. Ogden & I. A. Richards, *The meaning of meaning.* (3rd Rev. Ed.) New York: Harcourt, Brace.

Mandler, G.: 1962. From association to structure. *Psychol. Rev.,* 69, 415–426.

McCarthy, Dorothea.: 1954. Language development in children. In L. Carmichael (Ed.), *Manual of child psychology.* (2nd edition) New York: Wiley. Pp. 492–630.

McGranahan, D. V.: 1963. Some remarks on the human implications of technological change in undeveloped areas. *Soc. Problems,* 1, 13–16.

McNeil, D.: 1965. Anthropological psycholinguistics. Mimeo., Center for Cognitive Studies, Harvard Univer.

McNeill, D.: 1966. Developmental psycholinguistics. Mimeo., Center for Cognitive Studies, Harvard Univer.

Medawar, P.: 1963. Onwards from Spencer: evolution and evolutionism. *Encounter,* 21, 35–43.

Messick, S., & Hills, J. R.: 1960. Objective measurement of personality: cautiousness and intolerance of ambiguity. *Educ. psychol. Measmt.,* 20, 685–698.

Meumann, E.: 1908. *Die Entstehung der ersten Wortbedeutungen beim Kinde.* (2nd edition) Leipzig: Engelmann.

Miller, G. A.: 1956. The magical number seven, plus or minus two: some limits on our capacity for processing information. *Psychol. Rev.,* 63, 81–97.

Miller, G. A.: 1965. Some preliminaries to psycholinguistics. *Amer. Psychologist,* 20, 15–20.

Miller, G. A., & Chomsky, N.: 1963. Finitary models of language users. Chapter 13 in D. Luce, R. Bush, & E. Galanter, *Handbook of mathematical psychology.* Vol. II. New York: Wiley.

Miller, G. A., Galanter, E., & Pribram, K. H.: 1960. *Plans and the structure of behavior.* New York: Holt.

Miller, N. E.: 1934. The perception of children: a genetic study employing the critical choice delayed reaction. *J. genet. Psychol.,* 44, 321–339.

Miller, W., & Ervin, Susan.: 1964. The development of grammar in child language. In Ursula Bellugi & R. W. Brown (Eds.), The acquisition of language. *Monogr. Soc. Res. Child Develpm.,* 29, 9–34.

Mooney, C. M.: 1957. Age in the development of closure ability in children. *Canad. J. Psychol.,* 11, 219–226.

Mosher, F. A.: 1962. Strategies in the acquisition and use of information. Unpublished doctoral dissertation, Harvard Univer.

Mowrer, O. H., & Ullman, A. D.: 1945. Time as a determinant in integrative learning. *Psychol. Rev.,* 52, 61–90.

Neisser, U.: 1962. Cultural and cognitive discontinuity. In The Anthropological Society of Washington, *Anthropology and human behavior.* Washington, D. C.: Gaus. Pp. 54–71.

Olver, Rose R.: 1961. A developmental study of cognitive equivalence. Unpublished doctoral dissertation, Radcliffe College.

Piaget, J.: 1930. *The child's conception of physical causality.* New York: Harcourt Brace.

Piaget, J.: 1951. *Play, dreams, and imitation in childhood.* New York: Norton.

Piaget, J.: 1952. *The child's conception of number.* New York: Humanities Press.

Piaget, J.: 1954. *The construction of reality in the child.* New York: Basic Books.

Piaget, J.: 1961. *Les mécanismes perceptifs.* Paris: Presses Universitaires de France.

Piaget, J.: 1964. Personal communication.

Piaget, J., & Inhelder, Bärbel.: 1956. *The child's conception of space.* London: Routledge & Kegan Paul.

Piaget, J., & Inhelder, Bärbel.: 1962. *Le développement des quantitiés physiques chez l'enfant.* (2nd revised edition) Neuchâtel, Switzerland: Delachaux & Niestlé.

Piaget, J., & von Albertini, Barbara.: 1954. Recherches sur le développement des perceptions. XIX. Observations sur la perception des bonnes formes chez l'enfant par actualization des lignes virtuelles. *Arch. Psychol., Genève,* 34, 203–243.

Prentice, W. C. H.: 1954. Visual recognition of verbally labeled figures. *Amer. J. Psychol.,* 67, 315–320.

Price-Williams, D. R.: 1961. A study concerning concepts of conservation of quantities among primitive children. *Acta Psychologica,* 18, No. 4. Pp. 297–305.

Price-Williams, D. R.: 1962. Abstract and concrete modes of classification in a primitive society. *Brit. J. educ. Psychol.,* 32, 50–61.

Rasmussen, K.: 1931. *The Netsilik Eskimos: social life and spiritual culture.* (Report of the 5th Thule Expedition: 1921–1924). Vol. 8. Nordisk Verlag-Copenhagen, Denmark: Gyldendalske Boghandel.

Reichard, S., Schneider, M., & Rapaport, D.: 1944. The development of concept formation in children. *Amer. J. Orthopsychiat.,* 14, 156–161.

Richards, I. A.: 1966. Book review. *General linguistics: an introductory survey* by A. H. Robbins; *The linguistic sciences and language teaching* by Holliday, McIntosh, & Stevens. *New York Review of Books* (April 14, 1966).

Rigney, Joan C.: 1962. A developmental study of cognitive equivalence transformations and their use in the acquisition and processing of information. Unpublished honors thesis, Radcliffe College.

Sahlins, M.: 1966. Notes on the original affluent society. Paper delivered at the Conference on Hunting Societies sponsored by Viking Fund. Chicago, April, 1966.

Sapir, E.: 1921. *Language.* New York: Harcourt, Brace.

Saugstad, P.: 1955. Problem solving as dependent on availability of functions. *Brit. J. Psychol.,* 46, 191–198.

Schachtel, E. G.: 1947. On memory and childhood amnesia. *Psychiatry,* 10, 1–26.

Segers, J. E.: 1926. La perception visuelle et la fonction de globalisation chez les enfants. *Documents Pédotechniques,* 5me Annee, No. 2, Bruxelles.

Simon H. A.: 1962. An information processing theory of intellectual development. In W. Kessen & Clementina Kuhlman (Eds.), Thought in the young child. *Monogr. Soc. Res. Child Develpm.,* 27 (2), Serial No. 83, 150–155.

Slobin, D. I.: 1963. Grammatical transformations in childhood and adulthood. Unpublished doctoral dissertation, Harvard Univer.

Smock, C. D.: 1955. The influence of psychological stress on the "intolerance of ambiguity." *J. abnorm. soc. Psychol.,* 50, 177–182.

Smock, C. D.: 1957. The relationship between "intolerance of ambiguity," generalization and speed of perceptual closure. *Child Develpm.,* 28, 27–36.

Sokolov, Y. N.: 1963. *Perception and the conditioned reflex.* New York: Macmillan.

Sonstroem, Anne M.: 1966. Manipulation, labeling, and screening in the learning of conservation. Unpublished doctoral dissertation, Harvard Univer.

Spindler, G. D.: 1955. *Education and anthropology.* Stanford: Stanford Univer. Press.

Stern, C., & Stern, W.: 1907. Die Kindersprache: Eine psychologische und sprach-theoretische Untersuchung. (Monogr. seel. Entwick, Kindes, Vol. I.) Leipzig: Barth.

Tajfel, H.: 1957. Value and the perceptual judgment of magnitude. *Psychol. Rev.,* 64, 192–204.

Titchener, E. B.: 1908. *Lectures on the elementary psychology of feeling and attention.* New York: Macmillan.

Tolman, E. C.: 1932. *Purposive behavior in animals and men.* New York: Century.

von Senden, M.: 1960. *Space and sight.* Glencoe, Ill.: Free Press.

Vurpillot, Eliane, & Zoberman, Nicole.: 1965. Roles des indices communs et des indices distincts dans la différentiation perceptive. *Acta Psychologica,* 24, 49–67.

Vygotsky, L. S.: 1962. *Thought and language.* New York: Wiley.

Walk, R. D., & Gibson, Eleanor J.: 1961. A comparative and analytical study of visual depth perception. *Psychol. Monogr.*, 75, No. 15.

Wallach, L., & Sprott, R. L.: 1964. Inducing number conservation in children. *Child Develpm.*, 35, 1057–1071.

Wallach, M. A.: 1958. On psychological similarity. *Psychol. Rev.*, 65, 103–116.

Wallach, M. A.: 1963. Research on children's thinking. In *Child Psychology*, 62nd Yearb. nat. Soc. Stud. Educ., Part I. Pp. 236–276.

Wallach, M. A., & Kogan, N.: 1965. *Modes of thinking in young children.* New York: Holt, Rinehart & Winston.

Washburn, S. L., & Howell, F. C.: 1960. Human evolution and culture. In S. Tax, *The evolution of man.* Vol. 2. Chicago: Univer. of Chicago Press.

Weir, Ruth H.: 1962. *Language in the crib.* The Hague, Netherlands: Mouton.

Werner, H.: 1948. *Comparative psychology of mental development.* (Revised edition) Chicago: Follett.

Werner, H., & Kaplan, Edith.: 1950. The acquisition of word meanings: A developmental study. *Monogr. Soc. Res. Child Develpm.*, 15 (Serial No. 51).

Werner, H., & Wapner, S.: 1956. Sensori-tonic field theory of perception: basic concepts and experiments. *Revista di Psicologia*, 50, 315–337.

White, L. A.: 1949. *The science of culture.* New York: Farrar, Straus & Cudahy.

White, L. A.: 1960. Four stages in the evolution of minding. In S. Tax (Ed.), *The evolution of man.* Vol. 2. Chicago: Univer. of Chicago Press.

White, R. W.: 1959. Motivation reconsidered: the concept of competence. *Psychol. Rev.*, 66, 297–333.

Whorf, B. L.: 1956. *Language, thought, and reality: selected writings of Benjamin Lee Whorf* (Edited by J. B. Carroll). New York: Wiley.

Witkin, H. A., Dyk, R. B., Fattuson, H. F., Goodenough, D. R., & Karp, S. A.: 1962. *Psychological differentiation: studies of development.* New York: Wiley.

Wittgenstein, L.: 1953. *Philosophical investigations.* New York: Macmillan.

Wittgenstein, L.: 1958. *The blue and brown books.* Oxford: Blackwell.

Wohlwill, J. F.: 1959. Un essai d'apprentissage dans le domaine de la conservation du nombre. In A. Morf, J. Smedslund, Vinh-Bang, & J. F. Wohlwill, L'apprentissage des structures logiques. *Etudes d'epistémologie génétique.* Vol. 9. Paris: Presses Univer. France. Pp. 125–135.

Wohlwill, J. F.: 1960. A study of the development of the number concept by scalogram analysis. *J. genet. Psychol.*, 97, 345–377.

Wohlwill, J. F.: 1962. From perception to inference: a dimension of cognitive development. In W. Kessen & Clementina Kuhlman (Eds.) Thought in the young child. *Monogr. Soc. Res. Child Dev.*, 27, 87–112.

Wohlwill, J. F., & Lowe, R. C.: 1962. An experimental analysis of the development of conservation of number. *Child Develpm.*, 33, 153–167.

Wyatt, D., & Campbell, D.: 1951. On the liability of stereotype or hypothesis. *J. abnorm. soc. Psychol.*, 46, 496–500.

Young, J. Z.: 1964. *Model of the brain.* Oxford: Clarendon Press.

Index of Authors

335

Index of Subjects